IMPROVING SCHOOLS FOR AFRICAN AMERICAN STUDENTS

ABOUT THE EDITORS

Dr. Sheryl J. Denbo has been involved in civil rights and education for more than 30 years. She has a national reputation on issues of school reform with a focus on equity. Having worked with federally funded projects since the 1980s, she is frequently requested as a keynote speaker by educational and parent groups around the country. She co-authored a highly regarded work on equity and school reform entitled "Educate America: A Call for Equity in School Reform," which focuses on systemic reform efforts that prioritize the problems of low-income students. The author of numerous publications, her most recent article is "All Students Are Not Equal," which appears in *Challenges to Equality: Poverty and Race in America*, edited by Chester Hartman, 2001.

Lynson Moore Beaulieu is currently the Director of Race Equity Programs at the Mid-Atlantic Equity Center. Since coming to Washington, DC, in 1994, she has also served in senior staff positions at the Council of Chief State School Officers and in the U.S. Department of Education's Compensatory Education Programs (Title I) Division in Washington, DC. Her broad background in educational equity includes expertise in early care and education, as well as in elementary and secondary education. Ms. Beaulieu practices a systemic approach to institutional change and in recent years has focused her work on building the capacity of school leaders, educators, and institutions to more successfully serve children and families from diverse ethnic, cultural, and language backgrounds.

IMPROVING SCHOOLS FOR AFRICAN AMERICAN STUDENTS

A Reader for Educational Leaders

Edited by

SHERYL J. DENBO, PH.D.

Director
Mid-Atlantic Equity Center
Chevy Chase, Maryland

and

LYNSON MOORE BEAULIEU

Director
Race Equity Programs
Mid-Atlantic Equity Center
Chevy Chase, Maryland

Foreword by

Vinetta C. Jones, PH.D.

Dean
School of Education
Howard University
Washington, D.C.

Charles C Thomas
PUBLISHER · LTD.
SPRINGFIELD · ILLINOIS · U.S.A.

Published and Distributed Throughout the World by

CHARLES C THOMAS • PUBLISHER, LTD.
2600 South First Street
Springfield, Illinois 62704

ISBN 0-398-07281-7 (hard)
ISBN 0-398-07282-5 (paper)

Library of Congress Catalog Card Number: 2002020639

With THOMAS BOOKS *careful attention is given to all details of manufacturing and design. It is the Publisher's desire to present books that are satisfactory as to their physical qualities and artistic possibilities and appropriate for their particular use.* THOMAS BOOKS *will be true to those laws of quality that assure a good name and good will.*

Printed in the United States of America
MM-R-3

Cover illustration and design by Fransis Young.
franworks@aol.com

Library of Congress Cataloging-in-Publication Data

Improving schools for African American students : a reader for educational leaders / edited by Sheryl J. Denbo and Lynson Moore Beaulieu ; forward by Vinetta C. Jones.
p. cm.
Includes bibliographical references and index.
ISBN 0-398-07281-7 (hard) -- ISBN 0-398-07282-5 (paper)
1. African American--Education. 2. Academic achievement--United States. 3. Educational equalization--United States. I. Denbo, Sheryl. II. Beaulieu, Lynson Moore.

LC2717 .I46 2002
371.829'96'073--dc21 2002020639

This book is dedicated to the staff of the Mid-Atlantic Equity Center, without whose passion, talent, commitment, and hard work it would not have come to fruition.*

*The Center is federally funded to provide technical assistance and training on equity issues to educators in Delaware, the District of Columbia, Maryland, Pennsylvania, Virginia, and West Virginia. For further information about the Center, call 301-657-7741 or visit our website at www.maec.org

CONTRIBUTORS

A.Wade Boykin is a Professor and Director of the Developmental Psychology Graduate Program in the Department of Psychology at Howard University. He has published numerous articles on Black child development and related topics and is the co-editor of *Research Directions of Black Psychologists.*

James P. Comer is the Maurice Falk Professor of Child Psychiatry at the Yale University School of Medicine's Child Study Center. He is the author of hundreds of articles and several books on African American children and education, including *Waiting for a Miracle: Why Schools Can't Solve Our Problems and How We Can.*

Kayte Fearn is Special Assistant to the Executive Director for Diversity Affairs, Council for Exceptional Children. She has an extensive background in education at all levels, including as a university professor and federal employee. Her writings are done primarily for presentations, information sharing, and fundraising.

Donna Y. Ford is Associate Professor of Special Education, Ohio State University. She is widely published and is the author of *Reversing Underachievement Among Gifted Black Students* and *Multicultural Gifted Education Theory and Practice.*

Pat Burke Guild is on the faculty of Western Washington University. She is the co-author of *Marching to Different Drummers* and the author of many articles on learning styles and their applications.

Vinetta C. Jones is the Dean of the School of Education at Howard University and for eight years served as Executive Director of the EQUITY 2000 program. She has written and lectured widely on issues related to the education of diverse populations and is widely regarded as a leading authority on the education reform movement in this country.

Gloria Ladson-Billings is a Professor of Education at the University of Wisconsin, Madison. She is the author of several articles and *The Dreamkeepers: Successful Teachers of African American Children.*

Patricia E. Ortman is a Research Associate with the Mid-Atlantic Equity Center, Executive Editor of this volume, author or co-author of several articles on education and gender, and author of *Not for Teachers Only: Creating a Context of Joy for Learning and Growth.*

Mike Schmoker is a former teacher and school district administrator. Now a school improvement consultant, he is the author of several publications, including *Results: The Key to Continuous School Improvement.*

Susan Shaffer is the Deputy Director of the Mid-Atlantic Equity Center. She is the author or co-author of multiple publications related to gender and other equity issues. Her most recent publication is *Why Boys Don't Talk and Why We Care*, which she co-authored with Linda Perlman Gordon.

William Tate is Professor of Mathematics Education in the Department of Curriculum and Instruction at the University of Wisconsin–Madison. He has published numerous articles and book chapters focused on mathematics education and urban school reform. He is the co-author of an elementary mathematics textbook series.

Nathalie Thandiwe is a Research Associate at Mid-Atlantic Equity Center. She is also a freelance writer and herbalist and is delighted that "naturalist" has been added to the categories of Gardner's Theory of Multiple Intelligences.

Scott Thompson is the Assistant Director of the Panasonic Foundation, the editor of *Strategies*, an issue series by the Foundation and the American Association of School Administrators, and the vice president of the Glen Rock Public Education Foundation. Before joining Panasonic, he began his career as a high school English teacher and worked with the Institute for Responsive Education in Boston.

Belinda Williams is a psychologist with more than 25 years of experience studying the academic achievement patterns of culturally diverse and socioeconomically disadvantaged students in urban districts. She is the author of numerous publications on urban education and the editor of *Closing the Achievement Gap: A Vision for Changing Beliefs and Practices.*

Robert Witherspoon is Senior Research Associate with RMC Research Corporation in Arlington, Virginia. Some of his responsibilities include the Region III Comprehensive Center parent involvement issues team and the Goals 2000 Parent Information Resource Center. He is editor of The National Coalition of Title I/Chapter I Parents newsletter and author or co-author of several publications on parents and education.

Ray Yau is a Research Associate at the Mid-Atlantic Equity Center. He is also the in-house computer technology expert and has published in the field of educational technology.

FOREWORD

The most pressing challenge that this nation faces as we begin this new millennium is helping all of America's children meet the standards needed to live, learn, work, communicate, and be productive citizens in the highly technological, global community of the twenty-first century. Current demographics show students from diverse ethnic, cultural, and language backgrounds are in the majority in public schools in the states of California, New Mexico, Mississippi, and Louisiana, as well as in most large urban school districts. In addition, there are predictions of increases in these trends. America's very future depends on how quickly we can end the "savage inequalities," which produce inevitable achievement gaps resulting from the undereducation of African American and other students from diverse backgrounds. Many current school reform policies are causing achievement gaps to widen rather than close. These policies are focusing primarily on high standards and assessment while neglecting issues of access to high-quality education and curriculum taught by competent and caring teachers who hold high expectations for currently underachieving students.

Research shows that an effective school leader is key to any transformation of schools into places where all students from diverse backgrounds succeed academically. The challenge is great in this era of shortages of school principals, especially in urban areas. Into this breech comes *Improving Schools for African American Students: A Reader for Educational Leaders*; it brings together in one volume the accumulated knowledge, from research and experience, of cutting-edge ideas that advance our understanding of "what works." These outstanding researchers and practitioners highlight critical issues and provide proven practices that will be invaluable to those preparing to be school leaders in diverse settings, as well as for those creating policies to support the development of schools where *all* students reach high standards. This volume puts at the fingertips of education leaders and policymakers an institutional and cultural context from which to develop policies, practices, and programs that support high achievement among African American students.

Each author not only discusses what is not working in today's schools and classrooms but also provides the reader with specific examples of what is working and helps us to understand why. While acknowledging that African American students are frequently succeeding despite the institutional barriers they face, each article provides detailed discussions of what these barriers are and how to remove them. *Improving Schools for African American Students: A Reader for Educational Leaders* discusses key issues in educational reform, including the processes involved in reforming individual schools and whole school systems, academic standards and assessment practices, staff development, effective leadership, literacy, math education, and parent participation, all from the perspective of strategies that have been proven to work for African American students. Administrators and other educational leaders will be exposed to important new ideas and will revisit ideas of the past from a new perspective. The information presented in this volume is important for anyone who is struggling to improve our schools so that they become institutions that support the learning of all students.

VINETTA C. JONES

INTRODUCTION

> The question is not whether we can afford to invest in every child; it is whether we can afford not to.
>
> *Marian Wright Edelman*

Improving Schools for African American Students: A Reader for Educational Leaders provides education leaders with access to critical ideas, research, and knowledge across a broad range of educational issues that affect the successful schooling of African American children and youth. The articles that make up this book discuss generic education issues such as policy reform, the importance of high-quality teaching, and the improvement of schools from the perspective of the academic achievement of African American students. They explore the need to identify and redress policies and practices that hinder African American student achievement. They discuss effective teacher training programs, both pre-service and in-service, that focus on the academic and the ethical, social, political, and cultural dimensions of teaching African American students. These articles explore educational programs that build on the strengths that African American students bring to school, as well as how to create these programs in a wide variety of school settings, ranging from schools that serve predominantly African American students to schools in which African American students are a small percentage of the total school population.

The articles in this anthology were selected to provide concerned education leaders with a better understanding of how they can support high levels of academic achievement and social development for African American children and youth. *Improving Schools for African American Students: A Reader for Educational Leaders* contains articles that will help educational leaders to recognize the institutional barriers that present formidable stumbling blocks to successful educational outcomes; understand the diversity of strengths that their African American students bring with them to school; and become familiar with how successful educators use the strengths of African American students to improve achievement. Although many school leaders are already playing a key role in mobilizing teachers, parents, and other community stakeholders to work together to improve schools and achievement levels for African American students, they are the first to recognize that this is not an easy task.

Today's educational leaders must have skills that go far beyond management and budgets. In school systems where they are very likely to have accountability without authority, today's leaders must have the skills to make connections with a broad cross-section of education stakeholders, build a thriving school community, and facilitate effective communication and collaboration. A school leader must not only be knowledgeable about curricular and instructional choices, he or she must be an advocate for children. At the school level, this means that he or she must be able to create and maintain relationships: school to community, children to learning, teachers to children and parents, parents to school and children, teachers to teachers, and students to students. To gain the level of results we are seeking for African American and other students from diverse ethnic, cultural, and language backgrounds, educational leaders must be prepared to "create a web of support around children and their families" (Houston, 2001). The roles and duties of today's educational leaders are complex and challenging, often without obvious rewards. To do the job well, to be able to withstand adversity, requires a commitment not only of their time, energy, and professional resources but also of their heart and soul. Houston describes the job of school superintendent as a "calling"; Cornel West (cited in Houston, 2001) describes it as "soul craft."

To make schools work for African American and other students from diverse ethnic, cultural, and language backgrounds, a school's culture and structure must be built on a foundation of respect for diversity and support for the high achievement of all students. The institutional structures of schools must provide a variety of organizational options designed to support the high achievement of all students. The most effective educational leaders are collaborators, working with their staff, their students and their students' families to acquire the knowledge and skills necessary to establish educational climates that ensure the high achievement of African American students.

To assist school leaders in their efforts to more effectively serve African American students, this anthology highlights a wide variety of policies, programs, practices, and research that provide insight into how educators can successfully restructure their schools so that they offer teaching and learning environments that provide diverse pathways for African American students to meet high standards. Concentrating on African American students does not mean creating one separate pathway to success for African American students and another pathway for students from other backgrounds. It does, however, mean creating institutional infrastructures, cultures, and environments that support the many ways in which people learn. Such institutions effectively meet the needs of individuals and diverse groups of learners, ultimately promoting the educational success of all students.

If education leaders are to make substantial progress toward building, sustaining, and replicating effective programs for African American students, they need to understand the many dimensions of institutional racism. Oakes, Quartz, Ryan, and Lipton (2000) advise us that we must do more to address institutional racism than create effective schools. We must nurture new and existing local successes to prevent them from being undermined or dismantled. Part I, "Recognizing and Addressing Institutional Racism," provides readers with an opportunity to explore institutional racism in the context of America's public schools. It also provides suggestions for how education leaders can begin to eliminate harmful policies and practices within their educational institutions and settings.

The articles in Part II, "Institutional Change and Culturally Relevant Pedagogy: Two Sides of the Same Coin," discuss the kinds of institutional and instructional changes that are needed to support the successful schooling of African American children and youth. Part III, "Achieving Results," focuses on the challenges presented to African American students by the current high stakes testing environment that surrounds standards, assessment, and accountability. Through the articles in this chapter, we hope to stimulate education leaders to think more broadly about their approaches to defining and measuring the achievement of African American students. Part III also includes a review of the literature on schools that have succeeded in improving achievement for African American students at the elementary, middle, and high school levels, as well as districts that have moved toward narrowing the achievement gap.

Although evidence clearly shows that the past fifty years have brought tremendous educational, economic, and social gains for African American people as a whole, equally clear is that progress toward educational parity for most African American students has slowed. Large disparities in educational outcomes still persist between ethnic, cultural, and language-diverse groups, and by some indicators, educational gaps have widened in recent years. Overall, the data are not encouraging (Tidwell, 2000). Regardless, education remains the most effective road to success. Removing the barriers that prevent African American students from accessing a high-quality public education is an essential first step to achieving access to the economic, social, and political resources that are needed to support strong families and a truly democratic society.

There is no doubt that the most recent educational reform movement has helped uncover the contradictions between our desire to improve the overall quality of public education and our ability to do so for all groups of students. Changing the institutional culture of schools so that it focuses on achievement and other related outcomes is a good idea. Having universally high standards is another step in the right direction. However, there remains a powerful contradiction between establishing the goal of high achievement for all students and maintaining differential access to the kinds of educational programs and resources that are needed to support high achievement for all students. Although we have had many years of "school reform," most schools serving Black students and families still fail to provide them with a high-quality educational experience, as evidenced by reports from some urban school systems of dropout rates of up to 50 percent for their African American students. Other schools throughout the country continue to place a large percentage of their African American students into "lower ability" tracks. Even schools that redesign their policies so that African American students gain equal access to challenging educational programs often fail to address other important issues, such as access to effective prerequisite courses, the need for supportive and caring student-teacher relationships, and the need to increase the levels of parent and community involvement. Given the widespread cultural and academic disconnects between Black students and the schools they attend, it is safe to say that most of America's schools are still not supporting the high achievement of African American students.

Although we applaud universally high standards and a responsive and responsible system of assessment, our definition of effective schools must include the institutionalization of a variety of supports and pathways that enable students from all backgrounds to attain the high standards. The concept of multiple pathways to academic success is entirely consonant with the constructivist approaches to education now recommended by many experts. Among other things, constructivist approaches call for educators to build on the individual and cultural resources students bring with them to class. However, this proven strategy is made much more difficult to enact, given that the teaching workforce is largely White and middle class, and the nation's students are increasingly poor and from diverse ethnic, cultural, and language backgrounds. Simply put, most White, middle-class teachers do not have the knowledge or experience they need to build on the cultural resources of their African American and other diverse students. And not unlike their White, middle-class counterparts, many ethnically diverse teachers who also come from middle-class backgrounds frequently find themselves disconnected from the lived experiences and cultural backgrounds of their lower-income students and families.

Many of our widely publicized "successful" school reform models have been measured by how much they improve test scores. Even if we accept standardized test scores as a measure of improved achievement, we must still recognize that many of these reform models have not brought about the changes needed to close the achievement gap between African American and White students. Some schools have succeeded in generally improving achievement for many of their students, but such efforts have failed to decrease or eliminate existing gaps in achievement and dropout rates. When test scores rise more or less equally among African American and White students, the achievement gap is maintained, and unfortunately, rising test scores can be the result of increases in student dropout rates.

A singular focus on high stakes assessments and accountability practices as the only measure of school and student success has the power to undermine the entire school reform effort with a disproportionate negative impact on poor students of diverse ethnic, cultural, and language backgrounds.

Houston (2001) tells us, "If you lean your ladder against the wrong wall, you will paint the wrong house." He goes on to describe the problem with this wave of education reform as one that tries to force students to learn by giving them high-stakes tests and a narrow curriculum. Houston believes that this external pressure approach is doomed to failure. It certainly flies in the face of a constructivist approach by undermining efforts to encourage students to explore topics of interest in some depth and by subverting attempts to build diversity into the restructuring processes.

Many educators acknowledge the importance of authentically addressing diversity in school reform efforts. They often recognize that designing effective educational programs for African American students requires a great deal more than celebrating Black History month, having African American role models, or incorporating the historical contributions of people from diverse ethnic, cultural, and language backgrounds into the curriculum. They are not always sure, however, how to integrate issues related to differences in students' backgrounds and learning preferences into the overall reform effort.

In the pages of this book, education leaders will find the information they need to improve their understanding of the myriad issues and concerns surrounding the successful education of African American students. As educational leaders, we have the responsibility to lean our ladders against the right wall. We must use our knowledge, resources, and power to help ensure the academic success of all African American students. To do this, we must establish a climate of support and collaboration in which all teachers, students, and their families are valued, and each student's achievement and well-being is monitored and supported as part of a collective schoolwide, family, and community responsibility. As we go about our school change efforts, we must make the kinds of institutional changes that result in high achievement for all students. This anthology focuses on how we can best accomplish this goal for African American students.

REFERENCES

Houston, P. (2001, February). Superintendents for the 21st century: It's not just a job, it's a calling. *Phi Delta Kappan*, pp. 428–433.

Oakes, J., Quartz, K.H., Ryan, S. & Lipton, M. (2000). *Becoming good American schools: The struggle for civic virtue in education reform.* San Francisco: Jossey-Bass.

Tidwell, B.J. (2000) Parity progress and prospects: Racial inequalities in economic well-being. In L.A. Daniels (Ed.), *The state of Black America 2000.* Washington, DC: National Urban League.

ACKNOWLEDGMENTS

We are grateful for the support and encouragement of the entire staff of the Mid-Atlantic Equity Center. To Susan Shaffer, who participated in virtually every aspect of the publication's development, we want to thank you for your honest and sincere critique of our efforts. To Nathalie Thandiwe, we want to thank you for your honesty, careful research, and editorial assistance. To Ray Yau, we thank you for keeping us abreast of the most up-to-date data and information. Oluseyi Ojeifo, our student intern, we thank for her contagious enthusiasm, excellent skills, and the detailed care she took in all tasks, small and large. To Pat Ortman, who started out assisting with administrative tasks and ended up taking on the huge task of Executive Editor, we offer our undying gratitude for a difficult job well done.

To the education leaders who work every day on behalf of African American students, their families, schools, and communities, you remain an inspiration. To the researchers who have persisted despite a severe lack of funding and support for your efforts, we could not have done this book without you. To our African American students and their families, we want you to know that our work is driven by the need to right the injustices and inequitable conditions you face as students in America's public schools.

To our husbands, Steve and David, and our children, Nathan and Leah, and Micah, Adia, Dasan, and Orion, without whose ongoing support, inspiration, and love this project would not have been possible, we offer our most profound love and thanks. You are the light in our eyes.

SHERYL J. DENBO
LYNSON MOORE BEAULIEU

NOTE TO THE READER

The Mid-Atlantic Equity Center of the Mid-Atlantic Equity Consortium, Inc., is funded through a grant awarded by the U.S. Department of Education under Title IV of the Civil Rights Act of 1964. The content of this publication was developed under this grant. However, the opinions expressed in this publication do not necessarily reflect the position or policy of the U.S. Department of Education and no endorsement by the U.S. Department of Education should be inferred.

CONTENTS

IMPROVING SCHOOLS FOR AFRICAN AMERICAN STUDENTS

Part I

RECOGNIZING AND ADDRESSING INSTITUTIONAL RACISM

> O, let America be America again–
> The land that never has been yet–
> and yet must be–The land where *every* man is free.
>
> *Langston Hughes*

ALTHOUGH RACISM IS A FAMILIAR SUBJECT to many, the discussion of institutional racism may be overwhelming, stressful, or shocking to others. We believe, however, that it is important to understand both intentional and unintentional racism if we are going to create educational environments that support the high academic achievement of African American children. As Professor Asa Hilliard continues to tell us in speech after speech, many African American students have reached and continue to reach high levels of academic achievement. Our failure to replicate these successes has a great deal to do with institutional racism.

Racism has become institutionalized in American schools through hierarchical conceptions of intellectual ability. The bell curve, for example, assumes high levels of intellectual abilities for only a small percentage of the population. This assumption does not motivate educators to create and nurture intellectual ability. Instead, it supports the institutionalization of a hierarchical notion of innate mental ability through practices such as academic tracking. These hierarchical conceptions of intellectual ability have led to a focus on the individual and cultural characteristics of students rather than the ways that the social system structures academic success for some and academic failure for others. The result has been a variety of school policies and practices that foil the full development of the intellectual potential of African American children.

In Part I, "Recognizing and Addressing Institutional Racism," we address a wide variety of separate issues that together form many of the components of institutional racism. The section starts with James P. Comer's "My View" that is actually the first chapter of his wonderful book, *Waiting for a Miracle: Why Schools Can't Solve Our Problems and How We Can* (1997). Dr. Comer, clearly an old soul and a patriot who loves his country, recognizes that he is an example of the American dream come true. "The United States," he tells us, has "probably come closer to creating the 'good society' than any society of its complexity in the history of the world." Despite its complexity and history of slavery, the United States is a place where democratic ideals remain alive. Nonetheless, Dr. Comer presents his concerns about the inherent flaws in America's belief in a meritocracy and the damage that that has brought. Dr. Comer expresses the belief that we already have in place the strategies and practices that can be used to redress remaining inequities.

In the next two articles, "Why Can't We Close the Achievement Gap?" and "The Effects of Racism, Socioeconomic Class, and Gender on

Academic Achievement of African American Students," issues related to the effects of institutional racism are addressed. In "Why Can't We Close the Achievement Gap?" Sheryl Denbo presents an overview of institutional racism in America's schools and the resulting privileges experienced by White students. It is concise by design, because many of these issues are topics that educators have been struggling with for decades. It is helpful to look at them together to get a better understanding of what many of our African American students face. In "The Effects of Racism, Socioeconomic Class and Gender on Academic Achievement of African American Students," Susan Shaffer, Pat Ortman, and Sheryl Denbo address issues of gender and class as they relate to African American students. While critiquing the lack of research and data on African American students that is disaggregated by class and gender within race, they discuss what is known or theorized about poverty and its relationship to the achievement of African American students; middle-class African American student achievement; achievement of African American male students; and the achievement of African American female students.

In the final two articles, Donna Y. Ford and Kayte Fearn address the issues of special education and gifted education. In "The Recruitment and Retention of African American Students in Gifted Education," Donna Y. Ford helps to explain the causes of underachievement among African American students. The article suggests specific administrative solutions to decrease the identification of African American students in special education and increase their identification for gifted education. Kayte Fearn offers descriptions of programs that successfully reduce overrepresentation of African American students in special education programs.

Recognizing and addressing racism is an important priority to those who want to support the high achievement of African American students. Educators must recognize and incorporate the voices, experiences, and hopes of their diverse populations of students without labeling, devaluing or tracking them, or requiring them to be submerged into a bureaucratic melting pot. Although it is not easy to address racism and support diversity, it is imperative that these become widespread educational goals if we are to succeed in supporting high achievement among all of our students.

Article 1

MY VIEW*

JAMES P. COMER

I HAVE BEEN MORE FORTUNATE than most Americans. My experience as an African-American has been an expression of what America could be. And that is why I want to discuss how it still can become what it set out to be, the Good Society.

I am from a working-class family. On one side I am a generation removed from extreme poverty and abuse, with grandparents probably born into slavery. On the other side I had great-grandparents whose slave experience was less disorganizing, and a grandfather who was a small farmer and church minister.

My choice of child psychiatry as a career stemmed originally from my curiosity about why equally talented (sometimes more talented) black friends did not achieve their potential. In time, my work led to an effort to do something to improve the chances of such young people.

In many ways my life has been a journey from the margins of society toward the center. What I have been told along the way by various people has often been different from what I have observed and what I know will and will not work. So, throughout this book, I will use as a frame of reference my own life experience. This experience in general, and my work in schools in particular, has brought me to doubt that many institutional policies and programs being used and proposed to address our growing social problems–community and family deterioration, educational underachievement, ethnic and racial tensions, vandalism and violence–will succeed.

After several years as director of Yale's School Development Program, I with my colleagues learned how to significantly improve two schools, and then many more. But as we analyzed our work, troublesome questions began to arise. Why did some improve dramatically, some modestly, and some not at all? Why is it so difficult and why does it take so long to improve schools? And most important, why are there so many schools in trouble?

All along we have observed that most schoolteachers and administrators want to succeed. Most parents certainly want their children to succeed. And most students are able and struggling to succeed in all the ways available to young people. What, then, is the problem?

The question calls to mind an apocryphal story.

Two men in a boat rescued a child drowning in a river. As they rowed on, they saw three, then four, and finally a riverful of drowning children. As the man at the oars started for the shore, the other asked him where he was going: there were still so many children to be rescued. The reply was, "I'm going to find out who is throwing these children in the water, and stop them!"

No single person can "stop them"–put an end to institutional and individual problems. But it is

*"My View," from *Waiting for a Miracle: Why Schools Can't Solve Our Problems and How We Can* by James P. Comer, copyright 1997 by James P. Comer. Used by permission of Dutton, a division of Penguin Putnam, Inc.

important to point out that the state of our schools is not the problem itself, but a reflection of the condition of the larger society. It gradually became clear to me what the problem is.

In our culture we believe that the life outcome of an individual is due almost entirely to genetically determined intelligence and will. This central belief both flows from and contributes to the *individualism* that is so much a part of the American character. (The belief, not coincidentally, is fundamental to our "trickle-down" economic system, according to which, the brightest and the best create and manage economic enterprises and others fit into the system as they are able.) We deny or downplay all other determinants: child development, access to opportunity networks–educational, economic, political, social–and chance, particularly inheritance and the natural connections stemming from where you are born on the social scale.

I call this belief our First Myth.

The many roots of American individualism have been described, often, as both our major strength and our major weakness. The tension that sets individual effort and rights and interests against the common good is probably necessary and even useful–when in balance, and when all individuals have reasonable access to the same opportunities. But a serious imbalance or limited access, for whatever reasons, creates problems.

The notion that intelligence and will alone determine outcomes implies that everyone has similar opportunities and faces similar obstacles. It suggests that the cream rises to the top through superior intellect and exertion, and that is good for society. For their efforts, the best and brightest deserve all they can get. This creates a winner/loser rather than a win-win mentality. The focus on competition allows individualism to run amok–to be carried to extremes that endanger the common good.

Competition is a highly regarded American value. It is a product of the impulse for survival. But the winner/loser mind-set creates a need to find and attack "losers." The loser deserves disdain and exclusion. Gone is any emphasis on caring and on using individual talents to promote the common good. Gone is any recognition that human beings function best in caring societies–in win-win situations.

The universal human task is to find personal adequacy and meaning in life. These are found most often through pride in work, in care for self and/or family, and in being a valued and contributing citizen of a society–a winner. Some people, for a variety of reasons both personal and situational, are unable to achieve this. Yet the myth holds that they have brought all their problems on themselves.

Those who do not succeed at life's tasks often seek adequacy and meaning through behaviors that are troublesome to the society and the individual–that contribute to problems ranging from poor family functioning to undereducation, dependency, crime, and violence. Also, the fear of being a loser can evoke the immature but very powerful human urge to scapegoat others less able to defend themselves.

The effectiveness of this tactic should not be underestimated. Scapegoating is a primitive but natural response to threat and insecurity. A simple example from my own life illustrates this. As a student in graduate school at the University of Michigan with a 3½-year-old son, a newborn daughter, and a wife who had just given birth, I was under stress. One evening I snapped at my son unfairly. He was hurt. Without saying a word, he moved slowly the long way around the room until he reached the crib of his new sister. Then he reached in and hit her.

Because this kind of hurtful reaction is natural, a society must be structured to enable people to deal with insecurity in more mature ways. To minimize scapegoating and to promote the general well-being, a society must make it possible for most people to be successful most of the time. But for many reasons–size, wealth, and particularly the fact that we are a nation of immigrants–America has always resorted to scapegoating. Throughout our history, the latest immigrant group was blamed for any and all problems. The descendants of African slaves have been particularly vulnerable. This caste group would become for the nation what the "problem child" is to a family that is not functioning well–a permanent scapegoat. A common refrain in clinical practice is "There's nothing wrong with us, it's him."

This brings us to what I call the Second Myth–that whites have been successful, and blacks have not.

How is this explained in the face of contradictory evidence? Certainly a large factor has been the First Myth–that able individuals will rise by their own effort. And many whites maintain the myth through their identification with more highly successful whites and through their denial of significant black success.

There have been changes since World War II. A 1996 National Opinion Research Center report indicated that only 7 percent of Americans born after 1945 attribute lower average socioeconomic attainment among blacks to lesser intelligence, compared to 26 percent among those born before. But a sobering 47 percent attributed the disparity to a lack of motivation.

Implicit in this belief is the idea that everyone has had the same chance. This is clearly not true, yet it provides justification for limiting efforts to promote educational and economic opportunities. Racial abuse, even demonization, serves selfish political and economic purposes and encourages continued scapegoating. And blacks are the proxy for all vulnerable groups.

The front cover of the August 12, 1996, issue of *The New Republic* pictured a black woman smoking a cigarette, looking aimlessly into space, with a baby in her lap sucking on a bottle. Blazoned above were the words **DAY OF RECKONING**, and the story title below read "Sign the Welfare Bill Now." While the articles inside were balanced and thoughtful, the impact of the cover was much more powerful. It is flagrant scapegoating, for it blames people whom many already view as "bad" for the outcomes of past and present bad policies.

Opportunists have managed to convince the average American that "those people" are breaking the bank. In fact, Aid to Families with Dependent Children, Supplemental Security Income, and food stamps–programs for the most dependent–all together amount to 3.4 percent of the federal budget. And most of the recipients are not black, but it is easier to scapegoat them if the public thinks they are. The typical child on AFDC is white and lives in the rural South, Appalachia, or poor areas of major cities. Medicare, Social Security, and other middle-class benefits are actually much more costly than these programs.

The intelligence-determines-outcome myth, with attendant ramifications that are often played out without conscious awareness, permeates all our institutions–economic, political, educational–and affects the way we interact with each other. It affects our attitudes about health care, childcare, housing, recreation, and all the other things needed to promote child and youth development and expression and adequate family functioning.

Alas, it is often expressed most sharply and hurtfully in schools.

On a recent trip to Copenhagen, I told my hosts–a teacher and three administrators–about an incident in an American school: When a teacher brought her dog to school prior to the opening of the year, a colleague playfully commented, "I see you brought us another student," to which the dog owner replied, "Oh, no! This is a smart dog, not like our kids."

The Danish teacher, who had been sitting in a relaxed position, bolted erect and said sharply, "She should not be a teacher!" She added that in Denmark some teachers perform poorly but that she had never heard anyone make a remark like that about students in her many years in the profession. But when I recount the incident to American educators, there is little surprise or shock, even if they are distressed. Most have heard the dummy-loser attitude expressed time and again.

In this case the offending teacher was White and her school was predominantly Black. But in a recent *New York Times* article about moving her family to the exurbs of upstate New York, Francine Prose describes how a teacher there sprinkled a little water on the "slow" students while watering the classroom plants. She called this practice "watering the vegetables."

It would be easy to label these teachers "bad." And surely anything that hurts the development of students is bad pedagogical practice. But such teachers are products of a pervasive cultural belief. From their own childhood experiences through their professional preparation to our almost fanatical preoccupation with the highest test scores in school, they absorb the message that will and intelligence determine success.

In his book *Emotional Intelligence*, Daniel Goleman wrote, "One of psychology's open secrets is the relative inability of grades, IQ or SAT scores, despite their popular mystique, to predict unerringly who will succeed in life. . . . There are widespread exceptions to the rule that IQ predicts success–

many (or more) exceptions than cases that fit the rule. At best, IQ contributes about 20 percent to the factors that determine life success, which leaves 80 percent to other forces." Yale psychologist Robert J. Sternberg and University of Connecticut psychologist Joseph S. Renzulli point to a threshold level of intelligence needed for life success but indicate the importance of factors such as creativity, task commitment, and positive reinforcement as determinants also. I would add good social skills, good health, access to opportunity, and good luck.

As long as most people could work without a high level of education, we got away with the argument that the cream rises to the top. But child care, health care, and community renewal programs are needed to enable most families without education and skills to function well. When our failure to provide such support began to result in social problems ranging from welfare dependency to crime, we blamed and scapegoated the most vulnerable people rather than developing policies and practices needed to adjust to changes created by technological advances.

Now employment requires a higher level of education, so an understanding we have downplayed—that through good development most people can perform well—needs to permeate our institutions. For the common good, society needs to systematically promote adequate development. Blaming vulnerable groups only interferes with our ability to identify and overcome or limit system-level problems that are affecting *all* groups.

For example, the one-parent family incidence among blacks that Daniel Patrick Moynihan courageously pointed out as a problem about twenty-five years ago is now the rate among whites. The proportion of white one-parent families increased from 10 percent in 1970 to 25 percent in 1994. The *Trends* report issued by the U.S. Department of Health and Human Services indicates that the percentage of births to unmarried white teens rose by 284 percent between 1970 and 1992. In 1970, the rate of black unmarried teen births was three times that of whites. In 1992 it was only one and a third times that of whites.

Substance abuse, once thought prevalent mainly in black communities, is now high in all communities. *Youth Indicators* (1993) noted that in 1992, 88 percent of high school seniors acknowledged using alcohol, 62 percent cigarettes, and 33 percent marijuana. Because blacks make up only 12 percent of the population, these drugs must be in widespread use in the white community.

The arrest rate for violent crimes by white teens under the age of eighteen rose by 300 percent from 1970 to 1992, while the rate for nonwhites rose only 22.5 percent during the same period. And the homicide rate among white males fifteen to nineteen years old almost tripled in those years.

When social problems began to increase sharply in white suburbs and rural areas in the 1970s, it should have been clear that we had underlying structural and/or systemic problems. But it wasn't until the 1990s that policymakers and even social scientists began to give significant attention to these issues. Even now many insist that the problems are individual, unrelated to economic and social structures and processes.

To survive and thrive as a democracy, a society must attend to three areas.

- It must develop a *sound and growing economy* that permits the participation of all of its citizens.
- It must maintain *sound community and family functioning* so that critical tasks, particularly child rearing, can be well performed.
- It must have a *culture that values both* and facilitates the critical interaction between the two.

And do we need to attend to these three areas simultaneously? Yes; they are linked.

- When the economy works, heads of households can earn the resources to promote adequate family functioning.
- When families function well, children are more likely to grow up prepared for success in school, as citizens—and at work.

A serious and sustained imbalance of power and lack of attention to any of these critical areas can lead to big problems. Our society gives lip service to the critical relationship between individual development and opportunity, but does not promote such development widely enough to meet today's requirements. Traditional schooling and the imparting of social skills are both needed, as are the employment opportunities, health care, and child care that help families to make their children ready for school.

Unfortunately, we tend to leave these necessities to economic chance.

The fact that individual development is directly related to the quality of community and family functioning is only now being recognized, and even now by too few. Our societal problems, based on wrongheaded cultural beliefs, have indeed been self-inflicted.

Nonetheless, the United States has probably come closer to creating the Good Society than any society of its complexity in the history of the world-despite its huge size, its growing population, and its complicated history of immigration and migration and slavery. Our country is still a place where you can start with nothing and build a fortune. It is still a place where you can worship as you please, speak your mind about what you think is right, even write a book about what you think is wrong.

Even with our great diversity, the United States is still a place where the democratic ideal remains alive. Indeed, we have endured two centuries of turbulence and struggle–against slavery and for suffrage–times of economic upheavals and divisive wars, and remained strong in our ideals and institutions. America is an idea that has come close enough to its proclaimed promise to tease us into believing that, with just a little more effort, maybe we can get it right. But it is getting late in the day.

The beginning of the twenty-first century is going to be an important psychological watershed. Nations in which large numbers of people are in great trouble are going to go on a downhill course, slowly at first, perhaps, but then rapidly as an increasing percentage of each generation fails to make the grade. Nations that reach the twenty-first century with most of their people functioning well most of the time are going to thrive.

The First and Second Myths identified above stand firmly in our way. They prevent us from overcoming the ill effects of race-based past policies and practices. They prevent us from creating a system of schooling that is based on what we know about how children develop and learn. They prevent us from promoting the kind of community and family functioning that will enable most families to successfully carry out their critical tasks most of the time, now and in a future that will bring great changes and, probably, less work as we now know it.

Without significant change in our culture, neither schools nor any other institutions can solve our problems. Expecting schools to do so is like "waiting for a miracle." But we can change our beliefs and behaviors and begin to effectively address our problems.

We can't begin to make the degree of change that is needed, however, without dismantling our paralyzing myths. The myths affect even our tools of understanding. For example, accepting test scores as reliable measures of student ability, prominent researchers once argued that changing the schools couldn't make a difference. They concluded that what the students brought with them–their inherent ability and their early experiences at home–were all that counted. But subsequent studies have shown beyond any doubt that schools can and do make a difference. The social environment of schools can promote student development and effort and improve academic achievement.

The old research reminds me of the comment of a student who was so fed up with social-science thinking that he dropped out of graduate school. He asked, "Why is it that they look at the dying flower and ask what is wrong with it? Why don't they ask whether it has had enough sunlight and water, whether the roots have taken and the nutrition is adequate?" Because we believe it is all in the genes, we don't think enough about how societal factors and forces interact to make desirable outcomes possible.

The pervasiveness of our major myths has suggested the organization of this book in three sections: Perspectives, Winners and Losers, and Win-Win. As my argument goes against the cultural grain, I devote the first section, Perspectives, to grounding. In the second section I explore the myths built into our cultural foundation. In the third section I examine three problem areas we must address, and I propose processes we can put in motion that will allow each American to help prepare us all to meet the challenges of this age, and the new age bearing down on us.

In the first section I ask the reader to walk in my shoes, to see what I have seen, to experience what I have experienced. I do this by describing aspects of my own growing-up experience. I want you to meet my family and my friends, the people in my church and neighborhood and school. I want you to feel the support and opposition I experienced in the world beyond my family, and the critical role my family played. I want you to see how my experience was both comparable to and different from that of other young people of the same ability and economic level.

I want you to walk with me into schools where young people were not doing well. I want you to hear how lessons learned from my experience brought about improved outcomes where many said it couldn't be done.

Equally, I want you to feel the resistance to efforts to improve the outcomes of many more that was expressed by institutions and individuals from the schoolhouse to the White House of the 1970s.

Because of my experience I know that outcomes are determined by more than intelligence and will. From my perspective, winners and losers are made, not born, and there is no such thing as a self-made man or woman. Yet the critical role of political, economic, and social structures in individual performance is largely ignored. Therefore in the second section of this book I explore our First and Second myths, looking at the way development and performance of the individual is affected by powerful structures and conditions in the networks around them.

I also show how the African-American experience differs from that of other groups in the ways that count the most–cultural discontinuity, inadequate opportunity for family and community development, and exclusion from the economic mainstream over time. The way the black experience is different contributes to the myth of innate inferiority and to greater vulnerability of the group to economic and social problems. I show how rapid changes in the economy over the last fifty years have been particularly harmful, and I discuss how this vulnerability hurts the country as much as the black community.

The problem here is that African-Americans are not a separate country–not even the left arm of a right-handed Uncle Sam. The group is more like 12 percent of the nation's heart muscle. And when that much of our heart muscle is in trouble, we're at serious risk of a national heart attack.

In the third section, I will discuss how we can individually and collectively begin to bring about needed adjustments. First, the nation must find ways to decrease the scapegoating of African-Americans–and all other groups–so that we can focus our attention on the problems and opportunities that face us. Second, we must create a system of schooling that can help us solve societal and cultural problems rather than simply reflect them. Finally, we must find a way to promote a win-win culture–competitive but caring and enabling of all–the Good Society.

Our policies and practices are often labeled conservative or liberal. And we wallow in the debate of public versus private. These dichotomies are not helpful. What we do should flow from empirical evidence of what works, as well as from what is ethical and moral. And successful human systems, because of human nature, require constant efforts to maintain the delicate balance among economic, cultural, and community and family forces. This requires public and private interaction and cooperation–and an effort to promote participation and inclusion for all.

Fortunately, structures and practices that are already in place, or have been beneficially used previously, can be modified or used as models to address today's needs. We already spend a great deal of money on social programs; unfortunately, too little is spent to prevent problems in the first place. Our task is to change the cultural mind-set in all our institutions from "those who can, will" to "all can."

Although the school is a reflection of the problem, with adjustments it can become a significant part of the solution. There are studies that show that scientifically based structural changes–organized and managed, and working differently at every level–and not education gimmicks can make public schools effective. And this in turn can foster the broader national change that we need as we face the challenges of the twenty-first century.

A colleague has pointed out that if deep-seated beliefs and related dynamics are the problem, and cultural change is the key to solving it, we are in a tight spot. Culture change is difficult and slow. There can be no "magic bullet," no quick fix.

Yet I am optimistic. With effective mobilization, significant cultural change has already taken place in our country in a reasonable period of time. And as I will show, mechanisms *can* be put in place to begin to solve our problems, to create a good and caring society capable of adjusting in a future that will be changing ever faster.

ENDNOTES

A 1996 National Opinion Research Center report: Cross, Theodore L., Slater, Robert B., & Hoffman, Adonis E. "Vital Signs: Statistics That Measure the State of Racial Inequality." *The Journal of Blacks in Higher Education*, Autumn 1996, 67.

In fact, Aid to Families with Dependent Children: U.S. Congressional Budget Office. *Appendix J. Budget Tables, Major Spending Categories [by fiscal year, in billions of dollars].* Washington, DC: U.S. Government Printing Office, 1995.

The typical child on AFDC: U.S. Bureau of the Census. *Statistical Abstract of the United States 1995 (115th ed.).* Washington, DC: U.S. Government Printing Office, 1995.

But in a recent New York Times article: Prose, Francine. "Outer City Blues: What Began As a Country Utopia for the Parents Turned into a Nightmare for the Kids." *New York Times Magazine*, 21 April 1996, 68.

In his book *Emotional Intelligence*: Goleman, Daniel. *Emotional Intelligence.* New York: Bantam, 1995.

Sternberg, R. J. "Lies We Live By: Misapplication of Tests in Identifying the Gifted." *Gifted Child Quarterly*, 15: 7–61.

Renzulli, J. S. "Three-Ring Conception of Giftedness: A Developmental Model for Creative Productivity." *South African Journal of Education*, 1985, 1–18.

The proportion of white one-parent families: U.S. Bureau of the Census. "All Parent/Child Situations, by Type Race and Hispanic Origin of Householder or Reference Person: 1970 to Present." *Current Population Reports, Series P20-483: "Household and Family Characteristics March 1994," and earlier reports.* Washington, DC: U.S. Government Printing Office, 1994.

The *Trends* report: U.S. Department of Health and Human Services, Office of the Assistant Secretary for Planning and Evaluation. *Trends in the Well-Being of America's Children and Youth: 1996.* Washington, DC: U.S. Government Printing Office, 1996.

Youth indicators: U.S. Department of Education, Office of Educational Research and Improvement. *Youth indicators 1993: Trends in the Well-Being of American Youth.* Washington, DC: U.S. Government Printing Office, 1993.

Because blacks make up only 12 percent of the population: U.S. Bureau of the Census. *Statistical Abstract of the United States 1995 (115th ed.).* Washington, DC: U.S. Government Printing Office, 1995.

The arrest rate for violent crimes for white teens: Ibid.

Article 2

WHY CAN'T WE CLOSE THE ACHIEVEMENT GAP?

SHERYL J. DENBO

THERE ARE NUMEROUS EXAMPLES of school reform that have resulted in African American students rapidly and significantly improving their levels of academic achievement and thus closing the achievement gap (Bullard & Taylor, 1993; Hartmann, DeCicco, & Griffin, 1994; Hilliard, 1997; Oakes et al., 2000; Schmoker, 1999; Schmoker & Wilson, 1999; Sizemore, Brosard, & Harrigan, 1982; Viadero, 2000)

Central Park East Secondary School: East Harlem, New York

An alternative public high school that primarily serves African American students saw significant gains in test scores after adopting interactive teaching methods and learning activities through writing workshops, thematic units, discussion, and inquiry. (Schmoker & Wilson, 1999)

Montgomery County, Maryland

School officials retrained principals and teachers, increased class time and hired more teachers to reduce class size in order to improve reading skills. As a result, the proportion of Black 2nd graders who were reading at grade level rose form 45 percent to 68 percent between February and June of 1999, narrowing the gap between Black and White reading levels from 17 percentage points to 10, in five months. (Viadero, 2000)

In a study by Texas A&M University of the best schools for educating Blacks and Hispanics in their state, researchers found that solid, consistent implementation of curricular programs was more important than the programs themselves; thus, quality and consistency led to student success in a diversity of programs. In addition, researchers noted that long-term leadership that focused on quality, with high expectations of both teachers and students made a difference. "At the low end, districts give up and blame the environment," said Kenneth J. Meier, a professor who worked on the study. "You never see that in good districts. Their attitude is, 'We can teach anybody to learn'" (quoted by Viadero, 2000). In an evaluation of principals at high-performing, low-income, and predominantly minority schools, Samuel Casey Carter (2000) of the Heritage Foundation, a Washington, D.C. think tank, attributed the success of the principals to their having latitude in curricular and spending decisions, "tangible and unyielding goals," careful teacher recruitment, regular student assessments, and systematic parent outreach. Why, then, have we failed to make these successes the norm rather than the exception?

The success of such programs demonstrates how institutional practices can be used to expand educational opportunities and raise achievement levels among African American students. Conversely, they also demonstrate how the institutional practices they replace had previously limited the educational opportunities of African American students and resulted in their poor academic performance. Success stories like these are evidence that the high academic performance of African American students is the result of educators believing in their students' ability to learn and their own ability to teach and supporting those beliefs with a wide variety of opportunities to learn, innovative school policies, challenging curriculum, and effective teaching practices. Changing ineffective practices, rather than abandoning African American students to low-level, low-expectation learning environments, is the key to success. Unfortunately for every example of success there are literally thousands of examples of failure. Why is that? The answer, we believe, is that these successes live in a larger institutional and cultural environment that reinforces the failure of African American students, thus making success difficult to achieve and almost impossible to maintain and/or scale up. The overall result has been a pervasive achievement gap. If educational leaders are going to succeed in closing the achievement gap between White and Black students, while, at the same time, raising overall achievement, we must understand exactly how current institutional practices contribute to maintaining this performance gap.

Current institutional practices that discourage the achievement of African American students include but are not limited to the following:

- **Unequal Funding and Lack of Comparable Resources**. Schools are financed through local sources of revenue (i.e., local property, business taxes, and state taxes). In large part, this ensures unequal resource distribution among school districts. Districts that lack adequate revenue bases serve the largest number of students of color. African American students suffer from a lack of educationally related resources and inferior facilities, resulting in larger class sizes, less qualified teachers, inferior buildings, science equipment and labs, libraries and library materials, computers, textbooks, and other resources. They have fewer and less rigorous after school and summer programs (Center on Education Policy [CEP], 2001; Kozol, 1991, as cited by House, 1999; Taylor & Piche, 1991; USDOE, 2001; USGAO, 1997).

- **Inaccurate and Misused Assessments**. High stakes tests disadvantage non-White students for a variety of reasons. They do not provide a complete picture of student performances, particularly for those students whose knowledge and abilities are not accurately measured by tests; they may not be aligned with the curriculum, especially for those students tracked into lower ability classes; they may narrow the curriculum to teaching to the test, and they have cultural, class, and racial biases. These tests legitimize tracking and retention policies, contribute to high drop and push out rates, and perpetuate low test scores. Inaccurate assessment and scoring results in disproportionally high placement of African American students in special education and disproportionally low placement in gifted programs and advanced academic classes (CEP, 2001; Fordham, 1996; Haney, 1993, as cited by House, 1999; National Research Council, 1997).

- **Less-Qualified and Experienced Teachers**. Despite research that indicates teacher quality has a very significant effect on student achievement, the least-qualified teachers are assigned to the students faced with the greatest challenges. In addition, a decreasing number of African American educators and administrators are teaching and/or managing our public schools (CEP, 2001; Darling-Hammond, 1999; USDOE, 1997).

- **Lack of a Rigorous School Curricula and Lower Teacher Expectations**. Students in schools with large numbers of low-income students and students from diverse ethnic, cultural, and language backgrounds are taught through curricula that are geared to "slow" learners and are repetitious and boring, based on the presumed lesser abilities of these students. Students tend to take fewer and less rigorous academic courses and tend to receive watered-down instruction. Research demonstrates that teachers tend to have lower expectations for African American students. Curriculum, instructional materials, and instructional strategies continue to be largely Eurocentric and to devalue African American culture and contributions, ways of learning, and world views (Adelman, 1997; CEP, 2001; Darling-Hammond, 1999; Levin, 1993, as cited by House; Sleeter & Grant, 1993).

- **Tracking**. African American students in schools

with a diverse student population are often separated from the mainstream student population into less challenging classes and programs and assigned the least-qualified teachers. African American students tracked into lower groups and special education programs receive dumbed-down curricula and do not have access to the curriculum and instruction that supports high achievement and that leads to on-time graduation. Students placed in less-challenging programs experience diminished self-esteem, motivation for learning and engagement in school. In addition, African American students have less access to effective teaching practices using technology (CEP, 2001; Darling-Hammond, 1999; Oakes, 1985, as cited by House; Oakes et al., 2000; Wenglinsky, 1998; Wheelock, 1992, as cited by House, 1999).

- **Disproportional Retention**. African American students are disproportionately retained, despite the fact that being retained does not increase learning, but rather significantly increases the student's chances of dropping out of school (CEP, 2001; Shepard & Smith, 1989, as cited by House, 1999).

- **Disproportional Expulsion and Suspension**. A great disparity exists in the suspension rates for African American students and their peers. Nationally, African Americans made up about 17 percent of all students in 1998–1999, but accounted for 33 percent of all students suspended. White students made up 63 percent of enrollment and 50 percent of suspensions, and Latino students made up 15 percent enrollment and 14 percent of the suspensions. The rise of "zero-tolerance" policies that mandate suspension and expulsion for the possession of weapons and a wide range of student behaviors categorized as misconduct is attributed to furthering the racial disparities in discipline. According to researchers and civil rights advocates, racial discrimination in the application of the zero tolerance rules has led to more severe punishments for African American students compared with their White peers accused of the same or similar violations of the rule (CEP, 2001; Gordon, Della Piana, & Keleher, 2000).

- **Segregation**. Schools continue to be organized in ways that segregate African Americans and other minorities in large numbers. Segregation continues the tradition of racially identifiable schools, programs, and classrooms (CEP, 2001; House, 1999; Orfield, Arenson, Jackson, Bohrer, Gavin, & Kalejs, 1998; Orfield & Gordon, 2001).

School-Related Achievement Factors

- Unequal funding and lack of comparable resources
- Inaccurate and misused assessments
- Less-qualified and less-experienced teachers
- Lack of a rigorous school curriculum and lower teacher expectations
- Tracking and disproportional placement in special education
- Disproportional retention
- Disproportional expulsion and suspension
- Segregation

Local school district policies, local financing practices, standardized testing, tracking, retention, the discipline of students, and inadequate curricula and resources can be discussed without reference to race. However, any examination of how these policies and practices function together and whom they most negatively affect reveals that they isolate African American students and provide them with an inferior education. House (1999) has gone as far as proclaiming that whatever its virtue, "American education as a whole, functions as a racist system." The institutional practices discussed earlier have resulted in disempowering and devaluing African American students and have made White privilege the norm.

Feminist researcher Peggy McIntosh has pointed out that most White people are unaware of the privileges they receive by virtue of being White and provides readers with a detailed list of examples of White privilege (1988). Educator Ruth Anne Olson (1992) builds on McIntosh's model for describing White privilege by outlining examples of the privileges that her own White children have in school.

- Whatever topics my children choose to study, they are confident that they will find materials that link people of their race to the accomplishments in those areas.

- My children know that they will always see faces like their own liberally represented in the textbooks, posters, films, and other materials in the hallways, classrooms and media centers of their schools.

- When my children talk about celebrations, holidays, or family observances in show-and-tell or in other informal exchanges at school, they know that their teachers will have experienced similar events and will be able to reinforce their stories.

- My children are confident that the musical instruments, rhythms, harmonies, visual design forms, and dramatic traditions of their culture will be generously recognized in the formal and informal uses of music, theater, and visual arts in their schools.

- The color of my children's skin causes most adults in school offices, classrooms and hallways to have neutral or positive assumptions about them. My children know that most adults in their schools will be of their same racial background, even in classrooms where many or most of their fellow students are of races different from theirs.

- My children are confident that they will never be embarrassed by being called on to tell the class about their race, culture, or special ways of celebrating events.

- When I visit their schools, my children know that school staff members will reserve judgment about my economic class, my level of education, and my reason for being in the school until I make them known.

- My children take for granted that the color of any crayons, bandages, or other supplies in their classrooms labeled "flesh" will be similar to their own.

- I take for granted that the tests used to judge my children's achievement and to determine placement in special classes has been developed with groups that include significant numbers of students who share our racial history and culture.

- My children are confident that they will never be embarrassed by hearing others suggest that the problems of the school (low levels of achievement, the need for special support services, etc.) are caused by the high numbers of children of their race.

- I am confident that policy decisions that affect my children's school experience will be made by state and local bodies dominated by people who understand our racial history and culture.

These circumstances, taken for granted as the norm in many schools, have the effect of supporting White, middle-, and upper-class students safely and successfully through a public education system designed to ensure their success.

The effects of current institutional practices and the resulting White privilege on African American students include:

- **Persistent underachievement**, as measured by standardized tests, and participation in advanced placement and gifted and talented programs. Tracking and placement of African American students into educational environments that have less-qualified teachers and less-challenging curricula perpetuates lower test scores and higher dropout rates (Berlak, 2001; National Center for Education Statistics, 2001).

- **High student dropout rates** that are approaching 50 percent in some urban schools. The low expectations, poorly trained teachers, and weaker curricula that characterize both urban schools and lower-tracked classes are conditions that hinder student graduation (Fletcher, 2001; Gilbert & Gay, 1985; USDOE, 1999).

- **Student performance anxiety and challenges to psychological and emotional well-being**. Many African Americans live within a social context and attend schools where they are believed to be less intelligent. To protect their self-esteem, some African American students are unwilling to become academically engaged. For many of these African American students, respect and support for a positive self-concept is sought among peers, and the importance of school is devalued (Berlak, 2001; Fordham,

1996; Shaffer, Ortman, & Denbo, in press).

- **Lower levels of African American parent involvement**. The continued perception by African American parents that schools discriminate and are not accessible to them has resulted in lower levels of African American parent participation. Greater levels of family stress, less available time, fewer social and economic resources, and fewer positive memories with their own public education experiences also inhibit African American parents from being involved in their own children's educational experiences at home and in school (Witherspoon, 2000).

A high-performing, African American high school student offers the following view of why African Americans often underperform in school and also expresses doubt that his own school success will be rewarded.

"Well, we supposed to be stupid . . . we perform poorly in school 'cause we all have it thought up in our heads that we're supposed to be dumb so we might as well go ahead and be dumb," he said. "And we think that most of the things we learn (at school) won't help us in life anyway. . . . What good is a quadratic equation gonna do me if I'm picking up garbage cans?" (Berlak, 2001)

Increasing diversity, the widening gap between the rich and the poor, the changing economy, and the increases in academic standards have all helped to focus attention on equity in educational reform. Unfortunately, too often we fail to change the culture and structure of American schools and thus continue to have only isolated successes.

CONCLUSION

Current institutional practices limit educational opportunities for African American children and ultimately limit their socioeconomic potential as well. These practices leave a large number of African American students unprepared for higher education or skilled work, even as the demand for unskilled labor is disappearing. Although many school systems are maintaining practices that perpetuate underachievement among African American students, there are schools that are choosing to make cultural and institutional changes rooted in the belief that they can successfully educate all children. Many African American students continue to improve their performance despite pervasive institutional structures that create failure. The gains made among students in schools that transform their educational practices underscore the power of institutional change and its potential for raising African American student achievement levels and closing the achievement gap. (For a detailed discussion of how to solve these problems, see "Institutional Change and Culturally Relevant Pedgogy: Two Sides of the Same Coin," Part II, of this volume. For an excellent discussion of the achievement gap with data and tables, see "It Takes More than Testing: Closing the Achievement Gap: A Report of the Center of Educational Policy" available online at *www.ctredpol.org*.)

REFERENCES

Adelman, C. (1999). *Answers in the toolbox: Academic intensity, attendance patterns, and bachelor's degree attainment.* Washington, DC: U.S. Department of Education.

Berlak, H. (2001, Summer). Race and the achievement gap. *Rethinking Schools: An Urban Educational Journal*, Vol. 5, No. 4. Milwaukee, WI: Rethinking Schools.

Bullard, P., & Taylor, B.O. (1993). *Making school reform happen.* New York: Allyn & Bacon.

Carter, S.C. (2000). *No excuses: Lessons from 21 high-performing, high-poverty schools.* Washington, DC: The Heritage Foundation.

Center on Educational Policy. *It takes more than testing: Closing the achievement gap*. Washington, DC, 2001. Website: *www.ctredpol.org.*

Darling-Hammond, L. (1995). Inequality and access to knowledge. In J.A. Banks & C.A.M. Banks (Eds.). *Handbook of research on multicultural education*, pp. 524–547. New York: Simon & Schuster.

Darling-Hammond, L. (1999). *The right to learn: A blueprint for creating schools that work.* San Francisco: Jossey-Bass.

Fletcher, M.A. (2001, March 3). Progress on dropout rate stalls: Critics say test drive could worsen problem. *The Washington Post*, p. 1, 10.

Fordham, S. (1996). *Blacked out: Dilemmas of race, identity, and success at Capital High.* San Francisco: Jossey-Bass.

Gilbert, S.E., & Gay, G. (1985, October). Improving the success in school of poor Black children. *Phi Delta*

Kappan, pp. 133–137.

Gordon, R., Della Piana, L., & Keleher, T. (2000). *Facing the consequences: An examination of racial discrimination in U.S. public schools.* Oakland, CA: Applied Research Center.

Hartman, J.A., DeCicco, E.K., & Griffin, G. (1994, November). Urban students thrive as independent researchers. *Educational Leadership, 52*(3), 46–47.

Hilliard, A. (1997). *Tapping the genius and touching the spirit: A human approach to the rescue of our children.* The Ninth Annual Benjamin E. Mays Lecture. Atlanta, GA: Georgia State University.

House, E.R. (1999). Race and policy. *Education Policy Analysis Archives* 7(16), 1–15.

Johnston, R.C. & Viadero, D. (2000, March 15). Unmet promise: Raising minority achievement. *Education Week*, 1, 18–19.

McIntosh, P. (1988). *White privilege and male privilege: A personal account of coming to see correspondences through work in women's studies.* Wellesley, MA: Center for Research on Women.

National Center for Education Statistics. (2001). *The Nation's Report Card* (A Report of the National Assessment of Educational Progress). Washington, DC: Author. *http://nces.ed.gov/nationsreportcard/*

National Research Council. (1997). *Improving schooling for language-minority students: A research agenda.* Washington, DC: National Academy Press.

Oakes, J., Quartz, K.H., Ryan, S., & Lipton, M. (2000). *Becoming good American schools: The struggle for civic virtue in education reform.* San Francisco: Jossey-Bass.

Olson, R.A. (1992, Nov.). *Eliminating White privilege: An awesome challenge for White parents and educators.* Saint Paul, MN: The Saint Paul Foundation.

Orfield, G., Arenson, J., Jackson, T., Bohrer, C., Gavin, D., & Kalejs, E. (1998). Summary of _City-suburban desegregation: Parent and student perspectives in metropolitan Boston. A Report by the Harvard Civil Rights Project. *Equity and Excellence in Education 31*(3), 6–12.

Orfield, G. & Gordon, N. (2001, July). *Schools more separate: Consequences of a decade of resegregation.* Report of the Harvard Civil Rights Project. Cambridge, MA: Harvard University. Retrieved 7/24/2001 from The World Wide Web: *http://www.law.harvard.edu/civilrights/publications/schoolsseparate.pdf*

Schmoker, M. (1999). *Results: The key to continuous school improvement* (2nd ed.). Alexandria, VA: Association for Supervision and Curriculum Development.

Schmoker, M.J., & Wilson, R. (1999). *Total quality education: Profiles of schools that demonstrate the power of Deming's management principles.* Bloomington: Phi Delta Kappa.

Shaffer, S., Ortman, P., & Denbo, S. (In press). The effects of racism, socioeconomic class and gender on academic achievement of African American students. In S. Denbo & L. Beaulieu (Eds.), *Improving schools for African American students: A reader for educational leaders.* Springfield, IL: Charles C Thomas Publishers, Ltd.

Sizemore, B.A., Brosard, C., & Harrigan, B. (1982). *An abashing anomaly: The high achieving predominately black elementary schools.* Pittsburgh, PA: University of Pittsburgh Press.

Sleeter, C.A., & Grant, C.A. (1993). *Making choices for multicultural education - Five approaches to race, class, and gender.* Englewood Cliffs, NJ: Prentice-Hall.

Taylor, W.L., & Piche, D.M. (1991). *A report on shortchanging children: The impact of fiscal inequality on the education of students-at-risk.* Prepared for the Committee on Education and Labor, U.S. House of Representatives. Washington, DC: U.S. Government Printing Office.

U.S. Department of Education (USDOE). (1997). *Digest of education statistics 1997.* Washington, DC: National Center for Education Statistics.

U.S. Department of Education. National Center for Education Statistics. (1999). *Digest of Education Statistics 1998.* Washington, DC: U.S. Government Printing Office.

U.S. Department of Education (USDOE). (2001, January). *Data enclosure on disparities in educational and financial resources among racial and ethnic groups and between urban and non-urban districts.* (Paper accompanying letter from USDOE Secretary to State Governors.) Washington, DC: Author.

U.S. General Accounting Office (USGAO). (1997). *State efforts to reduce funding gaps between poor and wealthy districts.* Washington, DC: Author.

Viadero, D. (2000, March 22). Lags in minority achievement defy traditional explanations. *Education Week*, 1, 18–22.

Wenglinsky, H. (1998). *Does it compute? The relationship between educational technology and student achievement in mathematics.* Princeton, NJ: Educational Testing Service.

Witherspoon, R. (2000). The involvement of African American families in education: Whose responsibility is it? In S. Denbo & L. Beaulieu (Eds.), *Improving schools for African American students: A reader for educational leaders.* Springfield, IL: Charles C Thomas Publishers, Ltd.

Article 3

THE EFFECTS OF RACISM, SOCIOECONOMIC CLASS, AND GENDER ON THE ACADEMIC ACHIEVEMENT OF AFRICAN AMERICAN STUDENTS

SUSAN SHAFFER, PATRICIA E. ORTMAN, AND SHERYL J. DENBO

WHEN EDUCATORS AND RESEARCHERS examine issues related to the underachievement of African American students, differences in performance related to gender are often overlooked. Understanding how gender influences achievement is critical. Historically, institutional racism has effected Black males and females differently. Without an understanding of how gender shapes experience, educators do not have the information they need to create effective solutions to what are very complex educational challenges. The underachievement of African American students in today's schools is clearly related to the organization of schools and is associated with particular school practices, such as tracking. However, the impact of these practices, as well as students' responses to them vary by class and gender. To fully understand African American student achievement, it is essential to take into consideration the historical context of racial oppression and current conditions in schools that continue to support institutional racism. Current school conditions that have a negative impact on African American students are addressed in a number of articles in this anthology. This article focuses our attention primarily on contemporary issues related to the intersection between institutional racism, socioeconomic class, and gender and their effects on the academic achievement of African American male and female students.

SOCIOECONOMIC STATUS AND ACHIEVEMENT

Class is a difficult issue to discuss in America. On the one hand, Americans are likely to deny the existence of class differences. On the other, the belief of many Americans that they live in a meritocracy gets translated into a belief that those who succeed economically deserve their success, and those who do not deserve their failure. If we couple the denial of the lingering effects of slavery and racism with the view that America is a meritocracy, any discussion of poverty among African Americans can be viewed as an indictment of those who have already been victimized. From the perspective of the authors of this article, poverty is not an indictment of those who are poor but of the society that continues to allow widespread poverty in the midst of economic prosperity.

LOW-INCOME AFRICAN AMERICANS AND ACHIEVEMENT

Poverty has adverse effects on child development and has a disproportionate impact on African American children (Center on Hunger, Poverty and Nutrition Policy, 1995). In 1999, 32.7% of African American families with children younger than 18 lived on incomes that were below the poverty level. This is compared with 8.8% of White families (U.S. Bureau of Census). One of the more debilitating aspects of poverty is related to residential patterns that promote socioeconomic isolation. Low-income African American children are more likely than low-income White children to live in low-income communities (Orfield, Arenson, Jackson, Bohrer, Gavin, & Kalejs, 1998). In addition to a lack of jobs, low-income communities frequently lack the family support services and other resources such as high-quality health and child care or preschool programs that are common in middle-income communities. These services have been shown to have positive long-term effects on academic achievement (Pianta & Cox, 1999; The Center for the Future of Children, 1997). African American students from low-income families are likely to attend segregated urban schools that are funded at lower levels than those of their suburban counterparts. Urban students have less access to a variety of educationally important resources, such as small class sizes, highly qualified teachers, computers, advanced level courses, and other curriculum supports (Darling-Hammond, 1997).

The residential segregation and resulting social and economic isolation of large numbers of poor African American families, many of whom are experiencing multigenerational poverty, can exacerbate the harmful effects of poverty on African American children. Theorists and researchers seem to disagree about whether poor and nonpoor children enter school at similar developmental levels or whether there are sizable differences exist among different groups of children (Pianta & Cox, 1999). However, what is clear is that the longer African American children stay in school, the farther they fall behind. Even middle-class African American students with access to additional educational and familial resources fail to keep pace with their middle-class White peers (Viadero, 2000).

MIDDLE-CLASS AFRICAN AMERICANS AND ACHIEVEMENT

If poverty is a chief culprit in undermining African American student achievement, why are we also finding entrenched achievement gaps between middle-class African American students and their White counterparts? Middle-class African American students perform significantly better then their low-income counterparts, but they do not achieve as well as middle-class White students. Thus, the achievement gap is only partially explained by the effects of poverty. On some standardized tests, African American students from middle-class or wealthier families perform at levels commensurate with White students who are poor. Other data have suggested that at higher grade levels, the gap between African American and White student performance is wider than at lower levels (Johnson & Viadero, 2000, citing Philips). In a recent study on racial bias in special education conducted by the Civil Rights Project of Harvard University (cited by Mathews, 2001), one of the most disturbing findings is that African American males who live in wealthier communities with better schools are at greater risk of being labeled mentally retarded and sent to special education classes than those attending predominantly African American low-income schools.

The reasons for middle-class African American students underachieving are complex and varied. Although research that specifically examines the academic achievement of middle-class African American students is limited, a variety of theories are offered to explain the gap in achievement levels that is commonly found between middle-class White and African American students. These theories include continued institutional practices that negatively affect African American students (e.g., fewer African American students are placed in advanced classes, more are placed in special education programs); lack of culturally responsive curriculum and/or programmatic options to support high achievement; lower teacher expectations; peer pressure; first-generation middle-class status; and differences in parental involvement in schools and their child's learning (Belluck, 1999; The College Board, 1999).

Fordham (1996) suggests that middle-class African American parents socialize their children to identify with both middle-class and working-class African Americans. Thus, middle-class African American students who see their lower-income counterparts disengaged in school may feel that to excel too much is a "selling-out" of their identity.

The view that achievement is not "a Black thing" is reinforced by a Eurocentric curriculum and a color-coded tracking system. African American parents may also experience a conflict between upward mobility and a desire to stay close to their communities of origin. In addition, middle-class African American parents may assume that because they are sending their children to better schools in the suburbs, they do not have to monitor the school or their own children as carefully. They very well may be underestimating both the institutional racism that their children are experiencing and the level of their child's disassociation from school.

Researchers have pointed out that achievement is probably influenced by additional socioeconomic differences between racial/ethnic groups that are not typically measured by educational surveys. For example, children's achievement could be shaped by grandparent's level of education, accumulated family wealth and assets, household size, quality of the schools attended by parents, mother's perception of her own efficacy, and children's birth weight, among other factors (Center on Education Policy, 2001). If we had better measures for these factors, perhaps they could explain more of the gap. Additional research on the academic achievement of middle-class African American students is needed to improve their educational experience. It is estimated that family income and parental education can explain about one-third of the racial/ethnic achievement gap (Center on Education Policy, 2001). In other words, the gap shrinks, but does not disappear, when adjustments are made for family income and parental education.

RACE, GENDER, AND ACHIEVEMENT

Claude Steele (1992) agrees that African American student underachievement cannot be explained simply by poverty or inadequate academic preparation; he believes that it is also explained by a failure of African American students to identify with school. Doing well in school, he tells us, requires that students believe that school achievement can be a promising source of self-esteem and that belief must be constantly reinforced. He concludes that African American students are devalued at school. Steele explains:

> Like anyone, Blacks risk devaluation for a particular incompetence, such as a failed test or a flubbed pronunciation. But they further risk, that such performances will confirm the broader, racial inferiority they are suspected of. Thus, from the first grade through graduate school, Blacks have the extra fear that in the eyes of those around them their full humanity could fall with a poor answer or a mistaken stroke of the pen. (p. 6)

Society is preconditioned to see the worst in them, he tells us, leaving African American students "deeply vulnerable in America's classrooms."

To cope with how they are devalued at school and yet maintain a positive self-concept, many African American students disengage in school and seek their self-esteem elsewhere. This disconnection from school can spread so that those who do continue to work are criticized for "acting white." The disassociation or disconnection from school often seems to manifest itself, within race, in gendered ways (Fordham citing Watkins, 2001). Michael Kimmel, an internationally recognized sociologist specializing in the study of men and masculinities and a participant in the American Association of University Women's September 2000 symposium "Beyond the Gender Wars, "mentions (citing Fordham's 1996 study) that "Black girls who take school seriously are accused of 'acting White' and Black boys who take school seriously and do really well in school are accused of 'acting like girls'" (p. 5).

Although both African American males and females are disenfranchised, Kimmel claims that "men who feel powerless socially or economically nevertheless differ as a group from women in one crucial aspect–these men have a sense of entitlement. . . . They may feel powerless, but they also feel *entitled* to power" (AAUW, 2001, pp. 7–8). If indeed African American males have a sense of being denied male privileges that are the norm in mainstream America and African American females lack that sense of entitlement, this may, in part, account for gender differences in responses to racism within school systems.

It has been common for both educators and researchers to fail to take into account issues of gender when they look at the factors related to achievement. In addition, when researchers examine gender, it has been largely from the perspective of White females. All students must have the opportunity to develop positive self-concepts within the context of school if they are to become engaged in and responsible for their own learning. For that to happen, teachers, administrators, and parents need to address both male and female sex role development as it relates to the ethnicity and culture of each child. Gender identity becomes more important as students grow up; therefore, it should be taken increasingly into account as they progress to higher grades. Because both teachers and parents respond differently to African American males than they do to African American females, it is essential to understand the relationships between gender and achievement.

AFRICAN AMERICAN MALES

African American males are often held in high esteem by their peers. They are viewed as leaders, good athletes, and trend setters for youth culture. At the same time, African American males are sometimes feared by school officials who may consider them threatening. More than any other group of students, Black males experience negative school outcomes (Davis, 2000). As a group, they have lower standardized test scores, higher retention and dropout rates, more frequent placement in special education, lower participation in nonathletic extracurricular activities, less representation in advanced-level classes than their White counterparts or Black females, and are disproportionately disciplined for committing similar infractions.

The popularity of high stakes testing and accountability policies and practices means that schools are asking all students to work harder, invest in their own schooling, and demonstrate higher levels of achievement on standardized tests (Roderick, 2000). Societal stereotypes, together with a wide variety of social, political, and economic forces, interact to place African American males at a disadvantage in the educational system and in meeting these expectations. African American males not only face lower expectations from their teachers, they are also less likely than their White peers to see themselves as good students (Roderick, 2000, citing Hare & Castenell). Because of these factors, "Minority boys, more so than other adolescents, must cope with the dual stresses of academic challenge and negative stereotype about their group and these stresses can undermine their endorsement of achievement values" (Roderick, 2000, citing Graham et al., 1998, p. 618).

In a new article, Margaret Spencer, Gregory Seaton, and Vinay Harpalani from the University of Pennsylvania (2000) call African American males, "the most highly stigmatized and stereotyped group in America. Whether it is by images of super athlete, criminal, gangster, or hyper-sexed male, it seems that most of society's views of African American males are defined by these stereotypes" (p. 3). Dr. Martha R. Bireda (2000) says that, "Stereotypical images of African American males have over time become part of the cultural psyche of America" (p. 9). Bireda (2000) explains Boskin's description of the most predominant of these stereotypes: the "Sambo" and the "Brute." The "Sambo" image originated during slavery and characterizes African American males as lazy, unintelligent, irresponsible, and servile. The other archetype, the "Brute," depicts African American males as overly aggressive and needing to be controlled. They are portrayed as sexually impulsive, animal-like creatures, who can be dangerous, especially to White women. Contemporary images continue to support these stereotypes. According to Bireda:

> Unfortunately, the Sambo and Brute stereotypes survive in some form today and continue to have a negative impact on African American students. The Sambo image inhibits both the academic achievement of African American males and their relationships with their teachers, leading to low expectations as well as disproportionately high referrals to special education and low referral rates to higher level and gifted courses. In many instances, teachers are more comfortable with the playful, jovial African American male students than with the serious, quiet ones, who are perceived to have an "attitude." The Sambo image also creates greater acceptance for the African American male student who is submissive rather than assertive, the latter being perceived rather as aggressive or defiant.
>
> The Brute image leads to a preoccupation with control and unjust labeling. African American male students are held to a higher standard of behavior than their peers. They are most likely to be punished for minor infractions, and they receive penalties disproportionate to their conduct. In the same way that African American male students are tracked academically,

> they are tracked behaviorally. When one misbehaves, he is quickly branded a troublemaker and is henceforth never able to escape this label. In many instances, African American male students are set up for misbehavior. The teacher, knowing which "button to push," can easily provoke the student to an angry response and thus have cause to remove him from the classroom. (pp. 9–10)

Thus, while forming their adult identities, African American male adolescents must also cope with the negative feedback that comes from entrenched racism and stereotyping.

African American males with psychological adjustment issues are often referred to the criminal justice system, whereas their European American counterparts are often referred to mental health services (Spencer, Seaton, & Harpalani, 2000, citing Spurlock & Norris). Spencer, Seaton, and Harpalani (citing Jerrett & Oyemade) go on to say that, "Simply by their contrast to mainstream culture, the behaviors and practices that characterize African American communities are assumed not to be cultural but, instead deviant" (p. 17). In response to these social and developmental challenges, Black males develop coping methods that can lead to either adaptive or maladaptive solutions. In addition, a solution may be adaptive in one context, such as a neighborhood, and maladaptive in another, such as school. These coping strategies help to define how individual students view themselves as students, members of cultural and social groups, and individuals (Spencer, Seaton, & Harpalani, 2000).

Anderson (cited by Noguerra, 2001) claims that low-income Black males learn at an early age that by presenting a tough exterior, it is easier to avoid threats or attacks. Ron Ferguson (cited by Norguerra, 2001) found in his research in Shaker Heights, Ohio, that African American students were more likely than White students to cite "toughness" as a trait they admired. This particular coping strategy may have a negative effect on teacher-student relationships and academic performance.

However, Spencer, Seaton, and Harpalani (2000) and others believe that the problem may not be particular coping strategies so much as it may be society's view of African American males. Spencer explains that African American males are generally viewed through a lens of negative stereotypes associated with male adolescence in general, along with the added burden of the negative image of African American males. Asa Hilliard, a professor at the University of Georgia, has told numerous audiences that he believes the decisive academic downward turn at the age of nine or ten may be explained, at least in part, by the fact that at this age African American boys start to look like young men, and White female teachers are afraid of them. Others state that the demeanors of African American boys frequently are misunderstood by White middle-class teachers and are often seen as defiant, aggressive, and intimidating (Davis, 2000, citing Grant; Davis, 2000, citing Majors et al.; Davis, 2000, citing Slaughter-Defoe & Richards).

The link between school climate and student achievement is well documented (Davis, 2000, citing Irvine & Pallas); however, much more research is needed to understand how this specifically applies to African American boys. The research on African American boys in the early grades is limited, but what does exist provides some insights. Davis (2000, citing Slaughter-Defoe & Richards) suggests that as early as kindergarten, African American males are treated differently from other male and female students. Research indicates that although African American males share a desire for more personal and positive contact with their teachers, there is evidence that they do not receive positive contact (Davis, 2000, citing Davis). Throughout elementary and middle school, African American boys consistently receive lower ratings by teachers for social behavior and academic expectations (Davis, 2000, citing Irvine and Rong). In addition, it is widely believed that the disproportionate placement of African American boys in lower ability groups and their early placement in special education negatively affects their academic self-concept and results in lower achievement (Davis, 2000, citing Simmons & Grady; Darling-Hammond, 1997; Oakes, 1990; Oakes, Wells, Yonezawa, & Ray, 1997).

Adolescent males from diverse ethnic and cultural groups may feel they are forced to choose between their ethnic and cultural group identity and academic success. African American males can come to believe that to preserve and promote the value of their own identity, they must reject academic achievement (Tatum, cited by Noguerra,

2000). This belief is reinforced in schools by the failure of the educational system to engage African American students in the rich history of African American intellectualism and by the disproportionate tracking of African Americans into lower-level academic programs. Some researchers believe that for some African American students, doing well in school comes to be perceived as a sign that one has "sold out" or opted to "act white" for the sake of individual gain (Ogbu, cited by Noguerra, 2000; Fordham, 1996). In response to these dilemmas, adolescents may develop an oppositional identity (Tatem, cited by Noguerra, 2000). As Jon, an academically successful African American high school senior tells it:

> As a Black male, I know a little about this. I wouldn't say Black males are academic underachievers, but I would agree that right now we are underachieving. I mean it's hard to do anything else and give in to the same system that treats you like garbage. To get up every morning at six and go to school, saying yes sir, yes ma'am, and learn things about these same people that are doing this to you. It's hard.

This attitude is what some experts have labeled an oppositional identity. From the perspective of the African American students, even the academically successful ones, it is seen as fighting back against an oppressive system. Whatever the interpretation of the cause, this behavior can have a great impact on both academic achievement and students' interactions with the larger society. In addition, what is labeled an oppositional identity could be, in part, difficulties in cross-cultural communication between White teachers and Black students; or, based on an African American student's fear that any academic involvement might be seen by a White teacher as a confirmation of his or her racist assumptions about the student's abilities (Davis, 2000, Steele, 1992). Culturally dissonant pressures and expectations, as well as conflicts between home, community, school, and mainstream culture, are promoting misinformed, unhealthy, and unfair choices for African American adolescents (Shaffer & Gordon, 2000).

Spencer (2000) believes that some African American males, in their pursuit of justice and/or respect, may develop an interpersonal style or coping mechanism that has been labeled "hypermasculinity persona." Teachers, for their part, are likely to have uniform expectations for what is appropriate student behavior irrespective of the problematic school climate experienced by many African American males. For some Black males, the pursuit of respect, an important social value in the African American community, can take on more importance than the acquisition of academic skills. This hypermasculinity may be seen by youth as potentially more effective in generating respect than behaviors that are more likely to be associated with academic success. Academic success may be seen as beyond their reach or achieved only through selling out to a White, racist society.

We urgently need a better understanding of how African American males perceive their options, how they interpret their risks and stresses, and how they evaluate accessible supports and available coping methods. As many researchers have pointed out, we have had insufficient research on those students who have demonstrated resilience and have achieved in school (Spencer, Seaton, & Harpalani, 2000). Despite the social, psychological, and economic barriers that many Black males face, most do manage to graduate from high school, find employment, and support and take care of their families. We need to know more about the factors that contribute to their success in the face of significant adversity. Unfortunately, far more research seems to focus on examining the reasons for failure instead of the reasons for success.

AFRICAN AMERICAN FEMALES

By some measures it would seem that African American girls are doing better in school than African American boys. Evidence exists, however, that African American girls as a group suffer academically because of discrimination on the basis of both gender and race. African American girls are sometimes punished for being "loud," i.e., not conforming to teachers' expectations of "feminine" behavior (Fordham, 1996). Indeed, research shows that the "black girls who are outspoken and independent often find themselves (like some boys) cast as troublemakers rather than leaders" (AAUW, 1998, p. 25). But being assertive and outgoing often conforms to the home culture of Black girls

(Fordham, 1996).

As they reach adolescence, some African American girls, so as to be recognized in school, adopt what they call "attitude." One African American girl describes the reason why she has adopted this "attitude." Florence says, "It lets people know that I'm serious, that I'm not playing and it's a good way, you know, for people to listen, to know that I'm trying to get a point across" (Way, 1998). Although teachers may respond negatively to this voice, the girls who adopt an "attitude" believe it is necessary in order to encourage people to acknowledge and listen to them. Adolescent girls, especially Black girls from low-income families, realize that unless they speak up, they will be offered little from a society that continues to marginalize them. Because of this reality, it is not surprising that some African American girls may believe their academic achievement will not be rewarded commensurate with their efforts to succeed. Although some girls are adopting an "attitude" to cope with racism, others cope by "growing more passive and quiet than almost any other school group" (AAUW, 1998, pp. 48–49). And although much has been made of the 1991 AAUW findings (cited by Ward, 1996) that "Black girls . . . began with and were better able to retain higher levels of self-esteem through adolescence than their white and Latina counterparts," it is important to note that they were not relying on school to give them that positive sense of self (Ward, p. 88). In fact,

> . . . black girls showed evidence of a significant decline in their academic self-esteem over the course of their years in the school system. . . . (they) showed a drop in their positive feelings about their teachers and their school work. They were not feeling good about their academic performance nor about the evaluations and validations received from school personnel. Such a decline in academic self-esteem has serious implications for academic achievement and may engender apathy in school, resulting in low grades and poor academic performance." (Ward, p. 98)

It seems, then, that in order for African American girls to succeed at school, they must tread a very fine race and gender line. Indeed, Fordham (cited by Weiler, 2000) found that "the academically successful African American girls achieved their success by becoming or remaining silent or voiceless or alternatively by impersonating a male image" (p. 27). The silence of these girls, however, was not due to acquiescence to the idea that they lacked value but rather defiance of the schools' low expectations of them. Clearly, ". . . their academic success comes at great cost: alienation and isolation from their community's cultural system, and seemingly little support or reward from parents, in particular mothers, for maintaining their academic and 'nice girl' roles" (p. 27). In addition, they are also going through "a process of socialization toward a Black female role" by their teachers (Jones & Clark, 1986 and Fordham, 1993, as cited by Weiler, 2000). They are expected to serve as "social integrator," bringing children together from all different backgrounds because they are looked on by the teacher as mature, self-reliant, and helpful. At the same time, they are less likely to get the attention or recognition necessary to encourage their intellectual achievement. Their comments in class discussions may be ignored, and they may not receive the help they need in academics (Sadker & Sadker, 1994). In fact, gender interacts with race to determine who gets the most attention and results in Black females getting the least of any group (Sadker & Sadker, 1994). This dichotomy can encourage social skills at the expense of academic skills.

Despite the legacy of racial oppression, the challenges of contradictory expectations, and a lack of support for academic success, many African American girls recognize the strong connection between a good education and a good job (Mickelson, 1990). Most want, and expect, both. In a study of the aspirations of young women of African American and Puerto Rican descent, one African American high school girl exemplifies most of girls in the findings. She says, ". . . I want to go to a good college . . . [In five years] I'll be a career woman . . . I think I want to be a social worker or a doctor" (Weiler, 2000, p. 75). She recognizes the strong connection between acquiring a good education and getting solid future employment. At the same time, African American girls expect to assume the dual role of mother and worker. According to Collins (cited by Weiler, 2000),

> Black girls learn to expect to work, to strive for an education so they can support themselves, and to anticipate carrying heavy responsibilities in their families

> and communities because these skills are essential to their own survival and those for whom they will eventually be responsible. (p. 80)

These young women are attempting to contradict society's assumptions about the value low-income urban women attach to schooling and about how they think about the future. Despite the enormous barriers to achievement, most African American girls are motivated to achieve academically and to plan for the future. Unfortunately, for working-class young women, already at the margins in the larger world because of their social status, there is little room for error, and there are few resources (Taylor, Gilligan, & Sullivan, 1995). Gender bias, although detrimental to all, has a significantly greater negative effect on lower-income African American girls than on middle-class White girls (Davenport & Yurick, 1991; AAUW, 1998). Especially troublesome at this time is that education research is concentrated on White middle-class girls, and this does not adequately depict the meaning of social inequality and discrimination in the lives of girls and boys of color. In addition, data are not, for the most part, disaggregated by gender within race and/or class. This omission makes it difficult to draw conclusions.

Some researchers have begun to collect and examine data by gender within race, but these efforts are still quite limited (AAUW, 1998). The Educational Testing Service recently published an analysis of the data of standard educational and economic measures of success that look at gender across racial/ethnic groups. Overall, the study finds support for the fact that the "cross-cutting nature of gender differences across groups suggests that policies to remedy educational inequalities must treat gender, as well as race/ethnicity as a crucial factor" (Coley, 2001, p. 3) and provides evidence that attention must be paid to the unique challenges African American males and females face in school. It is very important, therefore, for school personnel to make a concerted effort to address issues related to the academic achievement of both Black males and females. To that end, we make the following recommendations, many of which are explained in great detail in other articles throughout Part II.

IMPLEMENT PRACTICES THAT SUPPORT THE DEVELOPMENT OF AFRICAN AMERICAN MALE AND FEMALE POSITIVE SELF-CONCEPTS AND ACADEMIC ENGAGEMENT

1. Establish a whole school climate that assists African American male and female students to identify with learning, in general, and school, in particular, by consistently pointing to the students' academic potential and the rich history of Black academic accomplishment.
2. Help teachers to understand the importance of establishing close personal relationships with their students so that, in doing so, they can assist them to become committed to their own intellectual development.
3. Establish mentoring, tutoring programs, and homework assistance programs that emphasize acceleration and enrichment.
4. Hold separate focus groups with African American male and female students to talk about their experiences and brainstorm effective responses to difficulties they may be experiencing.
5. Create after-school and summer programs, including multicultural clubs, Afro-centric clubs; Rites of Passage programs; professional and job-related clubs, i.e., future teachers or firefighters; talent or interest-related clubs, i.e., bands, composing rap music, dance, that become alternatives to gangs and that help students to identify their strengths and interests.
6. Create a violence-free and respectful climate around all peer relations.
7. Introduce sex education in middle school.

ESTABLISH SCHOOL POLICIES AND PRACTICES THAT SUPPORT THE ACADEMIC ENGAGEMENT OF AFRICAN AMERICAN MALE AND FEMALE STUDENTS

1. Assist teachers to incorporate culturally relevant curriculum and instruction in their everyday teaching and learning activities.

2. End tracking and ability group practices that permanently segregate students and introduce differentiated instruction.
3. Review all disciplinary policies, procedures, and practices and identify rates of referral for individual teachers.
4. Assist teachers who are experiencing consistent difficulties with the behavior of their African American students to develop new competencies for successfully managing African American students' behaviors.
5. Develop a prereferral process that reduces special education identification and placement for African American students and supports their success in mainstream classes.
6. Provide students and parents as early as elementary school with information and resources on preparing for college, financial aid, other postsecondary programs, and scholarships.
7. Encourage the participation of parents in their child's education through the use of student-parent teacher activities that keep parents informed on a frequent basis of their child's progress and build parent capacity to be involved.
8. Develop transition programs between elementary, middle, and high school that focus on supporting students who may be at risk for failing to make solid adjustments.
9. Collect data that are disaggregated by race and gender and within race by gender so that the particular issues related to African American male and female achievement will become apparent and appropriate intervention strategies can be introduced.

BUILD STAFF DEVELOPMENT PROGRAMS THAT SUPPORT THE ACADEMIC ENGAGEMENT OF MALE AND FEMALE AFRICAN AMERICAN STUDENTS

1. Help teachers and administrators to examine and, when necessary, to change their beliefs and attitudes about young African American males and females.
2. Assist teachers and administrators to better understand the home and community culture and language of African American girls and boys and how they can be effectively used to engage African American students in meaningful learning.
3. Assist teachers with accessing information about the contributions of African Americans to the social, economic, intellectual, artistic, scientific, and historical development of America and the world. Infuse this information into the curriculum, standards, and assessments.
4. Assist teachers with developing an understanding and capacity related to cross-cultural communications.
5. Help teachers to better understand their own ethnic roots and the similarities and differences among cultures.
6. Train teachers in culturally responsive pedagogy.

CONCLUSION

African American students face a complex combination of issues that affect their human development and academic achievement. What we have seen is that these issues are exacerbated as male and female students reach adolescence. Although we have examined some early childhood issues as they relate to poverty and parenting, we have not discussed here in any detail the myriad school practices, e.g., poorly equipped segregated schools, underqualified teachers, lack of culturally relevant pedagogy, tracking, retention, and other practices that increase dropout rates, unequal funding, high-stakes tests, that combine to create an institutional imperative for failure. These factors are discussed in many of the other articles in Part I. We have concentrated instead on the interaction between class, gender, identity, and institutional racism.

When adolescent males and females begin to develop abstract reasoning, they are likely, regardless of their socioeconomic class, to become painfully aware of injustices and hypocrisy. Black adolescents who are forming their identity in a culture that continues to devalue them are forced to fight the internalization of society's negative image of them and, at the same time, resist the institutional racism that surrounds them. Despite sometimes destructive school practices, the complex issues of adolescent development, and the struggle against internalizing society's negative definitions, most Black youth successfully manage the transition to adulthood. Under these circumstances, how have so many African American youth succeeded? How can we restructure schools to support the high achievement of increasing numbers of African American male and female students? How can we address the different issues that impact low-income and middle-income African American student achievement? These are some of the critical questions that we must explore if we are to improve the academic achievement of African American male and female students.

REFERENCES

American Association of University Women Educational Foundation. (1998). *Gender gaps: Where schools still fail our children.* Washington, DC: Author.

American Association of University Women Educational Foundation. (2001). *Beyond the gender wars: A conversation about girls, boys, and education.* Washington, DC: Author.

Belluck, P. (1999, July 4). Reason is sought for lag by Blacks in school effort. *The New York Times*, p. 1, 12.

Bireda, M. (2000, November). The mythical African American male. WEEA Digest, 9–10. Newton, MA: Women's Educational Equity Act Resource Center.

Center on Education Policy. (2001). *It takes more than testing: Closing the achievement gap.* Washington, DC: Author. www.ctredpol.org.

Center on Hunger, Poverty and Nutrition. (1995). *Statement on the link between nutrition and cognitive development in children* (2nd ed). Medford, MA: School of Nutrition, Tufts University.

Centers for Disease Control and Prevention. (1999, October 25). Declines in teenage birth rates, 1991–1998: Update of national and state trends. National Vital Statistics Reports, Vol. 47, No. 26. Hyattsville, MD: U.S. Department of Health & Human Services.

Coley, R.J. (2001). *Differences in the gender gap: Comparisons across racial/ethnic groups in education and work.* Princeton, NJ: Educational Testing Service.

Darling-Hammond, L. (1997). *The right to learn: A blueprint for creating schools that work.* San Francisco: Jossey-Bass.

Davenport, D.S., & Yurick, J.M. (1991). Multicultural gender issues. *Journal of Counseling and Development, 70,* 1, 64–71.

Davis, J.E. (2000). Early schooling and academic achievement of African American males. Paper presented at the Department of Education's Conference on African American Males, December 4, 2000.

Ferguson, A.A. (2000). *Bad boys: Public schools in the making of Black masculinity (law, meaning and violence).* Ann Arbor, MI: University of Michigan Press.

Fordham, S. (1993). Those loud black girls: (Black) women, silence, and gender "passing" in the academy. *Anthropology and Education Quarterly 2Y* (1): 3–32, 1993.

Fordham, S. (1996). *Blacked out: Dilemmas of race, identity and success at Capital High.* Chicago: University of Chicago Press.

Fordham, S. (2001). Why can't Sony (and Kwame) fail math? In W.H. Watkins, J.H. Lewis, J.H., & V. Chou (Eds.), *Race and education: The roles of history and society in educating African American students.* Needham Heights, MA: Allyn and Bacon.

Johnson, R.C., & Viadero, D. (2000, March 15). Unmet promise: Raising minority achievement. *Education Week, 19,* No. 27, pp. 1, 18–19.

Mathews, J. (2001, March 3). Study finds racial bias in special ed. Washington, DC: *The Washington Post.*

Mickelson, R.A. (1990). The attitude-achievement paradox among Black adolescents. *Sociology of Education, 63*: 44–61.

Noguerra, P. (2000). The role and influence of environmental and cultural factors on the academic performance of African American males. Paper presented at the Department of Education's Conference on African American Males, December 4, 2000.

Oakes, J. (1990). *Keeping track.* New Haven, CT: Yale University Press.

Oakes, J., Wells, A.S., Yonezawa, S., & Ray, K. (1997). Equity lessons from detracking schools. In A. Hargreaves (Ed.) *Rethinking educational change with heart and mind.* ASCD 1997 Yearbook. Alexandria, VA: Association for Supervision and Curriculum Development.

Orfield, G., Arenson, J., Jackson, T., Bohrer, C., Gavin, D., & Kalejs, E. (1998). Summary of "City-suburban desegregation: Parent and student perspectives in metropolitan Boston." A Report by the Harvard Civil Rights Project. *Equity and Excellence in Education, 31*(3), 6–12.

Pastor, J., McCormick, J., & Fine, M. (1996). Makin' homes: An urban girl thing. In Leadbeater, B.J. & Way, N. (Eds.), *Urban girls: Resisting stereotypes, creating identities.* New York: New York University Press.

Pianta, R.C., & Cox, M.J. (Eds.) (1999). *The transition to kindergarten.* Baltimore: Paul H. Brookes.

Roderick, M. (2000). What's happening to the boys? Early high school experiences and school outcomes among African-American male adolescents in Chicago. Paper submitted to the National Institute on the Education of At Risk Students, September 2000.

Sadker, M., & Sadker, D. (1994). *Failing at fairness: How*

America's schools cheat girls. New York: Charles Scribner's Sons.

Scott-Jones, D., & Clark, M. L. (1986, March). The school experiences of black girls: The intersection of gender, race, and socioeconomic status. *Phi Delta Kappa*, p. 520–526.

Shaffer, S. M., & Gordon, L. P. (2000). *Why boys don't talk and why we care: A mother's guide to connection.* Chevy Chase, MD: The Mid-Atlantic Equity Consortium, Inc.

Simmons, W., & Grady, M. (1992). Black male achievement: From peril to promise. *Report of the Superintendent's Advisory Committee on Black Male Achievement.* Upper Marlboro, MD: Prince George's County Public Schools.

Spencer, M. B., Seaton, G., & Harpalani, V. (2000). African American males' academic achievement experiences: Assumptions about "opportunities" and facts about normative developmental needs and inopportune structural conditions. Paper commissioned by the Department of Education's Special Task Force on African American Males. Presented at the DOE Conference, Washington, DC, December 4, 2000.

Steele, C.M. (1992, April). Race and the schooling of black Americans. *The Atlantic Monthly, 269*(4), 67–68. Retrieved on 4/09/2001 from the World Wide Web: *http://www.theatlantic...nbound/flashbks/steele.htm.*

Taylor, J.M., Gilligan, C., & Sullivan, A. (1995). *Between voice and silence: Women and girls, race and relationship.* Cambridge, MA: Harvard University Press.

The Center for the Future of Children. (1997, Summer/Fall). *Programs that mitigate the effects of poverty on children*, 7, 2: 103–104. Los Altos, CA: The David and Lucile Packard Foundation.

The College Board. (1999). *Reaching the Top: A Report of the National Task Force on Minority High Achievement.* Princeton, NJ: Author.

U.S. Bureau of Census. (2001). *Poverty 1999.* Washington, DC: Author *www.census.gov/hhes/poverty99/pv99est1.html.*

Viadero, D. (2000, March 15). Even in well-off suburbs, minority achievement lags. *Education Week, 19*, No. 27, p. 22–23. Retrieved on 6/28/2000 from The World Wide Web: *http://www.edweek.org/ew/ewstory.cfm?sl...%22closing%20the%20achievement%20gap%22*

Ward, J.V. (1996). Raising resisters: The role of truth telling in the psychological development of African American girls. In Leadbetter, B.J.R., & Way, N. (Eds.) *Urban girls: Resisting stereotypes, creating identities.* New York: New York University Press.

Watkins, W. H. (2001). *Race and education: The roles of history and society in educating African American students.* Needham Heights, MA: Allyn & Bacon.

Way, N. (1998). *Everyday courage: The lives and stories of urban teenagers.* New York: New York University Press.

Weiler, J.D. (2000). *Codes and contradictions: Race, gender identity and schooling.* Albany, NY: State University of New York Press.

Article 4

THE RECRUITMENT AND RETENTION OF AFRICAN AMERICAN STUDENTS IN GIFTED EDUCATION: BEYOND DEFICIT IDEOLOGIES

DONNA Y. FORD

WHY DO AFRICAN AMERICAN STUDENTS continue to be underrepresented in gifted education and the more challenging academic programs and courses? Although some explanations target testing issues, we believe that the first and foremost barrier to African American students participating in challenging academic programs is the pervasive deficit orientation that prevails in society and its educational institutions. After examining this orientation, we explore the *symptoms* of this orientation, such as the low referral rates of Black students for gifted education services, the heavy reliance on tests that do not capture the strengths and cultural orientations of Black students, and other factors.

DEFICIT IDEOLOGIES: LIMITING ACCESS AND OPPORTUNITY

The less we know about each other, the more we make up.

Reactions to differences among students manifest themselves in various ways. And these reactions have a powerful influence in educational settings. Boykin (1994) and others have studied the cultural styles of African American students, noting such characteristics as verve, mobility, oral tradition, communalism, spirituality, and affect. As Figure 4.1 illustrates, deficit thinking can contribute to misunderstandings of these cultural characteristics. For example, verve and movement (tactile and kinesthetic preferences) may be (mis)interpreted as hyperactivity; an affective orientation may be (mis)interpreted as immaturity, irrationality, and low cognitive ability; and communalism may be (mis)interpreted as dependence and immaturity.

Ideas about ethnicity (often used interchangeably with "race") have influenced the development of definitions, policies, and practices designed to deal with differences. For instance, Gould (1981, 1995) and Menchaca (1997) have noted that deficit thinking has contributed to past and current beliefs about ethnicity and intelligence. As school districts faced increasing ethnic diversity (e.g., because of immigration), educators resorted to increased reliance on standardized tests–biased standardized tests–which almost guaranteed low test scores for immigrants and culturally different groups who were unfamiliar with U.S. customs, traditions, values, norms, and language. As Gould (1995), Hilliard (1992), and others have noted, the tests measured familiarity with American culture, not innate intelligence. Nonetheless, the tests afforded school systems the opportunity to legitimize their efforts to separate children by ethnicity. In this respect, intelligence testing has become a theory of limits for diverse populations (Gould, 1995). Historical and contemporary abuses of intelligence tests with African

Characteristic	Description	Possible Misinterpretation
Oral tradition	Strong preference for oral modes of communication; students speak frankly, directly, and honestly; students enjoy playing with language (puns, jokes, innuendoes, storytelling, etc.)	Frankness and bluntness may be perceived as rudeness and lacking in social skills. Creative language may not be appreciated; if students speak Black English vernacular, they may be considered less intelligent.
Movement and verve	A strong need to be actively involved, mobile; psychomotor preferences	Student may be viewed as hyperactive, inattentive, and immature.
Communalism	Interdependence; preference to social or group learning; dislike for individual competitiveness	The desire to work with others may be perceived as immaturity and lacking independence.
Affective	Expresses self easily with emotions; feeling oriented	Student may be perceived as too emotional and immature; may be considered weak in cognitive skills.

Figure 4.1. Possible misinterpretations of cultural orientations.

Americans are too numerous to discuss here, but Gould (1995) has given it considerable attention. Ultimately, he likens current-day practices of intelligence testing to historical practices of craniology and craniometry. He states:

> The misuse of mental tests is not inherent in the idea of testing itself. It arises primarily from two fallacies, eagerly embraced by those who wish to use tests for the maintenance of social ranks and distinctions: reification and hereditarianism. (1981, p. 155)

Likewise, Menchaca (1997) states:

> Racial differences in intelligence, it was contended, are most validly explained by racial differences in innate, genetically determined abilities. What emerged from these findings, regarding schooling, were curricular modification that the "intellectually inferior" and the social order would best be served by providing these students concrete, low-level, segregated instruction commensurate with their alleged diminished intellectual abilities. (p. 38)

Most recently, the deficit orientation was resuscitated by the publication of *The Bell Curve* (Herrnstein & Murray, 1994), which sought to influence public and social policy. Their interpretations (or misinterpretation and misrepresentation) of data, like those of earlier centuries, confirmed all the common prejudices of comfortable White males–that Blacks and poor people occupy the subordinate roles by the harsh dictates of nature (Gould, 1981, p. 74). The hereditarian theory of IQ is a home-grown American product (Gould, 1981, p. 158), one that persists in current-day practices of testing, sorting, and discarding.

Menchaca (1997) also traces the evolution of deficit thinking and demonstrates how it influenced segregation in schools (e.g., *Plessy v. Fergusen*, 1896) and resistance to desegregation during the Civil Rights era and today. For instance, some scholars argue that educators continue to resist desegregation and use tracking and ability grouping to resegregate students by ethnicity (e.g., Oakes, 1985; Slavin, 1987). Furthermore, some educators argue that the underrepresentation of Black students in gifted education and their overrepresentation in special education are strongly related to efforts to continue segregation in school settings (Ford & Webb, 1995; Hilliard, 1992).

In the sections that follow, we discuss how the deficit orientation influences, directly and indirectly, myriad practices in gifted education. Specifically, deficit thinking limits access to gifted education for diverse students. The following paragraphs present an overview of critical issues related to the recruitment and retention of Black students in gifted education. This list is not exhaustive; instead, it is an overview of some of the major *symptoms* of deficit thinking:

1. Traditional IQ-based definitions, philosophies, and theories of giftedness
2. Identification practices and policies that have a disparately negative impact on Black students (e.g., a reliance on teacher referral for initial screening)
3. A heavy emphasis on productivity or achievement as a criterion for giftedness, which excludes gifted students who are underachievers
4. A lack of training among teachers, counselors, and psychologists in the area of gifted education
5. A lack of training among teachers to understand and interpret standardized test results;
6. Inadequate training of teachers and other school personnel in multicultural education;
7. Inadequate efforts to communicate with Black families and communities about gifted education
8. Black students' decisions not to participate in gifted education programs

TESTING AND ASSESSMENT BARRIERS. The use of tests to identify and assess students is pervasive in gifted education. Test scores play a predominant role in identification and placement decisions. For example, a study by VanTassel-Baska, Patton, and Prillaman (1989) revealed that 88.5 percent of states rely primarily on standardized, norm-referenced tests to identify gifted students, including those from economically and racially diverse groups. According to Colangelo and Davis (1997) and Davis and Rimm (1997), test scores are currently used by more than 90 percent of school districts.

Because of the high reliance on test scores for placement decisions, the demographics of gifted programs remain relatively White and middle class. Whereas traditional intelligence tests have been effective at identifying and assessing White students, they have not been as effective with African America students. This begs the question–so why do we continue to use these tests so exclusively or extensively? Educators and decision makers have at least three options from which to choose to explain the poor test performance of a disproportionate number of Black students: (1) the fault rests within the test (e.g., test bias); (2) the fault rests within the educational environment (e.g., poor instruction contributes to poor test scores); or (3) the fault rests within the student (e.g., he/she is cognitively inferior, "culturally deprived").

If the first two options were selected, educators would feel more obligated to making substantive changes in assessment and educational practices. The last explanation points directly to deficit thinking; educators who support this option abdicate themselves of any responsibility for minority students' lower test performance (e.g., Herrnstein & Murray, 1994). It is easy to blame the victim rather than to share some of the problem.

IQ-BASED DEFINITIONS AND THEORIES. Little consensus exists among educators regarding how best to define the terms "intelligent" or "gifted." Cassidy and Hossler (1992) maintained that most states continue to follow a 1978 (or older) definition of gifted. They reported that most states use either the 1978 federal definition outright or a modification of it; 30 states had made no definitional revisions in at least a decade, and only fifteen states had made revisions in the last five years. Essentially, most states continue to define gifted from a unidimensional perspective–that is, as a function of high IQ scores. Unidimensional assessments identify only some students as gifted and miss the rest. These definitions do a good job of identifying middle-class White students. Specifically, IQ-based definitions ignore those students who:

1. Perform poorly on paper-and-pencil tasks conducted in artificial or lablike settings
2. Do not perform well on culturally loaded tests (e.g., Kauffman, 1994)
3. Have learning and/or cognitive style differences (e.g., Hilliard, 1989, Shade, Kelly, & Oberg, 1997)
4. Have test anxiety (Ford, 1993)

5. Have low achievement motivation (e.g., Ford, 1996).

The use of dated definitions has many negative implications, first among them is the issue of validity. Given our increasing diversity, how can educators and decision makers continue to rely on definitions that do not reflect the most contemporary research and thought? Just as tests can become outdated so, too, can definitions. If definitions support static notions of human capacity and ability, they must be revisited and revised. In those schools that do not adopt more inclusive (and less hereditarian)definitions, such as those espoused by the USDE (1993) and Gardner (1983), the educational needs of many gifted students are likely to go unrecognized and unmet. The construct of giftedness is critical to identification practices.

INADEQUATE IDENTIFICATION PRACTICES/POLICIES. Procedural and policy issues also contribute to the underrepresentation of Black students in gifted education. Specifically, data indicate that teachers underrefer minority students for gifted education services (e.g., Ford, 1996; Saccuzzo, Johnson, & Guertin, 1994). Ford found many Black students in her study had high test scores but were underrepresented in gifted education, because teachers had not referred them for screening. In other words, when teacher referral is the first (or only) step in the recruitment process, gifted Black students may be underrepresented. Given that perceptions have a powerful influence on behavior and decisions, teachers who lack multicultural preparation may hold deficit ideologies about culturally, linguistically, and ethnically diverse groups.

LACK OF MULTICULTURAL PREPARATION BY TEACHERS. Few preservice teachers are exposed to multicultural educational experiences (e.g., multicultural curriculum and instruction, internships, and practica in urban setting) (see Banks & Banks, 1995). At institutions of higher education, most students graduate with a monocultural or ethnocentric curriculum. Thus, they are ill prepared to work with culturally, ethnically, and linguistically diverse students. Therefore, teachers may misunderstand cultural differences among Black students relative to learning styles, communication styles, behavioral studies, and so forth. Differences may be perceived as deficits, as illustrated in Figure 4.2.

For instance, several researchers have noted learning and cognitive styles that tend to be characteristic of Black children (e.g., Hale-Benson, 1986; Hilliard, 1992; Shade et al., 1997). Thus, teachers should be cognizant that many Black students tend to be concrete learners, social learners, field-dependent learners, and learners who value concrete, constructive feedback. Torrance's (1977, 1978) characteristics of gifted culturally diverse groups acknowledged how these differences are strengths that can be used to identify and nurture their gifts and talents. These differences and characteristics have numerous implications for the identification of gifted Black students. Specifically, the extent to which Black students are global versus analytic learners, visual versus auditory, highly mobile versus less mobile, and less peer-oriented versus more peer-oriented will affect their learning, achievement, motivation, and school performance. It may also inhibit their recruitment and retention in gifted education. Because many, if not most, Black students tend to be global and visual, they may not be identified as gifted by teachers (Figure 4.2).

INADEQUATE TEACHER PREPARATION IN GIFTED EDUCATION. Ford (1998) surveyed minority teachers about their decision to enter or not enter the field of gifted education. Many of these teachers reported having little exposure to gifted education in their teacher preparation programs. Most teachers, including those who held degrees in special education, did not have formal preparation in gifted education. This lack of preparation in the characteristics of gifted students, understanding the social and emotional needs of gifted students, understanding underachievement among gifted students, and understanding factors that hinder the representation of Black students in gifted education all hinder the competence of teachers to make fair and equitable referrals. Data indicate that teachers who lack preparation in gifted education are ineffective at identifying gifted students (e.g., Cox, Daniel, & Boston, 1985). Likewise, teachers unprepared to work with gifted students may hold stereotypes and misperceptions that negatively affect their ability to see the strengths of students who behave differently from teacher expectations. Teachers may use the behaviors of White students as the norm from which to compare Black students.

INADEQUATE TEACHER PREPARATION IN TESTING

AND ASSESSMENT. Teachers are directly responsible for providing services to gifted students based on assessed needs. Therefore, teachers require formal preparation in testing and assessment. Many teachers with whom we have worked have never seen a *WISC-III*, *Otis-Lennon School Abilities Test*, or other tests frequently used for identification and placement decisions. Accordingly, teachers cannot adequately interpret intelligence and achievement test scores. Given this lack of preparation, how can teachers adequately provide effective, high-quality gifted education services? How can they differentiate services for gifted students whose IQ and achievement scores vary?

Furthermore, teachers must understand the impact of culture on test scores to interpret the scores in meaningful ways. This means understanding how culturally loaded tests can decrease Black students' test scores or hinder their performance. Given that Black students tend to score lower on IQ and achievement tests than White students, how will teachers interpret and use test scores? What explanations will they give for the differential test scores? What alternative instruments and assessment practices will they adopt?

INADEQUATE COMMUNICATION WITH BLACK FAMILIES AND COMMUNITIES. Much work indicates that substantive family involvement in the educational process enhances student achievement. Karnes, Shwedel, and Steinberg (1984) noted that 90 percent of the parents of gifted students they surveyed involved themselves directly in their children's schooling by taking part in the teacher selection process and in parent organizations. Likewise, Scott-Jones (1987) found that academically successful Black students had mothers who provided more books, set clearer academic goals for their children, and were more involved in schoolwork than other Black parents. Slaughter (1987) suggested that Black parents must play at least four roles in their children's educational achievement–parent as decision maker; parent as supporter; parent as mediator; and parent as teacher.

However, Black families face numerous barriers to educational involvement. Black parents often express concerns that teachers and schools fail to acknowledge giftedness within the minority student population. They are apprehensive that school personnel may view them with suspicion because of less affluent economic backgrounds, different family values and structures, and lower educational attainment levels. Equally important, Black parents tend to distrust the school system when they become aware of the underrepresentation of Black students in gifted education programs. These concerns, real or perceived, cause Black parents to fear that their "different" children stand a better chance of being identified for special education rather than gifted education. These stressors and worries can be attributed, in part, to the deficit thinking that is prevalent in education.

SOCIAL-EMOTIONAL AND PSYCHOLOGICAL DEVELOPMENT OF BLACK STUDENTS. Perhaps the worst consequence of deficit thinking among educators is the impact that it can have on social-emotional and psychological development of Black students. Research by Fordham and Ogbu (1986) and others (e.g., Ford, 1993; Fordham, 1988; Suskind, 1998) reveals that many gifted Black students have internalized deficit thinking orientations. Many highly able Black students have begun to question their own abilities and to sabotage their achievement. For example, some Black students don the role of class clown or athlete to hide their academic ability and achievements, and these students are refusing to participate in gifted education programs. They also succumb to negative pressures to avoid achievement, particularly from other students; and they have come to associate or equate academic achievement with "acting White." Thus, many gifted African American students are underachieving and otherwise failing to reach their academic potential.

RECOMMENDATIONS FOR CHANGE: BEYOND DEFICIT THINKING

"Schools must eliminate barriers to participation of economically disadvantaged and minority students in services for students with outstanding talents . . . and must develop strategies to serve students from underrepresented groups" (USDE, 1993, p. 28).

To more effectively recruit and retain African American students in gifted education, educators must, of course, shed their deficit thinking. This will increase the probability that they will (1) adopt con-

Traditional Beliefs and Practices	Contemporary Beliefs and Practices
Focus on identification, which does not suggest how to meet students' needs.	Focus on identification, which does not suggest how to meet students' needs.
One test is sufficient to identify gifted students. One number (IQ or achievement test score) is used to identify gifted students. The best measure of giftedness is a test.	Giftedness is multidimensional; therefore, multiple methods (qualitative and quantitative) must be used, and information must be gathered from multiple sources (teachers, parents, etc.). There is no "one size fits all" test.
Giftedness is equated with a high IQ or achievement score. A cutoff score determines giftedness.	The limitations of test scores are recognized, especially with culturally diverse students. Gifted students can have low test scores.
Ability is rewarded; students must demonstrate their ability.	Effort is valued and rewarded. Educators recognize that high-quality educational experiences can help students to reach their potential.

Figure 4.2. Suggestions for change: From traditional to contemporary practices and beliefs.

temporary theories and definitions of giftedness; (2) adopt multicultural assessment instruments; (3) identify and serve gifted underachievers; (4) provide students with a multicultural education; (5) provide all school staff with multicultural preparation; and (6) create strong home-school partnerships. Figure 4.2 presents suggestions for moving away from traditional practices.

ADOPT CONTEMPORARY THEORIES AND DEFINITIONS. At least two recent theories of intelligence and giftedness promise to capture the strengths, abilities, and promise of gifted Black learners. Sternberg's (1985) Triarchic Theory of Intelligence proposes that intelligence can be revealed in at least three ways: contextually, experientially, and componentially. Componential learners are analytical and abstract thinkers who do well on standardized tests and in school. Experiential learners value creativity and like to deal with novelty. They dislike rules and have few of their own; they see rules as inconveniences meant to be broken. Contextual learners adapt to their environments (a skill not measured by IQ tests). They are street-smart, survivors, socially competent, and practical, but they may do poorly in school.

Gardner (1983) distinguished among seven types of intelligences (linguistics, logical-mathematical, interpersonal, intrapersonal, bodily kinesthetic, spatial, and musical), each of which entails distinct forms of perception, memory, and other psychological processes. Gardner's (1983) Theory of Multiple Intelligences defines intelligence as the capacity to solve problems or to fashion products that are valued in one or more cultural settings.

These two theories recognize that giftedness is a social construct and that giftedness manifests itself in multiple ways. The theories, therefore, are broad and comprehensive; they are flexible and inclusive.

The most recent federal definition of gifted appeared in 1993, and it is equally promising for broadening notions of giftedness:

> Children and youth with outstanding talent perform or show the *potential* for performing at remarkably high levels of accomplishment when compared with others of their age, experience, or environment. These children and youth exhibit high performance capacity in intellectual, creative, and/or artistic areas, and unusual leadership capacity, or excel in specific academic fields. They require services or activities not ordinarily provided by the schools. *Outstanding talents are present in children and youth from all cultural groups, across all economic strata, and in all areas of human endeavor* [italics added].

The words and statements in italics are especially meaningful for recruiting Black students into gifted education. First, the focus of the definition is on talent development, hence, the use of "potential" in the definition. In the definition, there is an increased recognition that many Black students are diamonds in the rough–they may not have had adequate opportunities to develop and perform at high levels. For example, some gifted Black students, especially those who live in poverty, may not be exposed to books and other literature, they may not visit libraries or bookstores, or they may not participate in meaningful educational experiences. The most encouraging aspect of the federal definition is, of course, its inclusion of the "potential." It seems to recognize a need to serve those students who have, for various reasons, yet to manifest their abilities. These students tend to include underachievers, minority students, economically disadvantaged students, and students with special education needs. For the most part, these students might not be identified and placed in gifted programs whose definitions and identification practices rely solely or primarily on intelligence or achievement test scores. Finally, the definition explicitly states that giftedness exists among *all* sociodemographic groups.

ADOPT MULTICULTURAL ASSESSMENT INSTRUMENTS. To date, the most promising instruments for assessing the strengths of Black students are nonverbal tests of intelligence. These tests, such as the *Naglieri Non-Verbal Abilities Test* and *Raven's Analogies Tests*, are considered less culturally loaded than traditional tests (see Kaufman, 1994; Saccuzzo et al., 1994); thereby, they are likelier to capture the cognitive strengths of Black students. Saccuzzo et al., for instance, identified substantively more Black and Hispanic students using the *Raven's* than using a traditional test. Specifically, they reported that "50% of the non-White children who had failed to qualify based on a *WISC-R* qualified with the *Raven*" (p. 10). They go on to state that "The Raven is a far better measure of pure potential than tests such as the *WISC-R*, whose scores depend heavily on acquired knowledge" (p. 10).

Educators must be aware that these tests assess intelligence nonverbally; this is not to say that students are "nonverbal"; rather, the tests give students an opportunity to demonstrate their intelligence without the confounding influence of language. This is certainly advantageous for students whose first language is not English or standard English. In essence, we must reexamine the purpose of identification and testing and use the information in diagnostic and prescriptive ways.

REVISE POLICIES AND PROCEDURES. Recruitment and retention is a process, not an event. For students requiring gifted education services to be identified, there must be multiple entry points that provide access to initial screening and assessment. Teacher referral and test scores are the primary entry points for screening students for gifted education, and screening and identification tend to occur one or two times per year. Of course, this can be problematic for diverse students. If teacher referral of minority students is low, then schools must seriously reconsider this as an initial step in the process. Likewise, if minority students score low on traditional tests, they cannot be the first entry point for screening. Schools must, therefore, consider nominations or referrals from families and community members, nominations must be ongoing, and educators must consider themselves to be talent scouts. Likewise, both accomplishments inside and outside of schools need consideration. In general, policies and practices must reflect a philosophy of equity and excellence.

IDENTIFY AND SERVE GIFTED UNDERACHIEVERS. There are philosophical differences about the goals of gifted education and the types of gifted students to serve. Specifically, some philosophies dictate that gifted students must be gifted *and* high achieving. Thus, giftedness is equated with achievement or demonstrated performance. In these schools, gifted students must demonstrate high achievement, otherwise they will not be identified initially or kept in gifted programs if the grades fall below a specified level. When giftedness is equated with high achievement (which is itself a relative term), gifted underachievers will not be recruited and retained. Given the unfortunate but persistent reality that many Black students are underachievers, they will not be identified; accordingly, their needs will not be recognized or met.

Some gifted underachievers are difficult to identify, particularly those who do not test well. In addition to examining why test scores show discrepancies, we must examine factors (such as prejudice and discrimination) that contribute to low academic performance. Therefore, we must use both quantitative and qualitative indices to more effectively identify gifted underachievers. When Black students' underachievement is being analyzed, we examine social-emotional and psychological factors, as well as teacher expectations (e.g., deficit thinking). These teachers are likely to provide minority students with poor or low-level curriculum and instruction.

ADOPT A TALENT DEVELOPMENT PHILOSOPHY. Students who live in poverty–many of whom are African American–are at risk for not reaching their potential. The impact of poverty on students' achievement and quality of life is obvious. Many low-socioeconomic status students will need to be identified early before the effects of poverty become increasingly difficult to reverse. Thus, it behooves educators to focus on the concept of talent development (Bloom, 1985; USDE, 1993). Bristow, Craig, Hallock, and Laycock (1951) noted this some years ago: "Giftedness appears in many different forms in every cultural group at every level of society. It is the source of power which has contributed most to progress at all times and in all places. Yet, like other human resources, it remains a potentiality until it has been developed" (p. 10).

PROVIDE MULTICULTURAL PREPARATION FOR EDUCATORS. To be successful in school and life, gifted Black students have been required to change and adapt to different settings. That is, Black students have borne the responsibility of being bicultural, bicognitive, and bilingual. Seldom are teachers required to be culturally responsive–to become bilingual, bicultural, or multicultural. With forecasts projecting an increased minority student population in the near future, teachers will have to bear a greater responsibility for demonstrating multicultural competence (Ford & Harris, 1999; Ford, Grantham, & Harris, 1998).

The recruitment and retention of Black students in gifted programs is influenced by the nature and extent of multicultural education preparation among all school personnel–teachers, counselors, psychologists, administrators, and support staff. This preparation–which focuses proactively on individual differences and cultural diversity–must be infused throughout the preparation of educators and in professional development.

Comprehensive preparation should reeducate educators and school personnel so that deficit-oriented philosophies do not impede Black students' access to gifted education. Children often fail because the culture of the school ignores or degrades their family and cultural backgrounds. Educators, reflecting the school's values, may single out for criticism Black children's behaviors and values; thereby unrecognizing and neglecting the strengths that these students bring to academic settings.

Kitano (1991) argued that gifted programs continue to espouse assimilationist rather than pluralistic approaches to cultural diversity. Assimilationists favor the relinquishment of a diverse student's original culture. These students are expected to adopt the values, attitudes, and behaviors of the predominant culture–the child must change. Conversely, pluralists support the retention of a student's original culture, so the school changes. Certainly, when the culture of the child is valued, educators are more likely to witness fundamental and essential changes in that student's achievement, motivation, and behavior. To become more culturally competent, educators must:

1. Engage in critical self-examination that explores their attitudes and perceptions concerning cultural diversity and the influence of these attitudes and perceptions on minority students' achievement and educational opportunities
2. Acquire accurate information about various cultural groups (e.g., history, historical and contemporary contributions)
3. Explore the range of diversity that exists within and between cultural groups
4. Learn how to infuse multicultural perspectives into curriculum and instruction to maximize the academic, cognitive, social-emotional, and cultural development of students
5. Build partnerships with diverse families, communities, and organizations

PROVIDE A MULTICULTURAL GIFTED EDUCATION FOR STUDENTS. The need for all students, but especially minority students, to be exposed to a multicultural education has been addressed by many scholars (e.g., Banks, 1999; Ford, 1998; Ford & Harris, 1999; Ford et al., 1998). Gay's (1990) article titled "Achieving Educational Equality through Curriculum Desegregation" holds important implications for gifted education. Gay argued that segregation of the curriculum and instructional inequities exist in a wide array of schools (and, by inference, gifted programs) where minority students are denied equal access to high-status knowledge and learning opportunities because of biases about their ethnicity, gender, nationality, cultural background, and/or social class:

> "Curriculum segregation" occurs when different course assignments, instructional styles, and teaching materials are routinely employed for different groups of students; it constitutes a form of discrimination that mirrors the prejudices and inequities in the larger educational system and in society. In the books and content that are regularly taught, the role models that are commonly presented, the way students are treated in classroom interactions, and the assignment of certain students to instructional programs all convey subtle–but powerful–messages about just how separate and unequal education is. (p. 56)

Because the infusion of multicultural education into the content is empowering for gifted Black students, multiculturalism must continually permeate the curriculum for gifted students. Ford and Harris (1999) provided numerous strategies and materials to help teachers and counselors as they design multicultural experiences for gifted students.

DEVELOP HOME-SCHOOL PARTNERSHIPS. In philosophy, school districts hold that family involvement is central to students' achievement. In practice, few schools consistently and aggressively build partnerships with Black families. During the first week of school and thereafter, teachers and administrators must ensure that African American families are aware that the school district has gifted education services, understand referral and screening procedures, and know how placement decisions are made. Just as important, Black families must understand the purpose and benefits of gifted education. These partnerships can only become a reality when schools:

1. Hold high expectations for Black students and communicate these expectations to families
2. Believe that African American families are an equal member of the school community
3. Respect Black families' right to define the nature and extent of their role in the school settings

The extent to which schools will be effective at recruiting and retaining Black students in gifted education rests heavily on critical self-examination and a willingness to move beyond deficit thinking (see Ford, 1996; Ford & Harris, 1999).

Assessing the Quality and Inclusiveness of Gifted Programs

1. What is the school district's philosophy of gifted education and its definition of giftedness?
   - In what ways are the philosophy and definition inclusive or exclusive? To what extent are the strengths of ethnically and culturally diverse students represented in the philosophy and definition?
   - Are contemporary definitions of giftedness adopted and/or applied?
   - Does the gifted education program and services address the community's needs? Are students "retrofitted" to the program or does the program accommodate the needs of the students?
2. Are assessment instruments and practices equitable?
   - Are the measures used valid and reliable for the student population? Are nonverbal instruments used?
   - Are there ethnic, cultural, or gender biases in the selection process? If so, what are they?
   - Which instruments seem to be most effective at identifying the strengths of minority students?
   - Is a combination of qualitative and quantitative assessment practices used? If so, is one type given preference or higher weight than another?
   - What are the primary purposes of assessment (e.g., to diagnose and prescribe or to label and segregate/separate)?
   - Are personnel trained to administer and interpret test results in a culturally fair manner?
   - Are the instructions on the tests and the manner in which the tests are administered accommodated to the students' learning styles?
   - To what extent are student's home language, culture, and background represented or not represented in the test questions?
   - Are tests biased (or culturally loaded) in favor

of students from wealthier and more economically privileged backgrounds?

3. Are the students in the gifted program representative of the community's demographics?
   - Are students of diverse backgrounds equitably represented according to criteria such as ethnicity and socioeconomic status?
   - Are there any disparities between the gifted program's demographics and the demographics of the school and community?
   - Is there evidence of increasing diversity among professionals in the gifted program?
4. Does the school district provide opportunities for continuing professional development in gifted and multicultural education?
   - Are faculty and other school personnel encouraged and given opportunities by administrators to participate in workshops, conferences, university courses, and so forth? Do administrators attend such professional development training? Do personnel seek or willingly take advantage of these opportunities?
   - Is there a commitment to multicultural education? If so, what are the indications? For instance, does a library exist for teachers and students that contains up-to-date multicultural resources (e.g., newsletters, journals, and books)?
5. What, if any, mechanisms are in place to assess and address the affective and psychological needs of minority students (i.e., social and emotional needs, racial identity, environmental and risk factors)?
   - To what extent are support personnel and test administrators trained in gifted education?
   - To what extent are personnel trained in multicultural assessment and multicultural counseling?
   - How diverse is the support staff?
6. To what extent are families involved in the formal learning process?
   - How diverse are the parents and families involved?
   - In what ways are African American families encouraged to become and remain involved? Are efforts to create home-school partnerships ongoing? How aggressive are efforts?
   - What is the nature and extent of family involvement in the classroom or school (e.g., serve on placement committee, help create curriculum)?
7. To what extent are curriculum and instruction grounded in multiculturalism?
   - Is multicultural content infused throughout the curriculum?
   - Is the multicultural content at the higher levels of multicultural education?
   - Is the content pluralistic (i.e., does it reflect diversity relative to ethnicity, socioeconomic status, and other sociodemographic variables)? Does the curriculum provide genuine options for all students to understand diverse cultures?
   - To what extent are learning style preferences and differences accommodated?
   - Are all students exposed to multicultural content, regardless of school or program demographics?
8. What policies are in place to support multiculturalism and diversity?
   - Are there published policies regarding multiculturalism?
   - If specific policies exist, to what degree are they observed in the school?
   - In what ways do policies and procedures about grouping, scheduling, and student assignments promote or inhibit interaction among white and minority students?

CONCLUSION

Much controversy exists in education over the nature and causes of Black student underrepresentation in gifted education, low achievement, and low test scores. The controversy focuses on whether the causes are deficiencies in the children and their families or the inadequacies of and discriminatory practices of schools and society that restrict the search for talent development (Passow & Frasier, 1996). As we have argued herein, decisions about giftedness are never more than predictions; therefore, wide nets should be thrown to increase the power of those predictions, erring on the side of inclusion rather than exclusion (Passow & Frasier, 1996).

The persistent and pervasive underrepresentation of Black students in gifted education is a tragedy. Many gifted Black students, for any number of reasons, are not being identified as gifted. Accordingly, they are not being provided an appropriate education. As noted in this chapter, much of the difficulty can be attributed to the deficit thinking that persists in education; deficit thinking limits access and opportunity. However, proactive steps can be taken to rectify this mindset and its consequences. For instance, traditional identification approaches can be improved by designing, adapting, modifying, and extending instruments, strategies, and procedures that take into account the influence of ethnicity, culture, caste, and socioeconomic status on behavior (Passow & Frasier, 1996, p. 201). The ultimate challenge is one of creating paradigms that take culture and context into account to enhance possibilities for diverse students. As the United Negro College Fund has recognized: "A mind is a terrible thing to waste." Should deficit thinking orientations continue, many more gifted Black students will atrophy in school settings.

REFERENCES

Banks, J.A. (1999). *Introduction to multicultural education* (2nd ed.). Boston: Allyn & Bacon.

Banks, J.A. & Banks, C.A.M. (Eds.). (1995). *Multicultural education: Issues and perspectives.* Boston:Allyn and Bacon.

Bloom, B. (Ed.). (1985). *Developing talent in young people.* New York: Ballantine.

Boykin, A.W. (1994). Afrocultural expression and its implications for schooling. In E.R. Hollins, J.E. King, & W.C. Hayman (Eds.), *Teaching diverse populations: Formulating a knowledge base* (pp. 225–273). New York: State University of New York Press.

Bristow, W.H., Craig, M.L., Hallock, G.T., & Laycock, S.R. (1951). Identifying gifted children. In P. Witty (Ed.), *The gifted child* (pp. 10–19). Boston: DC Heath and Co.

Cassidy, J. & Hossler, A. (1992). State and federal definitions of the gifted: An update. *Gifted Child Quarterly, 15*, 46–53.

Colangelo, N. & Davis, G.A. (1997). *Handbook of gifted education.* Boston: Allyn & Bacon.

Coleman, M.R. & Gallagher, J.J. (1992, Jan./Feb.). State policies for identification of nontraditional gifted students. *Gifted Child Today*, 15–17.

Cox, J., Daniel, N., & Boston, B. (1995). *Educating able learners.* Austin, TX: University of Texas Press.

Cross Jr., W.E. (1995). The psychology of Nigrescence: Revising the Cross model. In J.G. Ponterotto, J.M. Casas, L.A. Suzuki, & C.M. Alexander (Eds.), *Handbook of multicultural counseling* (pp. 93–122). Thousand Oaks, CA: Sage.

Davis, G.A. & Rimm, S.B. (1997). *Education of the gifted and talented.* Boston: Allyn & Bacon.

Educational Policies Commission. (1950). *Education of the gifted.* Washington, DC: National Education Association and American Association of School Administrators.

Ford, D.Y. (1993). An investigation into the paradox of underachievement among gifted, above-average, and average Black students. *Roeper Review, 16*, 78–84.

Ford, D.Y. (1994). *The recruitment and retention of African-American students in gifted programs.* Storrs, CT: The University of Connecticut, National Research Center on the Gifted and Talented.

Ford, D.Y. (1996). *Reversing underachievement among gifted Black students: Promising practices and programs.* New York: Teachers College Press.

Ford, D.Y. (1998). *Factors affecting the career decision making of minority teachers in gifted education.* Storrs, CT: The University of Connecticut, National Research Center on the Gifted and Talented.

Ford, D.Y., Grantham, T.C., & Harris III, J.J. (1998). Multicultural gifted education: A wakeup call to the profession. *Roeper Review, 19*, 72–78.

Ford, D.Y. & Harris III, J.J. (1999). *Multicultural gifted education.* New York: Teachers College Press.

Ford, D.Y. & Webb, K. (1995). Desegregating gifted education: A need unmet. *Journal of Negro Education, 64*, 52–62.

Fordham, S. (1988). Racelessness as a strategy in Black students' school success: Pragmatic strategy or pyrrhic victory? *Harvard Educational Review, 58*, 54–84.

Fordham, S. & Ogbu, J. (1986). Black students' school success: Coping with the "burden of 'acting white.'" *The Urban Review, 18*, 176–203.

Frasier, M.M., Garcia, J.H., & Passow, A.H. (1995). *A review of assessment issues in gifted education and their implications for identifying gifted minority students.* The University of Connecticut: National Research Center on the Gifted and Talented.

Frasier, M.M., & Passow, A.H. (1994). *Toward a new paradigm for identifying talent potential.* Storrs, CT: The University of Connecticut: National Research Center on the Gifted and Talented.

Gardner, H. (1983). *Frames of mind: The theory of multiple intelligences.* New York: Basic Books.

Gay, G. (1990). Achieving educational equality through curriculum desegregation. *Phi Delta Kappan*, 72, 56–72.

Gould, S.J. (1981). *The mismeasure of man.* New York: Norton.

Gould, S.J. (1995). *The mismeasure of man* (revised ed.). New York: Norton.

Hale-Benson, J. (1986). *Black children: Their roots, culture, and learning styles.* Baltimore, MD: The Johns Hopkins University Press.

Harris III, J.J. & Ford, D.Y. (1991). Identifying and nurturing the promise of gifted Black students. *Journal of Negro Education, 60,* 3–18.

Eerrnstein, R.J., & Murray, C. (1994). *The Bell Curve: Intelligence and Class Structure in American Life.* New York: The Free Press.

Hilliard III, A.G. (1992). The pitfalls and promises of special education practice. *Exceptional Children, 49*(4), 168–172.

Karnes, M.B., Shwedel, A.M., & Steinberg, D. (1984). Styles of parenting among young gifted children. *Roeper Review, 6,* 232–235.

Kaufman, A.S. (1994). *Intelligent testing with the WISC-III.* New York: John Wiley & Sons, Inc.

Kitano, M.K. (1991). A multicultural educational perspective on serving the culturally diverse gifted. *Journal for the Education of the Gifted, 15,* 4–19.

Menchaca, M. (1997). Early racist discourses: The roots of deficit thinking. In R. Valencia (Ed.), *The evolution of deficit thinking* (pp. 13–40). New York: Falmer.

Oakes, J. (1985). *Keeping track: How schools structure inequality.* New Haven, CT: Yale University Press.

Passow, A.H., & Frasier, M.M. (1996). Toward improving identification of talent potential among minority and disadvantaged students. *Roeper Review, 18,* 198–202.

Plessy v. Ferguson, 163, U.S. 537, 16 S. Ct. 1138; 41 L. Ed. 256 (1896).

Saccuzzo, D.P., Johnson, N.E., & Guertin, T.L. (1994). *Identifying underrepresented disadvantaged gifted and talented children: A multifaceted approach* (vols. 1 & 2). San Diego: San Diego State University.

Scott-Jones, D. (1987). Mother-as-teacher in the families of high- and low-achieving low-income Black first graders. *Journal of Negro Education, 56,* 21–34.

Shade, B.J., Kelly, C., & Oberg, M. (1997). *Creating culturally responsive classrooms.* Washington, DC: American Psychological Association.

Slaughter, D.T. (1987). The home environment and academic achievement of Black American children and youth: An overview. *Journal of Negro Education, 56,* 3–20.

Slavin, R.E. (1987). Ability grouping: A best-evidence synthesis. *Review of Educational Research, 57,* 293–336.

Sternberg, R.J. (1985). *Beyond IQ: A triarchic theory of human intelligence.* Cambridge, MA: Cambridge University Press.

Suskind, R. (1998). *A hope in the unseen: An American odyssey from the inner city to the Ivy league.* New York: Broadway.

Torrance, E. (1977). *Discovery and nurturance of giftedness in the culturally different.* Reston, VA: Council for Exceptional Children.

Torrance, E.P. (1978). Ways of discovering gifted Black children. In A.Y. Baldwin, G. H. Gear, & L.J. Lucito (Eds.). *Educational planning for the gifted: Overcoming cultural, geographic and socioeconomic barriers.* Reston, VA: Council for Exceptional Children.

U.S. Department of Education. (1978). *1978 Elementary and Secondary School Survey.* Washington, DC, Office of Civil Rights: Author.

U.S. Department of Education. (1993). *National excellence: A case for developing America's talent.* Washington, DC: Author.

VanTassel-Baska, J., Patton, J., & Prillaman, D. (1989). Disadvantaged gifted learners at-risk for educational attention. *Focus on Exceptional Children, 22,* 1–16.

White, J.E. (1999, March 8). Prejudice? Perish the thought. *Time,* p. 36.

Article 5

SPECIAL EDUCTION: WHAT CAN BE DONE? PROGRAMS THAT USE PROMISING PRACTICES IN EDUCATING STUDENTS WHO HAVE BEEN PLACED AT RISK

KAYTE FEARN

WHAT ARE EDUCATORS DOING to address the serious and longstanding issue of the over-identification of African American students to inappropriate and/or ineffective special education programs? This section provides school administrators with examples of promising programs.

THE CIRCLE PROGRAM (CHILDREN IN ROTATING CENTERS LEARN EARLIER): INTEGRATION OF CHILDREN WITH DISABILITIES WITH THEIR NON-DISABLED PEERS

The CIRCLE program at A. R. Davis Elementary School in the Garland, Texas, Independent School District integrates students and teachers in the school's Preschool Program for Children with Disabilities (PPCD) with mainstream prekindergarten (pre-K) and kindergarten (KN) classes. The following briefly summarizes the program's elements:

1. Integration includes preprimary child development, pre-K, and KN students.
2. Ongoing collaboration among regular and special education staff and related service providers makes a successful practice.
3. Campus-level administrative support ensures continuity and success.
4. Children are involved in mixed-age and heterogeneous groups for a one-hour rotation.
5. Designated classroom centers provide a variety of hands-on, multisensory educational experiences.

This campus-wide program involves the coordination of eight classrooms, 24 staff members, and approximately 100 children, for a total of eight centers or classrooms. The program was initiated to enhance communication, promote independence, and foster problem solving and creativity in children.

More than 100 students in mixed age and ability groups rotate through one of seven different classrooms. Children rotate through one center per day, usually for an hour a day, eight out of ten days, in a two-week period. Options for children to be included in general education classes and CIRCLE participation are based on committee decision. Each classroom represents a large "center" that has a particular educational focus that includes music, listening, art, literacy, mathematics, blocks/manipulatives, science, dramatic play, and active play. The rooms each have specific educational focuses to facilitate skills through developmentally appropriate environments and experiences. The activities in the centers change every two weeks. Play is an essential component of the program. Within each classroom "center," the students have the opportunity to interact with a variety of materials and be involved in a variety of experiences at activity stations (interest areas). The interest areas support the goals of each child's development, including the physical, social, communication, and cognitive domains. Related services are integrated into the children's natural activities during the center time.

The therapists and teachers work closely to adapt and modify instructional activities and environments for each child. The entire teaching team plans together twice a month. There is ongoing planning as needed on an individual basis. The librarian, physical education teacher, and music teacher are directly involved in the practice. The teachers, speech pathologist, and related services therapists facilitate the children's individual goals within the context of the daily routine. Instructional assistants follow a consistent group of children in the classroom rotations throughout the year. The teachers are very aware of each child's individual needs and goals and act as facilitators. The environments are well defined with well-equipped centers that support a variety of developmental levels and interests and that include adaptive devices and equipment to support the needs of particular children. To obtain additional information about this program, you may contact Alane Welch at 972-494-8205.

CHANTILLY HIGH SCHOOL (VA) ACADEMY SUPPORT TEAM (CAST)

The primary purpose of the CAST is to support students and teachers as they work together to develop the technical skills students need to achieve success in both the world of employment and higher education. The CAST staff of three learning disabilities specialists and two teachers who support ESL students focus primarily on providing services for students with special needs–both LEP students and those with disabilities. In addition to working directly with students in classroom, small group, and individualized instruction, they hold employability and career seminars, self-advocacy activities, behavior management, and technical reading and writing workshops. The CAST staff assists other teachers with teaching methods and adapting curricular materials as appropriate. CAST staff also assists teachers to establish advisory committees of community and business leaders to enhance career opportunities for the skilled workers they train. The goals of the academy are:

1. Development of opportunities for all students, including diverse and special populations
2. Selection of coursework experiences, made with the student, counselor, and/or parent, to fit the student's strengths, interests, and future-oriented goals
3. Support of students without labeling
4. Use of nontraditional instruction and support of students in the Academy courses
5. Support of potential learning expansion as students experience interning, job shadowing/professional mentoring

CAST serves academy students from 25 high schools in Fairfax County and serves as liaison with base schools, area offices, parents, business, and community leaders and thus helps to facilitate appropriate placements that meet the academic and career needs of students. Once a student decides to apply to the academy, CAST staff works in concert with instructional and guidance staff members and parents to identify and address student issues and problems.

The academy serves 25 high schools, with a total of 936 students, of which 225 are enrolled in special education classes. It offers Advanced Drawing, Animal Science, Auto Body and Design, Auto Technology, Computer Technology, Construction Technology, Cosmetology, Criminal Justice, Culinary Technology, Dental Careers, Engineering Physics, Engineering Systems, Hotel Management, Medical Health Technologies, Network Administration, Network Design and Engineering, and the Physics of Technology.

CAST staff are proud of the fact that 94 percent of the students make passing grades in their selected courses, and last year's students with disabilities earned more than $36,000 in scholarships. For more information about this program, contact John

Wittman, Administrator, Chantilly Academy, Chantilly High School at 703-222-7461.

PREREFERRAL ASSESSMENT MODEL (PROGRAM PAM)

Program PAM has been designed to address the prereferral to placement process of students identified with possible special education needs. The Prereferral Assessment Model was piloted during the past three years in a local school district in Louisiana. The model was developed by professionals with extensive input from the local education agency of St. Charles Parish and has been directed by consultants from The University of New Orleans and Louisiana State University. It centers around a problem-solving approach designed to validate teacher referral and, after a concern has been validated, to design and put in place an intervention within one to two weeks of validation.

The first part of the problem-solving approach consists of a Problem Validation Screening Model that uses systematic data collection procedures that include:

1. Classwide and individual assessments for academics and behavior
2. Measures to determine whether the problem is such that the student "can't" or "won't" meet teacher expectations
3. Decisions about next steps

The next part of this model involves designing an intervention based on screening results, as well as "how to coach cards," to assist teachers to implement individual and classwide interventions.

The third part of the model is designed to teach educators how to collect intervention data through continuous progress monitoring techniques, such as checklists, assessments, and direct observation. Coaching, feedback, and evaluation of the intervention implemented are other components of the PAM model. PAM provides an opportunity for educators to learn and to participate in decision-making on the basis of systematic data collection.

The outcomes of this model have been several.

1. There has been a reduction in inappropriate referrals. Data have documented that approximately 50 percent of minority students and 20 percent of white students were inappropriately suspected of having a disability and needing special education services.
2. Psychologists and educational diagnosticians have had 80 percent more direct contact with teachers and referred students. They have been assisting teachers by direct instructional methods in the implementation of interventions.
3. Teachers have begun to use systematic data to support decision making. Currently, Louisiana's program is among five other programs at either the state education agencies or the local education agencies across the United States in which approaches related to assessment and eligibility are being addressed. The Office of Civil Rights and Council for Exceptional Children have recognized the approach as one that may result in effective reduction of disproportionality. For more information on this program, contact Dr. Gale Naquin, PAM Project Director, University of New Orleans, Special Education Department ED 246, New Orleans, LA 70148, at 504-280-6833. E-mail: gnaquin@uno.edu

THE INSTRUCTIONAL SUPPORT PROCESS A SYSTEM THAT WORKS AT PERKIOMEN VALLEY SOUTH ELEMENTARY SCHOOL

Since South Elementary School replaced its Child Study Team with the Instructional Support Team (IST) process, special education referrals have decreased dramatically. The IST program is designed to support the regular education teacher who is frustrated by the child who exhibits academic and/or behavior problems. The goal of the IST is to maximize individual student success in the regular education classroom. When a student is referred to the IST, data are collected, and a goal is set. The IST meets, brainstorms strategies to meet the goal(s), and an action plan is developed. The strategies are in place for thirty school days. The team meets again to assess the progress that has been made and to determine what strategies will be continued. A "What Works" form ensures that successful interventions follow the student to the next grade level.

A systems change has taken place at South Elementary School from a "pull-out" remediation model to a program that is tailored to meet each student's individual needs. Supports include the ASSIST Team in the first and second grades, which is a "push-in" program that uses Title I funds. Project Silver is a 1:1 program that supports struggling readers in the first grade. A Homework Club and Study Skills groups are used in the intermediate grades. "Seedlings" is an adult/student mentoring program. Service agreements and 1:1 aides are used to support students who would have been placed in special education. The Instructional Support process is really a compilation of all of the support systems that are available at South Elementary School. The IST adapts the programs to fit the student's needs rather than placing the student in established programs.

Although Perkiomen Valley is not a racially diverse community, it is socioeconomically diverse, and poor students are also disproportionately represented in special education. This school is working hard to find solutions for every child through emphasizing the needs of each student and designing a program to fit those diverse individual needs. For more information about this program, contact Helen Bergey, Instructional Support Teacher, Perkiomen Valley South Elementary School, 200 E. Third Avenue, Collegeville, PA 19468; 610-489-2991 or 610-948-4047; hbergey@erols.com.

HOW DO YOU KNOW WHEN YOU'VE GOT DISPROPORTIONALITY? TWO MODELS USED FOR CALCULATING DISPROPORTIONALITY IN THE TEXAS EDUCATION AGENCY

Since the early 1990s, the Texas Education Agency (TEA) has examined issues of representation and disproportionality in special education as part of compliance monitoring in districts. The TEA analyzes representation of three student groups in special education:

1. Students from ethnic minority groups (Hispanic, African American, Euro-American)
2. Students who are economically disadvantaged
3. Students who are limited in English proficiency

The TEA conducts data analysis of these groups before scheduled monitoring visits and examines practices, procedures, and professional development on-site to determine how districts are addressing potential overrepresentation issues.

Two methods for determining potential overrepresentation in each of these groups have been used. Before the summer of 2000, TEA used the chi square data trial analysis to identify potential overrepresentation of these student groups in special education. In 2000, TEA determined that a "difference score" method would be used.

The chi square analysis helps determine whether something other than chance is contributing to differences in observed versus expected frequencies, given current demographic data. Observed frequencies indicate actual values (i.e., what is actually occurring); expected frequencies indicate anticipated values (i.e., what should be expected to occur given current data). Results of a chi square analysis indicate whether a finding is statistically significant for potential over- or underrepresentation of the targeted student group.

The difference scores method establishes a difference score for each of the targeted groups by determining:

1. The percentage of each student group in special education
2. The percentage of each student group in the general school population
3. The difference between these two percentages

A zero or positive number indicates expected representation; a negative indicates potential overrepresentation of the student group in special education.

A manual for conducting the chi square analysis, developed by Region IV Education Service Center (ESC), Houston, Texas, provides step-by-step directions and includes a software program. Another software product developed by Region IV ESC conducts risk analysis of several state-identified data elements in special education, including disproportionality of the student populations listed earlier. This process uses the difference score analysis. Both products can be used at the district or campus level.

Training is provided on using both products and also on strategies for supporting students in general education settings. For more information, you may contact Jamie Morris, Director, Accountability and Compliance Services, Education Services Division, Region IV Education Service Center, 7145 West Tidwell, Houston, TX 77092-2096, 713-744-6392; E-mail: Jmorris@esc4.net.

REDUCING BIAS IN SPECIAL EDUCATION ASSESSMENT FOR AMERICAN INDIAN AND AFRICAN AMERICAN STUDENTS: A MINNESOTA DEPARTMENT OF CHILDREN, FAMILIES & LEARNING MODEL

The Minnesota Department of Children, Families & Learning (MNCFL) was concerned about possible bias in the special education assessment process for two of the major ethnic groups in the state. To address that problem, the staff developed a notebook summarizing cultural, language, and socioeconomic differences that may have an impact on the special education referral and assessment process. The manual also details the process that should be used in assessment to avoid bias in its findings. Training on the manual has been conducted statewide. The manual has also been piloted in several districts. The *Reducing Bias* manual is currently being expanded to include materials and procedures for evaluating English language learners. In addition, the department is funding two research projects for prereferral interventions, one focusing on the needs of African American students and one focusing on American Indians.

The book describes changes in both referral and assessment procedures and includes a school system bias review. Strategies include (1) creating environments in which each student's diverse needs, gifts, and/or talents are known, valued, and developed; (2) involving all stakeholders in the student's interest; (3) disaggregating data regarding the impact of the practice on diverse populations; (4) providing data to show how the practice works for a variety of ethnic populations; (5) recommending appropriate culturally sensitive materials and resources; and (5) recognizing that there may need to be changes in various segments of the educational system.

The impact of the program on the prereferral/referral process has been impressive. The prereferral system ensures that before a student is referred for evaluation for special education services, appropriate interventions have been introduced, and referrals for assessment for special education have involved parents and ensured that language is not a problem. If a referral becomes necessary, the referral:

1. Contains data regarding the result of the interventions and describes why the intervention did not work
2. Indicates referrals to general education service programs before referral to special education (reading programs, special tutoring, etc.)
3. Includes parental connections and interventions
4. Identifies student strengths as well as weaknesses

Assessment processes include, among other features:

1. Assessment tied to curriculum
2. Assessment in several areas, not just cognitive/academic/psychological
3. Appropriate evaluations of students with limited English proficiency
4. Sensitivity to diverse cultures
5. Assessment reports that consider and honor cultural traditions
6. An analysis of teacher and student behavior

To download an order form for *Reducing Bias in Special Education for American Indian and African American Students*, please go to the website of CFL's Division of Special Education: *http://cfl.state.mn.us/speced/* and select "Written Guidelines." For further information, contact Elizabeth Watkins at 1-651-582-8678; or E-mail at Elizabeth.Watkins@state.mn.us.

Although not comprehensive, this list of programs should serve to provide school administrators with a variety of successful strategies they can adopt or adapt to address the special education challenges they face in their schools. This should ultimately lead to a reduction of referrals of students to special education.

Part II

INSTITUTIONAL CHANGE AND CULTURALLY RELEVANT PEDAGOGY: TWO SIDES OF THE SAME COIN

> If we are to successfully educate all of our children, we must work to remove the blinders built of stereotypes, monocultural instructional medthodologies, ignorance, social distance, biased research, and racism. We must work to destroy those blinders so that it is possible to really see, to really know the students we must teach. I pray for all of us the strength to teach our children what they must learn, and the humility and wisdom to learn from them so that we might better teach.
>
> *Lisa Delpit*

As "the body of learned beliefs, traditions, and guides for behavior that are shared among members of any human society" (Grant & Ladson-Billings, 1997), culture is a powerful experience in the everyday lives of individuals and groups of people. As an ever-evolving constellation of influences, culture shapes the essence, experiences, and worldviews of individuals, groups, communities, and institutions alike. No person or institution is exempt from its influences. Within the world of schools, cultural experiences have a profound effect on the ways in which students approach learning and the schooling experience, including their relationships with teachers and peers. Similarly, cultural experiences also affect the ways in which teachers approach both teaching and their own learning (i.e., professional development), as well as their relationships with students and colleagues. Every school and school system reflects an institutional culture that is represented by a set of beliefs, values, policies, and practices that either support and nurture students, families, and educators toward high performance or creates insurmountable barriers to success.

Culture mediates all learning–it is the lens through which all learning experiences are filtered. As a result, each member of the learning community brings to the schooling experience his or her own unique cultural style and ways of viewing the world and his or her place in it. Very often, there is discordance between the cultural styles and worldviews of African American students and their teachers, typically resulting in poor development and learning outcomes for the students and a less than satisfying teaching experience for the teachers. Even African American students and African American teachers who share a common ethnic heritage can be separated by cultural styles and worldviews that reflect individual class differences and the cultural discordance within the prevailing school culture. When teachers are in tune with their students' cultural styles and worldviews, they "understand their students' verbal communication and body language, preferred modes of discussion and participation, time and space orientations, social values and religious beliefs, and preferred styles of learning" (Grant & Ladson-Billings, 1997). They are better prepared to develop the kinds of learning opportunities that will engage and motivate their students to master challenging educational materials and goals. As such, education leaders–in the field, in academia, in communities, and in government–cannot have a meaningful conversation about improving education for African American students without having issues of culture–African American and otherwise–out in the open, at front and center stage.

Diverse cultural styles and worldviews have a profound influence on how people relate to one another. However, high-quality relationships between teachers, their students, families, and communities, built on a foundation of mutual knowledge, understanding, trust, and respect, are fundamental to an effective instructional program. The critical first steps on this journey for teachers who are seeking to acquire skills in culturally relevant pedagogy are to understand more about the concept of culture in general and then to explore their own cultural backgrounds, including how their own cultural experiences have worked to shape their belief systems about other people and their own worldviews. In a society in which assimilation and acculturation were the mainstay experience for large groups of America's early European immigrants, this becomes an especially difficult task, because many of the cultural rituals, practices, and belief systems of those early groups have been lost. The result is that many of today's descendents of northern European ethnic and cultural groups have been left without important knowledge about the intrinsic value of culture, in general, and their own ethnic and cultural heritages, in particular. However, to become more effective at meeting the learning needs of African American students, educators must commit to becoming more culturally knowledgeable and aware and specifically to gaining authentic cultural knowledge of the African American experience in America and the life experiences of their African American students. They must also work toward developing authentic relationships with their African American students, families, colleagues, and communities.

Part II, "Institutional Change and Culturally Relevant Pedagogy," brings together nine informative articles that help to demystify the role and importance of culture in improving educational opportunities and outcomes for African American students. Readers will gain tremendous insight into the power of culture as a necessary component of any school improvement effort by exploring its relationship to teaching, learning, leadership, and institutional change.

In "Institutional Practices that Support African American Student Achievement," Sheryl Denbo guides us through an institutional framework that allows us to see how a school's culture shapes the effectiveness of the school as an institution by influencing the nature and performance of its many parts. We see how institutional culture, manifested as an entrenched system of beliefs, traditions, policies, and practices, can affect the quality of a school's social/emotional climate, expectations for student achievement, student and adult relationships, community relationships, approaches to diversity, professional development opportunities, resources, scheduling, and more.

In "A No-Excuses Approach to Closing the Achievement Gap," Belinda Williams teaches us about a belief system that supports the educational success of African American children. In this system, "all children can learn" is more than rhetoric; it is a statement of real purpose, intent, and meaning. No excuses means just that–schools and teachers accept responsibility for education success by focusing on two essential institutional components: a shared focus on teaching and learning and pedagogical strategies that are specific to the needs of African American children as learners. She reminds us that any strategies that we develop for the improvement of educational outcomes for our nation's diverse student body must be grounded in a well-developed and understood theory of human development, one that acknowledges the role of culture and cultural environments in human development and teaching and learning.

In "Talent Development, Cultural Deep Structure, and School Reform: Implications for African Immersion Initiatives," A. Wade Boykin reminds us that "schools traditionally are not culturally neutral terrains." He makes a strong case for the educational and cultural empowerment of African American children through a model of comprehensive school change called the Talent Development Model, which maximizes every student's academic and social/emotional development through a rigorous curriculum and appropriate support, assistance, structure, and facilitating conditions. Citing the efficacy of building on the cultural assets of African American children in light of a growing body of research examining the interface of cognition and context, Dr. Boykin advocates for fusing such a model with teaching and learning practices we frequently see in African-centered approaches to schooling.

In "But That's Just Good Teaching! The Case for Culturally Relevant Pedagogy," Gloria Ladson-Billings helps us to recognize that when we unravel the intricacies of culturally relevant pedagogy, we find ultimately that it is "just good teaching." Defining culturally relevant pedagogy as a "pedagogy of opposition, not unlike critical pedagogy but specifically committed to collective, not merely individual, empowerment, " she tells us that culturally relevant teachers use students' culture as a vehicle for learning. To ensure that African American children have adequate opportunity to reach their greatest potential–as students and as members of familial and world communities–she argues that pedagogy must speak to the development of cultural competencies and the development of a broader sociopolitical consciousness, one that allows our students to engage the world and others critically.

Pat Burke Guild, in "An Educational Leader's Guide to Culture and Learning Style," helps us to understand what we mean when we talk about the intersection of culture and learning styles and the need to attend thoughtfully to the diversity of cultures and learning styles reflected in today's schools. She indicates that differences between the norms of students' homes and communities and the norms of most school cultures is seriously damaging to both students and teachers alike. And as we engage in efforts to respond to issues of culture and learning styles, she cautions us to remember that there are tremendous variations among individuals within groups and that if we are not diligent, we can be misled into stereotyping and labeling, ignoring the great differences within cultural groups, and mitigating the potential for making education meaningful to students with individual learning needs. Finally, she leaves us with specific administrative suggestions for making culture and learning style connections for students and teachers in our schools and classrooms that have been shown to improve learning outcomes for African American students.

In a trilogy of articles focused on literacy, Lynson Moore Beaulieu examines issues of language and literacy development for African American children over the course of their early childhood, elementary, and secondary schooling years. Language, literacy, and reading development pose some of the greatest challenges to the successful education of African American children. With consistently high rates of very low performance on language and literacy assessments and an African American adult illiteracy rate of 44 percent, these issues deserve serious attention within the context of a larger discussion on improving schooling for African American students. Failing to learn to communicate, read, and comprehend at levels commensurate with the demands of the "information age" is a prescription for immediate education failure and long-term social and economic marginalization. Each phase of the African American child's literacy growth, development, and learning requires that we pay close attention to specific literacy issues, challenges, and opportunities.

In "Moving Past the Ebonics Debate to a Common Understanding," Ms. Beaulieu explores the territory of African American Vernacular English (AAVE), also known as Ebonics. She proposes that it is an authentic issue of African American culture that is currently downplayed and/or ignored by the African American and mainstream education communities to the detriment of the successful education and cultural development of African American children. The result is poorly developed language arts programs for vernacular speakers and large-scale literacy failures throughout the African American community. Using the voices of prominent linguists and the authority of linguistic research, she attempts to reroute the debate over the legitimacy of AAVE/Ebonics. Ms. Beaulieu helps the reader understand the importance of Ebonics to cultural connections and its value to the African American community. She presents a discussion of the merits of language arts programs for African American students and other Standard American English language learners that incorporate the study and use of AAVE/Ebonics (and other native languages) as an integral part of the formalized study and mastery of SAE. This approach results in students who are "bidialectal," culturally competent, and equipped to successfully engage in native language and mainstream literacy activities.

In "Literary Development in the Early Childhood Years," Ms. Beaulieu plants the early childhood years firmly on the radar screen of public schooling issues and outlines some of the key factors in the early years that contribute to children having difficulties learning to read. Ms. Beaulieu looks at the challenges and promises of early childhood education and provides descriptions of public prekindergarten programs that are making a measurable difference in African American children's early language, literacy, and reading development.

In "Literacy Development Across the Elementary, Middle, and High School Years," Ms. Beaulieu explores the complex landscape of language, literacy, and reading development issues as they affect the successful literacy education of African American students throughout their formal schooling years. Using a standard of literacy that requires students to become learned and accomplished as readers, speakers, writers, thinkers, and technology users, and bidialectally proficient, she defines our task for the successful literacy education of African American children and youth.

For the middle and high school years, Ms. Beaulieu reminds us that the physical and psychosocial changes of adolescence must be taken into consideration as we develop and implement literacy education programs and opportunities for our older students. Helping students to define and embrace their "personhood," one of the most important tasks of adolescence, becomes an important avenue for literacy education. Literacy development in the secondary years is greatly enhanced by authentic classroom discourse and reading, writing, and thinking activities that connect and allow students to reflect on their cultural and social experiences.

She ends this article by posing and responding to four critical questions for schools and teachers that get at the heart of institutional change and culturally relevant pedagogy as strategies for improving literacy outcomes for African American youth. Ms. Beaulieu tests our knowledge of adolescence, requires that we learn about and identify student strengths, challenges educators to undergo personal and professional journeys to improve their success as educators of multicultural students, and queries our knowledge of successful teaching and learning strategies for secondary school students.

Finally, in "African American Children and Algebra for All," William Tate speaks to us cogently about the correlation between algebra and the achievement gap and the institutional and cultural barriers that must be overcome for the *Algebra for All* movement to succeed. Citing a shift from the basic skills movement of the '60s and '70s to a more demanding vision of mathematical literacy, he makes a strong case for changes in school systems that create mechanisms and for supporting policies that foster opportunities for all students, especially African American students, to participate in college preparatory courses, such as algebra and geometry.

What school administrators and teachers believe about the possibilities for teaching and learning for African American children has a profound effect on what they choose to teach, how they will teach it, and how they will determine what their children have learned. As things currently stand, students who are perceived to be culturally enriched and cognitively capable are afforded the most challenging and supportive opportunities to learn. Students who are perceived to be culturally and cognitively deficient, *as a result of their cultural differences*, are given less-challenging educational opportunities and support for their educational efforts. What teachers believe and think that they know about their students, the ways in which they interpret student behavior or respond to children's use of native languages, can significantly affect their approaches to discipline, the quality of their interactions with students during the learning process, and the quality of their relationships with colleagues, families, and members of the school community.

Successful institutional change needs the support of culturally relevant pedagogy to improve the school experiences and outcomes for African American students. Changes in institutional structures can enhance opportunities for African American students to meet and exceed high standards of learning *only if* issues of culture–as they affect the quality of teaching, learning, and human relationships–are simultaneously addressed. A culturally relevant school experience is important for all children, especially children from diverse ethnic, cultural, and language backgrounds. To this end, we must commit ourselves to acquiring the knowledge and skills needed to design and implement culturally relevant pedagogic strategies. Without them, we continue to consign a significant proportion of our African American children to an educational dead end and the social and economic consequences that invariably follow.

REFERENCES

Delpit, L. (1993). *Other people's children–Cultural conflict in the classroom.* NY, New York: The New Press.

Grant, C.A. & Ladson-Billings, G. (Eds.) (1997). *Dictionary of multicultural education.* Phoenix, AZ: The Oryx Press.

Article 6

INSTITUTIONAL PRACTICES THAT SUPPORT AFRICAN AMERICAN STUDENT ACHIEVEMENT

SHERYL J. DENBO

TRANSFORMING SCHOOL CULTURE AND STRUCTURE

According to Shade and Edwards (1987), culture is the collective consciousness of a community, representing the unique customs, rituals, communication styles, copy patterns, and social organization. School culture includes the values, beliefs, and norms that lay the foundation for a school's climate, programs, and practices. Unfortunately, one of the still prevalent underlying erroneous and harmful beliefs among both teachers and students in today's schools is that African American children come to school with cultural deficits. This belief all too frequently gets translated into assumptions about African American students' cognitive abilities and is reflected in common educational practices, such as assigning African American students to special education classes at disproportionately higher levels than their peers in other ethnic and cultural groups. Thus, for African American children, the school's negative perception of their ethnic group and culture creates a climate of low expectations and low performance that can evolve into self-degrading feelings (Pang, 1990). Claude Steele (1992) tells us, "For too many black students school is simply the place where, more concertedly, persistently, and authoritatively than anywhere else in society, they learn how little valued they are" (p. 13).

To create environments that support the high achievement of African American students, schools must transform their cultures in ways that result in the elimination of harmful institutional practices. School climate and practices must be shaped by a belief that African American students, like other students, can achieve to high standards and that the African American culture, like other cultures, is a rich one. This is not an easy task, but abundant research now shows that school cultures can be changed. This article discusses many of the factors involved in changing school culture and offers suggestions for implementation. Change itself, however, depends greatly on effective school leadership and diverse professional development opportunities.

TEACHER/STUDENT RELATIONSHIPS

Because research indicates that teachers, administrators, parents, and students operate more effectively in a supportive environment and that student identification with teachers and schools promotes learning, teachers are being asked to forge deep and meaningful relationships with their students (Harris & Associates, 1994; Hollins & Spencer, 1990). However, although student diversity in the United States is increasing, diversity within the ranks of the teaching workforce is declining (National Center for Education Statistics, 1998). Approximately 90 percent of teachers are White. It can be difficult for many European American teachers to create a nurturing environment for students whose cultures are unfamiliar and who come from communities that are often devalued by mainstream America. Teachers from middle-class European American backgrounds often have little personal or professional experience with African American children before they enter the classroom, and teacher education programs do not adequately prepare them to work with diverse student populations (Darling-Hammond, 1999; Dilworthy, 1992; Ladson-Billings, 1994; Zeichner & Hoeft, 1996). It seems clear, then, that to provide a foundation for creating meaningful relationships, teachers of all ethnicities and cultures need to examine their own ethnic and cultural roots, as well as their attitudes and beliefs about cultural diversity, in general, and the worthiness of African American culture, in particular. This is crucially important, because the value of their student-teacher relationships cannot be overstated. Nelson-Barber and Estrin (1995) emphasize that student-teacher relationships are as important as instructional strategy. Effective pedagogical techniques are not enough; teachers must also respect and value students. Specific teacher behaviors that demonstrate high expectations for students can have a positive effect on classroom climate and student achievement (Good & Brophy, 1994; McCormick & Noriega, 1986). A strong identification between students and teachers can result in significantly higher achievement, if that identification includes understanding and using student cultural values to support high achievement (Abi-Nader, 1993).

> I never thought I could learn French. No one in my family had ever spoken French. It seemed like too much work with all that memorization. But Mrs. Stern would not let me drop the class. If I didn't understand what she said she made a game or a song up that helped me. She simply would not let me fail. She insisted I could do it. And before you knew it, I was. She now says my accent is better than hers, can you believe that! *Shauna King, High School Student*

BUILDING A SCHOOL CULTURE THAT SUPPORTS RESILIENCE

For decades, researchers have been identifying risk factors that undermine academic success. These risk factors include, but are not limited to, poverty, exposure to drugs, violence, poor nutrition, high mobility, and homelessness. Although the relationship between such conditions and underachievement is significant, the overwhelming focus on risk factors has contributed to the view that African American students are unable to learn and prone to disruptive behavior. Although it is true that children with multiple risk factors develop a higher percentage of problems, it is also true that a greater percentage of these children become healthy, competent young adults (Bernard, 1991). To cultivate success and achievement among African American students in these circumstances, educators must begin to look beyond "risk factors" and learn how they can create schools and classrooms that help students gain "resilience" to succeed. Resiliency is the ability to bounce back from persistent stress and crisis. This characteristic is displayed in individuals as optimism, resourcefulness, and determination. Institutions such as families, schools, and community organizations demonstrate and cultivate resilience when they build caring support systems and solve problems sensitively and creatively. Institutions that promote resilience have the following characteristics:

- Promote close bonds
- Value and encourage education
- Use high-warmth, low-criticism style of interaction
- Set and enforce clear boundaries (rules, norms, and laws)
- Encourage supportive relationships with many caring others
- Promote sharing of responsibilities, service to others, "required helpfulness"
- Provide access to resources for meeting basic needs of housing, nutrition, employment, health care, and recreation
- Set high and realistic expectations for success
- Encourage goal setting and mastery
- Encourage development of pro-social values (such as altruism) and life skills (such as cooperation)
- Provide opportunities for leadership, decision making, and other meaningful ways to participate
- Support the unique talents of each individual

(Bernard, 1991; Hawkins, Catalano, & Miller, 1992; Werner & Smith, 1992)

School administrators and teachers can work together to promote these and other characteristics to create a school environment that will cultivate resilience among students. As with effective teaching, building resilience is rooted in developing close, meaningful relationships with students.

> It used to be that we were taught to build the student's self esteem, life skills, or academic skills. Now we are taught that they are interconnected. I think that is right. When you show students you like them and believe in their ability, then they begin to believe in themselves. That is the foundation to build academic skills. For students who did not believe in themselves, this foundation must be consistently reinforced. *Mary McGuire, Middle School Teacher*

INSTITUTIONAL PRACTICES THAT SUPPORT INCREASED ACHIEVEMENT

To implement a process of the magnitude required to make a difference for all African American children, it is necessary to create a powerful coalition among teachers, parents, students, communities, and administrators. This coalition should shape the mission and goals for transforming school culture and champion the change process. The following measures support the change process.

Develop school-community relationships:

- Establish open communication channels with all groups in the community that emphasize the support of diversity.
- Encourage the involvement of all groups of parents and community members and support parent education and involvement programs.
- Structure collaboration among principals, teachers, parents, and community stakeholders recognizing the joint responsibility of all stakeholders for student achievement.

Set rigorous academic achievement goals that are:

- Driven by data.
- Related to both increased achievement and closing of any existing achievement gaps.
- Designed to be measurable.
- Implemented incrementally

Prepare all students for a rigorous high school curriculum:

- Four years of English and math, including calculus.
- Three years of science, including biology, chemistry, and physics.
- Three years of social studies.
- At least one honors class.

Assess and meet student needs:

- Implement procedures to identify and address individual student needs and strengths.
- Assign teachers to ensure the best fit between teachers and students.
- Provide adequate resources–financial, academic support, social and emotional support, extended learning opportunities such as tutoring, after school programs, test preparation.

Cultivate teacher and administrator professional development:

- Provide professional development opportunities for teachers and administrators that are aligned with student achievement goals.
- Encourage teachers to take on leadership roles.
- Encourage teacher collaboration and build a professional learning community.
- Develop teacher schedules that support professional development, collaboration, planning, and more time for instruction.

Initiate innovative policies and practices that support African American student achievement:

- Experiment with research-based pedagogy and innovative instructional practices.
- Introduce action-based research to evaluate your own in-school innovations.
- Reduce class size. Small classes help to reduce the Black/White achievement gap.
- Expand access to high-quality preschools or all-day kindergarten programs.
- Identify and assign culturally competent and highly qualified teachers.
- Introduce challenging before and after school curricula, multicultural curricula, and summer long opportunities.

- Identify additional resources and monitor the equitable distribution of resources.
- Institute block scheduling in the higher grades to create opportunities for more in-depth learning and more efficient use of time available for learning.

INNOVATIVE EQUITY NETWORKS

Equity Networks in Student Achievement

Fowler-Finn is president of the Network for Equity in Student Achievement (NESA), a group of 15 larger urban school systems that share data, resources, and ideas with the ultimate goal of closing the racial gap and raising achievement for all students. Contact: Superintendent's Office, Fort Wayne Community Schools, 1200 S. Clinton St., Fort Wayne, IN 46802; 219-425-7200 (Sadowski, 2001, p. 3)

Minority Student Achievement Network

The Minority Student Achievement Network (MSAN) consists primarily of school districts in ethnically diverse suburban towns and small cities. Many MSAN member districts are located in university towns such as Ann Arbor, MI; Berkeley, CA: Cambridge, MA; and Madison, WI. The relative affluence of these communities means that member schools can study the achievement gap amid less interference from such factors as poverty and severe school underfunding. And, the location of the schools near major colleges and universities enables staff to work closely with key researchers in this field. Contact: Minority Student Achievement Network, Evanston Township High School, 1600 Dodge Ave., Evanston, IL 60204; 847-424-7000. *www.eths.k12.il.us/MSA/msanetwork.html* (Sadowski, 2001, p. 3)

Use multiple assessments to continuously evaluate outcomes, judge the efficacy of current instructional strategies, and change direction when needed:

- *For each student*, in-class assessment should be frequent, meaningful, aligned with curriculum and learning goals and objectives based on a reliable external scoring system, such as rubrics. Teaching methods and environments must change when progress is not being made.
- *For each educator*, assessment should be given several times a year. Peer coaching and professional development should be used to help teachers develop a variety of teaching styles to more effectively meet the needs of students with diverse learning styles.
- *For each school*, assessment should be a continuous process, resulting in both objective (e.g., test scores and enrollment data in key courses and programs) and subjective (e.g., attitudinal surveys of teachers, parents and students) data, used as the basis for deciding the direction of continuing improvement efforts.

Once school change efforts are underway, any obstacles to change stemming from policies, practices, or individuals should be identified and addressed. In addition, short-term accomplishments should be celebrated and rewarded. This helps to build the momentum for the "staying power" that will promote long-term results.

NURTURING LEADERS: EFFECTIVE PRINCIPALS, EFFECTIVE TEACHERS

Effective institutional change requires leadership. Although there is extensive literature on effective leaders, it is essential to understand that all educators have strengths and weaknesses. An effective leader who understands his or her strengths and weaknesses can collaborate with the leadership of others to support the change process. Interviews with principals have indicated that they are aware of the gap between what they actually do and what they ideally should be doing, and many believe that they do not have the time or skills to practice effective leadership.

Lieberman and Miller (1999) reported that principals in their study acknowledged the following:

- They should be leaders, but more likely they were managers.
- They should be helpers, supporters, and developers, but more often they were supervisors and evaluators.
- They should share knowledge, but they tended to keep secrets.
- They should be democratic, but circumstances sometimes forced them to be autocratic.
- They should show concern for individual problems and individual growth, but because they were in charge of the whole school, they had to

sacrifice personal vision for a more pragmatic view.

- They should do long-range thinking, but frequently they had to make short-range, even instantaneous, decisions to keep small brush fires from becoming conflagrations.
- They should be colleagues, but often they were bosses.
- They should be innovators, but they were maintaining the status quo.
- They should be champions of ideas; but in reality they were masters of the concrete, paying attention to detail before worrying about abstractions.

Principals can help nurture leadership among teachers, parents, students, and other community members by encouraging and providing opportunities for them to take various leadership roles related to their strengths and the needs of the school. The contributions of staff and community members will increase the level of leadership diversity and resources, as well as reinforce commitment to institutional changes among stakeholders. Encouraging leadership can be done in a variety of ways, including through professional development; opening formal and informal channels of communication; building personal and professional relationships; and providing opportunities for teachers to share their strengths with other teachers and schools. When principals make a conscious effort to acknowledge the strengths and talents of staff members and treat them with respect, they are more likely to take on additional leadership roles.

COLLABORATING TO BUILD NEW STRUCTURES

Although long-term transformation of school culture is the goal of all of our reform efforts, the momentum for making changes that will improve African American student achievement must be built on short-term, measurable successes (Schmoker, 1999). Research tells us that joint teamwork among teachers, administrators, and parents can facilitate both student achievement and the professional development of teachers (Little, 1990). This type of collaboration has been described by some educators as a "professional learning community."

Building a learning community requires an identification of both problems and opportunities, a belief that educational professionals have the ability to solve these problems and take advantage of opportunities, using thoughtful analyses, concrete solutions, and explicit goals. Teamwork may be more challenging. Conflict related to values and goals and the challenges of cross-cultural communication are likely to arise. This is part of the process of team building, and these issues must be addressed. It is helpful to bring in a skilled facilitator who has experience in building teams among people of different cultures to help the process move forward.

Linda Vista Elementary School
San Diego, California

Teachers work in teams, sharing the same students. They use their "prep" time to observe their colleagues' use of new instructional practices in the classroom. This process of working as a team, as well as the sharing of students, empowers teachers at Linda Vista to share resources and address problems collectively. Collaboration is instrumental in reinforcing changes in school culture. For example, collaboration was identified as the key means for resolving tension between the traditional class preparation ethic and new approaches. "Collaboration with fellow teachers in the day-to-day school context can have a powerful influence on teachers' values and beliefs as well as facilitate change in the technical dimension." (USDE, 1998)

Cooper Middle School
New Mexico

At Cooper, where curriculum and assessment activities cut across subject areas, success was found to hinge upon teachers having an opportunity to work together before implementing new instructional methods. As part of its reform effort, the school has organized itself into "families" of student and teachers who spend most of their day together. To assist teachers in planning their lessons, the school provides instructors with forty-five minutes of planning each day to organize integrated activities. Teachers note that without this time it would be much more difficult to implement their restructured educational program because this planning period provided them with a formal mechanism for sharing ideas and information. (USDE, 1998)

USING DATA TO IMPROVE TEACHING

If we want schools to improve for all students and to close the achievement gap between African American students and their peers, then teams of teachers need to use data to set goals for education. In that way, appropriate strategies can be chosen to meet particular needs of specific students.

For more than two decades, educators have recognized the importance of data in improving teaching practices (Brooks & Brooks, 1993; Bullard & Taylor, 1993; Glickman, 1993; Joyce, Calhoun, & Wolf, 1993; Wiggins, 1994). Collecting achievement, participation, attendance, and disciplinary data that are dissaggregated by race, gender, income, English language ability, and educational program (i.e., special education, gifted and talented, vocational education) helps to identify trends. This information should be used to monitor student progress, to identify student and teacher strengths and weaknesses, and to adjust the educational environment for each student whenever adequate progress is not being made.

The Maryland State Department of Education
The state is piloting a program to help schools pursue data-driven improvements. It has created a web page to help school teams analyze their students' state assessment data and identify best practices to support improvements in student performance. Maryland presents performance data on a variety of key dimensions in simple graphs for each school. Data are broken out by subject, gender, race, and grade, and allow school teams to compare results to similar schools in the state. The system includes worksheets that ask schools key questions about how their instructional practices influence assessment results, help schools chart questions raised by the data, and allow them to identify further data that they need to collect (USDE, 1998).

INCREASING EFFECTIVE LEARNING TIME

If African American students are not making progress, positive, constructive changes in the students' educational environment should be made. Students have different kinds of intelligences and learning styles, and, therefore, teaching must be designed to meet diverse cognitive and affective learning needs. Changes in a student's educational environment can include changes in teachers, teaching strategies, time of instruction, length of instruction, support activities, and curriculum materials. During the time structured for teacher collaboration, teachers should discuss ways to improve the educational environment for each child who is not making significant gains in his or her learning. Modification should be made, not at the end of the year, but when needed, as identified by regular, frequent assessments.

Increasing the time spent on focused learning activities is important for all students. Increased learning time should be incorporated into a regular part of the school schedule. It should not be a remedial add-on that is punitive in nature or directed only toward "teaching to the test." A year-round school schedule, block scheduling, summer school program used for remediation and enrichment, before and/or after school programs, and Saturday programs are all effective ways to increase learning. In Murfreesboro, Tennessee, a 5,300-student school district, all nine schools stay open twelve hours a day, year-round. The program began a decade ago to keep children safe after school. It now includes tutoring and serves almost half the district's students (USDE, 1998). Research indicates that focused learning is enhanced by teaching students in small groups and providing assessments based on objective, external criteria, such as rubrics. Small groups and frequent assessments help to identify individual skill development needs and make learning time more meaningful (Goodrich-Andrade, 2000; USDE, 1998). When additional learning time is required, there are a variety of ways to make that happen. In Halifax County, North Carolina, the district pays high school honor students to tutor younger students in reading one and a half hours per day. The district also hires retired teachers to work with struggling students.

Schools have had great success in increasing effective learning time by schedule changes that affect the size and length of classes. For example, schools that have designated a 90- to

120-minute period for language arts have had success in raising reading achievement when that schedule is supported with the following kinds of administrative policies: allowing no interruptions and assigning everyone in the school to teach language arts.

Some elementary schools have decreased the size of classes by scheduling only half the class to lunch periods or to special classes, such as gym, music, or recess time. This allows the primary teacher to teach language arts and mathematics to about half the students, while the specialty teachers (i.e., gym, music) receive half of a class from two different teachers. Computers, when available in the classroom, are used appropriately at all times on a rotating basis. This further reduces class size and provides students with more individualized support, especially in particular areas of identified need. In these ways, school schedules are being modified to support more instructional time and smaller group instruction.

EFFECTIVE PROFESSIONAL DEVELOPMENT

An important part of professional development is teacher collaboration. Additional time for teacher collaboration can be supported by schedule changes. Joint educational activities for two or more classes have been scheduled in some schools to provide teachers with additional time for professional development and collaborative planning. These large-group activities can be supervised by aides and/or volunteers. In this way, students can be provided with meaningful experiences in larger groups while teachers get much needed time for preparation and planning. At other schools, additional time for collaboration, professional development, or visits to other schools is found through "banking" an additional fifteen minutes per day, so that students can be dismissed early, one day per week. Finally, at many schools teachers are volunteering their time to make more time for planning.

Finding a Meeting Time	
Purchased time	Summer vacation or vacation planning
Borrowed time	Four days x 15-minute early arrival = 1 hour on Friday
Common time	Block scheduling
New time	Teacher incentives for their time
Free-up time	Parent volunteers or senior citizens
Tiered time	Lunch/brunch or breakfast club
Found time	Student teacher or unexpected time
Better-used time	Faculty and department meeting/memos
Rescheduled time	Back to back combining classes, common preparation period
Released time	Professional development days
Bought time	Substitutes

Adapted from *Time for Reform* by Purnell & Hill (1992).

Teacher collaboration and teacher training helps teachers and other staff to meet the needs of students who learn in different ways and who come from diverse cultural, linguistic, and socioeconomic backgrounds. Teachers who educate African American students must know the cultural context of their students. It is difficult to teach African American students effectively if those students are perceived through an ideology of deficits or the prism of Eurocentrism. To build on strengths that African American students bring to class, teachers must be able to recognize these strengths. Professional development must address both best practices for teaching and the deconstruction of deficit-focused cultural assumptions. It must provide a deeper understanding of African American cultures and students.

Recent studies indicate a direct relationship between teacher training and student performance. Research conducted on the importance of teacher quality in Alabama and North Carolina found that teachers who scored high on assessments of teacher quality tended to be more likely to produce significant gains in student achievement. In addition, a positive correlation has been found between teachers holding degrees in technical subjects (such as mathematics, physics, and biology) and student achievement (Darling-Hammond, 1998; Haycock, 1998). Several states and districts, motivated by new teaching standards, have implemented innovative professional development programs.

Tennessee Study

Significant academic improvement was found among low-achieving students by as much as 53 percent when taught by highly effective teachers compared with a maximum of a 14 percent increase by students taught by a less-effective teacher. This study concludes that the teacher can determine between a student being labeled remedial or placed in the accelerated of gifted track. (Haycock, 1998)

Dallas Independent School District

Two groups of students, with similar average reading scores, were evaluated over the course of three years. One group was assigned three teachers in succession who were evaluated as very effective. An increase from the 59th percentile to the 76th percentile was observed. Meanwhile, the other group of students were taught by three teachers in succession who were evaluated as ineffective, and their scores dropped from the 60th to the 42nd percentile by the end of sixth grade. Similar findings were also observed in mathematics. (Haycock, 1998)

A teacher's growth and development is important to all students and can be promoted in many ways. Teachers learn from outside knowledge; they also learn from each other and from looking at student work (Ayers, 1993; Cochran-Smith & Lytle, 1993; Schon, 1995). Attention to developing the collective ability of staff to solve problems and achieve goals should be assigned the highest priority.

States, including North Carolina, Ohio, New Mexico, and Kentucky, and school districts such as Los Angeles, St. Paul, Cincinnati, and New York City, provide incentives and salary increases to reward teachers who receive certification as master teachers from the National Board for Professional Teaching Standards (NBPTS). The St. Paul district is collaborating with the teachers' union and the University of Minnesota to support teachers through the NBPTS certification process. The district pays the application fees, and the university and other partners develop and conduct professional support programs for the candidates. Districts such as Toledo, Cincinnati, and Seattle, and the state of Connecticut have implemented peer review and assistance programs to help teachers, particularly new teachers, improve their classroom techniques. These programs help beginning teachers learn to teach and assist veterans who are having difficulty, improving their teaching or getting them to leave the classroom without union grievances or delays. In Columbus, Ohio, exemplary teachers are assigned as "consulting teachers" to mentor new teachers and intervene when teachers experience difficulty in the classroom (USDE, 1998).

The Southern Maine Partnership, established in 1985, was among the first in the country to develop the current model of school-university collaboration–one that fosters the renewal of educators in the schools and at the university simultaneously. The partnership links 30 school districts, three private schools, Maine College of Art, Southern Maine Technical College, and the University of Southern Maine. Its director, a professor at the university, is granted release time for partnership work and is aided by two partnership associates, both of whom are former teachers in partnership schools. Teachers

How Many of These Kinds of Professional Development Experiences Do You Have in Your School?

Direct Training	Out-of-School Professional Development	In-School Professional Development
9 Insirational awareness sessions 9 Motivational speakers 9 Conferences 9 Courses and workshops 9 Consultants/coaches	9 Immersion in community projects 9 Reform networks 9 School/university partnerships 9 Subject matter networks 9 On-line discussion groups 9 Study groups 9 Collaborations 9 Teacher centers 9 Writing for professional journals	9 Team teaching 9 Peer coaching 9 Peer collaboration 9 Dissemination of research & literature reviews 9 Problem-solving groups 9 Colleague review and assessment of teaching practices 9 Principal or specialized review and assessment of teaching practices 9 Peer review and assessment of student learning achievement 9 Case studies of practices 9 School site management teams 9 Collaborative review of data, priority objects & interviews

Adapted from Lieberman & Miller, 1999.

and administrators staff the partnership, because it is a school-based, educator-driven school reform effort. Accomplishments include:

- Developed collaborative work in the area of standards and assessments, such as the School Quality Review Initiative in which schools conduct self-assessments and respond to assessments by visiting teams
- Established linkages with local businesses and business leaders, such as a shadowing project between CEOs and superintendents
- Established a new teacher education program at the University of Southern Maine that is located in partnership schools and co-directed by university and school-based educators;
- Fostered and gave publication opportunities to teachers who wrote about their personal and school experiences with changes in practice
- Strengthened and expanded the conversation/networking purpose of the partnership.
- A growing number of districts are pooling their resources.

Professional development should:

- Result in a greater understanding of students' cultural backgrounds and cross-cultural communication issues
- Be based on research

- Have as its primary goal the improvement of student achievement
- Be rigorous and sustained
- Provide mentoring and coaching
- Be deeply embedded in daily work
- Result in reflection and dialogue
- Deepen subject matter knowledge
- Provide a better understanding of the learning and teaching processes
- Be evaluated at several different levels, but most important, for evidence of improved student performance, with the goal of closing existing performance gaps
- Foster renewal in teaching and greater commitment to students (USDE, 1998).

This checklist will help you to evaluate your professional development initiatives.

On the left, check those procedures your school follows.	**Do they incorporate issues related to becoming more effective with diverse students?**	
9 *Establish professional development priorities collaboratively by grade, subject, or department?*	**Yes**	**No**
9 *Have individual professional development plans developed with supervisor or subject coordinator?*	**Yes**	**No**
9 *Have professional development tied to school and department needs assessments?*	**Yes**	**No**
9 *Have professional development tied to teacher supervision?*	**Yes**	**No**

Check those professional development experiences your school has addressed:

9 Provide teachers with skills that allow them to teach diverse learners?
9 Are ongoing and concentrate on depth of teacher learning?
9 Increase the teachers' ability to introduce continuous embedded student assessment processes?
9 Reflect a design that encourages teachers and principals to work together to solve emerging problems?
9 Improve expertise in subject areas.
9 Provide mentoring and coaching.
9 Foster a renewal in teaching and dedication to students.
(Bennett, 1995; Ladson-Billings, 1999; Sleeter & Grant, 1987; Zeichner, 1992).

PROFESSIONAL DEVELOPMENT IS PARTICULARLY IMPORTANT TO THE ACHIEVEMENT OF AFRICAN AMERICAN STUDENTS

Although new teaching standards and innovative programs designed to help teachers reach these standards hold great possibilities for raising the quality of teacher preparation, they are not having a great effect on the quality of teachers in urban settings. School districts are continuing to hire teachers who are unprepared and disproportionately assigning them to teach urban students (Ladson-Billings, 1999). Even among the certified, few teachers have been provided the kind of training and experiences that will help them to teach African American students effectively. As Haberman (1995) states, "completing a traditional program of teacher education as preparation for working [in today's urban classrooms] is like preparing to swim the English Channel by doing laps in the university pool. Swimming is not swimming. . . . 'Teaching is not teaching' and 'kids are not kids.' Completing your first year as a fully responsible teacher in an urban school has nothing to do with having been 'successful' in a college preparation program."

In addition, teachers' experiences with diversity outside of the classroom are likely to have been very limited. Several studies have attempted to assess prospective teachers' knowledge about and attitudes toward student diversity and multicultural education. Sleeter (1993) found that student diversity was viewed as a problem rather than a strength or a phenomenon to be explored. Few teachers reported any desire to teach in urban areas or in schools populated by large numbers of children of color (Goodlad, 1990; Haberman, 1995). In addition, teachers are likely to have been trained by predominantly White middle-class professors. Eighty-eight percent of the full-time higher education faculties are White. Finally, they are likely to have been trained by older faculty who have less experience teaching children from diverse cultures. Eighty-one percent of the faculty are between the ages of forty-five and sixty (AACTE, 1994). Predominantly White faculty members are preparing predominantly White students to teach students who are racially, ethnically, linguistically, and economically different from them. Today's teachers are likely to have been miseducated in their own educational programs (Darling-Hammond, 1999; Ladson-Billings, 1999).

PROFESSIONAL DEVELOPMENT EXPERIENCES THAT MAXIMIZE THE ACHIEVEMENT OF AFRICAN AMERICAN STUDENTS

Identifying what works in settings of diversity is a necessary first step in developing effective professional development programs. Research indicates that teachers who are successful with African American students demonstrate the following:

- An interest in and dedication to teaching children of diverse cultures
  - High expectations for themselves and their students
  - A belief that they [teachers] can make a difference
  - A personal bond with their students
- Knowledge of subject area
- Intercultural competence
  - A sense of their own ethnic and cultural identities
  - An understanding of their own attitudes toward other cultures
  - An understanding of the damaging effect of class biases in navigating sociocultural and language issues in the classroom

  – Participation in the communities and cultures of their students

  – A knowledge of cross-cultural communication issues
- Knowledge of and willingness to confront racism and prejudice to
  - Assist students to recognize and combat racism
  - Integrate family and community issues into school curriculum
- Understanding of multiple historical perspectives
  - Knowledge of how to gain information about diverse communities
  - Ability to integrate the history and contribution of various groups into curriculum
  - An understanding of differences in epistemology and the social construction of world views, and
  - Strategies that maintain a student's sense or ethnocultural pride and identity
- Knowledge of effective instructional strategies for culturally diverse students
  - An understanding of learning style differences and how to use them in teaching
  - Use of a variety of successful instructional models
  - Use of scaffolding to link academically challenging curriculum to the cultural and personal resources that students bring to class
  - An understanding of the relationships among language, culture, teaching, and learning
  - An understanding of how to make learning tasks meaningful to students

– Willingness to involve parents and community members in the learning process. (Bennett, 1995; Ladson-Billings, 1994, 1999; Sleeter & Grant, 1987; Zeichner, 1992).

HOW CAN SCHOOLS AND SCHOOL DISTRICTS IMPROVE RECRUITMENT OF TEACHERS FROM DIVERSE ETHNIC, CULTURAL, AND LANGUAGE BACKGROUNDS?

According to the U.S. Department of Education, 36 percent of students only 10 percent of teachers are minority (NCES, 1998). The prospect for greatly increasing diversity in the teacher-candidate population seems minimal, unless specific and considerable actions are taken to train, recruit, and retain a diverse pool of teachers. Several factors inhibit such recruitment for teaching careers. These include (but may not be limited to): lack of adequate K to 12 preparation; the high cost of obtaining a college education; financial aid policies, increased opportunities for careers with greater financial rewards; institutional practices that promote the hiring of White teachers and administrators over teachers of other ethnic or racial groups (Sleeter & Grant, 1987; Recruiting New Teachers, Inc., 2000), discriminatory practices that prevent African American students from entering and completing teacher preparation programs; and work environments perceived to be hostile or unsupportive by teachers from diverse ethnic, cultural, and language backgrounds (Foster, 1997). In addition, it

How Many of These Strategies have You Tried In Order to Improve Your Diversity Recruitment Efforts?

9 Reach out to churches and community associations.

Yes **No**

9 Use local radio ads designed to reach a diverse group of grandparents and parents to encourage their children to become teachers.

Yes **No**

9 Build relationships with banks and other local businesses to create opportunities for housing, low-interest loans, and other incentives for teacher candidates.

Yes **No**

9 Build relationships with faculty and administrators at local colleges, encouraging professors to recommend promising minority students for teaching careers.

Yes **No**

9 Encourage liberal arts majors from local colleges to tutor in your schools.

Yes **No**

9 Prepare your recruiters with information about cross cultural communication and techniques to effectively attract individuals from different ethnic and racial groups.

Yes **No**

9 Give promising candidates the VIP treatment.

Yes **No**

From Recruiting New Teachers Inc., 2000.

stands to reason that high student dropout rates among students from diverse ethnic, cultural, and language backgrounds very likely severely diminish the potential pool of educators from diverse backgrounds.

There are tremendous benefits to increasing the number of teachers from diverse backgrounds, including:

- Teachers from diverse backgrounds serve as role models for students from diverse backgrounds.
- Teachers from diverse backgrounds challenge the hidden message that only Whites are best suited for positions of leadership and authority.
- Teachers from diverse backgrounds can serve as cross-cultural brokers and lessen the cultural isolation of White teachers, students, and parents. They can help all students learn to function effectively in an increasingly culturally diverse society.
- Teachers from diverse backgrounds have voices that are imperative for reforming school culture and curriculum (Ewing, 2000).

WHAT CAN SCHOOLS DO TO IMPROVE THE QUALITY OF TEACHING FOR AFRICAN AMERICAN STUDENTS?

There is a great deal that can be done to improve the quality of teaching for African American students. Let us start with what individual schools can do to improve professional development. In which areas do your teachers need more support to become culturally competent?

Linda Darling-Hammond (1999) clearly lays out an agenda for how school boards, superintendents, governors, state legislators, state boards of education, and state educational agencies can improve the quality of teaching in low-income and high-income areas. In her report published by the National Commission on Teaching and America's future, entitled, "Solving The Dilemmas of Teacher Supply and Demand And Standards: How We Can Assure a Competent, Caring and Qualified Teacher For Every Child," she outlines specific recommendations.

What school boards and superintendents can do to improve the quality of teaching:

- End the practice of assigning the most inexperienced teachers to teach the most disadvantaged students with the heavier loads and the fewest supports.
- Place beginning teachers with mentors and give them reduced loads.
- End the practice of hiring underqualified teachers and placing teachers out of field.
- Work with universities to create pathways into teaching for paraprofessionals and mid-career teachers and to create internships and student teaching assignments that provide students a cultural immersion experience that has adequate and appropriate supervision by the most successful teachers working with children of color.

What governors and state legislators can do to improve the quality of teaching:

- Increase the ability of financially disadvantaged school districts to pay for qualified teachers by raising and equalizing starting salaries and providing incentives (ranging from financial stipends to improved working conditions) for teachers to move to shortage areas. Then insist that school districts hire only qualified teachers.
- Provide incentives such as service scholarships and forgivable loans for teacher candidates who prepare to teach in high-need fields (e.g., mathematics, science, special education, ESL) and hard to staff locations (e.g., inner city or rural schools).
- Fund the development of high-quality pathways to teaching, including extending teaching preparation programs to include a year-long internship in a professional development school and/or a high-achieving urban school; and postgraduate options for mid-career changers, such as paraprofessionals already in the classroom, as well as military and government retirees.
- Make timely decisions about school budgets so that districts can recruit and hire qualified candidates in the spring of each year.
- Remove entrance barriers by ensuring pension portability, salary credit for experience, and acceptance of National Board Certification as portable license.
- Create mentoring programs for first-year teach-

Teachers' Needs Assessment

	Experienced			No Experience	
Immersion in the cultures of your students	1	2	3	4	5
Interactive workshop on understanding and reducing racism	1	2	3	4	5
Peer mentoring by a teacher who is successful with African American students	1	2	3	4	5
Attending courses on Afro-centric perspectives in math	1	2	3	4	5
Attending courses on Afro-centric perspectives in literature	1	2	3	4	5
Teaching through constructivist approaches	1	2	3	4	5
Training in using learning styles and multiple intelligences in teaching and assessment	1	2	3	4	5
Understanding cross-cultural communication issues	1	2	3	4	5
Integrating the contributions of diverse cultures into the curriculum	1	2	3	4	5
Using a student's culture and language as a resource resource upon which to build additional learning experiences	1	2	3	4	5
Integrating the family and the community into the learning process	1	2	3	4	5
Using a variety of instructional approaches	1	2	3	4	5
Embedding assessment into learning	1	2	3	4	5
Demonstrating high expectations and forming personal bonds with students	1	2	3	4	5
Understanding of one's own ethnic identity and attitudes toward other cultures	1	2	3	4	5
How to gain more knowledge of the ethnocultural communities of students	1	2	3	4	5
An understanding of epistemological differences among cultures and their importance to the learning process	1	2	3	4	5
Understanding the relationships among language, culture, and learning	1	2	3	4	5

ers to reduce attrition and enhance competence.

What state boards of education, state educational agencies, and professional standards can do to improve the quality of teaching:

- Establish rigorous standards for teacher education and licensing that are linked to student standards so that teachers are prepared to teach in ways that will enable students to learn as the new standards demand. This should include standards related to teaching diverse student groups.
- Support the creation of high-quality pathways into teaching for undergraduates, post-graduates, and paraprofessionals that meet rigorous accreditation standards and include standards for working with diverse populations. Then eliminate emergency, temporary, and alternative certificates that lower standards for teacher knowledge and skill.
- Conduct demographic studies that provide projections of anticipated teacher supply and demand by field and location and design policies, including scholarships and training grants, in high-need fields and locations to alleviate shortfalls before they become severe.
- Design mentoring programs that provide sustained support to beginning teachers and evaluate their teaching skills before granting a long-term professional license.

CONCLUSION

Creating a school that supports the high achievement of African American students requires a cultural transformation. To be sure change "takes" and is not dependent on one or a group of individuals, it is important to institutionalize change through the development and implementation of new policies and practices. These new policies and practices must support the cognitive and affective development of African American students and remain open to ongoing evaluation and revision. School and classroom schedules should be developed to support team teaching, collaboration, professional development, reduced class size, small-group instruction, frequent, embedded assessment, and increased instructional time, particularly in core subjects. Creating community and parent ties and working collectively with the community to build resources is essential. Many schools have succeeded, because they have established a process for identifying individual student strengths and needs and providing the resources to build strengths and meet student needs. Effective schools concentrate on achievement and provide a rigorous curriculum. They are successful at matching teachers to student needs. The teacher's abilities to meet student needs can be enhanced by the kind of professional development that assists teachers to effectively use a student's cultural identity to support his or her cognitive and affective growth. Finally, schools and school districts must pay attention to recruiting a highly qualified, culturally competent, and diverse teaching staff.

There is no doubt that school reform creates tension. Reform requires celebrating cultural diversity and recognizing cultural conflict. It requires a balance between content and process, teacher and student needs, action and reflection, pressure and support, responsibility and accountability. As Lieberman and Miller (1999) so eloquently tell us, school change must be characterized by the collective involvement of teachers, so goals for the school become greater than the personal goals of individual teachers:

> It happens as teachers get involved in collective struggles about student learning and engagement. It happens when student work can be discussed with colleagues rather than judged in isolation using one's intuition as a guide. It happens when teachers willingly engage in learning outside as well as inside their school and talk about it with their colleagues. It happens when a level of trust is sustained over a long period of time. It happens when the community recognizes that learning is not a one-time thing but is recursive, often stressful and challenging before it is rewarding. It happens when teachers struggle openly with a need to identify with their school or team or grade level but at the same time not give up their own sense of identity and strong feelings about being a teacher. It happens as teachers incorporate expanded strategies for student learning into their own repertoire and feel comfortable enough to talk about it, learn from it, and in some cases, teach it to others.

The transformation of school culture requires administrators to encourage teachers to assume leadership roles. Administrators and teachers must challenge their assumptions about themselves, their students, and their schools. School leaders must create new learning communities where high achievement is universal, but the roads to reach it are diverse, and principals, parents, and teachers advocate for African American students by helping them to believe in themselves. Students must be taught to use their own culture and learning styles to consciously learn how to learn, take responsibility for their own learning, and recognize the value learning has for their own communities and the larger society. Transformation of school culture requires a collective vision for not only improving achievement of all students but also closing the achievement gap between groups of students. It requires knowledge, passion, caring, honesty, inquiry, authentic relationships, and collective action.

REFERENCES

Abi-Nader, J. (1993). Meeting the needs of multicultural classrooms: Family values and the motivation of minority students. In S.J. Odell & J.M. O'Hair (Eds.), *Diversity and teaching: Teacher education yearbook 1* (pp. 212–236). Fort Worth, TX: Harcourt Brace Jovanovich.

American Association of Colleges of Teacher Education. (1994). *Briefing books.* Washington, DC: Author.

Ayers, W. (1993). *To teach: The journey of a teacher.* New York: Teachers College Press.

Bennett, C. (1995). Preparing teachers for cultural diversity and national standards of academic excellence. *Journal of Teacher Education, 46*, 259–265.

Bernard, B. (1991). *Fostering resiliency in kids: Protective factors in the family, school, and community.* Portland, OR: Western Regional Center for Drug-Free Schools and Communities, Northwest Educational Laboratory.

Brooks, J.G., & Brooks, M.G. (1993). *In search of understanding: The case for constructivist classrooms.* Alexandria, VA: Association for Supervision and Curriculum Development.

Bullard, P., & Taylor, B.O. (1993). *Making school reform happen.* Boston: Allyn & Bacon.

Cochran-Smith, M., & Lytle, S. (1993). *Inside/outside: Teacher research and knowledge.* New York: Teachers College Press.

Darling-Hammond, L. (1998, August). Alternatives to grade retention. *The School Administrator, 55.* Retrieved June 1999 from the World Wide Web: http://www.aasa.org/publications/sa/1998_08/Darling-Hammond.htm.

Darling-Hammond, L. (1999). *Solving the dilemmas of teacher supply and demand and standards: How can we assure a competent, caring and qualified teacher for every child.* Columbia University: National Commission on Teaching and America's Future.

Dilworthy, M.E. (Ed.) (1992). *Diversity in teacher education: New expectations.* San Francisco: Jossey-Bass.

Ewing, N.J. (2000). *Teachers of color: Why we need them.* Unpublished manuscript.

Foster, M. (1997). *Black teachers on teaching.* New York: The New Press.

Glickman, C.D. (1993). *Renewing America's schools: A guide for school-based action.* San Francisco: Jossey-Bass.

Good, T., & J. Brophy. (1994). *Looking in Classrooms* (6th ed.). New York: Harper Collins.

Goodlad, J.I (1990). Better teachers for our nation's schools. *Phi Delta Kappan, 72*: 185–194.

Goodrich-Andrade, H. (2000). Using rubrics to promote thinking and learning. *Educational Leadership,* Vol. 57(5), pp. 13–19. Arlington, VA: Association for Supervision and Curriculum Development.

Haberman, M. (1995). *Star teachers of children in poverty.* West Lafayette, IN: Kappa Delta Pi.

Harris, L., & Associates. (1994). *Dropping out or staying in high school: Pilot survey of young African American males in four cities.* New York: Commonwealth Fund.

Hawkins, J.D., Catalano, R.F., & Miller, J.Y. (1992). Risk and protective factors for alcohol and other drug problems. *Psychological Bulletin, 112*(1): 64–105.

Haycock, K. (1998, Summer). *Good teaching matters: How well-qualified teachers can close the gap. Thinking K-16.* (Report No. TK9802) Washington, DC: Education Trust.

Hollins, E.R., & Spencer, K. (1990). Restructuring schools for cultural inclusion: Changing the schooling process for African American youngsters. *Journal of Education 172*(2): 89–100.

Joyce, B., Calhoun, E. & Wolf, J. (1993). *The self-renewing school.* Alexandria, VA: Association for Supervision and Curriculum Development.

Ladson-Billings, G. (1994). *The dreamkeepers: Successful teachers of African American children.* San Francisco: Jossey-Bass.

Ladson-Billings, G. (1999). Preparing teachers for diverse student populations: A critical race theory perspective. In A. Iran-Nejad & P.D. Pearson (Eds.), *Review of research in education, Vol. 24.* Washington, DC: American Educational Research Association.

Lieberman, A., & Miller, L. (1999). *Teachers–Transforming their world and their work.* New York: Teachers College Press.

Little, J.W. (1990). The persistence of privacy: Autonomy and initiative in teachers' professional relations.

Teachers College Record, 91(4), 509–536.

McCormick, T.E., & Noriega, T. (1986). Low versus high expectations: A review of teacher expectations' effects on minority students. *Journal of Educational Equity and Leadership, 6*(3), 224–234.

National Center for Education Statistics. (1998). *The condition of education 1996.* (Supplemental Table 43-4). Washington, DC: Author

Nelson-Barber, S., & Estrin, E.T. (1995). Bringing Native American perspectives to mathematics and science teaching. *Theory into practice 34* (3):174–85.

Pang, V.O. (1990). Ethnic prejudice: Still alive and hurtful. In N.M. Hidalgo, C.L. McDowell, & E.V. Siddle (Eds.) *Facing racism in education* (pp. 28–32). Cambridge, MA: Harvard Educational Review.

Purnell, S., & Hill, P. (1992). *Time for reform.* Santa Monica, CA: Rand.

Recruiting New Teachers, Inc. (2000). *A guide to today's teacher recruitment challenges.* Belmont, MA: Author.

Sadowski, M. (2001, May/June). Closing the gap one school at a time. *Harvard Education Letter: Research Online.* Retrieved on 5/16/2001 from The World Wide Web: http://www.edletter.org/current.

Schmoker, M. (1999). *Results: The key to continuous school improvement.* Alexandria: Association for Supervision and Curriculum Development.

Schon, D. (1995, November/December). The new scholarship requires a new epistemology. *Change,* pp. 27–34.

Shade, B.J., & Edwards, P.A. (1987). Ecological correlates of the educative style of Afro-American children. *Journal of Negro Education, 56*: 88–99.

Sleeter, C., & Grant, C. A. (1987). An analysis of multicultural education in the United States. *Harvard Educational Review, 7*: 4221–444.

Sleeter, C. E. (1993) Multicultural education: Five views. Education Digest 58 (7): 53–57. Reprinted in Annual Editions: Multiculatural Education 94/95, First Ed., Guilford, CT: Dushkin Publishing Group, p. 147–149.

Steele, C.M. (1992, April). Race and the schooling of Black Americans. *The Atlantic Monthly,* pp. 68–78. Retrieved on 4/09/2001 from The World Wide Web: http://www.theatlantic_nbound/flashbks/blacked/steele.htm.

United States Department of Education. (1998). *Turning around low performing schools: A guide for state and local leaders.* Washington, DC: Author.

Werner, E.E., & Smith, R.S. (1992). *Overcoming the odds: High risk children from birth to adulthood.* New York: Cornell University Press.

Wiggins, G. (1994). None of the above. *The Executive Educator, 16*(7): 14–18

Zeichner, K. M. (1992). *Educating teachers for cultural diversity.* East Lansing, MI: National Center for Research on Teacher Learning.

Zeichner, K.M., & Hoeft, K. (1996). Teacher socialization for cultural diversity. In J. Sikula, T. Buttery, & E. Guyton (Eds.), *Handbook of research on teacher education* (2nd ed., pp. 525–547). New York: Macmillan.

Article 7

A NO-EXCUSES APPROACH TO CLOSING THE ACHIEVEMENT GAP

BELINDA WILLIAMS

IT IS CLEAR THAT A POWERFUL, transforming belief system exists in schools where teachers and students are succeeding; it's a belief system powerful enough to counter the statistical probability of school failure among lower-income children of color (Charles A. Dana Center, 1999; Corbett, Wilson, & Williams, 2000). This belief system is powerful enough to enable educators to go beyond rhetoric and slogans to actions that sustain focus on creating environments and structures that support success. How does such a powerful belief system develop? What enables teachers, administrators, students, and parents to succeed in some schools and fail in others? What might be done to set in motion a process of change, a shift from excuses to high expectations? Where does such a belief system exist? What do teachers, administrators, parents, and policy-makers need to know, do, and *be* to become advocates for the success of low-income students? To answer these questions, we must move away from excuses to a no-excuses approach.

Excuses	**No excuses**
Focusing on culture as deficits	Valuing cultural diversity
Limiting perceptions of ability	Defining and identifying multiple abilities
Assuming a lack of motivation	Engaging experiences and interests
Identifying risks	Fostering resilience

This article will explore how professional development, school environment, teaching and learning arrangements, and national policy can contribute answers to these essential questions.

PROFESSIONAL DEVELOPMENT

Successful education reform demands that all educators engage in comprehensive experiences of professional development (Darling-Hammond, 1997; Fullan, 1993, 1999). Researchers agree that among the most important elements common to effective teachers in urban schools are the belief that all students can be successful and the communication of this belief to students (Delpit, 1995; Ferguson, 1998; Ladson-Billings, 1994; Zeichner, 1996). If, as researchers have demonstrated, teachers have lower expectations for some children, and these expectations have on impact on achievement, it is important to provide teachers with experiences that effectively change these lower expectations (Ferguson, 1998; Pajares, 1992).

Recent research conducted with the support of a field-initiated OERI grant, suggests that most educators espouse the belief that "all children can learn," but that belief has multiple meanings (Corbett, Wilson, & Williams, 2000). The different meanings become clear in the qualifiers that people attach, such as "if their parents support education" and "if the students put forth the effort." A third qualifier should be, "and it's my job to make sure that they do." Educators making this statement refuse to allow home situations and student motivation to serve as reasons why students fail. Instead, they expect each student to complete schoolwork successfully and develop strategies that ensure that work is completed to high standards. Standards are clearly defined and communicated to staff, students, and parents. This approach has been labeled a "no-excuses" agenda.

"No excuses" depends on attitude as much as action. Professional development must go beyond the introduction of technical knowledge and skills to include developing a shared understanding and common values. Darling-Hammond (1997) cites Dewey's approach to the rich professional development of teachers, an approach that enables them to reach out to students who are difficult to know:

> . . . one that aims to empower teachers with greater understanding of complex situations rather than to control teachers with simplistic formulas or cookie-cutter routines for teaching: Command of scientific methods and systematized subject matter liberates individuals; it enables them to see new problems, devise new procedures, and in general, makes for diversification rather than for set uniformity . . . This knowledge and understanding render the teacher's practice more intelligent, more flexible, and better adapted to deal effectively with concrete phenomena of practice . . . Seeing more relations he sees more possibilities, more opportunities. His ability to judge being enriched, he has a wider range of alternatives to select from in dealing with individual situations. (p. 322)

Fullan (1993) cites Goodlad to illustrate how professional development experiences and change intersect to build an effective teacher-student connection:

> The moral responsibility of educators takes on its most obvious significance where the lives of teachers and their students intersect . . . The epistemology of teaching must encompass a pedagogy that goes far beyond the mechanics of teaching. It must combine generalizable principles of teaching, subject-specific instruction, sensitivity to the pervasive human qualities and potentials always involved. (p. 9)

SCHOOL ENVIRONMENTS THAT SUPPORT SUCCESS

There are two essential characteristics of schools that are successfully educating all of the children and closing achievement gaps: (1) a shared focus on teaching and learning; and (2) the existence of programs and strategies specific to engaging diverse learners. Rossi and Stringfield (1995), identifying overarching conditions in eighteen schools that had been designated as effective in educating diverse learners, conclude:

> Shared vision, shared purpose, and shared values were most often the result of efforts to define common goals for education and for working with students. [. . .]. Incorporation of diversity was a hallmark of all the successful sites we visited. Teachers and administrators actively sought out the distinctive talents of their students and they had come to see great value in a diversity . . . (p. 74)

Clearly, *no excuses* is hard work. Educators face challenges on many fronts, including the way the school day is organized, how teacher prep time is scheduled, and how students are disciplined. Furthermore, teachers are not able to sustain the effort necessary for student success without support. Working with low-performing students from low-income situations is hard work. An important characteristic of no-excuses structures is a common focus across all initiatives and programs. Fullan (1999) lists the need to attack incoherence and establish connectedness and knowledge creation as central to complex change:

> With change forces abounding, it is easy to experience overload, fragmentation, and incoherence. In fact, in education this is the more typical state . . . Many schools and school systems make matters worse by indiscriminately taking on every innovation that comes along–what Bryk et al. (1998) called "Christmas tree schools"–so many innovations as decorations, superficially adorned. (p. 27)

Fullan (1999) further describes "the deep meaning of inside collaboration":

> Collaborative organizations fan the passion and emotions of its members because they so value commitment and the energy required to pursue complex goals. But instead of leaving passionate teachers to sink or swim, the true value of collaborative cultures is that they simultaneously encourage passion and provide emotional support as people work through the roller coaster of change. In this sense these organizations foment moral purpose while providing support for its pursuit. (p. 38)

Teachers in schools where achievement gaps are closing make the following comments (Corbett, Wilson, & Williams, 2000):

> "Curriculum must be related to their own lives . . . the students can elect to portray meaning through art, a play, or a paper."
> "We just look at it as they have not had enough practice, not that they don't have the skills."
> "If we can pique their interest, they will be motivated."

Educators who make these statements recognize the importance of knowing the learners in their classrooms. Reducing class size enables these relationships if teachers are aware of the power of an interpersonal relationship that values the learner's experience, abilities, and interests, and uses this knowledge in instruction while providing a caring environment and communicating a sense of purpose and future (Ladson-Billings, 1994; Williams, 1999; Williams & Newcombe, 1994; Williams & Woods, 1997). Engaging all students in learning challenging standards in the regular education classroom is enhanced if teachers come to the instructional experience with varied strategies and with a belief that all children can learn challenging standards (Corbett, Wilson, & Williams, 2000).

The principal in one school where gaps in learning were closing was described by a teacher as bringing "a vision with him that kids are first. He instills that in others. He doesn't fall back on the excuse that they have bad family situations. He truly believes that all of them have the capacity, and we should be always searching for the right kid-based programs."

TEACHING AND LEARNING ARRANGEMENTS

Current proposals for improving the test performance of low-income students and closing the test score gap are numerous and varied, including expanding the availability of preschool, school-based management, and heterogeneous ability grouping. The recent Title I evaluation report, *Promising Results, Continuing Challenges* (USDE, 1999), states that student achievement has risen since 1992 and that we need to "stay the course" with the following strategies: standards, greater accountability for districts and schools, reduced class size, strengthened instructional abilities of teachers, improved parent involvement, and the introduction of research-based programs. However, we need to look again. I recently spoke with a researcher who was proudly reporting improvements in reading. I asked if he and his colleagues had considered what must be added to his model to improve the achievement of economically disadvantaged children to levels comparable to their more advantaged peers. He had to admit that he hadn't; for him, improvement was enough, but that improvement had not begun to close the gap between those children and high-resource children for whom the 50th percentile would not be considered an acceptable goal. Simple improvement is not enough. What is being touted as improvement frequently constitutes evidence of a widening gap between students in low-poverty and high-poverty schools. These recommended strategies may be necessary to improve achievement, but they are not sufficient to close the gap between those children who begin at the starting line and those who do not.

Standards, accountability, class size reduction, better teachers, parent involvement, and new research-based programs are important, positive strategies. But they are exactly that–strategies. In and of themselves, separate, fragmented strategies are not adequate (Fullan, 1993, 1999). They do not constitute a powerful integrating theory of learning that pulls together the best of what we know about human development (Bransford, Brown, & Cocking, 1999; Schoenfeld, 1999). Introducing standards assumes that the education community expects that all children are capable of learning challenging content and that educators know how to engage and interest all children in learning to high standards. Strengthening accountability assumes that districts and schools have sufficient knowledge and resources to do the job. Reducing class size assumes that teachers will know what to do differently in smaller classes. Allocating funds to schools to support the introduction of available program models without *rigorous* definitions of *research-based* or *comprehensive reform* assumes states, schools, and districts will develop and implement rigorous reforms that will not be limited to improving achievement but also close existing gaps in achievement between identified groups. My experiences with thousands of educators in state departments, districts, and schools across the country suggest that this is not necessarily so. Assuming that there is a critical mass of knowledge, skill, and will in every district and school where gaps in achievement exist leaves the successful education of all children to chance. Our goal must be to focus on closing the achievement gap.

Reform proposals must be defined by a solidly grounded theory of human development and not by narrowly conceived assumptions of individual researchers and model developers. The National Research Council has proposed a conversation to focus on the integration of research on human development with practice (Bransford, Brown, & Cocking, 1999). In addition, Alan H. Schoenfeld (1999), Past President of the American Education Research Association (AERA), has challenged the research community to move beyond narrowly defined conceptualizations to integrated social and cognitive theory and rejection of the deficit hypothesis:

> How do we begin to unravel the nature of the learning process, the relationship between the individual and the environment that results in the individual having new understandings and capacities? There are at present no good candidates for answers to this question. Moreover, a major reason for this state of affairs is the cognitive/social split . . . As I see it, no theory of learning is complete without a theory of mechanism–an elaboration in detail of the processes by which learning takes place. Whatever mechanism is proposed must, as noted above, apply to the broad range of ways in which learning takes place, both in and out of school. (p. 7)

What do we already know about human development and what influences achievement that is not consistently reflected in reform proposals? Maybe Dewey (1938) said it best more than sixty years ago:

> . . . be aware of the general principle of the shaping of actual experience by environing conditions . . . recognize in the concrete what surroundings are conducive to having experiences that lead to growth . . . know how to utilize the surroundings, physical and social, that exist so as to extract from them all that they have to contribute to building up experiences that are worth while . . . a system of education based upon the necessary connection of education with experience must on the contrary, if faithful to its principle, take these things constantly into account. (pp. 34–36)

Dewey's description of human development is supported by Piaget's notion of schemas and Vygotsky's notion of meaning being defined by the interpersonal cultural context and experience of the learner. Rigor across these theories is supported by recent cognitive theories suggesting the existence of the following: (1) multiple, modifiable abilities developed within the cultural context and experience (Gardner, 1999); (2) the power of engaging learners through the identification of intrinsic motivation and effort (Alderman, 1999; Resnick, 1995); and (3) the role of caring environments that support and respond to risk taking and errors in learning while promoting a sense of future (Nieto, 1996).

POLICY INITIATIVES

The fundamental question is not whether Title I should be continued. It must be continued–it is desperately needed. The question isn't whether the funds should be allocated by the federal government or by the states. We have learned from numerous studies of school-based management that simply shifting decision making does not ensure a focused step-by-step process of improved teaching and learning (Odden & Wohlstetter, 1995; Wohlstetter & Mohrman, 1996). The critical question concerns the adequacy of the current reform proposals and the models that guide our attempts to improve the education of all children.

Closing the academic and cognitive achievement gaps that exist between low-income and more advantaged students is tremendously complex and must be addressed at multiple levels: federal, state, and local policy levels, higher education, parents and community, and schools. Researchers target the schools, classroom teachers, and the practice of teaching and learning as the most powerful dynamic to be changed (Jencks & Phillips, 1998; Oakes & Lipton, 1999; Odden & Wohlstetter, 1995). In addition to the previously identified reform proposals, if we heed the recommendations of these researchers, pre- and in-service teacher preparation courses and experiences must include attention to understanding the role of culture and cultural environments in human development and teaching and learning. Newmann and Wehlage (1995) describe a revealing reality:

> We have seen that school restructuring can promote authentic teaching that helps to boost student achievement for all students. But this good news must be qualified: The tools of school restructuring do not assure a schoolwide focus on learning of high intellectual quality or authentic teaching. In fact, we found several schools in which restructuring activities did not advance the intellectual quality of student learning . . . Why? . . . We also found that restructuring initiatives themselves generated a host of new issues that could divert staff attention from the agenda for learning . . . student achievement gains and other benefits are influenced by organizational characteristics beyond the skills of individual staff . . . When schools are unable to coordinate teachers' diverse aims for students into a curricular mission focused on high quality student learning, when teachers have few opportunities to work together to devise approaches suited to the school's student body, or when schools pursue multiple innovations without sustained, long-term consistency, it is difficult for even the most gifted teachers to make a positive difference for students. (pp. 28–29)

Federal funding that recognizes the need to close the gap rather than just make progress doesn't exist. State policy that requires disaggregation of achievement data and comprehensive planning to address identified gaps does exist in a few states, but there is no nationally crafted policy that requires this focus. *The New York Times* (Belluck, 1999), and a recent series in *EdWeek* (Johnston & Viadero, 2000; Viadero, 2000b; Viadero & Johnson, 2000) alert us that the need to identify and formulate strategies to close achievement gaps is gaining attention. Haycock (Olson, 1996) warns, "Our silence as a profession about these numbers has let policymakers and others off the hook because we've allowed them to believe that these kids are doing as well as can be expected."

In an earlier article (Spray, 1992) I envisioned a comprehensive and systemic review and revision of policy:

> We are talking about the need for systemic change . . . There has to be a way of reaching consensus so that the curriculum reflects it, staff development addresses it at the district and the school levels, leadership manages it, states set up the regs and monitor them and federal funds support the effort. You can't have a school or district doing one thing, the state holding it accountable for something else, and the federal government funding something completely different. (p. 2)

Federal, state, and local policy must explicitly guide practice to make similar distinctions. Accountability must include (1) definition and activities that require disaggregation of achievement data and focused attention to existing patterns of achievement gaps; (2) professional development for all staff that ensures the classroom teachers' knowledge of content or outcome standards and current understandings of human development and expectations; (3) current conceptualizations of human development in courses required for certification; (4) parent involvement that introduces parents to understandings of the impact of cultural environments on learning and strategies to bridge the cultural gaps that exist between home and school; and (5) community support for children and families.

CONCLUSION

Clearly there is a need for additional resources to jump start the essential conversations of possibilities for improving the education of low-income racial and language minority students at federal, state, district, and local school levels. Formulations of school policies can do much to focus, facilitate, prioritize, and support the development and implementation of required structures, strategies, and programs to close the gaps in achievement, including:

- A powerful belief system of possibilities for low-income students
- Leadership and support
- School structures and arrangements that operationalize this belief system
- A collective and individually shared vision and responsibility for student success
- Clear definitions of standards and quality work
- Skilled, knowledgeable educators

In the end, institutionalizing a *no-excuses agenda* in schools serving low-income students across the country will require collaborative efforts for the entire education community: higher education; federal, state, district, and local school policy; and educators to ensure the existence of sustained structures, strategies, and programs that support the development and success of all students. There is much to be done at every level to silence the excuses and to create what Darling-Hammond (1997) has called a unified agenda for change.

This article was supported by a grant from the Office of Educational Research and Improvement, U.S. Department of Education. The opinions expressed are those of the author and do not represent policy of the U.S. Department of Education.

REFERENCES

Alderman, M.K. (1999). *Motivation for achievement: Possibilities for teaching and learning.* Mahwah, NJ: Lawrence Erlbaum Associates.

Belluck, P. (1999). Reason is sought for lag by blacks in school effort. *The New York Times, CXLVIII* (51, 573), p.1.

Bransford, J.D., Brown, A.L., & Cocking, R.R. (Eds.). (1999). How People Learn–Brain, Mind, Experience, and School. Washington, DC: National Academy Press.

Corbett, D, Wilson, B., & Williams, B. (2000). *Assumptions, actions, and performance: Final Report.* OERI Field-Initiated Studies Grant 1996–1999.

Charles A. Dana Center. (1999). *Hope for urban education: A study of nine high-performing, high-poverty, urban elementary schools.* The University of Texas at Austin.

Darling-Hammond, L. (1997). *The right to learn: a blueprint for creating schools that work.* San Francisco: Jossey-Bass.

Delpit, L. (1995). *Other people's children: Cultural conflict in the classroom.* New York: New Press.

Dewey, J. (1938). *Experience and education.* New York: Collier Books.

Ferguson, R.F. (1998). Teachers' perceptions and expectations and the black-white test score gap. In Jencks, C., & Phillips, M. (Eds.). *The black-white test score gap.* pp. 273–317. Washington, DC: The Brookings Institution Press.

Fullan, M. (1993). *Change forces: probing the depths of educational reform.* New York: The Falmer Press.

Fullan, M. (1999). *Change forces: the sequel.* New York: The Falmer Press.

Gardner, H. (1999). *Intelligence reframed: Multiple intelligences for the 21st century.* New York: Basic Books.

Jencks, C. & Phillips, M. (1998). *The black-white test score gap.* Washington, DC: Brookings Institution Press.

Johnston, R.C., & Viadero, D. (2000). Unmet promise: Raising minority achievement. *Education Week, 19*(27), 1.

Ladson-Billings, G. (1994). *The dreamkeepers: Successful teachers of African American children.* San Francisco: Jossey-Bass.

Newmann, F.M., & Wehlage, G.G. (1995). *Successful school restructuring: A report to the public and educators.* Washington, DC: The American Federation of Teachers.

Nieto, S. (1996). *Affirming diversity: The sociopolitical context of multicultural education.* White Plains, NY: Longman.

Oaks, J., & Lipton, M. (1999). *Teaching to change the world.* New York: McGraw-Hill College.

Odden, E.R., & Wohlstetter, P. (1995). How schools make school-based management work. *Educational Leadership, 52*(5), 32–36.

Olson, L. (1996). Achievement gap widening, study reports: Progress of minority students has stalled. *Education Week, XVI* (14), 31.

Newmann, F.M., & Wehlage, G.G. (1995). *Successful school restructuring: a report to the public and educators.* Washington, DC: The American Federation of Teachers.

Pajares, M.F. (1992). Teachers' beliefs and educational research: Cleaning up a messy construct. *Review of Educational Research, 62*(3), 307–332.

Resnick, L. (1995). From aptitude to effort: A new foundation for our schools. *Daedalus, 124*(4), 55–62.

Rossi, R.J., & Stringfield, S. (1995). What we must do for students placed at risk. *Phi Delta Kappan, 77*(1), 73–76.

Schoenfeld, A.H. (1999). Looking toward the 21st century: Challenges of educational theory and practice. *Educational Researcher, 28*(7), 4–14.

Spray, M. (1992). The other urban learner: Capable, motivated resilient. *R&D Preview, 7*(5), 2–3.

U.S. Department of Education (1999). *Promising results, continuing challenges: The final report of the national assess-*

ment of Title I. Washington, DC: U.S. Department of Education.

Viadero, D. (2000a). Lags in minority achievement defy traditional explanations. *Education Week, 19*(28), 1.

Viadero, D. (2000b). Minority gaps smaller in some pentagon schools. *Education Week, 19*(29), 1.

Viadero, D., & Johnston, R.C. (2000). Lifting Minority achievement: Complex answers. *Education Week, 19*(30), 1.

Williams, B. (1999). Diversity and education for the 21st century. In Marsh, D.D. (Ed.), *ASCD Yearbook: Preparing our schools for the 21st century.* Alexandria, VA: Association for Supervision and Curriculum Development.

Williams, B., & Newcombe, E. (1994). Building on the strengths of urban learners. *Educational Leadership, 51,* 75–78.

Williams, B., & Woods, M. (1997). Building on urban learners' experiences. *Educational Leadership, 54,* 29–32.

Wohlstetter, P., & Mohrman, S.A. (1996). *Assessment of school-based management.* Washington, DC: Office of Educational Research and Improvement, U.S. Department of Education.

Zeichner, K. (1996). Educating teachers to close the achievement gap: Issues of pedagogy, knowledge, and teacher preparation. In Williams, B (Ed.), *Closing the achievement gap: A vision for changing beliefs and practices.* Alexandria, VA: Association for Supervision and Curriculum Development.

Article 8

TALENT DEVELOPMENT, CULTURAL DEEP STRUCTURE, AND SCHOOL REFORM: IMPLICATIONS FOR AFRICAN IMMERSION INITIATIVES*

A. WADE BOYKIN

BY AND LARGE, AFRICAN AMERICAN children have not been well served by our nation's public schools. The push for African-centered infusion initiatives into public schools represents still another attempt to rectify this troubling situation. The major thesis of this article is that while there is wisdom and heuristic value in African-centered initiatives, such efforts must involve broader school reform. Comprehensive transformations, which impact the full range of school activities, outlooks, structures, and outcomes, are needed. The core assumptions, functions, and practices of schooling must change (Elmore, 1996; Goodman, 1995). Furthermore, this must be coupled with an understanding of the historical purposes that public schools have served in the American social order, the foundational problems of formal education, and an appreciation for the complexities and challenges of school reform (Boykin, 1994, 1996).

In this article, salient aspects of African-centered initiatives will first be identified. The larger questions of school reform will then be visited; this will lead to a plea for an alternative comprehensive model of schooling. A case will then be made that this talent development model of schooling can be successfully fused with African-centered initiatives. This fusion will transform the cultural deep structure of schooling, building on the cultural assets African American children bring with them to school and ultimately foster positive life transformations for Black children through cultural empowerment. Research consistent with these claims then will be presented. The article concludes with a distillation and summary of the line of argument that is advanced.

AFRICAN-CENTERED INITIATIVES

African-centered educational efforts typically strive to make salient, if not authenticate, canons and understandings that are African in origin and make these central to curriculum formulations. As Lee (1994) has persuasively argued, the goal is to legitimate "African stores of knowledge" (p. 297). African-centered infusion initiatives also tend to be transformative and "efficacy oriented" (Gordon, 1994; King, 1994). They operationalize "liberatory pedagogy" (Gordon, 1997) in that through the schooling process African American students are empowered to overcome the impediments of oppression, racism, low status, inadequate material

*Reprinted (with minor modifications) from *African-Centered Schooling in Theory and Practice*, edited by Diane S. Pollard and Cheryl S. Ajirotutu.

resources, and marginalization that have plagued African Americans for centuries. The formal education of African Americans is to be geared toward helping Black people overcome these obstacles.

Further, the goal is to enable African American children to have hope and to act to change their circumstances beneficially, to transform their lives and those of significant others, and to impact positively on their community as well as the wider society. Education should provide beacons toward bright futures. This concern resonates well with one offered by Carter O. Woodson over 60 years ago in his immortal work, *The Miseducation of the Negro* (1933) when he stated, "The mere imparting of information is not education" (x). In a related vein, African-centered infusion initiatives are geared toward rectifying the enduring impact of slavery's legacy on the lives of African Americans and American society at large. Defining people as property and treating people as though they were property are profoundly dehumanizing acts. An effort to dehumanize others is itself dehumanizing, both for those who engage in it and for a society that condones it. The humanity of this society cannot be completely restored until African Americans are fully participating partners in it. A people's humanity is effectively conveyed through their fundamental cultural expressions (Boykin, 1999).

The traditional cultural voice of African America was officially silenced through the institution of slavery, as this was a key mechanism in the effort to strip away their humanity (Akbar, 1985). Black Americans' participation in American society since the demise of slavery has been predicated upon embracing Anglo-EuroAmerican worldviews, values, and expressions. Yet the "unofficial" original cultural voice of African Americans was never fully silenced. African Americans as a whole, of course, with several individual exceptions, have never abandoned their cultural ties to their African past. They have just sought (even if tacitly) unofficial vehicles for its expression, even if such expression has not been officially sanctioned in mainstream attainment institutions such as public schools (Boykin, 1986; Boykin & Ellison, 1995).

> When the traditional cultural voice of African Americans is heard and authenticated by this society's institutions, the humanity of America at large will be more fully realized, the legacy of slavery will be more likely to be put to rest, and Black people will gain even greater access to their own humanity. African-centered infusion initiatives, by promoting and authenticating the traditional cultural expressions of African American people, provide a path for such realizations.

The transformations identified with African-centered approaches have merit in light of the historical and current circumstances in which African Americans find themselves. They suggest clear strategies and direction for school reform. But there are other, broader school reform considerations as well that must be considered if school reform is to be effective. Indeed, I argue that no effort at school reform will meet with success unless it is sufficiently appreciative of and responsive to several considerations. It must appreciate the historical purposes that schools have served in the American social order and the corresponding foundational assumptions upon which the schooling process is built. In doing this, it must address the full range of problems of schooling. It must provide change that is comprehensive, coordinated, and sustained. It must yield an assemblage of activities that permeate the many reaches of the schooling enterprise and do so in a conceptually coordinated, internally consistent fashion.

So what purposes have American public schools served? What is the historical context for current-day practices? These issues have been addressed persuasively by several authors (Goodman, 1995; Plank, Scotch, & Gamble, 1996; Tyack, 1974). Mass public education was established in the first two decades of the twentieth century in response to a convergence of cultural, economic, political, demographic, and social trends of the time period. This resulted in some strikingly consistent functions and operational modes for public schools that have persisted to the present day.

THE TRADITIONAL FUNCTIONS OF AMERICAN PUBLIC SCHOOLS

Perhaps most fundamentally, public education in America has performed a talent sorting and selection function. This was readily apparent as far back as the late eighteenth century when Thomas

Jefferson, arguing for public funding for "grammar schools," stated that their purpose should be to identify the few geniuses who "will be raked from the rubbish" (Spring, 1994). In this way, a "natural aristocracy" would emerge. It would be composed of only the best and brightest students, who would then lead and direct this nation. This premise has guided and informed educational policies and practices ever since. Traditionally, schools have played a gatekeeping role for society. They sort and weed out. They assess students for purposes of classifying and arraying them along a vertical pecking order from the most able to the least able, from the few who are deemed legitimately talented, to the bulk who are considered average, to the ones who are construed as intellectually handicapped. During the inception of the mass public education movement in the early twentieth century, the talent sorting paradigm was augmented by other principles and assumptions about the functions and purposes of public schools. Several references have documented and elucidated this formative process (Borrowman, 1965; Callahan, 1962; Cubberly, 1916; Curti, 1959; Karier, 1975; Lukes, 1973; Persell, 1977; Spring, 1994; Tyack, 1974).

One such additional function for mass public schooling was a mainstream acculturating function. Schools strove to bring the values and behaviors of immigrant children from southern and eastern European nations into conformity with Anglo cultural ideals–for example, to get them to appropriate such cultural themes as materialism, emotional containment, providence, competition, and particularly individualism in its many forms. As such, schools were conceived to perform a homogenization function, indeed, a cultural socialization function, that was officially and sharply at odds with principles of pluralism or diversity.

Public schools were also conceived to operate consistent with certain ways of conceptualizing learning and the learner arising from the emerging discipline of psychology. It is well documented that the functionalist principles espoused by William James, the behaviorist principles of John Watson, and especially the stimulus-response connectionist and law of effect principles of Edward Thorndike drove practices of pedagogy in this period (Borrowman, 1965; Goodman, 1995). Consequently, the learner was construed as passive; learning was to be imposed from outside the person and was driven by external motivation, in the form of rewards, incentives, and punishments. Schools were places where drill, repetition, and rote memorization prevailed and where an information accumulation approach to knowledge was promoted. The "proper" knowledge was gained in a piecemeal fashion, disconnected, largely formalized and abstracted from real life (Everhart, 1983; Lave, 1996; Rogoff, 1990).

Traditional Operating Functions of American Public Schools:

1. Sort and select students; weed out the best and brightest to lead the nation
2. Acculturate immigrants to the mainstream values and behaviors
3. Socialize a work force for factory work

Traditional Operating Assumptions of American Public Schools:

1. Learners are passive
2. Knowledge is accumulated by drill, repetition, and rote memorization
3. Schools should be run as bureaucracies

An additional objective of this model was to socialize a labor force to meet the manpower needs of a heavily industrializing society that was based on a factory work, manufacturing-driven economy. Consider that in a highly influential book on teacher training written during this era (William Chandler Bagley's *Classroom Management*, 1925) it was advocated that the chief purpose of schooling was to build habits of the kind needed to properly work on the assembly line. Students so trained would have the capacity to work long hours on repetitive, tedious tasks often unrelated to personal motives, interests, or desires. They would be punctual, do drill work, follow commands without hesitation, and generally conform to "company" rules.

Schools were also conceived to fit with the prevailing corporate-industrial model for institutional operation and to serve as bureaucratic institutions. Over time the preservation of the bureaucracy became an end unto itself and thus a purpose for schooling. As bureaucratic institutions, schools were characterized by centralization of authority, highly formalized organizational structures, and rule-governed social interactions, with authority residing in roles. Schools were supposed to be affect-neutral sites. There was standardization of procedures and practices. Further, there was a paramount concern with efficiency of institutional operation linked to an insistent preoccupation with quality control (Cubberly, 1916). Students who did not fit this mold were seen as threats to the system's efficiency; hence the problems of education came to be located inside students, inside their immediate families, or the proximal community. Thus, when things go wrong at school, it is attributed to students themselves who have learning problems, adjustment problems, behavior problems, or family problems, any or all of which would "naturally" impede the learning process (Karier, 1975; Spring, 1994, Chapters 9–10).

All in all, it can be argued persuasively that public education still operates largely according to these same premises. However, these premises and functions have receded from the spotlight of educational discussion and have been substantially blended into the ordinary, everyday routines of schooling where, all too often, they are unacknowledged. They are simply accepted as how schooling is supposed to be implemented. Unless a school reform initiative addresses these premises and purposes, reform cannot be fully responsive to the foundational problems of public schooling.

There is a need to change profoundly the way we school in America. Schools most surely need to be socially reconstructed. They must be reculturalized. The purposes and functions schools serve need to be redirected and reframed. A different set of operating assumptions is needed. This is so for several related reasons. These are discussed below.

THE PROBLEMS OF TRADITIONAL SCHOOLING APPROACHES AND THE TALENT DEVELOPMENT APPROACH

A talent-sorting, weeding-out approach to schooling may have outlived its usefulness. Considerable evidence supports this view (Boykin, 1994). Entry-level skills needed for employment have escalated. The cognitive and ethical demands for normal living and decision making are rising. The world is shrinking and global dependence is increasing. The labor pool, and indeed society at large, will increasingly rely on school graduates from groups that have had the most problematic schooling experiences. Resources are dwindling in our society. As a result of these changes, we will need substantially changed educational practices in order to educate a substantially greater proportion of our student population.

There may be many reasons why children fail to perform well in school. It may be that some are performing in a problematic manner that requires direct corrective intervention. But to reduce all the problems to this source and to invoke this single remedy is a narrow and myopic strategy. Surely, there might be multiple reasons why children fare poorly, and there may be multiple pathways that can lead to school success (Boykin, 1996).

There is real and profound pluralism in our society that should not be swept under the proverbial rug, cast in negative terms, or squashed by cultural imposition (Banks & Banks, 1995; Nieto, 1993). Schools are not culturally neutral terrains. A mainstream cultural socialization agenda still forms the backbone for the hidden curriculum of schooling (Carlson, 1982). As we have become more enlightened on the workings of culture, it is abundantly evident that the cultural terrain of schooling should be expanded. Concerted efforts must be made to become more inclusive and to take into account the experiences of domestic cultural groups whose origins are not European. In doing so, we can take fuller advantage of diverse cultural expressions in the promotion of widespread talent.

In a related manner, different types of learners and learning are demanded for the twenty-first century (Brooks & Brooks, 1993; Gordon, 1995; Wilson & Peterson, 1997). The learner must be active. Learning must be construed as a socially interactive process. Moreover, what is learned in school should also change. Especially for children from marginalized domestic cultural groups in this society, learning cannot consist of the accumulation and regurgitation of preprocessed facts or piecemeal, disconnected abstractions. Education should not be a passive experience in which students are taught to merely accept things as they are. Instead, it should be made meaningful to their lives, challenging them to be innovative about building a better tomorrow for themselves and others.

Schooling practices should be made more consistent with more recent conceptions offered by the social, behavioral, and human development sciences. In this regard, the importance of the intersection of culture, context, and cognition needs to be operationalized in schooling practices (Rogoff & Chavajay, 1995; Tharp & Gallimore, 1988). Ecological considerations need to be acknowledged as important. Moreover, greater focus should be on how a person can gain intrinsic enjoyment and stimulation from interaction with the environment (Deci, 1975; Hunt, 1965; Raffini, 1995). Finally, traditional conceptions of school learning did not address human development issues sufficiently. These need to be properly considered.

The economic order in our society has changed significantly since the inception of the traditionally dominant model of public schooling (Kearns & Doyle, 1991). We are living in what has been described as a post (manufacturing) industrial era. Today low-wage factory work forms a fairly small share of the available workforce options. More jobs are now available in the service sector. These new jobs require a particular focus on interpersonal and communication skills. We live in an era where information creation, management, analysis, utilization, and transmission are economic commodities, underscoring the importance of communication skills. There also is a premium on high levels of information technology. Fluency and competence with state-of-the-art electronic mechanisms and devices will be an increasingly common expectation in order to function in twenty-first century workplaces.

To improve the quality of life in schools for students and teachers alike may require less reliance on a strictly bureaucratic, early twentieth-century corporate model of systems operation. Strict adherence to impersonal guidelines for interpersonal exchanges, and casting students and their backgrounds in pejorative terms, may not create a socially conducive atmosphere for learning and for the nurturance of students' potential (Fine, 1994). Teachers who serve as rule enforcers and guideline implementers, who put meeting curricular datelines over genuine learning, and who feel little creative generative voice in the process can feel devalued and depersonalized in the process of teaching (Giroux & McLaren, 1986). While evaluation and assessment of students should no doubt continue, their role in support of a gatekeeping function needs to be reconsidered.

Indeed, an alternative overarching reform philosophy and corresponding model to guide schooling efforts have been formulated (Boykin, 1996). This alternative formulation asserts a different purpose for schooling. It is conceived to be comprehensive, farsighted, proactive, cohesive, and yet responsive to fundamental problems of formal education. The talent development model of schooling is proposed here. Incorporating this model would change the very core assumptions, functions, practices, schooling attitudes, and roles schools play in society at large.

The talent development model starts with the assertion that all students can learn to high standards in a demanding, high expectations academic setting.

This lofty goal can be achieved by any school that is committed to providing the appropriate support, assistance, structure, and facilitating conditions. This is a reachable goal for any school that strives to maximize every child's academic development. This then becomes the basis upon which a school and its classrooms are to be judged. *Talent* here refers to a high level of competence or performance, based upon an age-appropriate standard of excellence. Virtually any student, it is argued, can attain this standard of performance. *Talent* is not used here to refer to a specialized skill in a particular domain, but to general schooling competence and performance. It includes affective and interpersonal concerns, as well as community involvement. Development is meant to convey a host of considerations when it comes to talent. It includes identifying, cultivating, refining, sustaining, enhancing, and extending talent, providing opportunities for its expression and occurrence, and transferring this across different domains and settings, including in and out of school settings.

To fulfill its objectives, the **talent development** model advocates that a given school provides, simultaneously, multiple determinants for ensuring students' success. This means that the possibility of success for any given child is made redundant by ensuring that each of the major facets of the schooling process is reconstructed as an avenue for success. Specifically, the following steps should be taken:

1. Students should be fortified in those areas where they may be vulnerable to school failure. This would be achieved through providing access to supportive services, be they academic, social, health, and/or mental health; through tutorial assistance as needed; and through fostering a sense of resilience in them. Moreover, as appropriate, enrichment experiences that enhance schooling outcomes should also be provided.
2. Programs and activities should be implemented that ensure that peers, family members, and the local community are functionally supportive of students' success.
3. School personnel must become enabled to serve as advocates rather than adversaries for children. They must come to truly believe and be committed to the proposition that all children can learn, and they must receive sufficient and appropriate professional development activities to support the talent development model.
4. The content of the curriculum, pedagogical techniques, and learning contexts must be challenging, appropriate, effective, engaging, and responsive to the students' interests and needs.
5. Organizationally, the school must be configured and operated to ensure the delivery of successful schooling outcomes.

Overall, this model aims to provide appropriate activities and programs that are based on the best available documented evidence that they will lead to enhanced schooling outcomes for the population served by a given school.

The talent development model advocates several themes to inform schooling activities as well. These themes explicitly aim to redress the foundational problems of schools that have been identified earlier in this chapter, and they are conceived to give substance and focus to the activities that manifest the various successful pathways.

1. **In order to turn diversity into strength, the first talent development theme is building upon the assets that students bring with them to school**. Perhaps all children in America should become fluent in the dictates of mainstream society. Yet the integrity of diverse children's life experiences also should be capitalized upon to enhance educational outcomes and facilitate their beneficial participation in the larger society.
2. **A second talent development theme is that of helping children across key developmental transitions**. Schooling is a dynamic, not static, process, and there are changing developmental challenges along the way. From a talent development perspective, it is essential that children's schooling be consistently developmentally appropriate and that children make key transitions as successfully as possible.
3. **The third talent development theme emphasizes active, constructivist approaches to learning**. Passive rote learning and drill should be deemphasized. The learner should be construed as an active participant in the learning process, with knowledge acquisition viewed as a social construction and with a greater focus on active academic task engagement. Moreover, along with basic skills, there should be greater focus on higher-order thinking skills, critical thinking skills, and creative problem solving. Learning should not be construed as a pouring-in and subsequent pouring-out process.
4. Moreover, what children learn in school at all grade levels should not be so isolated, abstract, piecemeal, formalized, and disconnected. Instead, **a fourth talent development theme is the promotion of meaningful *and* connected learning**. Knowledge gained should be thematically connected across subject areas. It should be connected to the world outside of school in practical and meaningful ways. A child's formal education should be more greatly situated proactively in children's lived experiences. This should be done to generate greater interest level and also for purposes of cultural empowerment. For example, what a child acquires in school can be put to his or her other constructive benefit and to the benefit of his or her family community, and society at large.
5. **Still another talent development theme is the preparation of students for the twenty-first century**. For that matter, the focus should be on helping children to eventually prepare for the twenty-first century (Goodman, 1995). Children must be prepared for the information age, where information creation and transmission are major commodity products. They must function

in an economy more greatly dominated by the service industries. Schooling experiences must prepare students who can meet the intellectual challenge of high technology in their daily activities. Their world will be more socially and ethically complicated by the fact of global interdependence. Consequently, children must develop full-range communications skills. They must develop interpersonal negotiation skills and conflict-resolution skills. They must have high-level numeracy skills. They certainly must be multiculturally fluent. They must learn to apply the knowledge and information gained in creative and profitable ways. That is, they must become intellectual entrepreneurs.

6. **Still another talent development theme is the promotion of school as a community**. Schools should be personal and caring environments. Schools should be places where a sense of belonging is fostered among students and school personnel alike. There should be strong identification with the school. Students should feel they are wanted, desired, and honored in the schools they attend. Their well-being, interests, concerns, and development should be seen as central to the school's mission. Schools can serve as their sanctuaries, as places of hope. In all, schools should function more like small-scale communities, broken down perhaps figuratively into interconnected families and neighborhoods rather than large, impersonal bureaucratic machines. Efficiency of system operation should not be abandoned; such efficiency should be in the service of the promotion of a sense of community among all school participants.

AFRICAN-CENTERED INFUSIONS AND TALENT DEVELOPMENT

I posit that the thrusts of African-centered infusions are not inconsistent with certain themes of the talent development model. Indeed, manifestations of African-centered infusions can flesh out certain tenets of this reform model. Both African-centered infusions and the talent development model place premiums on building a sense of community in schools, the development of critical thinking skills, and understanding of learning processes, and knowledge acquisition which is meaningfully connected to children's lives. Both advocate that formal education should serve a transformative function in children's lives and lead to efficacy and empowerment for children, so that they can enhance life conditions for themselves and others. Both advocate building on the assets that children bring with them to school. The African-centered approach more obviously focuses on the factors as they serve to enhance life conditions for people of African descent. The talent development model addresses additional schooling concerns to which African-centered infusion initiatives should pay heed. These include a focus on human development considerations, especially as they relate to: school transitions, skill preparation of students for the twenty-first century, promotion of active academic task engagement, thematic learning across the curriculum, and actualizing a schooling framework that strives to overdetermine success so that virtually no children are left behind in the quest to develop pervasive high levels of performance and competence.

As mentioned above, both approaches promote building on the assets that children bring with them to school, assets that arise proactively out of the children's life experiences. This is a central consideration for reforming schools at the deep structure level. Quite frankly, it sounds laudable to proclaim that all children can learn. It surely seems like the appropriate thing for "concerned and committed" school personnel to advocate. Proclaiming this is one thing, but truly believing it and operating consistently with such a belief are other matters.

The efficacy of building on children's cultural assets is substantiated by the growing body of work examining the interface of cognition and context. It has been demonstrated that the quality of one's thinking in a given situation is tied to the quality of support that situation provides one's thought processes. Further, work on situated cognition reveals that scaffolding on current understanding or competencies leads to better results and produces more positive cognitive change than attempting to add on understanding or pour in competency, assuming a priori that none had existed (Greene, 1989; Greene & Middle School Group, 1997).

Moreover, other work suggests that children in school will be quite resistant to changing how they operate and even become alienated from the goals of the change process and those in school who promote it if the children's integrity or current ways of operating are dishonored through the proceedings (Fordham & Ogbu, 1986; Gilmore, 1985; Piestrup, 1973). More concrete elaboration is in order.

In the course of adapting and coping with life circumstances, it can be argued that many black children from low-income backgrounds acquire adaptive competencies that could be capitalized upon in school settings. The adaptive integrity plausibly can be scaffolded for cognitive enhancement and to fulfill a school's socialization agenda (John-Steiner & Mahn, 1996). In interviews conducted by a team of researchers at Howard, it was found that many fourth- and fifth-grade Black children have adult-like household responsibilities. They also have day-care responsibilities for their younger siblings or the younger children of their older siblings. These are potentially asset-laden experiences. These experiences have created opportunities for learning and cognitive skill development that are often overlooked by schooling processes. For example, family decision-making experiences promote a maturity in children that is not capitalized on in school settings.

We must also recognize that schools traditionally are not culturally neutral terrains. They were not conceived to be such. Certain cultural themes have come to dominate the extant contexts of schooling. The hidden curriculum is formed by such fundamental cultural themes as rugged or self-contained individualism, competition, and the sanctity of a bureaucracy orientation (Howard & Scott, 1981; Lukes, 1973; Sapon-Shevin & Schniedewind, 1991; Spence, 1985). Lack of mastery of this hidden curriculum has been used as a principal basis for weeding out children according to a talent-sorting model of schooling (Boykin, 1994). But evidence suggests that if we expand or alter the range of fundamental cultural themes that form the basis of the learning and performance contexts in school, we can capitalize upon the fundamental cultural assets of a wider range of children who participate in a more diverse set of cultural experiences and thereby enhance a larger number of children's learning and performance outcomes (Gay, 1988).

When this scenario plays out for a preponderant number of African American children from low-income backgrounds, it has very direct implications for African-centered infusion efforts. There are Afrocultural themes that permeate the lives of people of African descent throughout the Diaspora. These themes are considered Afrocultural, because it is posited that they are rooted in traditional African cultural legacy. These themes are considered fundamental because at base they are rooted in a worldview and belief system that addresses the fundamental philosophical foundations of life's purposes. They, in concert, form a blueprint for living and give substance and texture, indeed meaning, to one's existence.

Afrocultural themes include **communalism, a movement-expressive-percussive-polyrhythmic orientation, the co-importance and integration of cognition and affect, and spirituality**, and in the residue of such themes can be derived a premium placed on high levels of sensate stimulation or high psychological verve (Boykin, 1983; Boykin & Ellison, 1995). **By infusing such themes where possible into the differing contexts in which schooling gets done, we create changes at the deep structural level of schooling**. Making changes at this fundamental level when using African-centered infusion goes literally to the core of the schooling process.

These Afrocultural themes are available to be capitalized upon because they have shaped and informed contexts in which children have participated out of school (Boykin, 1999). Through such participation, the themes get yoked to children's values, perceptions, competencies, and their practice of various skills. These all become more available for constructive expression when schooling contexts are structured and informed by these Afrocultural themes.

A PROGRAM OF RESEARCH

Over the last several years, my colleagues and I have launched a basic (rather than applied) research program aimed at bringing empirical substance, clarity, and verification to these claims with respect to African American children from low-income backgrounds. We have focused in our work on the potential facilitating effects of three postulated Afrocultural themes. These we have labeled *communalism*, *verve*, and *movement expressiveness*. Communalism denotes the importance of social interdependence, social bonds, mutuality and identity, and duty tied to group membership. Verve refers to a premium placed on receptiveness to relatively high levels of physical stimulation, marked by receptiveness to variability and intensity in stimulation and to multiple sources of stimulation simultaneously present. Movement expressiveness connotes a premium placed on rich, complex, and expansive movement expression as it relates to the amalgamation of syncopation, percussion, music, and polyrhythm.

Since we have postulated that there is a distinctive cultural lens through which many African American children from low-income backgrounds view their schooling experience, we sought to discern the cultural character of their attitudes, preferences, and perceptions and how these may come into disaccord with those prevailing in their schools.

In our work, we have given low-income African American grade school students sets of scenarios depicting high-achieving peers who achieved via differing cultural means. We have found that, on average, these students are quite socially accepting of their peers who would achieve highly via communalism and verve and less accepting or even rejecting of peers who would achieve highly via conformity to mainstream cultural dictates of individualism and competition (Boykin, Bailey, Hurley, Miller, & Albury, 1998; Marryshow, 1995; Martin, 1994). Other work has shown that, on average, African American grade school students indicate high endorsement of learning environments where the academic practices are characterized by communalism and verve and rejection or no endorsement of such environments marked by individualism and competition (Martin, 1997). These results held for Black students in virtually all-Black inner-city schools and in suburban predominantly White schools. Intriguingly, in a study where grade school teachers of inner-city African American students were given depictions of students who preferred to learn via differing cultural modalities, it was found that the teachers expected children who were more attuned to individualism and competition to be more highly motivated and to attain higher academic levels in their classrooms than students who operated via communalism and verve (Walton, 1993). Of course, this is the opposite pattern to what was obtained when assessing the students' perceptions. Surely, this sets up a situation for potential discord in the classroom. This was more directly tested in another investigation (Miller, 1997). It was found that not only did Black grade school students on the average prefer academic practices consistent with themes of communalism and verve and reject those consistent with individualism and competition, but they perceived that their teachers preferred individualism and competition and that they would be likely to get into trouble or be punished if they exhibited behaviors consistent with communalism and verve. This occurred even though they further indicated that at home they would be encouraged to learn via communalism and verve and discouraged from learning via competition and individualism.

Taken together, the results from these studies give amplification to children's own voices about their classroom experiences. They seem to indicate that there is a systematic cultural character to the perceptions of at least the children that we have tested. These children display clear cultural preferences, and they seem sensitive to the potential schooling problems of not embracing Anglocultural themes. These results stand in striking contrast to the claims of Ogbu and others (Fordham & Ogbu, 1986; Ogbu, 1994) that black students simply reject high achievement and their high-achieving peers. Other work has more directly addressed whether African American children would actually perform better and be more motivated in contexts marked by Afrocultural themes.

One study (Albury, 1998) has shown that low-income African American grade school students perform significantly better on a vocabulary test when that test was preceded by a communal learning condition (children worked in groups of three with shared learning material and were prompted to help each other out for the good of the group, with no external incentive) than by conditions marked by individualism (children worked alone and were offered an external incentive for subsequent high test performance) or interpersonal competition (three children worked at same location under the promise that the one who performed best of the three on the subsequent test would receive a reward). Other studies have examined this communal theme as well.

Dill (1996) examined recall of information from printed text, Children first either worked alone or in dyads to study the text material. The study dyads were of two types. In one, students studied according to an orthodox approach to reciprocal peer tutoring. They took turns playing tutor and tutored and followed a script designed to structure the dyadic interactions. A reward was also offered contingent upon the pair achieving a designated high level of performance. The second peer tutoring condition was communal in nature. Pairs of children were simply told to work together for their mutual benefit, that they should do so because they are from the same community and should help each other out, so they could both do well. Performance on the subsequent recall test was substantially superior for communal peer tutoring in comparison to the other conditions, where performance levels were the same.

In another effort using Black grade school children from low-income backgrounds (Coleman, 1996), a communal study (groups of three) condition proved superior to an individual study condition in leading to greater subsequent individual performance on a creative problem-solving task. Students had to generate the number of exemplars that fitted a given concept such as naming reasons one should be proud of a person. Those who had been in the communal condition produced more thoughtful, interesting, and accurate examples than those from the individual condition. Other research has focused on additional Afrocultural themes. Speaking to the theme of verve, several investigations have documented that for low-income black children, problem-solving performance is greater when differing types of tasks are presented in varying sequential order regardless of task type, rather than when they are presented in a blocked fashion so that all of one type are first presented followed by all of a second type, followed by all of a third and fourth type (Bailey, 1993; Boykin, 1982; Boykin, Allen, Davis, & Senior, 1997; Tuck & Boykin, 1989; S. Walton, 1994, 1998). This result held even for academically relevant task types such as math, vocabulary, spelling, and logical picture sequencing (Bailey, 1993). Therefore, it proved more efficacious to present the children, for example, with a math task, followed by a spelling task, followed by vocabulary, followed by spelling, and then a picture sequencing than it was to give them first a set of math tasks and then a set of vocabulary, and so on. This effect was boosted when there was background music playing (Walton, 1994, 1998).

A series of studies has also been conducted demonstrating that for young Black children from low-income backgrounds, different forms of learning can be enhanced if the conditions for learning are characterized by opportunities for movement expression that is rhythmically joined to percussive, syncopated music. The beneficial effects of movement expression are also demonstrated when such expression punctuates the imagery of a to-be-recalled story's content. When there is movement imagery in the story and opportunities for movement expression are encouraged in the learning context, the beneficial effects are even more pronounced (Allen & Boykin, 1991; Allen & Butler, 1996; Cunningham, 1997; Mungai, 1997).

To be sure, these studies were done under controlled experimental conditions rather than in actual classrooms. But they do suggest that there are plausible benefits that accrue from the use of Afrocultural themes in learning and performance contexts. Beyond performance enhancement, across the range of these cited studies, children also consistently indicated greater preference and expressed more favorable attitudes for the Afrocultural contexts. They also indicated that their home environments are marked by the presence of such themes. Moreover, in general, there were positive intercorrelations among performance and motivation levels in Afrocultural contexts, children's perceptions of how present are Afrocultural themes in their home, and the level of expressed preference for these themes. That there are positive correlations among home perceptions, cultural theme preferences, and context-specific performance and motivational outcomes is consistent with the theoretical position proffered in this chapter on the connections among culture, context, cognition, and motivation.

A central thesis of this chapter is that success in school for poor African American children needs to be more pervasive, more widespread. Our empirical work on Anglocultural versus Afrocultural theme infusion signifies some ways that this can be more greatly accomplished. This line of work does not imply that if we don't teach Black children through Afrocultural themes, they cannot otherwise learn. Instead, our work suggests that intellectual competence as well as intrinsic interest in learning school-relevant tasks is potentially there for these children. It implies that academically valuable skills may go undetected or opportunities for the development of potentially valuable skills and competencies for some children may go unrealized in the absence of appropriately facilitating contexts. Moreover, such contexts may lead to children placing greater value on school tasks and to more favorable attitudes toward and investment in school. The implied prescriptions of this work may also reduce negative opinions about these children's academic potential.

REPRISE AND CONCLUSIONS

All in all, African-centered immersion efforts have much to recommend them. These are encouraging undertakings that have considerable potential heuristic value for African American children and communities. It is argued that such efforts should be situated in a somewhat larger analysis and informed by a broader set of concerns dealing with the nature and purposes of American public schooling. Instead, such efforts are encouraged to be talent development oriented. It is urged that such efforts be linked to schooling designed to ensure that all children can learn to high standards in an academically rigorous, high-expectation setting. This entails encompassing a framework where multiple means for ensuring success, covering all major facets of schooling, are present simultaneously. A merger of the tenets of talent development with immersion efforts should not be difficult to accomplish. To be sure, many of the operational themes of talent development such as building on assets, promoting critical thinking and pedagogy, enhancing communication and interpersonal skills, establishing a community of learners, promoting meaningful, connected learning, and striving for empowerment are quite convergent with the stated aims of African immersion initiatives.

Our empirical work on building on assets to change the deep structure of schooling lies squarely at the intersection of a talent development and an African immersion thrust. Additionally, the provision of cultural contexts in school that are linked to Afrocultural themes can make for more meaningful and connected learning experiences for many African American children. Moreover, as the themes are also made part of the content and substance of the curriculum, children further can become more consciously aware of these themes. This can serve as a springboard to critical analyses of the children's challenges in the American social order and thus promote these themes' efficacy in the children's lives. In turn, this can lead to discerning how such cultural themes can be used as vehicles for personal, familial, community, and societal enhancement. Such an enterprise surely can lead as well to a wider purpose for the schooling of African American children and enriches what is to be connoted by school success (Ladson-Billings, 1994).

Schools for Black children should be sites for talent development. They should accomplish a range of objectives. They should prepare these children to acquire a broad range of marketable skills; but they should also prepare them to appreciate their cultural legacy and to use it to be proactive contributors to changing their own life circumstances and to enhancing the life quality of others in their community if not in society at large.

Acknowledgment

Preparation of this article was supported by a grant from the U.S. Department of Education Office of Educational Research and Improvement (OERI) to the Center for Research on the Education of Students Placed at Risk (Grant Number Ri 1 7D40005). The views expressed in this chapter are those of the author. No GERI policy should be inferred.

REFERENCES

Akbar, N. (1985). *Chains and images of psychological slavery.* Jersey City, NJ: New Mind Productions.

Albury, A. (1998). *Social orientation, learning condition and learning outcomes among low-income black and white grade school children.* Doctoral dissertation, Howard University, Washington, DC.

Allen, B., & Boykin, A. W. (1991). The influence of contextual factors on Afro-American and Euro-American children's performance: Effects of movement opportunity and music. *International Journal of Psychology, 26,* 373–387.

Allen, B., & Butler, L (1996). The effects of music and movement opportunity on the analogical reasoning performance of African American and white school children: A preliminary study. *Journal of Black Psychology, 22*, 316–328.

Asante, M. (1987). *The Afrocentric idea.* Philadelphia: Temple University Press.

Bagley, W. (1925). *Classroom management.* New York: Macmillan.

Bailey, C. (1993). *The influence of cultural attributes and stimulus variability on the academically relevant task performance of African American school children.* Master's thesis, Howard University, Washington, DC.

Banks, J., & Banks, C. (Eds.). (1995). *Handbook of research on multicultural education.* New York: Macmillan.

Borrowman, M. (1965). *Teacher education in America.* New York: Teachers College Press.

Boykin, A. W. (1982). Task variability and the performance of black and white school children: Vervistic explorations. *Journal of Black Studies, 12*, 469–485.

Boykin, A. W. (1983). The academic performance of Afro-American children. In J. Spence (Ed.), *Achievement and achievement motives*, (pp. 322–371). San Francisco: W. Freeman.

Boykin, A. W. (1986). The triple quandary and the schooling of Afro-American children. In U. Neisser (Ed.), *The school achievement of minority children* (pp. 55–72). Hillsdale, NJ: Lawrence Erlbaum.

Boykin, A. W. (1994). Harvesting culture and talent: African American children and school reform. In R. Rossi (Ed.), *Schools and students at risk: Context and framework for positive change* (pp. 116–138). New York: Teachers College Press.

Boykin, A. W. (1996, April). *A talent development approach to school reform.* Paper presented at the annual meeting of the American Educational Research Association, New York.

Boykin, A. W (1999). *Culture matters in the development and schooling of African American children.* Paper submitted for publication.

Boykin, A. W., Allen, B., Davis, L, & Senior, A. M. (1997). Task performance of black and white children across levels of presentation variability. *Journal of Psychology, 131*, 427–437.

Boykin, A. W., Bailey, C., Hurley, E., Miller, O., and Albury, A. (1998). *The influence of culturally distinct learning orientations on the achievement perceptions of African American and European American grade school children.* Paper submitted for publication.

Boykin, A. W., & Ellison, C. (1995). The multiple ecologies of black youth socialization: An Afrographic analysis. In R. Taylor (Ed.), *African American youth: Their social and economic status in the United States.* Westport, CT: Praeger.

Brooks, J., & Brooks, M. (1993). *The case for constructivist classrooms.* Alexandria, VA: Association for Supervision and Curriculum Development.

Callahan, R. (1962). *Education and the cult of efficiency.* Chicago: University of Chicago Press.

Carlson, D. (1982). Updating individualism and the work ethic: Corporate logic in the classroom. *Curriculum Inquiry, 12*, 125–160.

Coleman, K. (1996). *The influence of a communal learning context on African American elementary students' creative problem solving.* Master's thesis, Howard University, Washington, DC.

Cubberly, E. (1916). *Public school administration: A statement of the fundamental principles underlying the organization and administration of public education.* Boston: Houghton Mifflin.

Cunningham, R. (1997). *The effects of contextual differentiation and content imagery on the cognitive task performance of African American and Euro-American working class children: Movement/music explorations.* Doctoral dissertation, Howard University, Washington, DC.

Curti, M. (1959). *The social ideas of American educators.* Patterson, NJ: Pageant Books.

Deci, E. (1975). *Intrinsic motivation.* New York Plenum.

Dill, E. (1996). *The influence of communal and peer tutoring contexts on the text recall learning of low-income African American students.* Master's thesis, Howard University, Washington, DC.

Elmore, R. (1996). Getting to scale with good educational practice. *Harvard Educational Review, 66*, 1–26.

Everhart, R. (1983). *Reading, un-icing and resistance.* Boston: Routledge & Kegan Paul.

Fine, M. (1994). Charter(ing) urban school reform. In R. Rossi (Ed.), *Schools and students at risk: Context and framework for positive change* (pp. 163–181). New York Teachers College Press.

Fordham, S., & Ogbu, J. (1986). Black students' school success: Coping with the burden of acting white. *Urban Review, 18*, 176–206.

Gay, G. (1988). Designing relevant curricula for diverse learners. *Education and Urban Society 20*, 322–340.

Gilmore, P. (1985). "Gimme room": School resistance, attitude and access to literacy. *Journal of Education, 167*, 111–128.

Giroux, H. & McLaren, P. (1986). Teacher education and the politics of engagement: The case for democratic schooling. *Harvard Educational Review, 56*, 213–238.

Goodman, J. (1995). Change without difference: School restructuring in historical perspective. *Harvard Educational Review, 65*, 1–29.

Gordon, B. (1994). African American cultural knowledge and liberatory education: Dilemmas, problems and potentials in postmodern American society. In M. Shujaa (Ed.), *Too much schooling, too little education.* Trenton, NJ: Africa World Press.

Gordon, B. (1997). Curriculum, policy, and African American cultural knowledge: Challenges and possibilities for the year 2000 and beyond. *Educational Policy, 11*, 227–242.

Gordon, E. (1995). Culture and the sciences of pedagogy. *Teachers College Record, 97*, 32–46.

Greene, J. (1989). A perspective on thinking. *American Psychologist, 44*, 134–141.

Greene, J., & the Middle School Mathematics through Applications Project Group. (1997). Theories and practices of thinking and learning to think. *American Journal of Education, 106*, 85–126.

Hilliard, A. (1995). *The Maroon within us.* Baltimore: Black Classic Press.

Howard, A., & Scott, R (1981). The study of minority groups in complex societies. In R. Munroe & B. Whiting (Eds.), *Handbook of cross cultural human development.* New York: Garland.

Hunt, J. McV. (1965). Intrinsic motivation and its role in psychological development. In D. Levine (Ed.), *Nebraska symposium on motivation* (pp. 189–282). Lincoln: University of Nebraska Press. 189–282.

John-Steiner, V., & Mahn, H. (1996). Sociocultural approaches to learning and development: A Vygotskian framework. *Educational Psychologist, 31*, 191–206.

Karier, C. (Ed.). (1975). *Shaping the American educational state: 1900 to the present.* New York: Free Press.

Kearns, D., & Doyle, D. (1991). *Winning the brain race: A bold plan to make our schools competitive.* San Francisco: ICS Press.

King, J. (1994). The purpose of schooling for African American children: Including cultural knowledge. In E. Hollins, J. King, & W. Hayman (Eds.), *Teaching diverse populations: Formulating a knowledge base.* Albany: Stare University of New York Press.

Ladson-Billings, G. (1994). *The dreamkeepers.* San Francisco: Jossey-Bass.

Lave, J. (1996) Teaching, as learning, in practice. *Mind, Culture and Activity, 3*, 149–164.

Lee, C. (1994). African-centered pedagogy: Complexities and possibilities. In M. Shujaa (U.), *Too much schooling, too little education* (pp. 295–318). Trenton, NJ: Africa World Press.

Lukes, S. (1973). *Individualism.* New York: Harper.

Marryshow, D. (1995). *Perception of future economic success and the impact of learning orientation on African American students' attitudes toward high achievers.* Doctoral dissertation, Howard University, Washington, DC.

Martin, S. (1994). *Children's attitudes and their parents' and peers' perceived attitudes toward culturally diverse high achievers.* Master's thesis, Howard University, Washington, DC.

Martin, S. (1997). *Students' attitudes toward four distinct learning orientations and classroom environments.* Doctoral dissertation, Howard University, Washington, DC.

Miller, .G. (1997). *Cultural influences on the classroom perceptions of African American grade school children.* Master's thesis, Howard University, Washington, DC.

Mungai, M. (1997). *Story-listening and off-task context effects on both the performance and motivation of African American and European American children.* Doctoral dissertation, Howard University, Washington, DC.

Nieto, S. (1993). *Affirming diversity: The sociopolitical context of multicultural education.* New York: Longman.

Ogbu, J. (1994). From cultural frames to differences in cultural frame of reference. In P. Greenfield & R. Cocking (Eds.), *Cross-cultural roots of minority child development* (pp. 365–392). Hillsdale, NJ: Lawrence Erlbaum Associates.

Persell, C. (1977). *Education and inequality: A theoretical and empirical synthesis.* New York: Free Press.

Piestrup, A. (1973). *Black dialect interference and accommodation of reading instruction in first grade* (Monograph No. 4). Berkeley: University of California, Language Behavior Research Laboratory.

Plank, D., Scotch, R., & Gamble, J. (1996). Rethinking progressive school reform: Organizational dynamics and educational change, *American Journal of Education, 104*, 79–104.

Raffini, J. (1995). *150 ways to increase intrinsic motivation in the classroom.* Boston: Allyn & Bacon.

Rogoff, B. (1990). *Apprenticeship in thinking: Cognitive development in social context.* New York: Oxford University Press.

Rogoff, B., & Chavajay, P. (1995). What's become of research on the cultural basis of cognitive development? *American Psychologist, 50*, 859–877.

Sapon-Shevin, M., & Schniedewind, N. (1991). Cooperative learning as empowering pedagogy. In C. Sleeter (Ed.), *Empowerment through multicultural education.* Albany, NY: SUNY Albany Press.

Shujaa, M. (Ed.). (1994). *Too much schooling, too little education.* Trenton, NJ: Africa World Press.

Spence, J. (1985). Achievement American style: The rewards and costs of individualism. *American Psychologist, 40*, 1285–1295.

Spring, J. (1994). *The American school: 1642–1993* (3rd ed.). New York: McGraw-Hill.

Tedla, E. (1995). *Sankofa: African thought and education.* New York: Lang.

Tharp, R., & Gallimore, R. (1988). *Rousing minds to life.* New York: Cambridge University Press.

Tuck, K., & Boykin, A. W. (1989). Task performance and receptiveness to variability in black and white low-income children. In A. Harrison (U.), *The eleventh conference on empirical research in black psychology.* Washington, DC: NIMH Publications.

Tyack, D. (1974). *The one best system.* Cambridge, MA: Harvard University Press.

Walton, S. (1994). *The influence of task variability and background stimulation on the task performance of low-income African American children.* Master's thesis, Howard University, Washington, DC.

Walton, S. (1998). *Verve effects: The influence of cultural attributes and two-dimensional physical stimulation on the task performance of African American and European American school-children.* Doctoral dissertation, Howard University, Washington, DC.

Walton, T. (1993). *Teachers' attitudes toward black students who display differing cultural orientations.* Master's thesis, Howard University, Washington, DC.

Wilson, S., & Peterson, V (1997). *Theories of learning and teaching: What do they mean for educators?* (Blue Ribbon Schools Working Paper). Washington, DC: U.S. Department of Education.

Woodson, C. (1933). *The miseducation of the Negro.* Washington, DC: Associated Publishers.

Article 9

BUT THAT'S JUST GOOD TEACHING! THE CASE FOR CULTURALLY RELEVANT PEDAGOGY*

GLORIA LADSON-BILLINGS

FOR THE PAST SIX YEARS I have been engaged in research with excellent teachers of African American students (see, for example, Ladson-Billings, 1990, 1992b, 1992c, 1994). Given the dismal academic performance of many African American students (The College Board, 1985), I am not surprised that various administrators, teachers, and teacher educators have asked me to share and discuss my findings so that they might incorporate them in their work. One usual response to what I share is the comment around which I have based this article, "But, that's just good teaching!" Instead of some "magic bullet" or intricate formula and steps for instruction, some members of my audience are shocked to hear what seems to them like some rather routine teaching strategies that are a part of good teaching. My response is to affirm that, indeed, I am describing good teaching, and to question why so little of it seems to be occurring in the classrooms populated by African American students.

The pedagogical excellence I have studied is good teaching, but it is much more than that. This article is an attempt to describe a pedagogy I have come to identify as "culturally relevant" (Ladson-Billings, 1992a) and to argue for its centrality in the academic success of African American and other children who have not been well served by our nation's public schools. First, I provide some background information about other attempts to look at linkages between school and culture. Next, I discuss the theoretical grounding of culturally relevant teaching in the context of a three-year study of successful teachers of African American students. I conclude this discussion with further examples of this pedagogy in action.

LINKING SCHOOLING AND CULTURE

Native American educator Cornel Pewewardy (1993) asserts that one of the reasons Indian children experience difficulty in schools is that educators traditionally have attempted to insert culture into the education, instead of inserting education into the culture. This notion is, in all probability, true for many students who are not a part of the White, middle-class mainstream. For almost 15 years, anthropologists have looked at ways to develop a closer fit between students' home culture and the school. This work has had a variety of labels including "culturally appropriate" (Au & Jordan, 1981), "culturally congruent" (Mohatt & Erickson,

*Ladson-Billings, G. (1995). But that's just good teaching! The case for culturally relevant pedagogy. *Theory into Practice, 34*: 159–165. (Theme issue on "Culturally Relevant Teaching").

1981), "culturally responsive" (Cazden & Leggett, 1981; Erickson & Mohatt, 1982), and "culturally compatible" (Jordan, 1985; Vogt, Jordan, & Tharp, 1987). It has attempted to locate the problem of discontinuity between what students experience at home and what they experience at school in the speech and language interactions of teachers and students. These sociolinguists have suggested that if students' home language is incorporated into the classroom, students are more likely to experience academic success.

Villegas (1988), however, has argued that these microethnographic studies fail to deal adequately with the macro social context in which student failure takes place. A concern I have voiced about studies situated in speech and language interactions is that, in general, few have considered the needs of African American students.[1]

Irvine (1990) dealt with the lack of what she termed "cultural synchronization" between teachers and African American students. Her analysis included the micro-level classroom interactions, the "mid-level" institutional context (i.e., school practices and policies such as tracking and disciplinary practices), and the macro-level societal context. More recently Perry's (1993) analysis has included the historical context of the African American's educational struggle. All of this work–micro through macro–level has contributed to my conception of culturally relevant pedagogy.

WHAT IS CULTURALLY RELEVANT PEDAGOGY?

In the current attempts to improve pedagogy, several scholars have advanced well-conceived conceptions of pedagogy. Notable among these scholars are Shulman (1987), whose work conceptualizes pedagogy as consisting of subject matter knowledge, pedagogical knowledge, and pedagogical content knowledge, and Berliner (1988), who doubts the ability of expert pedagogues to relate their expertise to novice practitioners. More recently, Bartolome (1994) has decried the search for the "right" teaching strategies and argued for a "humanizing pedagogy that respects and uses the reality, history, and perspectives of students as an integral part of educational practice" (p. 173).

I have defined culturally relevant teaching as a pedagogy of opposition (1992c) not unlike critical pedagogy but specifically committed to collective, not merely individual, empowerment. Culturally relevant pedagogy rests on three criteria or propositions: (a) Students must experience academic success; (b) students must develop and/or maintain cultural competence; and (c) students must develop a critical consciousness through which they challenge the status quo of the current social order.

ACADEMIC SUCCESS

Despite the current social inequities and hostile classroom environments, students must develop their academic skills. The way those skills are developed may vary, but all students need literacy, numeracy, technological, social, and political skills in order to be active participants in a democracy. During the 1960s when African Americans were fighting for civil rights, one of the primary battlefronts was the classroom (Morris, 1984). Despite the federal government's failed attempts at adult literacy in the South, civil rights workers such as Septima Clark and Esau Jenkins (Brown, 1990) were able to teach successfully those same adults by ensuring that the students learned that which was most meaningful to them. This approach is similar to that advocated by noted critical pedagogue Paulo Freire (1970).

While much has been written about the need to improve the self-esteem of African American students (see for example, Banks & Grambs, 1972; Branch & Newcombe, 1986; Crooks, 1970), at base students must demonstrate academic competence. This was a clear message given by the eight teachers who participated in my study.[2] All of the teachers demanded, reinforced, and produced academic excellence in their students. Thus, culturally relevant teaching requires that teachers attend to students' academic needs, not merely make them "feel good." The trick of culturally relevant teaching is to get students to "choose" academic excellence.

In one of the classrooms I studied, the teacher, Ann Lewis,[3] focused a great deal of positive attention on the African American boys (who were the numerical majority in her class). Lewis, a White woman, recognized that the African American boys possessed social power. Rather than allow that power to influence their peers in negative ways, Lewis challenged the boys to demonstrate academic power by drawing on issues and ideas they found meaningful. As the boys began to take on academic leadership, other students saw this as a positive trait and developed similar behaviors. Instead of entering into an antagonistic relationship with the boys, Lewis found ways to value their skills and abilities and channel them in academically important ways.

CULTURAL COMPETENCE

Culturally relevant teaching requires that students maintain some cultural integrity as well as academic excellence. In their widely cited article, Fordham and Ogbu (1986) point to a phenomenon called "acting White," where African American students fear being ostracized by their peers for demonstrating interest in and succeeding in academic and other school-related tasks. Other scholars (Hollins, 1994; King, 1994) have provided alternate explanations of this behavior.[4] They suggest that for too many African American students, the school remains an alien and hostile place. This hostility is manifest in the "styling" and "posturing" (Majors & Billson, 1992) that the school rejects. Thus, the African American student wearing a hat in class or baggy pants may be sanctioned for clothing choices rather than specific behaviors. School is perceived as a place where African American students cannot "be themselves."

Culturally relevant teachers utilize students' culture as a vehicle for learning. Patricia Hilliard's love of poetry was shared with her students through their own love of rap music. Hilliard is an African American woman who had taught in a variety of schools, both public and private for about 12 years. She came into teaching after having stayed at home for many years to care for her family. The mother of a teenaged son, Hilliard was familiar with the music that permeates African American youth culture. Instead of railing against the supposed evils of rap music, Hilliard allowed her second grade students to bring in samples of lyrics from what both she and the students determined to be non-offensive rap songs.[5] Students were encouraged to perform the songs and the teacher reproduced them on an overhead so that they could discuss literal and figurative meanings as well as technical aspects of poetry such as rhyme scheme, alliteration, and onomatopoeia.

Thus, while the students were comfortable using their music, the teacher used it as a bridge to school learning. Their understanding of poetry far exceeded what either the state department of education or the local school district required. Hilliard's work is an example of how academic achievement and cultural competence can be merged.

Another way teachers can support cultural competence was demonstrated by Gertrude Winston, a White woman who has taught school for 40 years.[6] Winston worked hard to involve parents in her classroom. She created an "artist or draftsperson-in-residence" program so that the students could learn from each other's parents and also affirm cultural knowledge. Winston developed a rapport with parents and invited them to come into the classroom for 1 or 2 hours at a time for a period of 2–4 days. The parents, in consultation with Winston, demonstrated skills upon which Winston later built.

For example, a parent who was known in the community for her delicious sweet potato pies did a 2-day residency in Winston's fifth grade classroom. On the first day, she taught a group of students how to make the pie crust. Winston provided supplies for the pie baking and the students tried their hands at making the crusts. They placed them in the refrigerator overnight and made the filling the following day. The finished pies were served to the entire class.

The students who participated in the "seminar" were required to conduct additional research on various aspects of what they learned. Students from the pie baking seminar did reports on George Washington Carver and his sweet potato research, conducted taste tests, devised a marketing plan for selling pies, and researched the culinary arts to find out what kind of preparation they needed to become cooks and chefs. Everyone in Winston's class was required to write a detailed thank you note to the artist/craftsperson.

Other residencies were done by a carpenter, a former professional basketball player, a licensed practical nurse, and a church musician.[7] All of Winston's guests were parents or relatives of her students. She did not "import" role models with whom the students did not have firsthand experience. She was deliberate in reinforcing that the parents were a knowledgeable and capable resource. Her students came to understand the constructed nature of things such as "art," "excellence," and "knowledge." They also learned that what they had and where they came from was of value.

A third example of maintaining cultural competence was demonstrated by Ann Lewis, a White woman whom I have described as "culturally Black" (Ladson-Billings, 1992b; 1992c). In her sixth grade classroom, Lewis encouraged the students to use their home language while they acquired the secondary discourse (Gee, 1989) of "standard" English. Thus, her students were permitted to express themselves in language (in speaking and writing) with which they were knowledgeable and comfortable. They were then required to "translate" to the standard form. By the end of the year, the students were not only facile at this "code-switching" (Smitherman, 1981) but could better use both languages.

CRITICAL CONSCIOUSNESS

Culturally relevant teaching does not imply that it is enough for students to chose academic excellence and remain culturally grounded if those skills and abilities represent only an individual achievement. Beyond those individual characteristics of academic achievement and cultural competence, students must develop a broader sociopolitical consciousness that allows them to critique the cultural norms, values, mores, and institutions that produce and maintain social inequities. If school is about preparing students for active citizenship, what better citizenship tool than the ability to critically analyze the society?

Freire brought forth the notion of "conscientization," which is "a process that invites learners to engage the world and others critically" (McLaren, 1989, p. 195). However, Freire's work in Brazil was not radically different from work that was being done in the southern United States (Chilcoat & Ligon, 1994) to educate and empower African Americans who were disenfranchised.

In the classrooms of culturally relevant teachers, students are expected to "engage the world and others critically." Rather than merely bemoan the fact that their textbooks were out of date, several of the teachers in the study, in conjunction with their students, critiqued the knowledge represented in the textbooks, and the system of inequitable funding that allowed middle-class students to have newer texts. They wrote letters to the editor of the local newspaper to inform the community of the situation. The teachers also brought in articles and papers that represented counter knowledge to help the students develop multiple perspectives on a variety of social and historical phenomena.

Another example of this kind of teaching was reported in a Dallas newspaper (Robinson, 1993). A group of African American middle school students were involved in what they termed "community problem solving." The kind of social action curriculum in which the students participated is similar to that advocated by scholars who argue that students need to be centered" (Asante, 1991; Tate, 1994) or the *subjects* rather than the objects of study.

CULTURALLY RELEVANT TEACHING IN ACTION

As previously mentioned, this article and its theoretical undergirding come from a three-year study of successful teachers of African American students. The teachers who participated in the study were initially selected by African American parents who believed them to be exceptional. Some of the parents' reasons for selecting the teachers were the enthusiasm their children showed in school and learning while in their classrooms, the consistent level of respect they received from the teachers, and their perception that the teachers understood the need for the students to operate in the dual worlds of their home community and the White community.

In addition to the parents' recommendations, I solicited principals' recommendations. Principals' reasons for recommending teachers were the low number of discipline referrals, the high attendance rates, and standardized test scores.[8] Teachers whose names appeared as both parents' and principals' recommendations were asked to participate in the study. Of the nine teachers' names who appeared on both lists, eight were willing to participate. Their participation required an in-depth ethnographic interview (Spradley, 1979), unannounced classroom visitations, videotaping of their teaching, and participation in a research collective with the other teachers in the study. This study was funded for two years. In a third year I did a follow-up study of two of the teachers to investigate their literacy teaching (Ladson-Billings, 1992b; 1992c).

Initially, as I observed the teachers I could not see patterns or similarities in their teaching. Some seemed very structured and regimented, using daily routines and activities. Others seemed more open or unstructured. Learning seemed to emerge from student initiation and suggestions. Still others seemed eclectic–very structured for certain activities and unstructured for others. It seemed to be a researcher's nightmare–no common threads to pull their practice together in order to relate it to others. The thought of their pedagogy as merely idiosyncratic, a product of their personalities and individual perspectives, left me both frustrated and dismayed. However, when I was able to go back over their interviews and later when we met together as a group to discuss their practice, I could see that in order to understand their practice it was necessary to go beyond the surface features of teaching "strategies" (Bartolome, 1994). The philosophical and ideological underpinnings of their practice, i.e. how they thought about themselves as teachers and how they thought about others (their students, the students' parents, and other community members), how they structured social relations within and outside of the classroom, and how they conceived of knowledge, revealed their similarities and points of congruence.[9]

All of the teachers identified strongly with teaching. They were not ashamed or embarrassed about their professions. Each had chosen to teach and, more importantly, had chosen to teach in this low-income, largely African American school district. The teachers saw themselves as a part of the community and teaching as a way to give back to the community. They encouraged their students to do the same. They believed their work was artistry, not a technical task that could be accomplished in a recipe-like fashion. Fundamental to their beliefs about teaching was that all of the students could and must succeed. Consequently, they saw their responsibility as working to guarantee the success of each student. The students who seemed furthest behind received plenty of individual attention and encouragement.

The teachers kept the relations between themselves and their students fluid and equitable. They encouraged the students to act as teachers, and they, themselves, often functioned as learners in the classroom. These fluid relationships extended beyond the classroom and into the community. Thus, it was common for the teachers to be seen attending community functions (e.g., churches, students' sports events) and using community services (e.g., beauty parlors, stores). The teachers attempted to create a bond with all of the students, rather than an idiosyncratic, individualistic connection that might foster an unhealthy competitiveness. This bond was nurtured by the teachers' insistence on creating a community of learners as a priority. They encouraged the students to learn collaboratively, teach each other, and be responsible for each other's learning.

As teachers in the same district, the teachers in this study were responsible for meeting the same state and local curriculum guidelines.[10] However, the way they met and challenged those guidelines helped to define them as culturally relevant teachers. For these teachers, knowledge is continuously recreated, recycled, and shared by the teachers and the students. Thus, they were not dependent on state curriculum frameworks or textbooks to decide what and how to teach.

For example, if the state curriculum framework called for teaching about the "age of exploration," they used this as an opportunity to examine conventional interpretations and introduce alternate ones. The content of the curriculum was always open to critical analysis.

The teachers exhibited a passion about what they were teaching–showing enthusiasm and vitality about what was being taught and learned. When students came to them with skill deficiencies, the teachers worked to help the students build bridges or scaffolding so that they could be proficient in the more challenging work they experienced in these classrooms.

For example, in Margaret Rossi's sixth grade class, all of the students were expected to learn algebra. For those who did not know basic number facts, Rossi provided calculators. She believed that by using particular skills in context (e.g., multiplication and division in the context of solving equations), the students would become more proficient at those skills while acquiring new learning.

IMPLICATIONS FOR FURTHER STUDY

I believe this work has implications for both the research and practice communities. For researchers, I suggest that this kind of study must be replicated again and again. We need to know much more about the practice of successful teachers for African American and other students who have been poorly served by our schools. We need to have an opportunity to explore alternate research paradigms that include the voices of parents and communities in nonexploitative ways.[11]

For practitioners, this research reinforces the fact that the place to find out about classroom practices is the naturalistic setting of the classroom and from the lived experiences of teachers. Teachers need not shy away from conducting their own research about their practice (Zeichner & Tabachnick, 1991). Their unique perspectives and personal investment in good practice must not be overlooked. For both groups–researchers and practitioners alike–this work is designed to challenge us to reconsider what we mean by "good" teaching, to look for it in some unlikely places, and to challenge those who suggest it cannot be made available to all children.

NOTES

1. Some notable exceptions to this failure to consider achievement strategies for African American students are *Ways With Words* (Heath, 1983); "Fostering Early Literacy through Parent Coaching" (Edwards, 1991); and "Achieving Equal Educational Outcomes for Black Children" (Hale-Benson, 1990).
2. I have written extensively about this study, its methodology, findings, and results elsewhere. For a full discussion of the study, see Ladson-Billings (1994).
3. All study participants' names are pseudonyms.
4. At the 1994 annual meeting of the American Educational Research Association, King and Hollins presented a symposium entitled, "The Burden of Acting White Revisited."
5. The teacher acknowledged the racism, misogyny, and explicit sexuality that is part of the lyrics of some rap songs. Thus, the students were directed to use only those songs they felt they could "sing to their parents."
6. Winston retired after the first year of the study but continued to participate in the research collaborative throughout the study.
7. Because the residency is more than a demonstration and requires students to work intensely with the artist or draftsperson, students must sign up for a particular artist. The typical group size was five to six students.
8. Standardized test scores throughout this district were very low. However, the teachers in the study distinguished themselves because students in their classrooms consistently produced higher test scores than their grade-level colleagues.
9. As I describe the teachers I do not mean to suggest that they had no individual personalities or practices. However, what I was looking for in this study were ways to describe the commonalties of their practice. Thus, while this discussion of culturally relevant teaching may appear to infer an essentialized notion of teaching practice, none is intended. Speaking in this categorical manner is a heuristic for research purposes.
10. The eight teachers were spread across four schools in the district and were subjected to the specific administrative styles of four different principals.
11. Two sessions at the 1994 annual meeting of the American Educational Research Association in New Orleans entitled, "Private Lives in Public Conversations: Ethics of Research Across Communities of Color," dealt with concerns for the ethical standards of research in non-White communities.

REFERENCES

Asante, M.K. (1991). The Afrocentric idea in education. *Journal of Negro Education, 60*, 170–180.

Au, K., & Jordan, C. (1981). Teaching reading to Hawaiian children: Finding a culturally appropriate solution. In H. Trueba, G. Guthrie, & K. Au (Eds.), *Culture and the bilingual classroom: Studies in classroom ethnography* (pp. 69–86). Rowley, MA: Newbury House.

Banks, J., & Grambs, J. (Eds.). (1972). *Black self-concept: Implications for educational and social sciences.* New York: McGraw-Hill.

Bartolome, L. (1994). Beyond the methods fetish: Toward a humanizing pedagogy. *Harvard Educational Review, 64*, 173–194.

Berliner, D. (1988, October). Implications of studies of expertise in pedagogy for teacher education and evaluation. In *New directions for teacher assessment* (Invitational conference proceedings). New York: Educational Testing Service.

Branch, C., & Newcombe, N. (1986). Racial attitudesamong young Black children as a function of parental attitudes: A longitudinal and cross-sectional study. *Child Development, 57*, 712–721.

Brown, C.S. (Ed.). (1990). *Ready from within: A first person narrative.* Trenton, NJ: Africa World Press.

Cazden, C., & Leggett, E. (1981). Culturally responsive education: Recommendations for achieving Lau remedies II. In H. Trueba, G. Guthrie, & K. Au (Eds.), *Culture and the bilingual classroom: Studies in classroom ethnography* (pp. 69–86). Rowley, MA: Newbury House.

Chilcoat, G. W., & Ligon, J.A. (1994). Developing democratic citizens: The Mississippi Freedom Schools as a model for social studies instruction. *Theory and Research in Social Education, 22*, 128–175.

The College Board. (1985). *Equality and excellence: The educational status of Black Americans.* New York: Author.

Crooks, R. (1970). The effects of an interracial preschool program upon racial preference, knowledge of racial differences, and racial identification. *Journal of Social Issues, 26*, 137–148.

Edwards, P.A. (1991). Fostering early literacy through parent coaching. In E. Hiebert (Ed.), *Literacy for a diverse society: Perspectives, programs, and policies* (pp. 199–213). New York: Teachers College Press.

Erickson, F., & Mohatt, C. (1982). Cultural organization and participation structures in two classrooms of Indian students. In G. Spindler, (Ed.), *Doing the ethnography of schooling* (pp. 131–174). New York: Holt, Rinehart & Winston.

Fordham, S., & Ogbu, J. (1986). Black students' success: Coping with the burden of "acting White." *Urban Review, 18*, 1–31.

Freire, P. (1970). *Pedagogy of the oppressed.* New York: Herder & Herder.

Gee, J. P. (1989). Literacy, discourse, and linguistics: Introduction. *Journal of Education, 171*, 5–17.

Hale-Benson, J. (1990). Achieving equal educational outcomes for Black children. In A. Baron & E.E Garcia (Eds.), *Children at risk: Poverty, minority status, and other issues in educational equity* (pp. 201–215). Washington, DC: National Association of School Psychologists.

Heath, S.B. (1983). *Ways with words.* Cambridge, U. K.: Cambridge University Press.

Hollins, E.R. (1994, April). *The burden of acting White revisited: Planning school success rather than explaining school failure.* Paper presented at the annual meeting of the American Educational Research Association, New Orleans.

Irvine, J.J. (1990). *Black students and school failure.* Westport, CT: Greenwood Press.

Jordan, C. (1985). Translating culture: From ethnographic information to educational program. *Anthropology and Education Quarterly, 16*, 105–123.

King, J. (1994). *The burden of acting White re-examined: Towards a critical genealogy of acting Black.* Paper presented at the annual meeting of the American Educational Research Association, New Orleans.

Ladson-Billings, G. (1990). Like lightning in a bottle: Attempting to capture the pedagogical excellence of successful teachers of Black students. *International Journal of Qualitative Studies in Education, 3*, 335–344.

Ladson-Billings, G. (1992a). Culturally relevant teaching: The key to making multicultural education work. In C.A. Grant (Ed.), *Research and multicultural education* (pp. 106–121). London: Falmer Press.

Ladson-Billings, G. (1992b). Liberatory consequences of literacy: A case of culturally relevant instruction for African-American students. *Journal of Negro Education 61*, 378–391.

Ladson-Billings, G. (1992c). Reading between the lines and beyond the pages: A culturally relevant approach to literacy teaching. *Theory Into Practice, 31*, 312–320.

Ladson-Billings, G. (1994). *The dreamkeepers: Successful teaching for African-American students.* San Francisco: Jossey-Bass.

McLaren, P. (1989). *Life in schools.* White Plains, NY: Longman.

Majors, R., & Billson, J. (1992). *Cool pose: The dilemmas of Black manhood in America.* New York: Lexington Books.

Mohatt, G., & Erickson, F. (1981). Cultural differences in teaching styles in an Odawa school: A sociolinguistic approach. In H. Trueba, G. Guthrie, & K. Au (Eds.), *Culture and the bilingual classroom: Studies in classroom ethnography* (pp. 105–119). Rowley, MA: Newbury House.

Morris, A. (1984). *The origins of the civil rights movement: Black communities organizing for change.* New York: The Free Press.

Perry, T. (1993). *Toward a theory of African-American student achievement.* Report No. 16. Boston, MA: Center on Families, Communities, Schools and Children's Learning, Wheelock College.

Pewewardy, C. (1993). Culturally responsible pedagogy in action: An American Indian magnet school. In E. Hollins, J. King, & W. Hayman (Eds.), *Teaching diverse populations: Formulating a knowledge base* (pp. 77–92).

Albany: State University of New York Press.

Robinson, R. (1993, Feb. 25). P.C. Anderson students try hand at problem-solving. *The Dallas Examiner*, pp. 1, 8.

Shulman, L. (1987). Knowledge and teaching: Foundations of the new reform. *Harvard Educational Review, 57*, 1–22.

Smitherman, G. (1981). *Black English and the education of Black children and youth.* Detroit: Center for Black Studies, Wayne State University.

Spradley, J. (1979). *The ethnographic interview.* New York: Holt, Rinehart & Winston.

Tate, W.F. (1994). Race, retrenchment, and reform of school mathematics. *Phi Delta Kappan, 75*, 477–484.

Villegas, A. (1988). School failure and cultural mismatch: Another view. *The Urban Review, 20*, 253–265.

Vogt, L., Jordan, C., & Tharp, R. (1987). Explaining school failure, producing school success: Two cases. *Anthropology and Education Quarterly, 18*, 276–286.

Zeichner, K. M., & Tabachnick, B.R. (1991). Reflections on reflective teaching. In B.R Tabachnick & K.M. Zeichner (Eds.), *Inquiry-oriented practices in teacher education* (pp. 1–21). London: Falmer Press.

Article 10

AN EDUCATIONAL LEADER'S GUIDE TO CULTURE AND LEARNING STYLE*

PAT BURKE GUILD

CAN WE ASSUME THAT STUDENTS who share cultural characteristics have common ways of learning? Does culture create a way of learning, and how would we know this? Do African American students have similar ways of learning? Although controversial, these questions are important for all educational leaders to grapple with. They are important because we need all the information we can get to help every learner succeed in school and because a deep understanding of the learning process should provide the framework for curriculum and instructional decisions.

They also are important questions, because success for the diverse student populations in today's schools calls for continual reexamination of educators' assumptions, expectations, and biases. Such questions are controversial, because information about a group of people often leads to naive inferences about individual members of that group. It is all too common to equate descriptions of differences with explanations for deficits. The questions also are controversial, because they force us to confront whether equality of instruction is synonymous with equity of educational opportunity for all. Is the purpose of public schooling to create a "melting pot" or "a salad bowl"? The relationship of the values of the culture in which a child is currently living, or from which a child has roots, and the learning expectations and experiences in the classroom are directly related to the child's school success academically, socially, and emotionally. A deep understanding of both culture and learning style differences is important for all educators, although the subject must be addressed carefully.

AFRICAN AMERICAN LEARNERS: SIMILARITIES AND DIFFERENCES

There are a variety of descriptions of typical learning patterns of African Americans (Hale-Benson, 1986; Hilliard, 1989; Shade, 1989) that report the students' desire for oral experiences, physical activity, and strong personal relationships (Hilliard, 1989; Shade, 1989). These patterns call for classroom work that includes collaboration, discussion, and active projects (Shade, 1989).

The same authors report that mainstream White male Americans value independence, analytic thinking, objectivity, and accuracy. These values translate into learning experiences that focus on information, competition, tests, grades, and critical thinking. It is no surprise that these patterns are prevalent in most schools, because they were established and are generally administered by mainstream White men. The further away from this style of education a student is, the more difficulty he or she has adjusting.

*Adapted from *Marching to Different Drummers* by Pat Burke Guild and Stephen Garger, ASCD, 1998, 2nd edition.

As well, reports about culture and learning style consistently agree that within a group, *variations among individuals are as great as commonalities.* Even as we acknowledge that culture affects learning styles, we know that distinct learning style patterns don't fit a specific cultural group. "Researchers have clearly established that there is no single or dual learning style for the members of any cultural, national, racial, or religious group" (Dunn, 1997, pp. 74–75). This important point is often verbally acknowledged but ignored in practice. Cox and Ramirez (1981) explain the result:

> Recognition and identification of these average differences have had both positive and negative effects in education. The positive effect has been the development of an awareness of the types of learning that our public schools tend to foster . . . . The negative effect[,] . . . arising primarily from common problems associated with looking at mean differences[,] is [that] the great diversity within a culture is ignored and a construct which should be used as a tool for individualization becomes yet another label for categorizing and evaluating. (p. 61)

Many reports contend that African Americans or Hispanic Americans or girls learn in certain common ways. Where is this information coming from? In general, there are two sources of information about learning styles and culture. The first source includes descriptions and profiles of learners of certain cultural groups written by people familiar with these groups to sensitize those outside the culture to children's experiences within the culture. Descriptions of minority students' learning patterns often are contrasted with the "majority" White Anglo students' ways of learning and with expectations in the schools designed by this majority group.

Another way we know about the links between culture and learning style is research study descriptions of specific groups. In this class of inquiry, researchers administer learning/cognitive style assessments to produce a profile of a particular cultural group to make comparisons with previously studied groups (usually mainstream White Americans) or to validate a particular instrument for cross-cultural application. Although a variety of published studies use this approach, it is important to realize that they are based on various assessment instruments that "measure" learning styles in different ways. Even though different assessment instruments are used, results of different studies are often compared, ignoring or diminishing the relevance of the type of assessment instrument in the report of the findings. The variation in type of assessment instrument used often accounts for the seemingly contradictory information reported about groups of learners.

From both sources of "research" we see that culture and learning style are connected, but cautions about specific application of this information are necessary. When educators apply knowledge of culture and learning style to the classroom, they face a number of unresolved issues and differences of opinion. Cox and Ramirez (1981) observe:

> The concept of cognitive or learning styles of minority and other students is one easily over-simplified, misunderstood, or misinterpreted. Unfortunately, it has been used to stereotype minority students or to further label them rather than to identify individual differences that are educationally meaningful. (p. 61)

One unresolved issue is how much should a teacher and a school know about each of their students? Should there be full information in a student's file that is shared with everyone who works with the student? Even when such information exists, some teachers intentionally don't read students' files. They argue that they want to form their own impressions of each learner. Other educators believe that a comprehensive background and educational history of each student is invaluable for helping the learner be successful. Why waste time reinventing the wheel? When these issues are applied to knowledge relating to a specific cultural group, there is also lack of agreement. "The greatest care must be taken to use the concepts as tools for growth and individualization and to avoid their use as labels or stereotypes" (Ramirez, 1989, p. 5).

The relationship of culture and learning style is also addressed in reference to student achievement. Most researchers believe that learning styles are neutral, meaning that all learning styles can be successful. However, they can also become a stumbling block when overused or applied inappropriately. This concept explains the success or failure of different learning approaches with different tasks, especially as they relate to expectations in schools.

There is evidence that students with specific learning style patterns (kinesthetic, field-dependent, sensing, extraversion) underachieve in school. Regardless of their cultural background, students who have these dominant learning style patterns have limited opportunities to use their style strengths in the classroom.

Although relating culture, style, and achievement requires much more examination (Guild, McKinney, & Fouts, 1990; Myers, 1974/1980), serious inequity results if schools undervalue behaviors that certain cultures foster. Gardner (1991) advises that cultural practices yield "[c]hildren and adults who are characteristic of their own culture and who may appear dysfunctional in a culture that embraces a divergent or opposing set of assumptions" (p. 53). This appearance of dysfunction affects the student's potential for successful achievement. Some students are caught in a no-win situation, unable to be true to their culture or meet school expectations. Irvine and York (1995) are blunt: "The cultures of students of color or their 'way of life' are often incongruous with the expected middle-class cultural schools. These cultural differences are major contributions to the school failure of students of color" (p. 489).

It is also important to be willing to confront the issue of cultural identity and self-esteem. Many large city school systems struggle with the appropriateness of ethnically identified schools, such as an African American academy. Bilingual education programs are continually forced to debate the priority of instruction in students' first languages. All-girl schools, math classes, and science classes are promoted for their affirmative action approach. The goal of encouraging positive self-esteem would lead one to argue for like groups at certain stages of development. An acceptance of learning style differences demands an approach that develops skills through strengths. Should the same not be said of cultural identity?

TEACHERS' CULTURES

Another unresolved issue is how teachers working from their own cultures and teaching styles can successfully reach the diverse populations in most schools today. What training do teachers need for this challenge? Bennett (1986) is not the only one who believes that "to the extent that teachers teach as they have been taught to learn, and to the extent that culture shapes learning style, students who share a teacher's ethnic background will be favored in class" (p. 96). Bennett also warns that ignoring the effects of culture and learning style affects all students:

> If classroom expectations are limited by our own cultural orientations, we impede successful learners guided by another cultural orientation. If we only teach according to the ways we ourselves learn best, we are also likely to thwart successful learners who may share our cultural background but whose learning styles deviate from our own. (p. 116)

Some argue that teachers should play a special role in representing their own culture. For example, Hale-Benson (1986, p. xiii) posits that, "It is incumbent upon Black professionals to identify the intelligences found especially in Black children and to support the pursuit of their strengths." Even so, we all have learned successfully from teachers who differed from us in learning style and/or culture. Often, these were masterful, caring teachers. Sometimes our own motivation helped us learn despite the teacher. Regardless, teachers of all cultural backgrounds and style will have to work conscientiously to provide equity for students as classrooms increasingly reflect the diversity of our society.

THE NATURE VERSUS NURTURE ISSUE

If a classroom teacher is to facilitate successful learning opportunities for all learners, he or she must "know" the learner. This includes knowing about innate personality and also learned cultural values that affect behavior. The learner, of any age, is a product of nature and nurture. We each are born with predispositions for learning in certain ways. We also are products of external influences, especially within our immediate family, extended community, and culture.

Researchers confirm that learning patterns are a function of both nature and nurture. Myers (1990) asserts: "Type development starts at a very early age. The hypothesis is that type is inborn, an innate predisposition like right- or left-handedness, but the successful development of type can be greatly helped or hindered by environment from the beginning" (p. 176). Many researchers describe the importance of socialization within the family, immediate culture, and wider culture. They agree with Ramirez (1989) that "cultural differences in children's learning styles develop through their early experience" (p. 4). Gardner (1991) echoes this perspective: "[W]e are as much creatures of our culture as we are creatures of our brain" (p. 38).

Sometimes people wonder which is more important: innate personality traits or the influence of culture? This question has no clear answer. The most accurate response is probably "it depends." Variables such as the congruence of innate traits with cultural influences; the support, or lack of it, within the environment for preferred behaviors and for taking risks; and general life successes will influence how learning patterns are shaped. When my culture supports my individuality, I grow and develop in healthy ways. When my family encourages my uniqueness, I learn to trust my own innate predisposition. If, however, I do not innately fit the expectations of a "typical girl" or "typical African American," I become aware of the lack of congruence of my inner self with external expectations, and I have to reconcile those differences. Sometimes that reconciliation gives me more strengths and a wider range of behaviors. At other times, it leads to conflict and uncertainties. Both results confirm the important roles of nature and nurture in shaping a person's approach to life and to learning.

Every child of every culture, race, ethnicity, socioeconomic status, gender, age, ability, and talent deserves to have an equal opportunity to be successful in school. Knowing each student's culture is essential for providing successful learning opportunities. Understanding learning differences will help educators facilitate, structure, and validate successful learning for every student.

ATTENDING TO DIVERSITY

There is an urgent need to address the balance between uniformity and diversity within our schools, because the current imbalance is seriously damaging to many learners and teachers. The emphasis on uniformity creates serious disadvantages for students whose culture has taught them behaviors and beliefs that are different from the norms of the majority culture most often emphasized in schools. Students whose families value collaboration are told to be independent. Students whose culture values spontaneity are told to exercise self-control. Students who are rewarded in their families for being social are told to work quietly and alone. Hale-Benson (1986) points out: "A duality of socialization is required of Black people. Black children have to be prepared to imitate the 'hip,' 'cool,' behavior of the culture in which they live and at the same time to take on those behaviors that are necessary to be upwardly mobile" (p. 62). This cultural clash often causes students to struggle in school, and yet their individual strengths, if valued, respected, and promoted, would bring them success and increase their self-confidence.

Currently, our limited awareness and understanding of individual learning differences encourages a continual search for the one "best" way for students to learn and be assessed, teachers to teach, and the curriculum to be studied. There is ample proof over the years–in reading, mathematics, writing, and foreign language instruction, for example, that it is futile to search for the single best way to achieve a broad educational outcome, in large part because learners do not fit a single mold. Students who do not learn through whatever the current "best approach" happens to be are too often labeled "disabled," because their way of learning does not respond to that particular method. To further complicate the situation, the method becomes the identified deficit and the target for remediation. For example, in reading, remediation in phonics, which is a strategy, often becomes the target for learning. In a typical situation, a young learner who initially was not successful learning to read with a phonics-based approach receives additional instruction in phonics. The overarching goal, in this case the ability to read, is lost as the school emphasizes the specific practice of the deficit technique. Remediating a deficit rather than teaching the desired skill through the student's strength is the norm in too many schools.

The same pattern is evident in behavioral areas

where, for example, an active, hands-on learner who does not have the opportunity to use that approach in a positive way in the classroom is described as lacking self-control and labeled disruptive or hyperactive. It disturbs many educators to see the tremendous increase in the number of students medicated for attention deficit disorder (ADD) and attention deficit hyperactivity disorder (ADHD) without an examination of their learning styles. Thomas Armstrong, a former special education teacher and a proponent of the multiple intelligences theories, addressed this issue. He says,

> The traits that are associated with ADD-hyperactivity, distractibility, and impulsivity can result from a number of causes. For example, a child may be hyperactive or inattentive because of being bored with a lesson, anxious about a bully, upset about a divorce, allergic to milk, temperamental by nature, or a hundred other things. Research suggests, though, that once adults have labeled and medicated the child–and the medication works–these more complex questions are all too often forgotten. By rushing to drugs and labels, we may be leaving more difficult problems to fester under the surface. (1995, p. 42)

Teachers, too, suffer from the imbalance between uniformity and diversity, especially when they are evaluated with uniform processes. Numerous educators, including John Goodlad, Roland Barth, and Ted Sizer, have written eloquently about the value of diversity of teaching styles. We do not have evidence of one best way to teach, just as we don't know of one best way to learn. An emphasis on uniformity creates competition rather than collaboration among teachers. Although identification of specific teaching skills can be uniform, diversity of teaching styles can and should be a school's strength. For example, all teachers can be held accountable for thoughtful planning, but that planning could be linear and sequential for one teacher and holistic and conceptual for another. The plan books of these teachers would look very different, and they should be evaluated differently, too.

Distinct approaches to teaching methods, content instruction, curriculum organization, and special education programming come and go over the years. It is unrealistic to expect that a particular approach will be successful for all learners. This expectation only leads to disappointment and another swing of the education pendulum. Instead of an either/or mentality, many experienced teachers know that using the best of a variety of approaches benefits many learners. Instructional tools must be carefully and intentionally adapted to accommodate individual learners. Only in this way will African American, and all, students have an opportunity for success.

EQUITY AND EQUALITY

There is a need to understand the difference between equity and equality. We often justify uniformity in education with the explanation that the goal of schooling is to offer equal learning experiences for all students. We value equality and applaud examples as a confirmation of fairness to all. Yet, equal experiences do not provide equality for diverse learners. The word equity is far more significant and appropriate in this case.

Equity means "fair" and "just," implying equal opportunity, which often means unequal action. Felix Frankfurter wrote, "It is a wise man who said that there is no greater inequality than the equal treatment of unequals" (1949, p. 184). David Elkind echoes that same sentiment in his book *The Hurried Child*: "Recognizing special needs is not discriminatory; on the contrary, it is the only way that true equality can be attained" (Elkind, 1981, p. 22).

Administrators and school boards grapple with the equity issue each time they address the "fairness" of standard class sizes, when some schools and some classes have more children who need special attention from the teacher. Should schools with large immigrant populations, and the concurrent special language instruction requirements, be staffed with the same formula as a school with a homogeneous English-speaking student body? Should students at both of these schools be required to take the same curriculum and the same tests? What is "fair?" What is "equitable?"

In the classroom, teachers regularly confront issues of equity with assignments and quizzes. Is it "fair" to adapt an assignment, expecting some students to produce more in quantity, such as longer essays, or in quality, such as completing harder geometry proofs? Many schools and teachers think so, and they regularly diversify expectations for students.

ENDS VERSUS MEANS

It is important to have a distinction between the ends and the means. It is possible to strive for uniform outcomes but to intentionally diversify the means for achieving them. Schools can identify basic skill and knowledge goals for all students, yet these uniform expectations do not automatically dictate a uniform approach, or a uniform curriculum, for reaching the goals. In an extensive argument for national and state standards, Paul Gagnon (1995) states:

> When is a subject-matter essential, or "standard," and when is it not? . . . [T]he word "framework," too, means what it says; it leaves the third step–course design and pedagogy–to the school and the teacher. They must have the authority to make the choices most important to them and to their students: the topics and questions by which to teach the essentials, the day-to-day content of instruction, the materials and methods best suited to their students and to their own strengths. (p. 72)

As has been discussed earlier, educators have debated phonetic versus meaning-based approaches. The research, presented articulately and convincingly by proponents of both approaches, usually cites a successful achievement statistic of 65 to 70 percent. If we accept that students learn in different ways, it should be evident that different approaches to reading work for different students. Is it possible that most students can learn to read with a phonetic approach and also most students can learn to read with a meaning-based approach? Probably yes, especially with good instruction. There is undoubtedly an overlap of 35 to 40 percent of students who learn with either approach and who seem as successful statistics in both studies. However, if you view this research by looking at those who are not successful, the 30 percent minority, you see students who need attention. These students are probably not as flexible in their ways of learning and will learn best when their dominant style is accommodated.

Indeed, the cognitive style research on field-dependence-independence (global/analytic) supports this conclusion. Field-independent (analytic) learners profit from a part-to-whole approach like phonics, whereas field-dependent (global) learners are more successful with the whole-to-part approach of a meaning-based strategy. Because this cognitive style dimension is bipolar, we would expect 25 to 30 percent of a class to strongly represent each specific learning style pattern, with the remaining 40 percent in the middle. When the learners with a strong, specific learning style approach are forced to learn in a manner opposite their style preference, they must put energy into shifting approaches before they can concentrate on the skill to be mastered. This is similar to trying to learn to write calligraphy with your less preferred hand. Eventually you would gain some skill, but your learning would have been more efficient, enjoyable, and successful if you used your strength–your preferred hand–in the first place.

In a final example, teachers often debate the value of specific grammatical instruction. How much time should be spent teaching punctuation skills, or are they best learned in context of written work in the classroom? Is it "best" to teach the rules for math computation, and then apply them in practice problems? Or would tackling a problem initially give students a reason for knowing the rules? Most textbooks have answered these questions by consistently building from the part to the whole, the simple to the more complex. But teachers often find that teaching "backward" in the text responds to many students' ways of learning. Many adults exhibit this style of learning when they try skiing a few times before taking lessons or when they "teach" themselves a new program on the computer, then read the manual. Students need similar options.

DISTINGUISHING SKILL AND STYLE

It is important to distinguish between skill and style. It is possible for all students to be skilled in basic areas that educators agree on, for example, that all students would be competent readers, writers, and spellers. The practice of diversity implies that there are a variety of ways to achieve these required skills and individual ways to demonstrate achievement. Uniform competencies and skills can be articulated, but educators can honor stylistic learning differences for achieving and demonstrating those skills.

UNDERSTANDING LEARNING STYLE DIFFERENCES

To provide an equal opportunity for all students to be successful in school, educators must first develop a deep understanding of individual differences in learning. The research and theories on culture and learning style adequately document learning differences among individuals. Although these theories are familiar to many educators, and generally accepted, their application is relatively shallow. For example, many teachers know that it is important to provide a "visual" learner with visual information. But if the visual is words on an overhead projector mimicking the words spoken orally, this is a superficial accommodation of the learner's style. Far more significant would be an image, symbol, or visual representation of the information so that the visual learner could learn through his or her strengths.

Many teachers know that the active, kinesthetic learner needs hands-on experiences. A deeper understanding of these learners tells us that the experiences should come early in the process while the initial understanding of the concepts and skills are being developed, not just during practice time. Yet many times these learners are asked to "understand" first, then "do" later. The kinesthetic learner needs to manipulate the science equipment to understand the concepts, and she will learn abstract math concepts while doing the measurement project or even after it's completed. The kinesthetic learners' impatience to get started sometimes causes teachers to demand that they explain what they will do before they start. This is difficult for these students, because the doing leads to the understanding and the explaining.

Learning styles research and resources are rich with examples to help develop appropriate activities for different learners. But if the activities are not guided by a consistent and deep understanding of the significance of learning differences, the activities will be a cursory attempt to implement these concepts. Learning styles labels are simply a tool; the diverse behaviors we see in the classroom are reflections of much deeper cognitive processes.

Not all learners who share a certain label are alike. A "visual" learner who is also "concrete sequential" seeks visual order and would benefit from a linear diagram of material. A "visual" learner who is also "abstract random" responds to design and would be drawn to a mind-map format for organizing information. A careful study of the major concepts of learning styles is necessary for the practical application of these theories in schools.

DEFINING LEARNING STYLES

To understand people's behaviors, we need to look at the roots of their actions. One way to do this is to consider several basic ways in which we all interact with a situation, a person, information, or ideas. First we take in the occurrence; then we think about it, react to it, and ultimately act upon it. These basic functions guided us to create four categories of style differences.

- Style is concerned with cognition: People perceive and gain knowledge differently.
- Style is concerned with conceptualization: People form ideas and think differently.
- Style is concerned with behavior: People act differently.
- Style is concerned with affect: People decide and feel differently.

Below, we examine two approaches to understanding learning styles: Witkin's Field-Dependence-Independence and Gardner's Multiple Intelligences.

Field-Dependence-Independence

In his research, Witkin defined two extreme indicators of the extent to which the surrounding field influences an observer's perception of an item within it. A person with a field-dependent (FD/global) mode of perception is strongly influenced by the prevailing field, whereas the field-independent (FI/analytical) person experiences items as more or less separate from the surrounding field. Diagnosis of adults and students for field-dependence-independence is now possible with validated nonverbal paper-and-pencil instrumentation.

Witkin's work has a variety of messages for educators. His studies have consistently demonstrated cognitive styles to be independent of intelligence, and thus "field-dependence-independence appears to be more related to the 'how' than to the 'how much' of cognitive function" (Witkin, et al., 1977). Because cognitive style is neutral, both field-dependent and field-independent people, according to studies, make good students and good teachers. However, because style does affect success in specific kinds of situations, educators must be sensitive to style-related demands in teaching and learning.

In offering advice to educators for responding to cognitive style differences, Witkin and his colleagues urge us to consider the advantages of both matching and mismatching. He points out that the "development of greater diversity in behaviors within individuals seems as important an objective as the recognition and the utilization of diversity among individuals" (p. 53). Ultimately, he wants knowledge of field-dependence-independence to contribute to teachers' and students' abilities to use their own style strengths and then develop more diverse strategies to facilitate success in learning.

Multiple Intelligences

Howard Gardner first articulated his theory describing multiple perspectives on intelligence in his 1983 book *Frames of Mind.* He took to task the narrow view of Western society's emphasis on linguistic and mathematical intelligence and added and named several more intelligences.

Gardner's message also reinforces the call for understanding and accommodation of diverse ways of learning. When various intelligences are respected and valued, students of all cultural identities

HOW STUDENTS LEARN

Field Dependence	Field Independence
Perceive globally	Perceive analytically
Experience in a global fashion, adhere to structures as given	Experience in an articulated fashion, impose structure or restrictions
Make broad general distinctions among concepts, see relationships	Make specific concept distinctions, see little overlap
Have a social orientation to the world	Have an impersonal orientation to the world
Learn material with social content best	Learn social material only as an intentional task
Attend best to material relevant to own experience	Interested in new concepts for their own sake
Seek eternally defined goals and reinforcements	Have self-defined goals and reinforcements
Want organization to be provided	Can self-structure situations
More affected by criticism	Less affected by criticism
Use spectator approach to concept attainment	Use hypothesis-testing approach to attain concepts

have an opportunity for success.

The eight intelligences are:

- *Linguistic intelligence*, in which a person is facile with language and words. This person generally has a highly developed vocabulary, an ability to communicate in a clear and interesting way orally or in writing, and a sophisticated receptivity to language.
- *Logical-mathematical intelligence*, in which a person is especially competent in discerning quantitative relationships and connections, particularly related to calculations and scientific areas. This person is skilled in recognizing and developing logical systems.
- *Spatial intelligence*, in which a person skillfully manipulates images, recognizes, and creates visual forms mentally as well as on paper, and in designs of various kinds.
- *Bodily kinesthetic intelligence*, in which a person has graceful body movements and an awareness of his or her own and others' positions in space. This person has a physical agility that is often illustrated by an extraordinary ability in particular physical areas.
- *Musical intelligence*, in which a person exhibits acute sensitivity to sound and an ability to create and communicate through tones and rhythmic patterns.
- *Interpersonal intelligence*, in which a person perceptively understands the perspective of another person, relates to others easily, and is skilled at working cooperatively.
- *Intrapersonal intelligence*, in which a person reflects on himself or herself thoughtfully, is perceptive about personal abilities, and attuned to personal history.
- *Naturalist intelligence*, in which a person is interested in and knowledgeable about the natural world and effectively discriminates among sensory things.

Finally, for a more complete discussion of learning styles that includes a wider variety of learning style models (i.e., Myers-Briggs, 4MAT, Modalities, and Gregorc's Mind Types) and concrete examples of specific ways to assess that students' learning styles, we recommend *Marching to Different Drummers*, 2nd edition, by Pat Burke Guild and Stephen Garger. It is well worth reading the entire book.

ADMINISTRATORS' SUPPORT FOR TEACHING THROUGH LEARNING STYLES

How should we accommodate differences in style? Must schools and other institutions adapt to the diverse styles of the people who work and study there, or must the people who come to an institution meet its demands? In an individual teaching and learning situation, does the teacher adapt to the student, or the student to the teacher? Do parents adapt to the styles of each child, or do the children adapt to the parents' styles? One could argue that with the large numbers of people who learn and work in schools, uniform approaches are justified. But when we choose a uniform curriculum program, we definitely decide that students must adapt their styles to the demands of a particular approach. When we require all teachers be evaluated in the same way, we demand that they fulfill the style requirements of that specific evaluation process.

Although using variety in teaching methods is certainly not a new idea, most educators would agree that we have a long way to go to adequately provide for diversity in learners' styles. Seldom is there only one way to learn. It is this understanding that should encourage us to value students' and colleagues' various styles. Teachers and administrators who understand these concepts consciously attempt to respond to the diversity they regularly encounter in schools. Practical implementation of learning styles, concepts, and research challenges us to develop two things: understanding of individuality and a commitment to help each individual do his or her best in the learning and teaching process.

ADMINISTRATORS CAN INCREASE AWARENESS THROUGH PROFESSIONAL DEVELOPMENT

The very first practical application is awareness of style and cultural differences. When we accept that people learn in different ways, we face daily decisions about uniformity and diversity. But, a deep awareness of diverse learning styles requires a commitment to the belief that all students can be successful learners. If a learning experience is adjusted to accommodate diverse styles, students will be able to use their strengths to achieve this success. We know that currently not all learning styles are equally valued in schools. Most schools do a more effective job with learners who are reflective, linear, or analytic than those who are active, holistic, personal, or practical. Learners whose styles are accommodated more frequently in school achieve more immediate success. Students who struggle to adapt to an uncomfortable way of learning often underachieve.

Awareness of learning differences results in educators working together on various programs with a learning style perspective. As new curriculum materials are selected, discipline policies formed, and staff development goals set, questions of individual diversity and style will be prominent. The concepts of learning styles will be discussed on a regular basis, and opportunities for learning more about the theories and research will grow from these discussions.

Belief in learning differences becomes a rationale for many educational decisions. It is particularly important for teachers to adapt new techniques through an understanding of learning styles. In other words, a teacher would be motivated to apply a new method with the goal of accommodating the needs of certain students in the classroom. By focusing on learning styles, teachers would understand that a specific technique is successful, because it provides the opportunity for approaching a task in a way that is important for certain, although not necessarily all, learners.

For example, cooperative learning is successful not just because it is an alternative to lecture but because it allows some students the opportunity to process externally, to work with their peers, and to share responsibility for a task. Integrated curriculum is successful, because it offers opportunities for connections that are made naturally in some students' minds and for the chance to study a topic in depth, which is appreciated by other students. Indeed, educational innovations that have "worked" can trace a relationship to some students' learning patterns.

Teachers who understand learning style differences will strive for intentional variety in instruction, curriculum, classroom management, and assessment. Administrators who believe in learning styles actively value differences in teaching styles. Curriculum specialists who practice a learning styles approach encourage diverse programs in classrooms, schools, and the district. Administrators can increase awareness of individual learning styles and cultural differences through encouraging and supporting appropriate professional development experiences for all levels of school personnel, including their own.

REFERENCES

Armstrong, T. (1995). *The myth of the ADD child.* New York: A Dutton Book, Penguin Group.

Barth, R.S. (1980). *Run school run.* Cambridge, MA: Harvard University Press.

Bennett, C. (1986). *Comprehensive multicultural education, theory and practice.* Boston: Allyn & Bacon.

Butler, K. (1995). *Learning styles, personal exploration and practical applications: An introduction to style for secondary students.* Columbia, CT: The Learners Dimension.

Butler, K.A. (1984). *Learning and teaching style in theory and practice.* Maynard: MA: Gabriel Systems, Inc.

Cox, B., & Ramirez, M., III (1981). Cognitive styles: Implications for multiethnic education. In J. Banks (Ed.), *Education in the 80's.* Washington, DC: National Education Association.

Dunn, R. (1997). The goals and track record of multicultural education. *Educational leadership, 54*(7), 74–77.

Elkind, D. (1981). *The hurried child: Growing up too fast too soon.* Reading, MA: Addison Wesley Publishing Co.

Frankfurter, F. (1949). *Dennis v. US,* US Report, Vol., 339, p. 184.

Gagnon, P. (1995). What should children learn? *The Atlantic Monthly, 276*(6), 65–78.

Gardner, H. (1991). *The unschooled mind: How children think and how schools should teach.* New York: Basic Books.

Glatthorn, A.A. (1984). *Differentiated supervision.* Alexandria, VA: ASCD.

Goodlad, J.I. (1984). *A place called school: Prospects for the future.* New York: McGraw Hill Book Company.

Gregorc, A.F. (1982a). *An adult's guide to style.* Maynard, MA: Gabriel Systems, Inc.

Gregorc, A.F. (1982b). *Gregorc style delineator: Developmental, technical, and administration manual* (Rev. ed.). Maynard, M.A: Gabriel Systems, Inc.

Guild, P., McKinney, L., & Fouts, J. (1990). *A study of the learning styles of elementary students: Low achievers, average achievers, high achievers.* Seattle: WA: The Teaching Advisory.

Guild, P.B. & Garger S. (1998). *Marching to different drummers* (2nd Ed). Alexandria, VA: ASCD.

Hale-Benson, J.E. (1986). *Black children: Their roots, culture, and learning styles* (Rev. ed.). Baltimore: Johns Hopkins University Press.

Hilliard, A.G., III (1989). Teachers and cultural styles in a pluralistic society. *NEA Today* (January), 65–69.

Irvine, J.J., & York, D.E. (1995). Learning styles and culturally diverse students: A literature review. In J.A. Banks & C.A. Banks (Eds.), *Handbook of research on multicultural education.* New York: Macmillan.

Myers, I.B. (1980). Taking type into account in education. In M.H. McCauley & F.L. Natter, *Psychological (Myers-Briggs) type differences in education* (2nd ed.). Gainesville, FL: Center for Applications of Psychological Type, Inc.

Myers, I.B. (1990). *Gifts differing* (2nd ed). Palo Alto, CA: Consulting Psychologists Press, Inc.

Oltman, P.K., Raskin, E., & Witkin, H.A. (1971). *Group embedded figures test.* Palo Alto, CA: Consulting Psychologists Press, Inc.

Ramirez, M. III (1989). Pluralistic education: A bicognitive-multicultural model. *The Clearinghouse Bulletin, 3,* 4–5.

Shade, B.J. (1989). The influence of perpetual development on cognitive style: Cross ethnic comparisons. *Early Child Development and Care, 51,* 137–155.

Sizer, T.R. (1984). *Horace's compromise: The dilemma of the American high school.* Boston: Houghton Mifflin Company.

Tobias, C., & Guild, P. (1986). *No sweat! How to use your learning style to be a better student.* Seattle: The Teaching Advisory.

Witkin, H.A., Moore, C.A., Goodenough, D.R., & Cox, P.W. (1977). Field dependent and field-independent cognitive styles and their educational implications. *Review of Educational Research, 47,* 1–64.

Article 11

AFRICAN AMERICAN CHILDREN AND LITERACY: MOVING PAST THE EBONICS DEBATE TO A COMMON UNDERSTANDING

LYNSON MOORE BEAULIEU

BECOMING A FLUENT SPEAKER, reader, and writer in the languages of a child's home and broader communities is key to the success of children's social, emotional, and academic development, and ultimately their economic success. This article is about the journey that many African American children take toward literacy in two "required" languages–African American Vernacular English (AAVE, sometimes called Ebonics) and what is commonly called Standard English (SE–referred to as "standard" American English or SAE in this article). For many of the approximately eight million African American children whose primary language is AAVE, learning to read, write, and speak SAE can be difficult, especially when appropriate instructional method are not used (Perry & Delpit, 1998).

This article will explore some of the issues of language learning as they relate to African American children and the learning of both AAVE and SAE. It will examine how attitudes about language, such as the ongoing "inferior versus superior" debate about the relative value of different languages and dialects, affect children's motivation and abilities to learn and their opportunities for positive learning and interactions in both languages. This article will also explore the impact of early childhood, including how parenting practices and children's involvement in early care and education programs can influence African American children's early language and literacy development, experiences, and opportunities. And finally, it will share some of the successful strategies currently being used around the country that are helping many African American children become bidialectal–knowledgeable and skillful in the use of both the language of their homes and their schools. In those schools, African American children are learning to read and write well, and academic achievement is improving.

IS IT A LANGUAGE OR IS IT A DIALECT?

In a traditional way of thinking, the terms "language" and "dialect" confer a certain level of status to a form of language. Often the term "dialect" implies a lesser status than the term "language." AAVE is most often referred to as a "dialect," whereas SAE enjoys the status of being called a "language." Whether a language is considered a dialect or a language more often depends on sociohistorical and political considerations than purely on the rules of linguistics (Perry & Delpit, 1998; Rickford, 1997b).

Based on the rules of linguistics, dialects and/or languages must both meet the same stringent predictability criteria, which indicates that they are systematic and rule-governed. Both AAVE and SAE meet the predictability criteria and are referred to interchangeably throughout the linguistic research and literature as both dialects and languages (Adger, Christian, & Taylor, 1999; Perry & Delpit, 1998; Rickford, 1998; Smith, 1999). All dialects/languages, when systematic and rule-governed, are equally "standard" in their structures, patterns, usage, and reliability to the groups who use them.

Even though those who study language as a science have declared that all systematic, rule-governed languages are equal, SAE is commonly accepted by people without linguistic training or an awareness of their own language prejudices to be a language that is "superior" to AAVE (Adger et al., 1999). One result of this widespread belief in the concept of language superiority is that it is difficult for those who do not speak, read, and/or write SAE well to gain access to mainstream educational, social and economic opportunities.

SUPPORT FOR AAVE-SPEAKERS FROM THE PROFESSIONAL LINGUISTIC COMMUNITY

In support of the equality of all systematic, rule-governed languages, a number of linguistic organizations have offered a series of resolutions over the years aimed at promoting respect for language diversity. Three of these documents are discussed briefly below.

"The Students' Right to Their Own Language" resolution was passed by the Conference on College Composition and Communication (CCCC), an NCTE-affiliate organization in 1972 and reaffirmed by a vote of the membership at its annual business meeting in 1974. In addition to affirming the rights of children to their own patterns and varieties of language, this resolution also stresses the equality of all languages/dialects, and the need for teachers to have adequate experiences and training so that they can support student diversity and uphold student's rights to their own languages.

The CCCC went on to develop and adopt a National Language Policy in 1988. The policy with three inseparable parts addressed the issue of resources, programs that support native languages for native speakers, and the teaching of languages other than English for native English speakers (Adger et al., 1999).

In 1997 the Linguistic Society of America passed its own resolution regarding languages and dialects in support of the Oakland (California) Public School Board's 1996 controversial policy to implement a "standard" American language support program for African American students. Their resolution confirmed the wisdom and pedagogically sound decision of the Oakland School Board to implement a districtwide language strategy that recognized the vernacular of African American students in teaching them "standard" American English (Perry & Delpit, 1998).

In addition, in their January 1999 Position Statement on Ebonics, the University of Massachusetts Working Group on African American English reiterates the social, political, and economic power of American Standard English (as they call it) and the need for African American children to have the opportunity to add SAE to their repertoire of language competence, not subtract AAE (African American English). They also share that, "After all, no one is asked to disparage English in order to learn French." They support John Rickford's position that the goal should be to assist African American children with becoming bidialectal, "in the inspiring tradition of the many African Americans who have achieved success in America through that path" (University of Massachusetts National Institutes of Health African American English Working Group [UMASS NIH AAE Working Group], 1999).

For the large numbers of African American AAVE-speaking children in our public schools today, working toward a common understanding of the equality of all regular languages/dialects is critical. Given that classroom discourse is increasingly being promoted as a key teaching and learning tool for helping children reach academic excellence, it is especially important to appreciate the legitimacy of AAVE as a spoken and written language and to respect the communication styles of AAVE-speaking children.

In her review of research on variation in language structure and style in classroom discourse, Courtney Cazden (as cited in Adger et al., 1999) shares that "classroom talk assumes greater importance in the current understanding of how cognitive development occurs and in some of the high stakes testing associated with school reform. Educators' attitudes toward language differences thus have an increased potential to influence educational outcomes. Positive attitudes reinforce opportunities for students to build on the language skills they bring to school; negative attitudes increase the risks often associated with language differences."

SUPPORTING YOUNG CHILDREN'S LITERACY DEVELOPMENT

Although the differences between AAVE and SAE present a significant complication to the language and literacy development of many African American children, additional issues are also important to consider as we help African American children become proficient readers. Ensuring that children learn to read, write, and speak fluently in any language is like a well-choreographed dance with key cast members in starring and supporting roles. Families, early care and education providers and educators, schools and other public and private family supporting community organizations and resources, including churches, family resource centers, and health care programs, share in the responsibility for the successful education and socialization of children. Everyone who comes into contact with children in those earliest years has obligations and responsibilities in that dance.

Parents and other nuclear and extended family members are children's first and most important teachers, and the experiences of family and community life provide the first opportunities for babies and young children to practice emerging language skills, develop vocabulary and knowledge, and establish important relationships that begin to tell them about who they are and their relationship to the world. All of this early language and literacy activity begins and becomes grounded in the culture and languages of that child's immediate family and surrounding community.

The nature of parent-child interactions in the early years has an important effect on children's language development. Research conducted by Hart and Risley (1995) confirms that there are some important differences in parenting styles that are related to family income levels. For example, some parenting styles, found most often in lower-income families (which are disproportionately African American), place a substantial proportion of "prohibitions" on children's activities. Prohibitions can hinder children's speech development by reducing opportunities that children have to interact with their parents and other adults with language. Low-income parents have also been found to spend less time playing and verbally interacting with their children (Hart & Risley, 1995).

The nature of adult-child interactions is important, because young children acquire vocabulary, language skills, and knowledge about themselves, their families, and the world by engaging in interesting, child-centered conversations with responsive, caring adults. These early conversations and interactions provide access to the development of the early language and literacy skills that are important precursors to successfully learning how to read (Burns, Griffin, & Snow, 1999). Although Hart (1982), as cited in Novick (1996), found that the language of poor children had as much variety and complexity as middle-class children, they used complex structures less frequently and added new words and structures more slowly than advantaged children, creating an ever-widening vocabulary gap between poor and nonpoor children.

As we explore issues of literacy development for African American children and families, it is important to remember that African American families are not always "traditional," as traditional is typically viewed. In 1998, approximately 51 percent of African American children lived primarily with their mothers only (compared with 15 percent of White children and 27 percent of Hispanic children) (Federal Interagency Forum on Child and Family Statistics [FIFCFS], 1999). Single-parent, mother-headed families are known to be among the nation's poorest. Many fewer African American children (4 percent) live primarily with their fathers only. Nine percent of African American children live without any parent (compared with 3 percent of White children and 5 percent of Hispanic children) (FIFCFS, 1999).

Increasing numbers of African American mothers and fathers fill our jails, prisons, and the dockets of criminal justice court systems. Disproportionate numbers of African American children live in foster homes and other institutions, including youth jails, without their birth parents at all, an almost sure guarantee of less than optimal early care and education. In sometimes better situations, many of our children are in the homes of extended family members, with significant numbers of our children being raised by their grandparents (and great grandparents) as their primary caregivers. Loving, nurturing, and providing for their grandchildren to the limits of their economic and physical resources, African American grandparents, as the primary caregivers of their grandchildren, are likely to be poor, have significant health issues, and have completed lower levels of formal schooling (Casper & Bryson, 1998).

On the road to language and literacy development, large numbers of African American children begin life and experience early childhoods filled with poor health, family disruptions, violence, loneliness, hunger, and limited experiences for safe, complex, extended, fun, relational, and diverse cognitive and language challenges. *For these children, and many others who are just "simply" poor, high-quality early care and education interventions and programs that also include their families in literacy and other family strengthening activities are as necessary as water and food.* The early childhood brain research of the 1990s has helped to make this point explicitly and urgently clear. High-quality early care and education interventions and programs must become a part of the notion of a "Right to Learn." Promising early interventions, both before and after school entry, must be child, family, and community sensitive and focused. They must be culturally and language appropriate, educationally challenging, and able to help children build strong foundations for learning, academic mastery, and the resilience that we know serves children under stress well throughout their childhoods, adolescence, and young adult years.

THE SCHOOLS

Educational institutions and teachers share another important role in the dance of children's language and literacy development. By the time young children enter preschool or school, studies confirm that all children, regardless of their economic, ethnic, cultural, or language backgrounds, possess complex language skills and a wealth of knowledge, skills, and information about themselves, their families, their communities, and even some aspects of the larger society. Children come to school eager to learn, excited about going to school, but that excitement is extremely vulnerable to children's lack of success with classroom language and literacy experiences, especially with learning how to read.

In research conducted by Frank Vellutino and Donna Scanlon on kindergarten–first grade interventions, they expected to find that mid-first grade was soon enough for interventions with children experiencing early reading difficulties. However, what they found instead were many first graders who believed that they were not good at reading and had already decided that they were not going to engage in the activity (National Center on English Learning and Achievement [NCELA], 1999).

Because of differences in the way their language and language development presents itself, teachers of young dialect-speaking African American children often fail to recognize the language learning resources that the children bring with them to school and fail to use those resources as the foundation on which they, and the children, can build new knowledge and skills. For example, research on language socialization and uses in African American communities (e.g., Ball, 1992; Edwards, 1992; Gaunt, 1997; Goodwin, 1990; Hale-Benson, 1982; Heath, 1983; Labov, 1972; Morgan, 1994; Vernon-Feagans, 1996, as cited by Adger et al., 1999) highlights linguistic strengths that Ebonics-speaking children are likely to acquire in their communities, including sophisticated storytelling abilities; skillful use of word play, rhyme, and rhythm; use of vivid metaphors and analogies; skill in indirection; the ability to think quickly on their feet; and facility in adjusting to different audiences. These researchers go on to say that, "by the time they enter kindergarten, African American children are likely to have formed a sense of identity and self-efficacy strongly linked to their ability to use language in highly sophisticated and stylized ways. In their communities, they are applauded for quick verbal responses, creative plays on words and sounds, imaginative improvisations of familiar stories and themes, and their ability to best an opponent through superior verbal reasoning" (Adger et al., 1999).

Although it is clear that linguists do not view

AAVE as an accumulation of errors caused by the failure of their speakers to master "standard" English (Labov, 1972), many people, including educators of all ethnic and cultural backgrounds, continue to view AAVE negatively, referring to it as ignorant, corrupt, junk, gibberish, deficient, or akin to some kind of disease–a virus or the plague (Adger et al., 1999). This notion could not be farther from the truth, nor more damaging to the sense of self and internal motivation that helps African American children establish and remain engaged in long-term educational goals. In describing why he coined the term Ebonics more than twenty-five years ago, Black psychologist Robert William stated, ". . . My language is me. It is an extension of my being, my essence. It is a reflection and badge of my culture. Criticism of my language is essentially a direct attack on my self-esteem and cultural identity" (Adger et al., 1999).

As a result of the negative attitudes toward their vernacular language and serious difficulties learning to read well, many African American children do not have confidence in their classroom language skills. Although SAE is not the primary language spoken at home and in their communities, AAVE-speaking children are not typically viewed or treated as the standard English language learners that they are, as are other children whose primary languages are other than SAE. The dismal results, found in the consistently low scores on standardized language arts assessments of large numbers of African American children throughout their elementary and secondary school experiences point to large numbers of African American children (and later adults) who never grasp the complex rule-governed differences between their home languages and SAE.

African Americans have a rich, creative, and abundant history of complex language development and usage steeped in the traditions of great oratory, literature, and music, including the modern-day systematic, rule-governed language/dialect known as AAVE or Ebonics (Adger at al., 1999). In addition, there is a thirty-year body of research, knowledge, and understanding about the language development, experiences, and skills of African American children. This knowledge must be incorporated into the culture and work of schools. Currently, this information is widely ignored, and teachers continue to identify many African American children as having learning and language delays and disabilities early in their school careers. Because of *language differences*, many African American children are referred for evaluation and placement in special education programs. These programs rarely respond to what is most likely a central problem–the lack of appropriate and sensitive strategies for helping AAVE-speaking children understand the systematic, rule-governed nature of their own language *and* learn and master the SAE language of their schools and classrooms. Thus begins for many African American children, a downward academic spiral into the abyss of educational despair and failure.

Why has learning to read, write, and speak SAE been such a challenge to African American people? Although the answer is complex and multifaceted, researchers and scholars know that an important part of the answer lies in prevailing societal beliefs, values, and attitudes about the notion that some languages are better than others. In turn, these beliefs affect attitudes about language differences and learning in schools and classrooms and, in particular, how teachers support (or do not support) AAVE-speakers and their efforts to learn to speak, read, and write SAE. The answer has nothing to do with the ability of our African American children to learn and use SAE, but everything to do with the ability and willingness of today's schools and classroom teachers to accept and respect AAVE as a vibrant and important part of the heritage of African American children and to *effectively* teach SAE to AAVE-speaking children.

HELPING AAVE-SPEAKERS LEARN TO READ

Accountability pressures associated with school reform and its mantra of educational success for all children, in tandem with a renewed focus on the analysis of disaggregated achievement and student conduct data, persistently reveal the continuing academic underperformance of large numbers of African American children, particularly in the area of language arts. One appropriate and constructive response to this challenge is for educators to seek out and use strategies proven to help African

American children achieve mastery in the SAE forms of speaking, reading, and writing–the language of learning and performance in most public schools.

According to Dr. John Rickford, Department of Linguistics, Stanford University, in his article "Language Diversity and Academic Achievement in the Education of African American Students–An Overview of the Issues," ". . . a program that takes the linguistic background of AAVE speakers into account in teaching reading and the language arts is likely to be more successful than one that does not," and he goes on to further state that there is ". . . good evidence of this effect." As such, ". . . The real debate is, or should have been, about the means of teaching SE (*standard English*)" (Adger, et al., 1999).

He advocates in his revised (March 25, 1998) article, "Using the Vernacular to Teach the Standard," three approaches for helping African American children acquire the skills and knowledge of SAE:

1. **The linguistically informed approach** where teachers use strategies that are embedded in the knowledge of the intricacies and rules of AAVE (and SAE);
2. **Contrastive analysis** where students' attention is drawn specifically to the differences between the vernacular and the standard language which leads to a much greater metalinguistic awareness of similarities and differences between the vernacular and the standard, and allows children to more effectively negotiate the line between the two; and
3. **Introducing reading in the vernacular, then switching to the standard** that follows a principle for language learning that was established from research dating back to the 1950s. (Rickford,1998)

Wolfram (1990), as cited by Adger (1997) further argues that, "Dialect awareness is not just for vernacular dialect speakers learning standard English as an additional dialect. All students need language education that includes the facts about language variation if they are to engage sensibly in discussions about dialect differences . . . and to get along in a dialectally diverse world."

It seems clear, then, based on the weight of the research to date, that dialect awareness programs, which help children become bidialectal in both AAVE and SAE, can accomplish important goals for African American children, their families, and their communities. Importantly, African American children can:

- Learn the skills and knowledge of both AAVE and SAE in its spoken, read, and written forms
- Learn to enjoy reading and understand its purposes and uses
- Learn to read, interpret, and comprehend at higher levels

The potential is much greater that African American children will do better academically and socially (improved behaviors and attitudes toward learning and other social activities because of greater academic success) in school, at home, and in their communities, because they are engaged and being *fully* supported early in their language and literacy learning and throughout their school careers.

Fortunately for students, some school systems serving large numbers of vernacular-speaking African American children (Los Angeles Unified School District in California and DeKalb County Schools in Georgia) have paid heed to this valuable research information. They are successfully using English language arts programs for African American children that acknowledge and address issues of the vernacular through culturally, linguistically, and pedagogically sound and sensitive approaches to SAE language and reading development.

LOS ANGELES UNIFIED SCHOOL DISTRICT'S ACADEMIC ENGLISH MASTERY PROGRAM

Authorized for districtwide implementation in 1989, The Los Angeles Unified School District's Academic English Mastery Program (AEMP), strategically located in the Division of Instructions' Language Acquisition Branch for Standard English Language Learners, is a comprehensive and research-based instruction model designed to serve the language needs of students who are not proficient in SAE. It currently operates in thirty-one elementary and middle schools, and the program supports the language learning needs of African American, Mexican American, Hawaiian American, and Native American students who are not proficient in SAE. The program's primary goal is to ensure that students will learn to use "standard" American and academic English proficiently and, in the process, experience increased literacy acquisition and greater academic achievement.

A recent evaluation of the AEMP was conducted by the Center for Research, Evaluation, Standards, and Student Testing (CRESST) at the University of California, Los Angeles, for the purposes of determining the effectiveness of the AEMP in increasing students' general and academic use of Mainstream English Language (MEL) as measured by the Language Assessment Writing and Speaking Measures. Three instruments were used to collect data from a random sample of AEMP and comparable schools as a control group: the Writing and Speaking Language Assessment Measures, a teacher survey, and an observation checklist.

The evaluation results are encouraging. AEMP students outperformed those who did not participate in the program on the Language Assessment Writing Test. Evaluators also found statistically significant, but moderate, correlations between (1) some elements of program implementation such as "building upon the learning styles and strengths of African American Standard English learners" and student outcomes and (2) years of teaching experience in general, years of employment in LAUSD, level of education, and student outcomes.

On the basis of these and other results, the authors of this study concluded that the program *is* effective in improving academic use of the English language for speakers of nonmainstream English, that program effectiveness can be improved if teachers are motivated to implement and use program principles to their fullest extent, and that teachers with more experience and education are more successful in improving student achievement (CRESST, 2000).

DEKALB COUNTY SCHOOLS, DEKALB, GEORGIA

For more than ten years, DeKalb County schools have been using a bidialectic-focused language learning program that teaches mainstream communication skills to African American students without devaluing the language skills they learn at home. Students in the program learn that communication is sensitive to the relationship of the speakers, the purpose of speaking, and the context for communicating, helping them to become competently bidialectal without having to shed or subvert their African American identities as a prerequisite for learning SAE (Adger et al., 1999).

The DeKalb program is student-centered and uses performance-based assessments throughout the school year to help teachers and students measure student progress in acquiring SAE knowledge and skills. Students use videotaping, role planning, and peer critiquing and support to achieve their individual language development goals. Parents also attend classes on bidialectal communication. Test scores have been impressive. Students in the bidialectal program show higher test score gains in reading comprehension than comparable Title I students not in the program.

These examples of public school systems implementing dialect-sensitive "standard" English language learning programs for African American (and other) "standard" English language learners is still the exception rather than the rule. Most African American dialect-speaking children continue to face powerful obstacles to their literacy development. Young dialect speakers face the possibility that they will be labeled as "learning disabled" and/or language delayed even as they enter the public school system. By fourth grade, many dialect speakers begin to "drop out" of classroom and school learning and social activities, because their attempts to participate and communicate in the dialects of their home languages are constantly criticized, ridiculed, and devalued by teachers and peers (de Villiers et al., 1997). They fail to learn to read at levels that allow their successful engagement with increasingly more complex reading-based academic learning.

The consequences of children's failure to learn to read are costly to the individual in terms of lost personal and professional potential and costs to society. Surveys of adolescents and young adults with criminal records show that about half have reading difficulties. Nearly one in three African American male youths and adults is currently involved in the criminal justice system, and significantly large numbers of them have underdeveloped "standard" English language skills. About half of youths with a history of substance abuse have reading problems (NICHD, 1998). Clearly, the need to address issues of language and literacy development for African American children is urgent. Our past and current strategies for helping low-income African American children who are dialect speakers learn to read and communicate in SAE are not working for large numbers of children.

These challenges to the acquisition of mainstream literacy for African American children, an old struggle but newly emphasized civil right, called so eloquently by Linda Darling-Hammond in her book of the same name, *The Right to Learn*, give us an important national education goal for the twenty-first century. The "right to learn" must include for all AAVE-speaking African American children, at a minimum, the promise and accomplishment of bidialectal literacy.

CONCLUSION

Developing adequate early childhood literacy skills and knowledge in both the languages used at home and in school, learning to read well, and then mastering those skills over the course of a preK through grade 12 education career, will most assuredly produce improved academic achievement and long-term life outcomes for African American children and youth. As adults, it is more probable that they will be readers and lifelong learners, have stronger, more stable families, and possess greater earning power and a greater sense of connection to their families, communities, the nation, and the world. The key to ensuring that African American children have access and opportunity to engage in rich language and literacy experiences in both the languages of home and the larger society is the strength of our commitment as educators, schools, and families to making that happen.

REFERENCES

Adger, C.T. (1997, March). Dialect education: Not only for Oakland. *ERIC/CLL News Bulletin, 20*, 2. Retrieved 8/16/99 from World Wide Web: www.cal.org/ericcll/News/9703Dialect.html

Adger, C.T., Christian, D., & Taylor, O. (Eds.).(1999). *Making the connection: Language and academic achievement among African American students.* McHenry, IL: Center for Applied Linguistics and Delta Systems, Inc.

Burns, M. S., Griffin, P., & Snow, C. E. (Eds.) (1999). *Starting out right: A Guide to promoting children's reading success.* Washington, DC, National Academy Press.

Casper, L.M. & Bryson, K.R. (1998, March). *Co-resident grandparents and their grandchildren: Grandparent maintained families.* (Working Paper No. 26). Washington, DC: U.S. Census Bureau, Population Division.

Center for Research, Evaluation Standards, and Student Testing, 2000. Executive Summary of the evaluation of Los Angeles Unified School District's Academic English Mastery Program. Los Angeles, CA: Author (CRESST).

de Villiers, J. Roeper, T., Seymour, H.N., de Villiers, P., Dicky, M.W., & Donahue, M. (1997, January 9). *An open letter to "Dear Colleagues."* Retrieved on 12/2/99 from The World Wide Web: www.tnellen.com/cyber eng/nyt/openlet.htm

Federal Interagency Forum on Child and Family Statistics (1999). *America's children: Key national indicators of well-being.* Washington, DC: Author.

Hart, B., & Risley, T. R. (1995). *Meaningful differences in the everyday experience of young American children.* Baltimore, MD: Paul H. Brookes Publishing Company.

Labov, W. (1972, June). Academic ignorance and Black intelligence. *The Atlantic Monthly*, Retrieved on 12/3/99 from The World Wide Web: www.theatlantic.com//issues/95sep/ets.labo.htm

The National Research Center on English Learning and Achievement, University at Albany. (1999, Spring). *An interview with Frank Vellutino and Donna Scanlon: Kindergarten intervention shows promise in preventing first-grade reading difficulties.* Albany, New York: Author.

National Institute of Child Health and Human Development. (1998). *Why children succeed or fail at reading–Research from NICHD's program in learning disabilities.* Washington, DC: Author.

Novick, R. (1996, April). *Developmentally appropriate and culturally responsive education: Theory into practice.* Portland, OR: The Northwest Educational Laboratory.

Perry, T. & Delpit, L. (Eds.) (1998). *The real Ebonics debate–power, language, and the education of African American children.* Boston, MA: Beacon Press.

Rickford, J.T. (1997a). *Using the vernacular to teach the standard.* Revised (March 25, 1998) remarks delivered at the California State University Long Beach Conference on Ebonics, March 29, 1997. Retrieved 12/2/99 from The World Wide Web: ww.stanford.edu/~rickford/papers/VernacularToTeachStandard.html

Rickford, J.R. (1997b, December). Suite for ebony and

phonics: Commentary. *Discover Magazine.* Retrieved on 12/2/99 from The World Wide Web: www.standord.edu/~rickford/papers/SuiteForEbonyAndPhonics.html

Rickford, J. (1998). The creole origins of African American vernacular English: Evidence from copula absence. In S. S. Mufwene, J.R. Rickford, G. Bailey, & J. Baugh (Eds.), *African American English.* London: Routledge.

Smith, V. (1999, December 19). Linguist fights unfounded stigma of Appalachian speech oddities. *The Prince George's County The Sunday Journal.* Lanham, MD: Associated Press.

University of Massachusetts National Institutes of Health African American English Working Group. (1999, January). *Position statement on Ebonics (also known as African American English).* Amherst, Massachusetts: Author. Retrieved on 7/20/00 from The World Wide Web: http://www.umass.edu/aae/position_statement_.htm

Article 12

AFRICAN AMERICAN CHILDREN AND LITERACY: LITERACY DEVELOPMENT IN THE EARLY CHILDHOOD YEARS

LYNSON MOORE BEAULIEU

ACCORDING TO DR. REID LYON of the National Institute of Child Health and Human Development (NICHD), only about 5 percent of children find learning to read an effortless journey. Another 20 to 30 percent learn to read relatively easily once exposed to formal instruction. However, for approximately 60 percent of all children, "learning to read is a formidable challenge, and for at least 20-30% of these youngsters, reading is one of the most difficult tasks that they will have to master throughout their schooling" (Lyon, 1997). For disproportionate numbers of African American children, the road to reading is long and filled with frustration and failure, as they frequently encounter roadblocks and barriers that are historical, environmental, and institutional in nature.

In their synthesis of the extensive research on early reading development, Snow, Burns, and Griffin (1998) share that most reading problems faced by today's adolescents and adults are the result of problems that might have been avoided or resolved in the early childhood years. Because the early years have such a powerful influence on the trajectory of children's language, literacy, and reading development, there is a great urgency to explore the terrain with a wider audience of educators. For K through 12 educators, the years of early childhood, as they relate to the work of teaching and learning, are typically foreign territory.

ON THE ROAD TO READING–WHAT DO WE KNOW?

Many issues arise as we examine the problem of reading failure. In addition to the dialect/language challenges discussed in the previous article, African American children who are "standard" American English (SAE) language learners are faced with myriad challenges that first surface during the early childhood years. Learning to read is also impacted by such factors as:

- Family poverty
- Children's overall health and development
- Oral language development
- Early care and education experiences both inside and outside of the home
- Quality of teaching and learning interactions

By no means an exhaustive list, other critical factors that present additional obstacles to reading and learning success for many African American children include exposure to high rates of violence, low birth weight, homelessness and high rates of institutional placement, and prenatal drug and alcohol exposure.

Family Poverty

African American children and youth are affected by poverty at far higher rates than their White counterparts (Parham, White, & Ajamu, 1999) and are at greater risk of reading failure, because they are disproportionately affected by the many economic and social disadvantages linked to poverty. The effects of poverty place heavy added burdens and stresses on children, their families, and communities, often interfering with children's access to resources and growth opportunities. Historically, African American children experience the most long-term poverty, comprising almost 90 percent of all children who have experienced poverty for at least five years during their childhoods (Center for the Future of Children, 1997).

Children's Overall Health and Development

Poor children typically have lower-quality diets and experience hunger more often and more intensely than nonpoor children. Even moderate undernutrition, the type most frequently seen in the United States, can have lasting effects on the cognitive development of children (Federal Interagency Forum on Child and Family Statistics, 1999). However, improving children's nutritional and environmental conditions can modify the effects of early undernutrition (Center on Hunger, Poverty, and Nutrition Policy, 1995). For millions of low-income children, federally funded nutrition programs that children access through child care, school, and community-based programs are a critical intervention and provide a significant proportion of their daily nutritional and caloric intake.

Hunger can affect the outcome of children's schooling in many ways. Hungry and undernourished children have more difficulty fighting infections and are more likely to become sick, miss school, and fall behind. Growth retardation and iron deficiency anemia, two common nutrition-related disorders, affect poor children at two to three times the rate of their nonpoor peers (Center on Hunger, Poverty, and Nutrition Policy, 1995) and can adversely affect children's growth, development, and learning. Iron deficiency anemia affects 25 percent of all poor children in the United States (Center on Hunger, Poverty, and Nutrition Policy, 1995) and can lead to a shortened attention span, irritability, fatigue, and difficulty with concentration and memory functions. As a result, anemic children tend to do poorly on vocabulary, reading, and other tests. Making sure that children have enough water to drink is also important, because dehydration affects children's attentiveness and can cause lethargy (Jensen, 1998).

Paying attention to children's early development is critical, because many aspects of children's development help to prepare children to become readers. Understanding the role of development in helping children learn to read provides us with additional tools for ensuring that greater numbers of children–from all ethnic, cultural, and language backgrounds–become successful readers.

The first three years of a child's life contain critical "windows of opportunity," during which children's brains create important neural networks that pave the way for learning and build important foundations for many aspects of their development. For example, some researchers believe that many of today's children don't get the early motor stimulation needed for basic, much less optimal, school success. Early motor stimulation promotes brain, physical, and emotional development and occurs when children are held, rocked, carried, or otherwise moved about. In fact, touch has been identified as the first and most fundamental means of communication and interaction between parents (and other caregivers) and their children (Pribram & Rozman, 1998). Children also need everyday experiences of sight, sound, and touch or the brain regions that process information from the eyes, ears, and skin senses do not develop properly (Institute for Families in Society, 1997). Many poor families find themselves in situations in which they face chronic physical and/or mental distress or are forced to use (because of a lack of real options) childcare or other caring arrangements that provide minimal care and stimulation throughout the day. Many of the children in these families are at risk of not receiving adequate early stimulation.

Children's emotional development is also important to children's later school and reading success and is strongly influenced by their experiences with parents and other caregivers in the earliest periods of life. Infants and young children need warm, caring, and nurturing environments, where they are free to explore their world with confidence and are responded to sensitively in stressful situations. Chronic emotional stress, both prenatally and after birth, can stimulate the production of large amounts of hormones, such as adrenaline and cortisol, that affect the connectors and neural networks in the brain and can lead children to engage in violent and other inappropriate behaviors.

Our efforts to help more children learn to read successfully must incorporate strategies that engage the sum total of children's development and provide an integrated approach to growth and learning that provides protection against chronic stress and the right kinds of stimulation, at the best possible times, in all areas of children's development.

Oral Language Development

Large numbers of African American children develop their oral language skills in response to hearing and learning the sounds and language patterns of African American vernacular English (AAVE), which are distinct in many ways from the sounds of SAE. As such, many young African American children who are dialect speakers face challenges similar to those faced by speakers of other languages (Snow, Burns, & Griffin, 1998) when they begin to learn to read. Most teachers are unable to properly evaluate African American children's language development status at the time the children start school and, as a result, their language learning needs are met with limited (if any) interventions designed to appropriately help young AAVE speakers begin the process of becoming bidialectal in both AAVE and SAE. In support of such interventions, research on reading for SAE language learners provides evidence that SAE language learners should have opportunities to develop literacy skills in their native language and SAE before learning to read in SAE (Basterra, 1998; Snow, Burns, & Griffin, 1998).

Children who are most vulnerable to reading failure are those who enter school with a limited sensitivity to the concepts and sounds of language (for example, an awareness of the alphabetic principle, phonemes, and phonics) and limited verbal skills and vocabulary (Snow, Burns, & Griffin, 1998) in whatever language they speak. Some young children, especially those whose families have fewer economic and human resources, get fewer opportunities to practice their developing oral language skills (Hart & Risley, 1995). They also have fewer opportunities to engage in the type of learning experiences that would equip them with the knowledge domains and related vocabulary skills that most often are a part of the expectations for readiness that meet children when they enter school.

Attending to vocabulary development is very important. According to Robbins and Ehri (1994), as cited by Snow, Burns, and Griffin (1998), "Even at the youngest ages, the ability to understand and remember the meanings of new words depends quite strongly on how well developed one's vocabulary already is." The more words a child learns, the more new words he or she will be able to acquire. Well-developed vocabularies in the child's home language are important for building well-developed vocabularies in the child's second language. A child's verbal skills and vocabulary help us learn about what children know and can do and also about their interests. Well-developed vocabularies lead to children's greater success with word recognition when they begin to read (National Research Council, 1999). A generous amount of early language and literacy experiences, including frequent, complex, and meaningful conversations with adults and interesting interactions with their environment and literature, helps young children to develop and improve their vocabulary skills.

Early Care and Education Experiences

High-quality early care and education program experiences are important to large numbers of children, especially those who are poor, come from diverse ethnic and cultural backgrounds, are SAE language learners, and/or have parents who work and/or participate in adult education and employment training activities. Increased federal and state expenditures are enabling many low-income African American children to participate in early care and education programs, including Head Start, Even Start, child care, and other public preschool programs, in unprecedented numbers. In 1996, 63 percent of African American children were enrolled in center-based preschool programs, a higher percentage than White (54 percent) and Hispanic (37 percent) children (Federal Interagency Forum on Child and Family Statistics, 1999). However, simply increasing participation rates does not necessarily produce the results we are seeking. Although significant numbers of African American children attend center-based preschool programs, very few of these programs are considered to be of high quality.

Ongoing studies of the quality of out-of-home early care and education settings indicate that most children are not receiving the quality of care and education that will help them get ready for school. Studies on both center-based and home-based programs indicate that most environments where children are enrolled are of substandard quality and in many cases endanger children's health and safety (Kagan & Cohen, 1997). Many children attend such programs for nine to ten hours a day, five days per week.

Most parents, especially those who live in low-income, isolated communities, have few, if any, choices. Better quality care has long waiting lists, is simply not available, or if it is, is unaffordable. Families are required to pay more for preschool care and education than they do for tuition at many public colleges and universities, largely because of greater state and private subsidies for higher education (Hinkle, 2000). Longitudinal research, including such well-known early childhood studies as The Cost, Quality, and Outcomes Study of 1995 and the Abecedarian Project report, shows us that high-quality early care and education programs and experiences can be highly beneficial to children's immediate and long-term developmental and educational outcomes, especially for low-income children (Hinkle, 2000).

The Quality of Teaching and Learning Interactions

As in any other educational setting, high-quality teaching and learning activities contribute to high-quality programs, services, and results. As a result of recent brain research and other quality-focused studies, more attention and resources are being given to early childhood provider and educator professional development. Effective reading instruction and support requires that teachers be well informed and well trained in child development and research-based and proven approaches to early language, literacy, and reading development.

All early childhood educators must have access to training that supports their ability to effectively teach children from diverse cultural, language, and learning style backgrounds. Teachers must be prepared to use a combination of approaches and strategies that incorporate bilingual and bidialectal language learning, phonemic awareness, phonics, and a variety of teaching and learning styles, including direct instruction and whole language strategies, so that they can meet the needs of all learners. Young African American children bring with them to early care and education a wealth of experiences that need to be recognized for the value they can provide to support learning in the formal school setting. Teachers need to build on the spoken language, knowledge, and skills African American children develop at home and in their own communities. Teachers must be provided the professional development that will help them to create bridges between the languages and cultures of the home and school. This will reinforce motivation, compatibility between home and the schooling experience, and self-concept (Parham, White, & Ajamu, 1999).

Early Childhood and the Public Schools

Although most early care and education programs have limited connections to their neighborhood public schools, many individual schools and whole school districts are becoming increasingly involved in providing school-based and school-linked full-day childcare and preschool programs and services to the children and families in their neighborhoods. In addition to school-based programs, public schools are also reaching out and building relationships and partnerships with the other child care and preschool programs that are also providing services to community children who will one day attend their schools. Public schools and community-based programs are joining together in increasing numbers to build early care and education systems that provide high-quality childcare and preschool programs and connect families to much needed resources. Forty-two states reported funding prekindergarten initiatives as of 1998–1999 with an estimated one million children being served in public school prekindergarten programs (Hinkle, 2000).

Bright Beginnings–Charlotte-Mecklenburg Public Schools

The public school prekindergarten program in Charlotte, North Carolina, is called *Bright Beginnings* and is funded mainly through federal Title I elementary and secondary education program funds. The program serves eligible children who are selected through an assessment process that uses developmentally sensitive measures.

The full-day program revolves around four literacy circles. Teachers read storybooks out loud to the children and engage them in conversations about various aspects of the story. The literacy circles provide the children with regular opportunities to practice their emerging reading and literacy skills. In a large group setting, children become familiar with a wide variety of literature, learn the rhythms of reading, and build vocabulary and critical thinking skills. Staff at Bright Beginnings actively engage families in their children's learning at home and at school, and parents report tremendous satisfaction with their involvement with the program and in their children's growth, development, and learning. The program provides a caring, educational environment, is literacy-focused, and provides four-year-olds with a literacy-rich, resource-rich, full-day prekindergarten experience.

All teachers are early childhood specialists with at least a four-year degree and are certified to teach by the state. They are paid on the district's teacher salary schedule. Professional development is a continual process. Each classroom of eighteen to twenty children includes a teacher and teacher's aide.

The program uses a "home-grown" curriculum, with content and performance standards in the areas of social and personal development, language and literacy, language and literacy writing, mathematical thinking, scientific thinking, social studies, the creative arts, physical development, and technology.

Assessments of children participating in Bright Beginnings show that the program is having a positive effect on children's development and learning. Their approach to assessment is continuous and relies on appropriate and typical classroom activities. Data are gathered through observations and interactions with the children and are gathered from multiple sources. Findings on the 1997–1998 cohort of students indicate that the skills that the children learned during their year in the Bright Beginnings program were retained when assessed at the beginning of the kindergarten year and that the children showed sustained success throughout kindergarten into first grade. Bright Beginnings children outperform their eligible nonparticipating peers on the kindergarten assessment in both literacy and math (Bucci, et al., 2000).

Norfolk (VA) Public Schools' CoZi Program

CoZi is an initiative that brings together the school reform models of two Yale professors. It combines Dr. James P. Comer's School Development Program (SDP) and Dr. Edward Zigler's School of the 21st Century (21C). SDP offers a process for authentic family and community involvement, and 21C offers early childhood and family support services that enable children to build the foundation they need to take advantage of the school program and families to function with less stress. The SDP guiding principles of collaborative partnerships, no-fault problem solving, and consensus decision making help to ensure that the whole community has a stake in the initiative.

The School of the twenty-first Century program model brings a variety of child care and family support services under one roof: the neighborhood school. The school reaches out to families beginning in the third trimester of pregnancy and provides needed support services beginning at birth until the child is twelve years old. The model is built on the assumption that when families, schools, health care, and child care systems work together, children and families benefit in various ways. Having access to younger children and their families earlier makes it possible for the SDP to reach its goals.

Norfolk's CoZi schools operate under the vision that "language mediates all learning" and use the language of the children to facilitate the motivation and action necessary to lead caring adults to value literacy and create a culture of listening, speaking, reading, and writing for children. Toward that goal, CoZi schools involve families in literacy activities and provide outreach professional development services to neighborhood family child care homes to help improve the quality of early childhood literacy experiences for the children enrolled in their programs. The Parents As Teacher (PAT) program provides a PAT lending library, where child care providers can borrow books, videotapes, laptop computers, and educational CDs for use in the child care setting. In Norfolk, CoZi uses African American literature to connect preschool children to their identity to help foster an understanding of cultural heritage and promote student achievement.

Parents at Bowling Park Elementary school created a program called the Family Literacy Breakfast Club in which parents met monthly to discuss children's books. The group adopted a method of discussing books that uses five key prompts that help to bridge the material to the child's real-life experiences, promotes recall, discussion, and a focus on details, and builds vocabulary. Parents are given the books to take home to read and discuss with their children. Started seven years ago, the club still exists today.

CoZi Results

Between 1996 and 1998, a pilot study was conducted by Yale Bush Center in Child Development and Social Policy on the CoZi initiative at Bowling Park CoZi Community School in Norfolk. The evaluation revealed increased school readiness and student achievement. CoZi preschool and kindergarten students scored higher on the nationally recognized Peabody Picture Vocabulary Test, Revised, than students in the comparison school. Reading and math scores for students in grades 3 and 4 increased significantly over the five-year period of CoZi implementation, outscoring all schools in the district with similar student populations. Teachers and parents reported significantly better school climate levels, and evaluators noted dramatically higher and more effective levels of parent and community involvement. Program activities were also found to positively affect parents' interactions with their children at home. The study also showed an impact of the program's implementation on several classroom practices–specifically the teachers' use of comprehension and inferential thinking in their teaching of literacy and teachers meeting together to discuss students and other school matters.

CONCLUSION

The early childhood years provide many important opportunities to help young children develop early language and literacy skills, get ready for school, and excel at their studies. As we have seen, there are a wide range of developmental challenges that they face that can powerfully influence the trajectory of their formal educational experiences. To help them on their way, children's earliest experiences with reading and writing should allow them to "experience the joy and power associated with reading and writing while mastering basic concepts about print that research has shown are strong predictors of achievement" (IRA/NAEYC, 1995).

Understanding the importance of the early childhood years to all further learning is important for all educators, regardless of the ages and grades they teach. For educators of older children, knowledge of the early childhood years can provide important clues and contexts for understanding the literacy development needs of older students. Our job of helping young African American children lay strong foundations and skills for their language, literacy, and reading development in the years before they enter school is critical but made much more difficult by the overwhelmingly large numbers of poor African American children (40 percent or more) and a lack of high-quality local early care and education resources for supporting and supplementing parental efforts. Although there is still time during the formal schooling years to promote the literacy development and learning of children who have missed out on enriched, early childhood experiences, prevention and early intervention provide the greatest chances for the long-term academic and social success of the greatest number of children at the lowest cost to all parties involved–the children, families, schools, communities, states, and the nation.

REFERENCES

Basterra, M. R. (1998). *Excellence and equity for language minority students: Critical issues and promising practices.* Chevy Chase, MD: Mid-Atlantic Equity Center.

Bucci, F., Edmonds, E.O., Sims, J.G., & Hamilton, F. (2000). *Charlotte-Mecklenburg schools, bright beginnings–Title I: A catalyst for building dreams.* Slide presentation.

Center for the Future of Children. (1997). Children and poverty (Executive Summary). *The future of children,* 7(2). Los Angeles, CA: The David and Lucile Packard Foundation.

Center on Hunger, Poverty, and Nutrition Policy. (1995). *Statement on the link between nutrition and cognitive development in children* (2nd ed). Medford, MA: School of Nutrition, Tufts University.

Federal Interagency Forum on Child and Family Statistics. (1999). *America's children: Key national indicators of well-being.* Washington, DC: Author.

Hart, B., &. Risley, T.R. (1995). *Meaningful differences in the everyday lives of young American children.* Baltimore, MD: H. Brookes Publishing Co.

Hinkle, D. (2000). *School involvement in early childhood.* Washington, DC: U.S. Department of Education, Office of Educational Research and Improvement, National Institute on Early Childhood Development and Education, U.S. Government Printing Office.

Institute for Families in Society. (1997). Attachment and early brain development. University of South Carolina. Retrieved on 4/20/01 from the World Wide Web: *www.sc.edu/ifis/aaebd.htmrl.*

Institute for Families in Society. (1998). Promoting brain development. University of South Carolina. Retrieved on 4/20/01 from the World Wide Web: *www.sc.edu/ifis/pbd.htmrl.*

International Reading Association and the National Association for the Education of Young Children (1995). Overview of learning to read and write: developmentally appropriate practices for young children (official position statement adopted May 1998). National Association for the Education of Young Children, Washington, DC.

Jensen, E. (1998). *Teaching with the brain in mind.* Alexandria, VA: Association for Supervision and Curriculum Development.

Kagan, S.L., & Cohen, N.E. (1997). *Not by chance–Creating an early care and education system for America's children.* New Haven, CT: The Quality 2000 Initiative, The Bush Center in Child Development and Social Policy, Yale University.

Lyon, G.R. (1997, July). *Hearing on literacy: Why kids can't read.* Presented to the Committee on Education and the Workforce, U.S. House of Representatives, Washington, DC.

National Research Council (1999). *Starting out right–A guide to promoting children's reading success.* Washington, DC: National Academy Press.

Parham, T.A., White, J.L., & Ajamu, A. (1999). *The psychology of Blacks: An African centered perspective* (3rd ed.). Englewood Cliffs, NJ: Prentice Hall.

Pribram, K., & Rozman, D. (1998). Early childhood development and learning: What new research on the heart and brain tells us about our youngest children. Institute of HeartMath. Boulder Creek, CA. Retrieved 4/20/01 from the World Wide Web: *www.webcom.com/hrtmath/IHM/ResearchPapers/kids.htm.*

Quigg, C. The development of the human brain: Implications for parenting in the early years. Baby Talk, Inc., Decatur, IL. Retrieved 4/20/01 from the World Wide Web: *www.babytalk.org/essaybrain.html.*

Snow, C.E., Burns, M.S., & Griffin, P. (Eds). (1998). *Preventing reading difficulties in young children.* Washington, DC: National Academy Press.

Article 13

AFRICAN AMERICAN CHILDREN AND LITERACY: LITERACY DEVELOPMENT ACROSS THE ELEMENTARY, MIDDLE, AND HIGH SCHOOL YEARS

LYNSON MOORE BEAULIEU

TO SIGNIFICANTLY IMPROVE THE LIFE chances and living conditions for African American people, African American children must learn to read, write, and speak "standard" American English at levels commensurate with the broad societal goals of economic and social well-being. Because literacy is socially constructed, students must also be encouraged to discover the personal value inherent in becoming a truly literate person. Our literacy strategies for African American children must lead to children and youth who not only read well but are well read. African American youth, like other youth, must be able to read, write, and speak fluently and knowledgeably, from a place of personal meaning, about many subjects in their own and the "standard" American English language of the mainstream society.

HELPING AFRICAN AMERICAN CHILDREN LEARN TO READ

Attaining literacy is a lifelong journey, one that for large numbers of African American students continues to be stifled during the all-important elementary and secondary school years. Nearly seven in ten fourth graders in the nation's poorest urban schools (which are attended by large numbers of African American children) fail to read at the basic level needed for school success (U.S. Department of Education, 1999). Our ongoing efforts to help African American children achieve the mainstream American standard of literacy–becoming learned and accomplished as readers, speakers, writers, *thinkers*, and technology users–must significantly improve and continue in earnest throughout their schooling years.

Regardless of children's backgrounds or where they live, most children learn to read in much the same way. The basic school and classroom conditions necessary to help children excel in their language and literacy development efforts are similar for all children. The intensity, level, or type of instruction and support, however, must be varied based on children's individual prior language and literacy experiences, native cultural and language backgrounds, current skill levels, and learning needs.

Three decades of reading research have helped to identify key reading strategies that will ensure that more children are competent, fluent readers. It is important to focus on teaching children discrete but interrelated literacy skills, such as phonemic awareness, the alphabetic principal, decoding skills and recognizing sight words, *and* how to think about and develop understanding about what they are reading. Because developing speed is important for comprehension, it is also important to provide multiple opportunities for children to practice reading–independently, out loud, in pairs, and as a chorus, during the school day and to encourage reading for pleasure and learning in the hours that children are not in school.

Learning to Read in the Elementary School Years

Kindergarten is a critical year in children's reading development, and *all children*, regardless of where they fall on the language and literacy development and learning continuum, are ready for kindergarten when kindergarten time arrives, usually around the age of five years. They are ready to be engaged in the processes of early language and literacy development and, eventually, in learning how to read.

However, pressures from the standards-based movement and what is commonly referred to as an "academic-focused trickle-down curriculum" for kindergarten children are causing increasing numbers of age-eligible children to be screened out of kindergarten entry, because they are deemed not to be ready for school (Kelly, 2000; National Association of Early Childhood Specialists in State Departments of Education [NAECSSDE], 2000). These children are often screened using poorly constructed or misused instruments and measures whose results are then inappropriately used (Kelly, 2000; Nurss, 1987; Shepard & Smith, 1989) to deny children access to kindergarten programs. These assessment procedures are likely to screen out those children who would be most likely to benefit from a high-quality kindergarten experience. Although parents of children from more socioeconomically advantaged families often voluntarily delay their children's entry into kindergarten, low-income African American children (and other ethnic and language-diverse children) are especially vulnerable to being screened out of entry to kindergarten programs, because they typically perform poorly on these screening tests (National Center for Education Statistics [NCES], 1997) because of biases and misperceptions about their status as poor children and because of the nature of their early language and literacy development. Many African American children face the very real risk as they enter school that because of language differences, they will be stigmatized as "learning disabled" and "language delayed (de Villiers, Roeper, Seymour, Dicky, & Donahue, 1997).

Research clearly indicates that kindergarten retention does nothing to improve student's academic performance (NAECSSDE, 2000; NCES, 1997; Shepard & Smith, 1989) and has been shown, in fact, to significantly increase the likelihood that children will eventually drop out of school. Regardless, many schools and school districts actively employ a variety of kindergarten "retention" practices, including raising the kindergarten entrance age, placing children in transition programs (an additional year of prekindergarten or an extra year between kindergarten and first grade), or making children repeat kindergarten (NAECSSDE, 2000; NCES, 1997; Nurss, 1987; Shepard & Smith, 1989). Like older students, kindergarteners and primary grade students are also affected by being retained in grade, are frequently categorized as "slow learners" (NAECSSDE, 2000), and often personalize retention to mean that something is wrong with them. Even in the earliest years of schooling, children are aware when they are not making "normal" progress. Clearly, these practices should be of great concern, because African American and other ethnic and language-diverse children experience much higher rates of grade retention than other groups of children.

African American children have been shown to respond positively to literacy teaching and learning strategies that are responsive to their language and cultural needs. From an African American culture- and language-centered perspective, Noma LeMoine, the Director of Los Angeles Unified School District's *English for Your Success (EYS)* mainstream English mastery program, lays out expansive language and literacy goals for African American children during the early and middle schooling years:

- Goals for prekindergarten, kindergarten, and grade 1:
  - Acquiring an awareness and appreciation of (for) the language and culture of the home
  - Developing receptive language in mainstream American English (MAE)
  - Acquiring basic literacy skills
  - Developing an awareness and appreciation of language and cultural diversity

- Goals for grades 2 and 3
  - The four goals listed previously plus
  - Recognizing and labeling the differences between African American language (AAL/AAVE/Ebonics) and mainstream American English (MAE/SAE)
  - Expanding a personal thesaurus of conceptually coded word concepts
  - Analyzing linguistic differences between MAE and AAL
  - Using MAE structure functionally in oral and written form
- Goals for grades 4 and 5
  - The eight goals listed previously plus
  - Recognizing the language requirements of different situations
  - Demonstrating proficient use of MAE in written and oral form
  - Developing an expanded knowledge and appreciation of AAL and the languages and cultures of others
  - Communicating effectively in cross-cultural environments
- Goals for grades 6 though 8
  - All twelve of the previously listed goals

The *English for Your Success* goals and curriculum respond to the notion that children learn best in schooling environments that are culturally congruent with their own experiences. *EYS* provides African American students with language and literacy development opportunities and activities that embrace their home language and acknowledge, respect, and celebrate who they are as African American people. The goals and curriculum reflect research-based strategies that promote greater learning and achievement, ensuring that African American children are:

- Engaged in learning that has personal meaning (learning is culturally embedded)
- Assisted effectively to learn MAE (mainstream American English), the main language of instruction and learning in the classroom
- Offered multiple approaches for acquiring basic literacy skills (including whole language, print-rich environment, small group activities, schoolwide literacy focus, more time to read, technology, and integrated learning)
- Adept and knowledgeable at navigating diverse and multicultural situations
- Skilled in the proficient use of both the home and mainstream languages (bidialectal/bilingual)and able to demonstrate that proficiency. (LeMoine, 1999)

Elementary Schools with Effective Literacy Programs

Studies seeking information on practices that support high levels of literacy learning have traditionally looked separately at school organizational practices and classroom practices. Recent studies of reading instruction in the early elementary years (Fisher & Adler, 1999; Taylor, Pearson, Clark & Walpole, 1999) have looked at the effect of both school and classroom change on improvements in literacy achievement. School level change has been found to be as important in helping schools to produce notable results as are changes within the classroom (Taylor et al., 1999). As a result, there is a better understanding of how changes in the overall school environment combine with changes in classroom practice to produce the best results. Braunger (1995) suggests that school staff begin a process of school-level change by collaborating to explore their current classroom practices in the context of their personal and collective beliefs about language and literacy. From that experience, they are better able to develop a philosophy about language and literacy that can then serve as a template for teachers to consult in reflecting on their own classroom practices.

In their review of several studies on school effects with special attention to reading programs, Hoffman and Rutherford (1984) (as cited in Fisher & Adler, 1999) concluded that three categories of characteristics contributed to the success of reading programs:

- *Program characteristics* that include explicitly articulated objectives and role expectations, provision for continuous student progress, flexibility in matching materials and instruction to student needs, and stability of programs over several years;
- *Leadership behaviors* that include establishing reading improvement as a school priority, being knowledgeable about reading instruction, actively facilitating instructional decisions, establishing and maintaining monitoring of student progress, and evaluating teachers; and

- *Psychological conditions* including high expectations for students, calm and business-like school climate, staff commitment to the reading program, staff cooperation, parental involvement, and attribution of reading failure to program defects. (Fisher & Adler, 1999)

Professional Development for Effective Leadership and Teaching

Principals, as well as teachers, have a need for quality professional development opportunities so that they can continue to grow as school leaders. In addition to administrative duties, many principals of high-achieving, high-poverty schools act in the capacity of program and academic leaders, as well, and have usually been involved in their schools–as teachers and administrators–for a significant number of years. Veteran, knowledgeable staff members are a particularly important resource for building strong, successful early reading programs (Cawelti, 1999; Fisher & Adler, 1999; Taylor et al., 1999).

The principal of a high-poverty (50%), high-mobility (40%) elementary school located in a Midwest urban fringe school district indicated in a study of her school's successful early reading program that she considered it a part of her responsibility as an administrator to be involved in ongoing professional development. She described her recent participation in a conference sponsored by a nationally recognized education organization as an opportunity to expand her understanding of curriculum integration, the focus of a major project at her school at the time (Fisher & Adler, 1999). For both principals and teachers, professional development focused on improving the quality of literacy instruction in the primary grades must be regular, ongoing, research-based, and tailored to respond to the diverse and complex schooling contexts in which these school leaders operate.

Several decades of research have underscored the importance of "effective and powerful instruction as the key to successful early reading achievement" (Fisher & Adler, 1999). Recently, the influential national report *Preventing Reading Difficulties in Young Children* concluded that the "quality of instruction in kindergarten and the primary grades is the single best weapon against reading failure" (Taylor et al., 1999). Even though a recent study of 1,000 school districts found that every additional dollar spent on developing the qualifications of teachers netted improvements in student achievement greater than any other use of school resources, districts currently spend less than one half of 1 percent of their resources on staff development (Burns, Griffin, & Snow, 1999). High teacher mobility also affects the quality of instruction children receive and has a negative impact on their learning (Taylor et al., 1999).

Learning to read is a complex process in and of itself. When learning to read is combined with the demands of a multicultural, multilanguage, and multilevel "readiness" student population juxtaposed with an underprepared, monolingual/monocultural teaching workforce, challenges to effective teaching become monumental, and learning to read becomes much more difficult for the children. To better meet the literacy teaching and learning needs of children from diverse cultural and language backgrounds, schools of teacher education must improve the quality and quantity of preservice literacy and reading education and "real world/real time" mentored/supervised teaching experiences for the teachers-in-training enrolled in their programs.

Schools and school systems must also make significant investments in in-service teacher education, professional development, and training that helps teachers to understand:

- A variety of strategies for working with diverse learners
- The process of how children learn to read
- Concepts of language
- Child, cognitive, and behavioral development
- Diverse strategies for effective assessment and monitoring of student progress
- Strategies for building strong, professional learning communities within their schools–for planning and coordination, problem solving, mutual support, and ongoing professional development

Schools are also making good use of mentoring. For example, some help newer teachers get acclimated to the school's early reading programs by linking more experienced teachers with less experienced teachers and ensuring that newer teachers receive assistance from many sources (Fisher & Adler, 1999).

Effective Curriculum and Instructional Practices in Early Reading Programs

Approaches to curriculum and instructional practices for African American children that address issues of culture and language indicate the greatest promise for helping African American children to become successful readers. In the absence of such practices, African American children can benefit significantly when schools implement research-based curriculum and instructional practices that have proven to improve reading outcomes for all children. Encouraging schools that serve African American students to explore research-based early reading programs is an important step toward better reading outcomes for African American children.

Successful early reading programs have identifiable characteristics that in many cases are developed jointly by administrators and teachers as part of their collaborative, team-centered efforts and are a combination of both packaged and home-grown programs and practices (Taylor et al., 1999). They use small-group learning activities, dedicate significant portions of the school day to reading and writing activities, have garnered a schoolwide buy-in and focus on literacy learning, and focus jointly on basic skills and reading comprehension. They also have comfortable, well-thought-out literacy learning spaces, a wide variety of multicultural books and materials of interest to students, in addition to textbooks and adequate instructional tools and resources for teachers. Children learn to read better when they have an interest and can see themselves reflected in the books and activities being used to teach them.

In schools with successful reading programs, children are highly engaged in classroom learning activities almost all of the time. Everyone in the school community takes responsibility for student learning (student learning failure is attributed to instructional failures, not attributed to the student or the student's family), and children experience a coherent, orderly program of literacy learning experiences across the grades. Student progress is continuously monitored, and changes are made in the instructional program whenever needed. In the most effective schools, interventions are not limited to first grade but span the primary grades (Taylor et al., 1999). Regular and adequate time is created and set aside for teachers to plan, review, and discuss individual student work and progress; problem solve; and confer with families (Burns, Griffin & Snow, 1999; Cawelti, 1999; Fisher & Adler, 1999; LeMoine, 1999; Pressley et al., 1998; Snow, Burns & Griffin, 1998; Taylor et al., 1999).

The benefit of small-group instruction in early reading programs is substantial, and effective literacy programs ensure regular small-group learning experiences, along with large-group, and individualized instruction when needed. Small group learning allows students to benefit from the social nature of learning while allowing teachers to tailor instructional activities to suit student's individual learning needs. It also allows teachers to identify the need for interventions quickly, make adjustments in the program, and change a student's group placement as soon as the student is ready to take on additional skills. A student's individual learning needs are more easily identified and met when teachers have adequate time to interact with individual learners.

Recent studies are clearly identifying ability-grouping practices in schools with effective early reading programs, and it is important to note how these practices differ from the ability-grouping practices of the past. They are no longer a one-way ticket into a watered-down, second-tier curriculum for "slow learners." Instead, they are skill-based groupings that provide intensive, small-group, and individualized instruction toward a single high standard of reading proficiency for all students. Toward that goal, systematic evaluation of student progress through teacher observations and curriculum-based classroom assessments is ongoing, and interventions are available and applied immediately when needed. As students master the reading skills and performance levels that are the focus of the skills being taught and reinforced in their current groups, they are moved along to other small groups where students are acquiring additional skills and working toward more proficient performance levels. Student placement within ability groups is flexible and specifically focused on the task at hand–the acquisition of targeted literacy skills and learning to read. In balance, significant parts of children's school days are also spent in large-group learning activities.

The Importance of "Time on Task"

Time on task, the actual amount of time that children spend engaged in literacy learning activities, is one of the most important characteristics of successful programs and improved outcomes for students learning to read (Cawelti, 1999; Fisher & Adler, 1999; LeMoine, 1999; Pressley et al., 1998; Taylor et al., 1999; U.S. Department of Education 1999). It is not unusual for students in grades 1 and 2 to spend up to 50 percent of the school day on literacy activities (Fisher & Adler, 1999). Children with more early literacy experiences have an easier time learning to read. Schools doing a good job of helping children learn to read in the primary and elementary school years spend significant amounts of time every day in fun, interesting, personally meaningful, and appropriately challenging language development, reading, and writing activities.

Many schools that have managed to "beat the odds" and produce children who are proficient readers despite serious challenges have had school leaders in place for a decade or more and have been engaged in a variety of school improvement efforts over similar lengths of time. They have worked consistently over the years to:

- Positively improve school culture and the quality of instruction
- Build communities of educators committed to ongoing learning
- Test, discard, adapt, and improve on a variety of programs and practices
- Strengthen partnerships with families and the community
- Invested significant amounts of time and available financial and material resources to institutionalize promising programs and practices

Although their journeys have not been easy, it is the schools that have been most persistent in their efforts at implementing special strategies that are showing the greatest gains (Taylor et al., 1999).

Literacy Development in the Middle and High School Years

Schools are failing to teach even basic reading skills to large numbers of African American students who are preparing to leave fourth grade. In America's poorest schools (attended by many African American students), an astounding 68 percent of fourth graders fail to reach the *basic* level of reading achievement. Only one in ten fourth graders at these schools can read at the *proficient* level (National Center for Education Statistics, 1999).

By middle school, a number of things typically occur for struggling readers: (1) they continue to slip further and further behind their grade-level reading peers and continue to disconnect from the learning and schooling process (many eventually drop out–up to 50 percent in inner-city high schools [Workshop on High Schools of the millennium, 2000]–when they get so far behind that going through the motions of schooling no longer makes any sense), (2) many students get referred to and placed in special education programs, (3) many children get retained, and (4) behavior problems begin to escalate and students begin to get suspended and expelled more frequently. Large numbers of African American students eventually drop out or are "pushed out" of school. Even though none of these outcomes is acceptable for African American students, in most cases appropriate interventions and remedial efforts are nonexistent or those that are available are ineffective.

A number of critical issues continue to make reading a major concern at the middle and high school levels:

- Reading in content areas demands higher-level reading skills
- Older students become less interested in reading
- Large numbers of secondary students are at risk of reading failure and require targeted reading instruction
- Secondary school teachers have less time to implement reading strategies, even if they believe that improving older student's reading skills should be a part of their content-specific classroom curriculum (Wilson, 1999)

In light of such a system-wide failure, there are a number of questions we must ask and seek answers to if schools and teachers are to prevent the continuation of such discouraging outcomes for African American students:

- What bodies of knowledge are important for educators to understand about children's growth and development during the preadolescent and adolescent years?

- What student strengths can educators build on to accelerate literacy learning during the late elementary, middle, and high school years?
- What are some of the changes that educators need to undertake on a personal and professional level to improve their success as educators of African American preadolescent and adolescent students?
- And what are some of the successful teaching and learning strategies that engage and accelerate learning for older African American students?

What bodies of knowledge are important for educators to understand about children's growth and development during these particular years?

Educators who want to work successfully with African American adolescents need to have more than just strong content and skill knowledge in the field that they teach. Educators who aspire to work effectively with adolescents must also be knowledgeable about the varying aspects of adolescent development. Children entering the preadolescent and adolescent phases of development are undergoing a number of important psychological, social/emotional, and physiological changes that need to be understood by educators so that the experience of language arts learning can be shaped to respond positively to those changes and can support student's engagement in the development of their "personhood" (Egan-Robertson, 1998). Educational strategies that take these developmental differences, along with cultural differences, into account provide the greatest opportunity to get struggling learners back on task and continuing to make progress in the full complement of literacy skills, the bedrock of academic learning.

For example, new hormones are released during adolescence that create emotions children have never experienced before. These hormones precipitate changes in children's sexual and affective development and "neurons in the central nervous system make new connections in the brain that change forever the quality of thought. Old ways of thinking, feeling, and behaving are discarded in middle school and are replaced by radically different modes of operating" (Cohen, 1999). Driven by biological changes, children begin to seek, discover, and establish their own identities, and in doing so, they attach new meaning to all of their experiences, including learning. Relationships become critically important, and peer relationships, especially, take on greater importance as children begin to question those adult influences that have previously dominated their entire relationship to the world. Although children continue to need the support and guidance of caring, responsible adults during their adolescent years, by the very nature of adolescence, they must also seek to separate themselves and/or reduce the intense and highly dependent nature of those previous relationships (Cohen, 1999). Understanding the difference between puberty (the physiological aspects of adolescent development) and adolescence (the psychological events brought on by puberty) is important for educators, because although they cannot change anything about puberty, they can have a powerful influence on the meanings that children eventually attach to the experiences brought on by puberty (Cohen, 1999).

For the successful education of adolescent African American students, educators must develop an awareness of and understanding about how the experience of being African American in America additionally shapes and influences the adolescence experience. In the course of their teaching, many educators fail to fully understand and appropriately respond to the added complications of having a race-impacted developmental experience (i.e., multigenerational and widespread schooling failures, multisource discrimination, race-based profiling, stereotypic media imaging of African American youth, violence, isolation, disproportionate involvement with the criminal justice system, single-parent families, family displacement and homelessness, parental incarceration, multigenerational poverty linked to chronic under- and unemployment). Working with African American students requires that educators examine their own awareness, assumptions, and experiences related to the realities of growing up African American in America and the resulting beliefs and attitudes that shape their classroom practices and, ultimately, the success or failure of their students. In particular, educators must examine (1) how this knowledge affects their ability to develop "alliances and personal relationships" (Cohen, 1999) with African American adolescent students, an aspect of the schooling experience that is critical to students' engagement in learning and their ultimate educational success, and (2) whether they believe that African American adolescents are capable of continuing to make progress with their reading and other literacy skills during adolescence, regardless of their previous academic experiences. Is learning relative to a student's perceived ability and/or past experiences, or does the educator believe that learning results from the student's current efforts and the success of the educator to engage and interest the student in the learning task at hand?

Educators must use this awareness and knowledge of the African American experience to reflect on their own pedagogy and devise strategies for helping African American students make sense of the curriculum in the context of their unique ethnic, cultural, social, and political identities (Cohen, 1999) and experiences, so that they can remain engaged in and committed to authentic academic study. Educators must know their students on a deep personal and group level and be very clear about the curriculum, teaching, learning, and social/political dynamics within their classrooms, the school, and the broader community. With the appropriate kind of knowledge, educators can prepare themselves to build mutually respectful relationships, a relevant pedagogy, and a course of learning with African American adolescent students that steers their developmental energies toward positive intellectual, cultural, and social/emotional learning experiences and academic success.

What student strengths can educators build on to accelerate literacy learning for older students?

Building on students' strengths is a key strategy for helping students to find meaning in their learning and identifying relevant learning activities for individual students. Students entering the adolescent years bring with them a rich repertoire of life experience that can be built on in the learning environment. In trust-bearing situations, students are extremely social and verbal during their adolescent years and will readily share information on their preferred ways of learning and being taught. Indeed, in "High Schools of the Millennium," *student voices* in support of the redesign of the high school experience are called for at all levels of change: federal, state, and local (Workshop on High Schools of the Millenium, 2000). Student's voices should be used to gather important information for successfully shaping language, reading, and writing experiences in the middle and high school years.

Collective socialization and the development of social relationships are important developmental goals for children and youth in many ethnically and culturally diverse families. Not surprisingly, African American students have been shown to prefer learning environments that are organized around social relationships and activities, not around competitive or individual endeavors. Schools and classrooms serving African American students that have organized learning in this manner–where students are encouraged to support one another's learning and work collectively and collaboratively on learning tasks–have achieved tremendous gains in academic achievement (Cohen, 1999).

Students can also talk about the kinds of teachers they prefer. Studies on African American male adolescent students indicate that they prefer teachers who are strict and caring–personally supportive, but who are insistent that their students perform academically. Other African American adolescent male students have identified preferred teacher qualities that include firmness, compassion, and an engaging style of teaching and have indicated that their best teachers respect them, inspire them to work hard, and make learning interesting and relevant (Cohen, 1999).

Students' social and verbal proclivity provides a great resource for promoting classroom discourse–a powerful strategy for engaging students and strengthening the impact of literacy learning activities. Egan-Robertson (1998) reminds us that African American students frequently find themselves stigmatized in regard to their language practices, oftentimes leading to silence among African American students in the context of classroom discourse. African American students are not encouraged to call on their cultural competence as African

Americans as they participate in school-based learning (Egan-Robertson, 1998). Negating or devaluing the linguistic resources of a community can be understood as a way of negating an attribute of personhood (Egan-Robertson, 1998), the attainment of which is one of the main goals of adolescent development.

During the adolescent years, students are typically struggling to define their own personhood and to make sense of life and world events. Gloria Ladson-Billings argues that establishing teaching and learning practices that critically examine the broader society helps successful teachers of African American students to meet the twin goals of academic achievement and cultural competence (Egan-Robertson, 1998). Opportunities for formal and informal small- and large-group discussions often result in "greater student mastery of the subject, an increase in the quality and number of ideas, creative insight, and student enjoyment" (Wilson, 1999).

Educators can give students a voice by gathering information on "attitude surveys" and "interest inventories," which are two student attributes identified as key to improved reading outcomes. Information provided through these sources can provide important tools for mediating weaknesses in a key reading skill–comprehension (Wilson, 1999). Reading comprehension–understanding at a deep and meaningful level what one has read–is the key measure of a skilled reader. Toward better reading outcomes for struggling readers, researchers and practitioners have become increasingly interested in how "attitudes and interests" ultimately affect student's reading achievement.

Because there is a strong relationship between reading attitude and reading comprehension, researchers have been looking at student's beliefs about their own reading abilities. O'Sullivan (1992) studied students' motivational beliefs about their reading ability–beliefs that they could "take control of their reading, set high standards, and achieve their goals" (cited in Wilson, 1999). What she found was that student's own attitudes significantly influenced their reading achievement and also that student's beliefs about their own abilities were heavily influenced by the beliefs of teachers and parents (Wilson, 1999). Second, the degree of interest in reading materials has also been linked to comprehension. Students comprehend material better when it is more interesting to them (Wilson, 1999).

What are some of the changes that educators need to undertake on a personal and professional level to improve their success as language arts educators of African American preadolescents and adolescents?

Viewing adolescence as a positive, though challenging, phase of a child's development can encourage educators to seek out the assets of adolescence and build on their student's strengths during that time. Understanding the intricacies of adolescence and the experiences of their students' lives, and providing opportunities for students to share their voices and have power in their learning, can help educators uncover many assets and strengths that can be used to support student achievement.

Many teachers meet, and will continue to meet, tremendous diversity in their classrooms, in part because there is so little cultural and ethnic diversity in the teaching workforce. Less than 10 percent of teachers are from ethnic, cultural, and language-diverse backgrounds, even though ethnic, cultural, and language-diverse students in the decades ahead will approach 50 percent of the student population. In most classrooms throughout the country, teachers are poorly prepared to work with student populations whose cultures, life experiences, and languages are significantly different from their own. As a result, both students and teachers experience language and cultural disconnections within school and classroom contexts that jeopardize the learning process and affect student progress and achievement, as well as teachers' effectiveness and satisfaction in their work. Helping teachers to reconstruct their knowledge and beliefs about the education of African American and other diverse students, and then reformulate their school and classroom practices to support successful learning outcomes for these students, is challenging for most. Within the process of change, educators must learn to approach teaching and learning from new and very different perspectives, including reexamining what they believe and think they know about "knowing" and "learning."

In a common contrast of epistemological orientations, Johnston, Woodside-Jiron, & Day, 2000, use the terms, "received knowing" and "constructed knowing," to identify working distinctions between the two very different ways of experiencing "knowing" within the context of literacy and language arts learning in the fourth grade. "Received knowers feel that knowledge is "out there" and that someone in authority will give them the knowledge they need. Constructed knowers view knowledge as constructed by individuals in interaction through language, thus discussion is valued as a tool for learning and knowledge is more properly thought of in the active sense of knowing" (Johnston, Woodside-Jiron, & Day, 2000). Epistemological studies are rare in the elementary grades and much more common in high school and with postsecondary education students, but the researchers wanted, in fact, to discover how discourse environments affected the development of children's literate epistemologies in the earlier years.

Epistemologies are important to consider, because they are the lens through which an individual accesses, interprets, and applies knowledge. In the classroom, epistemologies determine in large part what teachers believe about their students as learners, what teachers will teach, how they will teach it, and how they will measure student knowledge. Student-literate epistemologies help to reveal how students view themselves as speakers, readers, and writers; how they will construct and interpret

Identifying Features of Epistemological Stances

Received knowing	Constructed knowing
Believe in a single Truth that is made up of facts discovered by authorities.	Belief in context-bound knowledge constructed by communities of users.
Answers/facts are simply right or wrong.	Believe that the significance and meaning of facts/answers is affected by the circumstances.
Uncomfortable with and avoids controversial and complex issues.	Welcomes controversial and complex issues.
Teacher's role is to ensure the delivery of content/facts to the children.	Teacher's role is to help expand children's independnet and interdependent thinking.
Relies on single sources of information.	Encourages multiple, and potentially conflicting, sources of information.
Teaching emphasizes facts and memory.	Teaching emphasizes process of knowledge construction.
Learning is individual enterprise.	Learning is social enterprise.
Knower and known are separate.	Knower and known are connected.
Teacher is sole authority with respect to knowledge in the classroom.	Authority for knowledge is distributed in the classroom as experience is deemed evident.

From *Teaching and Learning Literate Epistemologies*, by Peter Johnston, Haley Woodside-Jiron, and Jeni Day, National Research Center on English Learning & Achievement (CELA), University at Albany, State University of New York, Albany, NY, 2000.

knowledge encountered through the literacy process; and how they will approach literacy learning (Johnston, Woodside-Jiron, & Day, 2000). In this study, the classrooms of two teachers were compared. One teacher held a "received" view of knowledge and the other held a "constructed" view. The ways in which these very different teacher-literate epistemologies interacted with student-literate epistemologies affected the quality of classroom interactions and levels and types of learning. They also produced very different kinds of classroom literacies. The students in each of the two classrooms "held different views of what it means to be competent, the significance of technical competence, the significance of literate activity, the sense of agency in learning and knowledge production, and the significance they place on their own and others' experience" (Johnston, Woodside-Jiron, & Day, 2000). Not surprisingly, in most cases, their views conformed to or were influenced by the epistemological stances of their respective teachers.

And what are some of the successful teaching and learning strategies that engage and accelerate learning for adolescent African American students?

Successful strategies abound. Individual teachers in their own classrooms, whole schools, and even whole school districts are designing and implementing changes in their approaches to the literacy education of middle and high school students that reflect significantly improved practices.

A study of effective middle and high school language arts teachers in high-poverty/high-performing schools, many of which serve large numbers of African American and Hispanic students, identified six distinguishing features of effective instruction:

1. Skills and knowledge are taught in multiple types of lessons.
2. Tests are deconstructed to inform curriculum and instruction.
3. Within curriculum and instruction, connections are made across content and structure to ensure coherence.
4. Strategies for thinking and doing are emphasized.
5. Generative learning is encouraged.
6. Classrooms are organized to foster collaboration and cogitation.

These features dominated the higher-achieving English and language arts programs in the schools studied and created successful results only because they were used in conjunction with one another to form a supportive web of related learning. Langer (1999) states, "The overriding contributor to success was the whole-scale attention to students' higher literacy needs and development throughout the curriculum, which shaped what students experienced on a day-to-day basis in their regular classrooms."

Other researchers (Snyder, 1999) studied exemplary language arts teachers in the Dade County, Florida school district, where 87 percent of the students are from ethnic, cultural, and language-diverse backgrounds. In particular, they looked at the substantial support teachers received from the school district's Division of Language Arts/Reading, especially in the form of consistently high-quality, relevant professional development opportunities. Support from the school district has evolved over time to reflect changes in:

1. The structure of the Division of Language Arts/Reading.
2. The basic philosophy that underpins what happens in the division.
3. Ways in which division staff stay on the cutting edge of language arts instruction.
4. The process by which staff development and curriculum materials are developed and delivered.

In addition, over the years, the lines between elementary and secondary supervision, and between the curricular areas of reading and language arts, have blurred considerably, and all supervisors now work in both elementary and secondary arenas as well as in both reading and language arts. One of their most powerful professional development activities is their Writing Institute that which trained more than 2,000 teachers over fifteen years. Teachers spend two weeks in what most have called a life-changing experience (Snyder, 1999).

Their reading and language arts curriculum is driven by literature that moves ". . . students to an understanding of how the world works and how they can find their place in it, both in terms of what they are able to do, and in terms of who they are and can become. . . . The insights that students gain from their encounters with literature in our programs–from the silent reading they do during 'Sustained Silent Reading,' to the small group 'literature circle' discussions they regularly engage in, to the 'Grand Conversations' that up to 60 Highland Oaks Middle School students attend several times a year at the local Borders Book Store–are great, ongoing, and powerful" (Snyder, 1999).

A series of fourteen principles guide the development and support of their language arts/reading program.

CONCLUSION

This article by no means provides a complete picture of the qualities of effective literacy education for students in the elementary, middle, and high school years. It does, however, provide an overview of important characteristics and practices of effective literacy instruction and learning as gathered from a variety of studies of effective schools, programs, and teaching. This overview seeks to connect those effective characteristics and practices to the unique needs of African American learners in the context of their language, literacy, and reading development experiences across the full expanse of their elementary and secondary education experiences.

Most of America's public schools have a long way to go before African American students have an equitable learning experience in their language and literacy education. It seems, however, that an expanding body of research and knowledge, both on reading development in general and African American students and their learning in particular, is available to help schools and teachers redefine the nature and scope of their charge as teachers of reading and language arts and to redesign more effective curricula and instructional strategies–a highly doable task.

Helping children learn to read and develop strong reading and language arts skills requires that teachers and other school leaders become knowledgeable and skillful in issues of child, youth, reading, and language arts development across the years of children's schooling experiences. In an introduction to the listing of the fourteen Guiding Principles that support their districtwide elementary and secondary education language arts program, the Dade County Schools describes a series of profound goals for an effective reading and language arts program–one that is successfully serving an extremely diverse student population.

> The English language arts include a knowledge of language, the development of its use as a basic means of communication, and an appreciation of its artistry as expressed in literature. Toward this end, schools should develop richly literate environments in which students become effective users of language, information, and ideas. The language learning process should be a joyful experience in which students develop a variety of strategies to fulfill their educational and personal goals.
>
> An outstanding language arts program reflects critical and creative thinking and a harmonious balance of its several components: reading, writing, speaking, listening, and viewing. Language skills are inseparable from their contexts, from the actual speaking, writing, and reading experiences. The principles guiding the development and support of the language arts/reading program must provide fertile ground in which the program can not only exist, but continuously grow and inspire teachers and students." (Snyder, 1999)

REFERENCES

Braunger, J. (1995). *Tensions to resolve: Improving literacy programs in the context of school reform.* Portland, OR: Northwest Regional Educational Laboratory.

Burns, M.S., Griffin, P., & Snow, C.E. (Eds). (1999). *Starting out right–A guide to promoting children's reading success.* Washington, DC: National Academy Press.

Cawelti, G. (1999) *Portraits of six benchmark schools: Diverse approaches to improving student achievement.* Arlington, VA: Educational Research Service.

Cohen, J. (Ed.). (1999). *Educating minds and hearts–Social emotional learning and the passage into adolescence.* New York: Teachers College Press.

de Villiers, J., Roeper, T., Seymour, H.N., de Villiers, P., Dickey, M.W., & Donahue, M. (1997, Jan;uary 9). An open letter to "Dear Colleagues." Retrieved on 12/2/99 from the World Wide Web: www.tnellen.com/cybereng/nyt/openlet.htm

Egan-Robertson, A. (1998). *Learning about culture, language, and power: Understanding relationships among personhood, literacy practices, and intertextuality.* Madison, WI: National Research Center on English Learning and Achivement (CELA), Wisconsin Center for Educational Research.

Fisher, C., & Adler, M.A. (1999). *Early reading programs in high-poverty schools: Emerald elementary beats the odds.* (Report #3-009). Ann Arbor, MI: Center for the Improvement of Early Reading Achievement (CIERA), University of Michigan.

Hart, B., & Risley, T.R. (1995). *Meaningful differences in the everyday experience of young American children.* Baltimore, MD: Paul H. Brookes Publishing Company.

Johnston, P., Woodside-Jiron, H., & Day, J. (2000). *Teaching and learning literate epistemologies.* Albany, NY: National Research Center on English Learning & Achievement (CELA), University at Albany, State University of New York.

Kelly, K. (2000). *Preserving kindergarten in a high-stakes environment.* Harvard Education Letter, Research Online. Retrieved on 4/18/01 from the World Wide Web: *www.edletter.org/past/issues/1999-mj/kindergarten.shtml.*

Langer, J.A. (1999). *Beating the odds: Teaching middle and high school students to read and write well.* Albany, NY: National Research Center on English Learning & Achievement (CELA), University at Albany, State University of New York.

LeMoine, N. (1999). *English for your success–A language development program for African American children grades preK-8.* Maywood, NJ: The Peoples Publishing Group, Inc.

National Association of Early Childhood Specialists in State Departments of Education. (2000). *Still! Unacceptable trends in kindergarten entry and placement, 2000 Revision and Update.* Author. Retrieved on 4/18/01 from the World Wide Web: http//ericps.crc.uiuc.edu/naecs/position/trends2000.html.

National Center for Education Statistics. (November 1997). National Household Education Survey. The elementary school performance and adjustment of children who enter kindergarten late or repeat kindergarten: Findings from national surveys. NCES 98-097, U.S. Department of Education, Office of Educational Research and Improvement.

National Center for Education Statistics. (1999). *NAEP 1998 reading report card.* Washington, DC: U.S. Department of Education, Office of Educational Research and Improvement.

Nurss, J. R. (1987). *Readiness for kindergarten.* ERIC Clearinghouse on Elementary and Early Childhood Education, Urbana, IL. OERI- U.S. Department of Education, Washington, DC.

Pressley, M., Allington, R., Morrow, L., Baker, K., Nelson, E., Wharton-McDonald, R., Block, C.C., Tracey, D., Brooks, G., Cronin, J., & Woo, D. (1998). *The nature of effective first-grade literacy instruction.* (Report Series #11007). Albany, NY: The Center on English Learning & Achievement (CELA), University at Albany, State University of New York.

Shepard, L.A., & Smith, M.L. (1989). *Escalating kindergarten curriculum.* Urbana, IL: ERIC Clearinghouse on Elementary and Early Childhood Education.

Snow, C.E., Burns, M.S., & Griffin, P. (Eds). (1998). *Preventing reading difficulties in young children.* Washington, DC: National Academy Press.

Snyder, S. (1999). *Beating the odds over time: One district's perspective.* Albany, NY: National Center on English Learning & Achievement (CELA), University at Albany, State University of New York.

Taylor, B.M., Pearson, P.D., Clark, K.F. & Walpole, S. (1999). *Beating the odds in teaching all children to read.* (Report #2-006). Ann Arbor, MI: Center for the Improvement of Early Reading Achievement (CIERA), University of Michigan.

U.S. Department of Education. (1999). *Start early, finish strong–How to help every child become a reader.* Washington, DC: Author.

Wilson, E.A. (1999). *Reading at the middle and high school levels: Building active readers across the curriculum* (2nd ed.). Arlington, VA: Educational Research Service.

Workshop on High Schools of the Millennium. (2000). *High schools of the millennium.* Washington, DC: American Youth Policy Forum.

Article 14

AFRICAN AMERICAN CHILDREN AND ALGEBRA FOR ALL

William Tate

IN THE LATEST WAVE OF SCHOOL REFORM, driven by high-stakes standardized tests and school system accountability for results, an *"Algebra for All"* movement has emerged. For years in the United States, algebra has been strongly associated with a set of students designated as college-bound, most of whom are white. This *Algebra for All* movement has placed a new, yet appropriate, burden on schools to provide traditionally underserved poor and minority students with real opportunities to learn in the mathematical sciences and to close the achievement gap between African American students and their White peers. To succeed, the *Algebra for All* movement requires major changes in thinking about school mathematics and in improving the educational infrastructure of schools. The purpose of this chapter is to explore the correlation between algebra and the achievement gap and to discuss the institutional and cultural barriers that must be overcome for the *Algebra for All* movement to succeed.

A key feature of the *Algebra for All* movement is the emphasis on algebraic thinking as an essential theme in the elementary and middle school curriculum. This represents a shift from the basic skills movement of the late 1960s and 1970s, which also focused on elementary and middle schools (NCTM, 1980). The back to basics movement was a product of efforts to achieve educational equality through compensatory education. The back-to-basics discourse called for teaching a core set of rudimentary mathematics objectives–largely procedures and facts–often to the exclusion of more advanced mathematical concepts. Although the basic skills movement influenced much of the U.S. educational system, it arguably had its greatest impact in low-income urban schools populated by significant numbers of African American students (Strickland & Ascher, 1992). The legacy of this movement is that it is credited with improving standardized mathematics test scores for African American students (Secada, 1992). However, few gains have been made in African American standardized test scores since the late 1980s (Jencks & Phillips, 1998). Perhaps the best lesson learned from the Basic Skills movement is that it illustrates that when teachers and administrators understand and support a common goal in mathematics, students will learn the content. The *Algebra for All* vision has shifted what it means to be mathematically literate to a more demanding set of K through 12 standards (NCTM, 2000). The shift is consistent with policy research that examines the relationship between mathematics course-taking patterns and postsecondary opportunities of African American teenagers.

The study *High School and Beyond* by Pelavan and Kane (1990), confirmed that although more White than African American students attend college within four years of high school graduation overall, this difference was eliminated among students who took geometry, the prerequisite for which is algebra. In fact, 80 percent of the African American students in the group that took these math courses attended college. Moreover, even for the students living at poverty level, taking geometry *halved the gap in college attendance.*

Pelavin and Kane's findings are especially significant given the strong relationship between the postsecondary education of African Americans, their economic prospects and their family stability (DaVanzo, 1992; Kujovich, 1987; Margo, 1990; Miller, 1995). Thus it is critical for school systems to create mechanisms and support policies that foster opportunities to take college preparatory courses such as algebra and geometry.

The importance of algebra and other college preparatory mathematics is apparent in other studies of course-taking effects, suggesting that the differences between African American and White students in mathematics achievement in grades 9 through 12 is a product of the different mathematics courses that these students take during secondary school. Hoffer and colleagues (1995) reported that when African American and white students completed the same courses, the differences in average achievement gains from the end of grade 8 to grade 12 were smaller than in other circumstances, and none was statistically significant.

Smith (1996) investigated the effects of early access (eighth grade) to algebra and found that it has an effect beyond increased achievement, and in fact, it may create a kind of sponsored mobility for the student within the school system. In essence, having credit for a year of algebra at the beginning of high school is a credential, regulating access to more advanced coursework in mathematics. Furthermore, having this credential increases both the students' and system actors' expectations about how much mathematics the student will take in high school, providing greater longevity in the college prep track and producing higher achievement as a result.

Given that algebra-based advanced math courses are taught exclusively to students selected for a college track curriculum, most of whom are White, and the evidence that differences in mathematics course taking is a significant factor in the skills, achievement, and college attendance gaps between Blacks and Whites, it is clear that access to algebra is vital to the overall success of African American students. A simple, yet limited, response to these findings is to mandate an algebra course for all students by eighth grade and implement a high-stakes student accountability system designed to assess students' mastery of algebra. These are trademarks of the *Algebra for All* movement that are appearing in many school districts. For example, in Texas, students are required to pass a high school exit examination that includes both algebra and geometry (see Texas Senate Bill 103). Students who fail the examination will not receive high school diplomas. However, mandating algebra without systemic efforts to change the elementary school mathematics program is problematic. Improved African American performance in algebra and algebraic thinking will require deeper changes across grades pre-K through 12.

The remainder of this article is devoted to a discussion of this kind of change effort. First, I will provide a brief summary of two views of algebra–traditional and dynamic. Second, I will describe two factors–cultural and fiscal–that must be addressed if opportunities for African American students to learn algebra are to be realized in the *Algebra for All* movement. My discussion is focused on two exemplary algebra programs–one traditional in content and the other more dynamic. My goal is to provide greater insights to teachers and administrators seeking to design learning opportunities in algebra for African American students.

WORKING DEFINITION OF ALGEBRA

A dangerous myth associated with school algebra and accepted by many educators is that algebra is a subject taught only in grades 7 through 12, when, in reality, algebra is a theme throughout most elementary school curriculum programs. This is more apparent if a working definition of algebra is available for teachers and administrators. The origins of all of algebra and traditional school algebra are rooted in the following:

- The basic number systems–integers and real numbers and those derived from them, such as the rational and complex numbers.
- The arithmetic operations (+, –, x, ÷) on these number systems.
- The linear order and resulting geometric structure defined on the real line. For example, notions of size (whether one number is larger or

smaller than another) and of distance between numbers.

- The study of algebraic equations that arise naturally in these systems.[1]

This working definition of algebra reflects traditional notions about the subject. Curriculum writers often operationalize this definition of algebra or other very similar interpretations of the domain with a central focus on the following topics:

- Algebra is viewed as generalized arithmetic. Here variables represent pattern generalizations.
- Algebra is viewed as the study of solving equations (at this level, linear equations) and translating well-defined problems into equations (with the intent to solve the equations). Here variables are either unknowns or constants.
- Algebra is viewed as the study of functional relationships. (Under this view, a variable is an argument representing the domain value of a function or a parameter representing a number on which other numbers depend).
- Algebra is viewed as the study of structure or properties of numbers and operations.[2]

Absent from our working definition of algebra (derived from traditional notions of algebra) or the aforementioned views of algebra is a more recent perspective on algebraic thinking and reasoning that is linked to a dynamic viewpoint of the subject.

The dynamic view is part of the historical evolution of school algebra. The following quote from a document produced by the National Council of Teachers of Mathematics Algebra Working Group (2000) provides insights into foci recently associated with the construction of school algebra:

> As school algebra evolved over time, the themes used to organize the subject have changed. The "new math" of the 60s was based on structure. This was followed by a "back to basics" movement, based heavily on thinking of algebra as a language. In the 90s, with the emergence of the graphing calculator, the concepts of function and modeling have become points for conceptualizing algebra.

Some curriculum development efforts are more consistent with the dynamic perspective of algebra. The organizing themes of the dynamic view of algebra are listed as follows:

- **Modeling**. Algebraic relations are viewed in terms of the phenomena they model. The goals for modeling include
  - Representing quantity and relationships among quantities
  - Predicting what happens in quantitative settings
  - Controlling, where possible, the outcomes of quantitative processes
  - Extending the applications and establishing the validity of new relationships in the structure of algebra[3]
- **Functions and Relations**. Functions can be expressed in virtually all the representational systems of algebra. Change and variation are important ideas within this theme.
- **Structure**. The study of algebraic structure implies thinking how systems operate; for example, what enabling characteristics of a system allow for operations on fractions or equations to be solved. The key aspect of the study is to build on generalized arithmetic to formulate and manipulate general statements about numbers.
- **Language and Representation**. Algebra is viewed as the study of language with "dialects" of literal symbols, graphs, tables, words, and other visual displays. Different representations express and reconfigure quantities in a wide variety of situations.

For purposes of clarity, I will reference any curricular programs described in the remaining discussion with the labels "traditional view" or "dynamic view" of algebra. This dichotomy provides greater insight into the programmatic goals. However, many curricular features are subtle and have aspects of both the traditional and dynamic view of algebra.

CULTURAL FACTORS IN MATHEMATICS EDUCATION

What type of mathematics pedagogy, curriculum, and assessment practices must an African American student in an urban school negotiate to be successful? Traditionally, mathematics pedagogy has emphasized whole-class lectures, with teachers modeling one strategy for solving a problem and students listening to the explanation. Generally, this is followed by students working alone on a large set of problems from a worksheet or textbook (Fey, 1981; Porter, 1989; Stodolsky, 1988). The intent of this teacher-directed model of instruction is to prepare students to produce correct answers to narrowly defined problems. The curriculum often includes a tracking system, with many African American students being selected to participate in compensatory mathematics programs. The focus of these back-to-basics type programs has been the mastery of low-level computational skills (Strickland & Ascher, 1992). Typically, these programs have portrayed mathematics as disconnected from the learner and void of real social context (LeTendre, 1991). Woodson (1933/1990) described the presentation of abstract and disconnected mathematical facts as a "foreign method" incapable of preparing the African American student for life in the United States.

Today, the foreign method of mathematics education delineated by Woodson erects barriers to equity in school mathematics, such as: (1) persistent tracking, (2) fewer opportunities for African American students to learn from the best-qualified mathematics teachers, (3) less access to technology in school mathematics, and (4) cultural discontinuity between school mathematics and African American student life outside of school (NSB, 1991; Oakes, 1990; Piller, 1991; Stanic, 1991). The first three of these barriers to equity, which can be captured with statistical methods, are considered "acceptable" evidence of unequal conditions within the traditional models of mathematics education. In contrast, the fourth barrier–cultural discontinuity–is more subtle and cannot be objectified with numbers.

Stiff and Harvey (1988) reported that African American students who incorporated discussions of their lives and experiences within mathematics classroom discourse risked being dismissed from the communication process for digressing on and belaboring "extraneous matters." Similarly, Tate (1994), Silver and Nelson (1995), and Glaser and Silver (1994) discuss how a group of African American middle school students who integrated their out-of-school experiences into mathematical problem solving were penalized for not using a White, middle-class perspective. Many scholars have argued that mathematics pedagogy and assessment are more closely aligned with European culture and the experiences of White children (e.g., Anderson, 1990; Apple, 1992; Berlak, 1992; Ernest, 1991; Garcia & Pearson, 1994; Joseph, 1987, Stiff & Harvey, 1988; Tate, 1994). More recently, mathematics textbook publishers have attempted to resolve this problem by including pictures of and historical information about African Americans. This is a progressive move; however, many scholars contend that much more is necessary to connect the pedagogy of mathematics to the thinking and experiences of African American students (Carey, Fennema, Carpenter, & Franke, 1995; Fennema, Franke, Carpenter, & Carey, 1993; Tate, 1994).

Linguistic research also has provided insight into the African American experience in mathematics. Orr (1987) claimed certain differences between Black English Vernacular (BEV) and "standard" English can have an impact on the way a BEV speaker views quantitative relationships. Orr argued that, for a student whose first language is BEV, language is a barrier to mathematics learning. However, Orr's argument has not been universally accepted. Baugh (1994) examined the relationship among African American English (AAE), mathematical logic, and academic learning. He posited that standard English, as a dialect, is more archaic than AAE, but not more logical. Moreover, the development of English has not been guided by tenets of mathematics. Therefore, speakers of AAE should be as capable of logical thought and mathematical cognition as speakers of standard English.

One mathematics program that has directly supported Baugh's thesis, related to African American students in mathematics and algebra in particular, is Project SEED. Project SEED has a long history of improving student performance in mathematics, demonstrated through both educationally and statistically significant achievement gains, and has been replicated across a variety of school settings and diverse student demographic groups with success. In a recent book entitled, *"Show Me the Evidence: Proven and Promising Programs for America's Schools,"* Project SEED is one of six classroom instructional programs recognized nationally as effective and replicable, demonstrating a viability and consistency that is not often seen among K through 12 mathematics programs in the United

States. Project SEED is an enrichment program designed to teach elementary school students, particularly low-income and African American students, abstract and advanced mathematics using the Socratic method of teaching. Project SEED hires and trains mathematicians, scientists, and engineers to teach students algebraic ideas. The mathematical focus is more consistent with the traditional view of algebra. Algebra as generalized arithmetic is a central feature of the program. This view of mathematics is very consistent with traditional assessments of mathematical ability.

Webster and Chadbourn (1992) examined the effect of one semester of Project SEED as part of a longitudinal evaluation study. The evaluation included eleven elementary learning centers in South and West Dallas. The South Dallas Learning Centers consisted of 80 percent African American students, and the West Dallas Learning Centers were mostly Latino. There were a total of 10,890 Project SEED and matched comparison students. The treatment group students were involved in Project SEED for at least one semester between 1982 and 1991. The test scores of the control and experimental groups were equivalent at the beginning of the evaluation. Project SEED students significantly outscored the non-SEED students on mathematics scales. As I noted earlier, there has been extensive evaluation evidence that suggests Project SEED is an effective intervention for African American students in third through eighth grade.

Important Characteristics of Project SEED

1. Employs teachers with equivalent of undergraduate degrees in mathematics
2. Employs rigorous ongoing professional development
3. Includes regular peer visitation to the classrooms of colleagues
4. Solicits continual feedback from students to optimize their opportunities to learn
5. Offers all students a curriculum that goes beyond traditional notions of elementary mathematics, yet reinforces important arithmetic concepts and operations
6. Uses a spiral curriculum model for appropriate repeat investigations of concepts at each grade level
7. Enculturates students into the norms of mathematical engagement, engages students in intellectual struggles over important mathematical ideas and principles

There are features of Project SEED that can serve as lessons for teachers and administrators charged with achieving the "algebra for all" goal. Project SEED assumes that all students can learn algebra from a qualified professional. Thus, the program only employs teachers with the equivalent of an undergraduate degree in mathematics. There is a simple theory undergirding this practice: "You can't teach what you don't know." Thus, Project SEED instructional specialists begin the profession of teaching with greater subject matter knowledge than the typical elementary teacher, and in many cases secondary certified mathematics teachers.

The strong content knowledge of the Project SEED instructional specialist is enhanced by a rigorous ongoing professional development component. Each day of the week, specialists participte in workshops related to both university-level or school mathematics, curriculum development, questioning techniques, or other pedagogical strategies. Part of the program's design includes regular peer visitations to the classrooms of colleagues. Each peer visitation results in a detailed report of the strengths and weaknesses of a classroom episode. Often, the classroom episodes are revisited during daily afternoon debriefings. For example, the specialists conduct dry runs that closely replicate the classroom episodes. During this time, other specialists offer suggestions for handling potentially difficult situations. The situations could involve the appropriate development of questions to illicit students' understanding of mathematical concepts or how to handle a lively group of fourth graders. Every problematic situation is dealt with, and specialists are expected to report back immediately the results of changes in their pedagogical approach.

Project SEED breaks the cultural stereotype that teaching is a private act. Instead, this program has created and established a culture of shared responsibility. In Project SEED teaching is a public act that requires continuous feedback to optimize students' opportunities to learn algebra. In this way, the methods and pedagogical strategies that have proved successful with diverse student groups are transmitted to a new generation of specialists.

Project SEED establishes high expectations by offering all students a mathematics curriculum that exceeds traditional notions of elementary school mathematics, and yet reinforces important arithmetic number concepts and operations. Recent international studies of the U. S. elementary mathematics curriculum have characterized it as "a mile wide and an inch deep." It is a cultural reality that most elementary students in this country receive instruction on a poorly constructed isolated set of mathematical topics. A report on the *Third International Mathematics and Science Study* (TIMMS) stated:

> In the U.S., school mathematics has a long history of fragmenting content and gradually building up central topics. Traditionally, mathematics concepts and skills have been considered difficult in "large pieces." However, when broken into smaller facts and subskills, these smaller pieces are more easily mastered. They can build up and accumulate facts and skills incrementally. In theory, if not always in fact, we occasionally provide experiences designed to integrate these smaller facts and skills into larger concepts and more complex skills. This conventional practice may work for simpler facts and routine skills. It certainly seems less appropriate for more complex, integrated mathematical expectations recommended in current mathematics reform proposals. (Schmidt, McKnight & Raizen, 1997, p. 17)

Project SEED rejects this cultural artifact of U. S. school mathematics practice. Instead, at each grade level the curriculum is carefully crafted to involve students in an in-depth mathematical analysis of a unified body of concepts. The curriculum is presented in a spiral format allowing for repeat investigations of concepts with the goal of connecting them to new ideas and principles. In the third through sixth grades, SEED students are taught algebraic structure through the study of integers and rational numbers, exponentiation and logarithms, summations and limits. In the seventh and eighth grades, these areas of study are continued and extended through the study of the complex number system, analytic geometry, number theory, combinatorics, probability, and other branches of mathematics.

Another important feature of Project SEED is that students are enculturated into the norms of mathematical engagement. Project SEED instruction looks to prepare students for the structured conflict of the mathematics community and develops their confidence to communicate with technical ideas. The very nature of mathematical production involves structured conflict (Ernest, 1991). The mathematics community is governed by stated rules and a more covert value system. Within this community, individuals and groups of mathematicians have a history of struggling over what is accepted knowledge for the discipline (Eves, 1983). Other issues over which conflicts have emerged in the mathematics community include interpretation of data, credit for discovering mathematical relationships, and censorship. Hidden from the typical elementary school student is the role of structured conflict in mathematics. Project SEED represents one exception to this practice. Students are required to provide written "proofs" of their mathematical conjectures. Classmates are taught to use hand signals to agree, partially agree, or disagree with peer conjectures. Students are asked to give answers on their fingers, to chorus respond as a group, or to answer on paper. These techniques serve several purposes. First, this provides a forum for all students to engage in classroom activities. Many students begin participating in the class by using nonverbal or choral responses. These techniques help to develop the confidence of many students to communicate their position within the mathematical debates of the Project SEED classroom. Second, the specialist is able to get important feedback related to student understanding. Third, the strategies are used as classroom management techniques. Finally, the practice of debating the accuracy of mathematical conjectures is consistent with the norms and practices of mathematicians. In essence, Project SEED is not a traditional elementary mathematics class, instead it is a place where students engage in intellectual struggles over important mathematical ideas and principles.

Project SEED represents a cultural shift from typical elementary school mathematics. This shift requires teachers with significant mathematical expertise, high expectations for students and staff, ongoing professional development, a coherent curriculum, and pedagogical techniques that support the establishment of a culture consistent with the practice of mathematics. Real change in the mathematics performance of African American students in elementary school requires a similar cultural shift.

WHICH SCHOOL DISTRICTS CAN AFFORD TO IMPLEMENT ALGEBRA FOR ALL?

Longstanding cultural artifacts of school mathematics such as limited teacher knowledge, lack of curricular focus, and few professional learning opportunities for teachers are compounded by inequitable distribution of revenue and inappropriate investment of resources. The question, "Which school districts can afford to implement the *'Algebra for All'* reform recommendation?" is a critical issue in the equity debate. A 1990 national assessment of eighth grade mathematics programs found a strong relationship between students' economic status and the level of resources provided for their classroom experience. More than 80 percent of teachers in schools with middle to upper-class students received all or most of the materials or resources they requested for instructional purposes. In stark contrast, only 41 percent of teachers in schools with the largest concentrations of poor students received all or most of the instructional materials they requested (ETS, 1991). Furthermore, the students whose teachers reported having limited materials or resources had lower mathematics achievement than those whose teachers indicated their materials or resources were sufficient. The group of students with lower mathematics achievement was disproportionately African American (NCES, 1993).

The call for new mathematics standards represents an epistemological shift in school mathematics from shopkeeper (basic skills) mathematics to technology-driven mathematics (Devaney, 1991; Friske, 1988; Smart, 1987). The fiscal appeal of a basic skills mathematics curriculum is its low cost. However, the technology-based vision of school mathematics may require urban schools to reallocate funds and/or seek additional funding to improve teachers' mathematics qualifications, update instructional materials (e.g., textbooks, science laboratories, and computer facilities), provide summer mathematics programs, and enhance the quality of many other resources (e.g., deteriorating classrooms and buildings) (Entwisle & Alexander, 1992; Kozol, 1991; NCTM, 1980; NCTM, 1989; NCTM, 1991; Tate, 1994).

In my role as a school administrator, I experienced the challenges of implementing a technology-based mathematics program first hand when I considered launching the Carnegie Learning's *Cognitive Tutor Algebra* program in my school district. The program, commended as exemplary by the U.S. Department of Education's Mathematics and Science Expert Panel, is a full-year, first-year algebra course that integrates technology in its instructional design. It is clearly more consistent with the dynamic view of algebra. The following is a description of the program:

The mathematical content of the *Cognitive Tutor Algebra* program is sound and follows the NCTM standards, for instance, by asking students to use variables and functions to model mathematical situations. It also integrates other major strands of mathematics, such as statistics and geometry, with algebra focusing on depth rather than breadth of coverage. The program is built around active learning as evidence by an activity-oriented student text. Many of the problem-solving activities use real-world situations. These problem-solving activities require that students use written and oral communication and technology. The program provides familiarity and practice with problem-solving methods, algebraic notation, algorithms, and geometric representations (U.S. Department of Education, 1999).

Consider the costs associated with the implementation of the *Cognitive Tutor.* The program is driven by a software package that is purchased at a rate of $25,000 per site license. A site license is issued to a specific school building. In my case, we have thirty-five high schools. To outfit each high school with a site license would cost the school district $875,000. The student books are $5.00 a piece. These are disposable and must be purchased yearly. Carnegie Learning's School Care program provides initial teacher preparation (a four- to five-day, centralized trainings course), ongoing updates and upgrades to the software and the printed curriculum materials, and help-desk telephone and e-mail weekday support (another expense if it does not exist). The annual cost of this program is approximately $2,500 per site. To operate efficiently, the

Cognitive Tutor requires up-to-date computers and specific networking capabilities. Moreover, a classroom setting supporting the *Cognitive Tutor* should have a computer for every student in the class. For my district, this is part of the startup cost of operating the learning environment. It is worth noting that should you have the ability to secure the funding for the site license, technical support, books, professional development (that often includes teacher pay), and additional computers; there is another possible hidden cost–wiring. I found that most of our middle and high schools did not have the electrical infrastructure to support this exemplary technology-driven program. As a result of the infrastructure problem, many of the schools can implement the *Cognitive Tutor* with a limited number of students. However, the cost to the district is almost identical to full implementation cost (minus the cost of upgrading the electrical infrastructure). This is a type of hidden cost. Upgrading the electrical infrastructure would require a tax increase and/or be included in bond vote. The other option in times of level budgeting is to take from another program.

Imagine attempting to implement the *Cognitive Tutor* in algebra, geometry, algebra II and pre-calculus. These mathematics subjects exist in the *Cognitive Tutor* environment. To fully take advantage of these tools would require a rethinking of middle and high school as organizations. Furthermore, it is reasonable to assume upper elementary schools being outfitted with similar technology. Ultimately, this kind of technological tool would require significant financial resources.

A pre-K–12 technology-driven algebra program that is consistent with the dynamic view of algebra will require school districts to:

1. Adopt a set of mathematics standards
2. Identify the resources necessary for achieving these standards
3. Formulate a long-term plan for developing an instructional program that incorporates the standards and for allocating the aligned resources
4. Have an implementation plan in place before money is spent
5. Adopt the necessary structural changes to maximize cost-effectiveness

FINAL REMARKS: WHERE IS THE INFRASTRUCTURE?

The *Algebra for All* movement represents a major change in thinking about school mathematics. If all students are to learn algebra, it can no longer be seen as the domain of the mostly white, college-bound students to whom it has been offered exclusively in the past, and the basic skills math curriculum that has left most African American students behind their white peers must be dismantled in favor of a single, all-encompassing algebra-based curriculum. This shift in goals cannot be accomplished without major improvements involving the educational infrastructure. I have intentionally provided you with two examples of exemplary algebra programs from two different paradigmatic views of algebra–Project SEED and the *Cognitive Tutor.* Project SEED represents a cultural shift in thinking about school mathematics for elementary school students. This program stresses high expectations for students and staff, ongoing professional development, and a coherent curriculum focus. In contrast, most elementary schools, especially those serving African American students, lack these basic elements associated with excellence in elementary school mathematics. I submit we have a need for a major cultural revolution in elementary schools if algebra for all is to be achieved. We simply lack the infrastructure to achieve this goal without major organizational changes.

The calls for a more dynamic view of algebra will require significant investments in upgrading the facilities of many school districts. Moreover, this view of algebra also requires investment in the professional development of teachers. The call for a more dynamic view of algebra without careful attention to fiscal support can be illustrated with a simple analogy (Tate, 1995). If drivers are to benefit from a toll road, they must be able to afford the fee. Similarly, those school districts that want to adopt the dynamic view of algebra must be able to afford the implementation costs. Many school districts that are predominantly African American are hampered by local fiscal constraints that may impede this kind of reform. If the dynamic view of algebra represents the future in mathematics education, the question is, "Will African American students experience the world of mathematics based on a toll road principle or based on solid principles of fiscal governance that support the development of basic infrastructure for living in the twenty-first century?"

ENDNOTES

1. This definition is taken from Bass, H. (1997). *Algebra with integrity and reality. The nature and role of algebra in the K-14 curriculum.* Washington, DC: National Research Council.
2. These views of algebra are more fully articulated in Usiskin, Z. (1988). Conceptions of school algebra and uses of variables. In A.F. Coxford (Ed.), *The ideas of algebra, K-12.* Reston, VA: National Council of Teachers of Mathematics.
3. These goals for algebra are discussed in Dossey, J. (1997). Making Algebra Dynamic and Motivating: A National Challenge. *The nature and role of algebra in the K-14 curriculum.* Washington, DC: National Research Council. Perhaps the best example of this perspective is found in the document produced by the Algebra Working Group of the National Council of Teachers of Mathematics entitled, "A Framework for Constructing a Vision of Algebra: A Discussion Document."

REFERENCES

Anderson, S. E. (1990). Worldmath curriculum: Fighting Eurocentrism in mathematics. *Journal of Negro Education, 59,* 348–359.

Apple, M. W. (1992). Do the standards go far enough? Power, policy, and practice in mathematics education. *Journal for Research in Mathematics Education, 23*(5), 412–431.

Bass, H. (1998). Algebra with integrity and reality. *The nature and role of algebra in the K-14 curriculum: Proceedings of a national symposium* (pp. 9–15). Washington, DC: National Academy Press.

Baugh, J. (1994). New and prevailing misconceptions of African American English for logic and mathematics. In E. T. Hollins, J. E. King, & W. C. Hayman (Eds.), *Teaching diverse populations: Formulating a knowledge base* (pp. 191–206). Albany, NY: SUNY.

Berlak, H. (1992). The need for a new science of assessment. In H. Berlak, F. M. Newmann., E. Adams, D. A. Archbald, T. Burgess, J. Raven, & T. A. Romberg (Eds.), *Toward a new science of educational testing and assessment* (pp. 181–206). Albany, NY: State University of New York.

Carey, D. A., Fennema, E., Carpenter, T. P., & Franke, M. L. (1995). Cognitively guided instruction: Equitable classrooms in action. In W. G. Secada, E. Fennema, & L. Byrd (Eds.), *New directions for equity in mathematics education* (pp. 93–125). Cambridge: Cambridge University Press.

DaVanzo, J. (1992). Families, children, poverty, policy. In J. B. Steinberg, D. W. Lyon, & M. E. Vaiana (Eds.), *Urban America: Policy choices for Los Angeles and the nation* (pp. 83–104). Santa Monica, CA: RAND.

Devaney, R. L. (1991). Puttng chaos into the classroom. In M. J. Kenney, (Ed.), *Discrete mathematics across the curriculum, K-12* (pp. 184–194). Reston, VA: National Council of Teachers of Mathematics.

Dossey, J. (1998). Making algebra dynamic and motivating: A national challenge. *The nature and role of algebra in the K-14 curriculum: Proceedings of a national symposium* (pp. 17–22). Washington, DC: National Academy Press.

Educational Testing Service (1991). *The state of inequality: A policy information report.* Princeton, NJ: Author.

Entwisle, D. R., & Alexander, K. L. (1992). Summer setback: Race, poverty, school composition, and mathematics achievement in the first two years of school. *American Sociological Review, 57*(1), 72–84.

Ernest, P. (1991). *The philosophy of mathematics education.* London: Falmer Press.

Eves, H. (1983). *An introduction to the history of mathematics* (5th ed.). New York: Saunders.

Fennema, E., Franke, M. L., Carpenter, T. P., & Carey, D. A. (1993). Using children's mathematical knowledge in instruction. *American Educational Research Journal, 30,* 555–583.

Fey, J. T. (1981). *Mathematics teaching today: Perspectives from three national surveys.* Reston, VA: National Council of Teachers of Mathematics.

Friske, J. S. (1988). Using computer graphing software packages in algebra instruction. In A. F. Coxford (Ed.), *The ideas of algebra, K-12* (pp. 181–184). Reston, VA: National Council of Teachers of Mathematics.

Garcia, G. E., & Pearson, P. D. (1994). Assessment and diversity. In L. Darling-Hammond (Ed.), *Review of research in education* (pp. 337–391). Washington, DC: American Educational Research Association.

Glaser, R., & Silver, E. (1994). Assessment, testing, and instruction: Restrospect and prospect. In L. Darling-Hammond (Ed.), *Review of research in education* (pp. 393–422). Washington, DC: American Educational Research Association.

Greenes, C., & Findell, C. (1999). Developing students' algebraic reasoning abilities. In L.V. Stiff (Ed.),

Developing mathematical reasoning in grades K-12 (pp. 127–137). Reston, VA: National Council of Teachers of Mathematics.

Hoffer, T., Rasinski, K., & Moore, W. (1995). *Social background differences in high school mathematics and science coursetaking and achievement.* Washington, DC: National Center for Educational Statistics.

Jencks, C., & Phillips, M. (1998). *The Black-White test score gap.* Washington, DC: Brookings Institution Press.

Joseph, G. C. (1987). Foundations of Eurocentrism in mathematics. *Race and Class, 28,* 13–28.

Kozol, J. (1991). *Savage inequalities: Children in America's schools.* New York: Crown.

Kujovich, G. (1987). Equal opportunity in higher education and the Black public college: The era of separate but equal. *Minnesota Law Review, 72,* 29–172.

LeTendre, M. J. (1991). The continuing evolution of a federal role in compensatory education. *Educational Evaluation and Policy Analysis, 13,* 328–334.

Margo, M. (1990). *Race and schooling in the South, 1880–1950: An economic history.* Chicago: University of Chicago Press.

Miller, L. S. (1995). *An American imperative: Accelerating minority educational advancement.* New Haven. CT: Yale University Press.

National Center for Education Statistics. (1993). *Youth indicators 1993.* Washington, DC: U.S. Government Printing Office.

National Council of Teachers of Mathematics. (1980). *An agenda for action: Recommendations for school mathematics of the 1980's.* Reston, VA: Author.

National Council of Teachers of Mathematics. (1989). *Curriculum and evaluation standards for school mathematics.* Reston, VA: Author.

National Council of Teachers of Mathematics. (1991). *Professional standards for teaching mathematics.* Reston, VA: Author.

National Council of Teachers of Mathematics (2000). *Principles and standards for school mathematics.* Reston, VA: Author.

National Research Council. (1989). *Everybody counts.* Washington, DC: National Academy of Sciences.

National Science Board (1991). *Science & engineering indicators (NSB 91-1).* Washington DC: U. S. Government Printing Office.

Oakes, J. (1990). Opportunities, achievement, and choice: Women and minority students in science and mathematics. In C. B. Cazden (Ed.), *Review of Research in Education, 16,* 153–222.

Orr, E. W. (1987). *Twice as less: Black English and the performance of Black students in mathematics and science.* New York: W. W. Norton.

Pelavin, S., & Kane, M. (1990). *Changing the odds: Factors increasing access to college.* New York: College Entrance Examination Board.

Piller, C. (1991, September). Separate Realities. *Macworld,* 218–230.

Porter, A. C. (1989). A curriculum out of balance: The case of elementary school mathematics. *Educational Researcher, 18*(5), 9–15.

Schmidt, W., McKnight, C., & Raizen, S. (1997). *A splintered vision: An investigation of U. S. science and mathematics education.* Boston: Kluwer Academic Publishers

Secada, W. G. (1992). Race, ethnicity, social class, language, and achievement in mathematics. In D. A. Grouws (Ed.), Handbook of research on mathematics teaching and learning (pp. 623–660). New York: Macmillan.

Silver, E., & Nelson, B. S. (1995). The QUASAR project: Equity concerns meet mathematics education reform in middle school. In W. G. Secada, E. Fennema, & L. Byrd (Eds.), *New directions for equity in mathematics education* (pp. 9–56). Cambridge: Cambridge University.

Slavin, R., & Fashola, O. (1998). *Show me the evidence: Proven and promising programs for America's schools.* Thousand Oaks, CA: Corwin Press.

Smart, J. R. (1987). Implications of computer graphics applications for teaching geometry. In M. M. Lindquist (Ed.), *Learning and teaching geometry, K-12* (pp. 32–36). Reston, VA: National Council of Teachers of Mathematics.

Smith, J. B. (1996). Does an extra year make any difference? The impact of early access to algebra on long-term gains in mathematics achievement. *Educational Evaluation and Policy Analysis, 18,* 141–153.

Stanic, G. M. A. (1991). Social inequality, cultural discontinuity, and equity in school mathematics. *Peabody Journal of Education, 66,* 57–71.

Stiff, L. V., & Harvey, W. B. (1988). On the education of Black children in mathematics. *Journal of Black Studies, 19,* 190–203.

Stodolsky, S. (1988). *The subject matters: classroom activity in mathematics and social studies.* Chicago: University of Chicago Press.

Strickland, D. S., & Ascher, C. (1992). Low income African-American children and public schooling. In P. W. Jackson (Ed.), *Handbook of research on curriculum* (pp. 609–625). New York: Macmillan.

Tate, W. F. (1994, February). Race, retrenchment, and the reform of school mathematics. *Phi Delta Kappan,* 477–484.

Tate, W. F. (1995). Economics, equity, and the national mathematics assessment: Are we creating a national tollroad? In W. G. Secada, E. Fennema, and L. Byrd (Eds.), *New directions for equity in mathematics education* (pp. 191–206). Cambridge: Cambridge University.

U.S. Department of Education. (1999). *Exemplary & promising mathematics programs.* Washington, DC: Author.

Usiskin, Z. (1988). Conceptions of school algebra and uses of variables. In A. F. Coxford (Ed.), *The ideas of algebra, K-12* (pp. 8–19). Reston, VA: National Council of Teachers of Mathematics.

Webster, W. & Chadbourn, R. (1992). *The evaluation of Project SEED (Technical Report # EPS91-043-2).* Dallas TX: Dallas Public Schools, Department of Evaluation and Planning Services.

Woodson, C. G. (1990). *The mis-education of the Negro* (orginally published in 1933). Trenton, NJ: Africa World Press.

Part III

ACHIEVING RESULTS

If you don't know where you are going, then any road will take you there.
African Proverb

IF EDUCATORS ARE TO BE SUCCESSFUL in assisting African American students to achieve specific academic and developmental goals, then we need to examine what we mean by results. We need to know which schools are supporting high achievement of African American students and, therefore, which policies, programs, and practices are effective for teaching African American students. Educators must have specific ideas about where they want to go if they are to get there. One important reason why most American public schools have failed to close the achievement gap between White students and students from diverse ethnic, cultural, and language backgrounds is that their goal, more often than not, has been simply to raise standardized test scores. The model programs identified by the federal government as "research-based models" have been effective models insofar as they have been able to raise standardized test scores. Very often, however, they have raised test scores but failed to narrow the gap between African American and White students. Many believe that the increased pressures from high-stakes tests and the close alignment of curriculum and tests is narrowing the curriculum, in some cases, to teaching the test. The result can be that higher test scores are being accepted in lieu of children's access to more authentic learning opportunities.

Goals cannot be limited to raising standardized test scores, nor can our goals only focus on closing the achievement gap. After all, we can raise test scores and close the gap in ways that do not improve the academic achievement of African American and other poorly served students. For example, test scores can be raised by narrowing the curriculum to teach the test; the gap can be decreased by a decline in the test scores of White students; or test scores can appear to be increasing and the gap decreasing by eliminating the low test scores of academically neglected students through increased dropout and pushout rates. We also believe that however educators decide to define and measure results, unless one of the primary goals is to close the achievement gap between Black and White students, the gap will not be closed.

To achieve improved results for African American students, we must focus our school change efforts not only on key aspects of whole school improvement but also on individual students, particularly those students who are either not making gains at all or are not making gains fast enough to close the achievement gap within a reasonably short time. This does not mean that we should cancel programs that are currently working for some of our students. It does mean, however, that while we work toward the achievement of uniformly high results for all students, we must be aware that the pathways to high achievement will not be the same for every student. Systematic reform, if it is to succeed, cannot mean one size fits all. The systematic reform movement must not continue to focus on equal access to the same high-quality programs. What constitutes a "high-quality" program for some students may not serve the needs of others.

Accountability, "an obligation or willingness to accept responsibility or to account for one's actions," (*Webster's Tenth Edition*, definition) is an important part of achieving results. Educational leaders must be as willing to claim responsibility for student failure to learn as well as for student success. Accountability must be data driven, with data derived from multiple sources, including standardized test scores, ongoing classroom curriculum-based assessments, grades, teacher and parental observations and reports, and other anecdotal accounts of student development and learning. High-stakes decisions determining such life-altering courses as promotion and graduation must not be based on a single data source. Ongoing analysis of disaggregated student data at the school level–achievement data broken down by student ethnic groups, gender within ethnic groups, English language proficiency, income levels, and enrollment in educational programs, such as special education, talented and gifted, and advanced placement programs–is essential. Ongoing analysis of each student's academic progress is also essential. If a group of students or an individual student is not succeeding, then changes have to be made. A student or a group of students may not be able to learn to read through concentration on a whole language approach alone. For some students, phonetic-based learning strategies may also need to be integrated into the reading program. A student or a group of students may have a problem with a particular teacher or may not be able to concentrate before lunch or at the end of the school day. On the basis of an ongoing analysis of the various categories of disaggregated data, educators and educational leaders must be ready and willing to make adjustments in the curriculum, instructional strategies, class schedules, teacher assignments, or any other relevant aspect of the educational program to gain the results they are seeking for their African American students.

Strong positive relationships among administrators, teachers, parents, and students are key to accomplishing the agreed on results that educators, students, and their families are seeking. When parents are not available to assume their partnership roles, for whatever reason, it becomes even more important for school personnel to work cooperatively to establish caring, supportive, and respectful relationships. This enables students to gain the self-confidence and skills necessary to take responsibility for their own learning. Teacher relationships with African American students should be based on mutual respect developed through an understanding of and appreciation for the student's cultural and individual identity. Teachers and students must both accept responsibility for improving achievement, and this is best accomplished through caring, mutually respectful, and cooperative teacher-student relationships.

Achievement Facts

- The achievement of all students has improved over the past 25–30 years.
- When achievement goes up in all subgroups, African American students must improve at a more accelerated pace in order to close the achievement gap.
- Differences in family income between African American and White families contribute to, but does not fully explain the achievement gap.
- During the 1970's and 1980's, the federal government introduced and continued to fund programs that were designed to reduce poverty and improve educational opportunities for students from diverse ethnic, cultural, and language backgrounds. During this time period, the achievement gap declined.
- Since 1988, the Black/White achievement gap has stayed about the same. The gap appears to widen as a cohort of students moves through school.
- African American students lose more ground during the summer months than their White peers.
- Several states have made gains in their NAEP scores at about twice the rate of other states, including North Carolina, Texas, Michigan, Indiana, and Maryland. In these states, students

from diverse ethnic, cultural, and language backgrounds are improving at rates greater than the national averages. The greatest gains have occurred in states that have:
— the highest per pupil expenditures
— lower pupil-teacher ratios in the lower grades
— greater numbers of children participating in public preschool programs, and
— higher numbers of teachers reporting that they have adequate resources.

- In Connecticut, Texas, Delaware, Rhode Island, and North Carolina students from diverse ethnic, cultural, and language backgrounds are improving at faster rates than similar students in other states involved in the same project. These states:
  — have made considerable effort to improve teacher quality
  — hold schools accountable for progress by subgroups, and
  — focus rigorous initiatives on students needing extra educational support.

- Urban schools and districts with high poverty and large numbers of ethnic, cultural, and language diverse students have succeeded in raising achievement by:
  — designing instruction and assessment around standards, not tests
  — devoting increased time to reading and math instruction
  — investing in high-quality teacher professional development, and
  — involving parents in their school improvement efforts.

Adapted from *It Takes More than Testing: Closing the Achievement Gap*, A Report of the Center on Educational Policy (2001).

In Part III, "Achieving Results," we present a variety of articles that are designed to help educational leaders achieve and measure results. These articles raise and answer the question of how to define and measure results, describe schools that are supporting the high achievement of African American students, and outline the role African American parents must play in achieving results.

In "The Authentic Standards Movement and Its Evil Twin," Scott Thompson compares the pedagogical effects of test-based assessment with the standards movement. Test-based assessment, he tells us, encourages teachers to "teach the test," and this often results in "dumbing down" of the curriculum. An authentic standards-based curriculum, on the other hand, encourages thinking skills. Although Mr. Thompson does not discuss the implications for African American students, per se, he does point out the implications for equity.

In "Redefining Results," from his excellent book, *Results: The Key to Continuous School Improvement* (2nd Ed.) (1999), Mike Schmoker states, "By failing to supplement standardized tests with richer, more meaningful alternatives, we unwittingly invite our communities to use only test scores to judge us. We set ourselves up to be judged by an assessment that few of us believe is adequate." He continues by discussing how rubrics can be used not only to evaluate instruction and performance but also to improve it.

In "The Involvement of African American Families and Communities in Education: Whose Responsibility Is It?" Robert Witherspoon addresses the importance of parental involvement and provides the reader with specific suggestions for what schools and African American parents can do to improve the quality of involvement that parents must have in their children's learning and in their schools.

In addition, Part III includes articles on the programs and practices of successful elementary, middle and high schools that serve African American students. In "High-Achieving Elementary Schools with Large Percentages of Low-Income African American Students: A Review and Critique of the Current Research," Ray Yau not only summarizes the components of successful elementary schools that serve African American students, he discusses examples of particularly successful strategies from individual schools. In "Middle Schools: African American Children at the Crossroads," Nathalie Thandiwe provides the reader with a discussion of both the middle school movement and the developmental issues of adolescents from the perspective of African American students, giving us a better understanding of why middle schools are failing to support the high achievement of African American students and what can be done about it. In "Making

High Schools Work for African American Students," Pat Ortman and Nathalie Thandiwe discuss the situation of African American students in traditional American high schools, including the specific ways in which schools are most clearly failing them. More importantly, Ortman and Thandiwe outline recent practices at a number of high schools that seem to have promise for increasing the achievement of African American students. It is essential to point out that the research on successful schools and programs that these authors have found focuses primarily on schools serving low-income students. Although there are high percentages of African American students in the identified schools and programs, we are at a disadvantage, because we are left not knowing which specific policies, programs, and strategies work best for African American students.

Finally, Vinetta Jones' article, "District-wide Systemic Reform: Equity 2000 Shows Promise in Narrowing Achievement Gaps," provides information about the successful efforts to reform whole school districts. The importance of this work is not only that it is district-wide, but also that it concentrates not only on improving achievement but also on closing the achievement gap.

As each of us struggles to design the best possible educational environments for all of our students, it is essential that we continue to measure our own success in doing so. We need to remain aware that without both disaggregated data and curriculum-based student assessment, we will not know which policies, programs, and strategies are working best for each student and for each group of students. It is our role as educational leaders to continue to evaluate and improve the overall success of our schools and ensure that each individual student's successes and challenges are identified, so that we can address these appropriately. Our future depends on it.

REFERENCE

Center on Education Policy. (2001, April). *It takes more than testing: Closing the achievement gap.* Washington, DC: Author.

Article 15

THE AUTHENTIC STANDARDS MOVEMENT AND ITS EVIL TWIN*

SCOTT THOMPSON

ONE THING THE STANDARDS MOVEMENT will never be accused of is a lack of critical opposition. But for all the fiery rhetoric that critics direct against this powerful, nationwide movement, there is perhaps no greater threat to standards-based reform than much of what is being perpetrated in the name of standards-based reform. The so-called movement–so-called, because it is not truly a single movement but twin movements bearing the same name–has become its own worst enemy.

If giving twins the same name is a recipe for confusion, consider the havoc that gets unleashed when one of them proves to be an "evil twin."[1] In the case of the standards movement, the evil twin is the more visible and powerful of the siblings, and so its authentic namesake is in an increasingly perilous situation. In fact, the problem is even worse: the two are essentially joined at the hip.

So what are these twin movements? First, let's distinguish them by name. I would rename the evil twin "test-based reform" or more specifically "high-stakes, standardized, test-based reform." The sibling, then, is "authentic, standards-based reform." The defining distinction between them is their respective influence on the instructional core of schooling and on equity issues.

When academic progress is judged by a single indicator and when high stakes–such as whether a student is promoted from one grade to the next or is eligible for a diploma–are attached to that single indicator, the common effect is to narrow curriculum and reduce instruction to test "prepping." What gets lost when teachers and students are pressured to make students better test-takers is precisely the rich, high-level teaching and learning that authentic, standards-based reform aims to promote in all classrooms and for all students.

Authentic, standards-based reform is fundamentally concerned with equity. It departs radically from the tracking and sorting carried out by the factory-style school of yore. Instead, it aims to hold high expectations and provide high levels of support for all students, teachers, and educational leaders. Under the evil twin's (per)version of standards and accountability, we see students retained in grade because of a single test score, and we typically see a corresponding increase in dropout rates where such worst practice is in place.[2] Equity then becomes the casualty rather than the fruit of reform. And as Sandra Feldman, president of the American Federation of Teachers, recently observed, "When tests are allowed to become the be-all and end-all, they deform, not reform, education."[3]

In its influence on both the instructional core of schooling and on equity, the evil twin constitutes an inversion of the "real thing." It is a politically

---

*Thompson, S. "The Authentic Standards Movement and Its Evil Twin." *Phi Delta Kappan* (January, 2001), pp. 358–362.

warped variation on what is arguably among this nation's most powerful and promising education reforms. Although the evil twin purports to be standards-based, it actually flies in the face of research-based standards on the appropriate use of testing. Consider, for example, the conclusions of the National Research Council's Committee on Appropriate Test Use, which are being systematically, if not willfully, ignored by many education policy makers, especially at the state level: "An educational decision that will have a major impact on a test taker should not be made solely or automatically on the basis of a single test score."[4]

There are many reasons not to use any single assessment as the basis for assigning high-stakes consequences. Not only does such a practice tend to diminish curriculum and instruction, but most psychometricians will tell you that the assessment has yet to be created with a high enough level of validity and reliability to justify its use as the sole basis for making consequential decisions about the test-taker. This problem is not unique to education. Consider the words of Lt. Gen. Ronald Kadish, director of the Ballistic Missile Defense Organization: "I don't think we should draw conclusions from any one test that are irrevocable. No one test tells you everything you need to know."[5]

Another problem is that tests are frequently misused. Standardized tests designed for national comparisons between students, without reference to a particular school's curriculum or content standards, are, for example, too often used to evaluate teachers and schools. As I have noted elsewhere, that's a bit like trying to use a jigsaw and screw driver to eat a plate of angel hair pasta. The tools are not necessarily bad in themselves, but they are certainly ill-suited to the task.[6]

High-stakes, test-based reform is an approach that is most often driven by state-level mandate, and it suits the political appetite for rapid, quantifiable (hence readily digestible by the public) results.[7] Test-based reform represents a potentially lethal threat to its authentic twin. Whether by design or happenstance, it is effectively sabotaging the authentic standards movement. And not surprisingly, it is unleashing a swelling and intensifying backlash against standards and testing that is taking form legally and politically, as well as through mobilized grassroots opposition.[8]

It is the combination of test-based reform, in the name of standards, and the wholesale backlash that such practice provokes that is placing the authentic standards movement in peril. Not only in the general media, but also in specialized education media, one can see that the war between proponents and opponents of high-stakes testing tends to define the entire standards movement in such a way that its actual nature and potential, which some school districts are beginning to demonstrate, gets buried under an avalanche of rhetoric.

A RATIONALE FOR AUTHENTIC, STANDARDS-BASED REFORM

Too few children in many of our public schools are receiving the quality of education needed for successful life and work in a rapidly changing world. The imperative to provide them with a high-quality education is not so much economic as moral. Given what we know of the lifelong consequences for individuals of educational deprivation–not to mention the broader consequences for society and democracy–providing a high-quality education for all children is quite simply the right thing to do.

We know that some good schools have succeeded in providing a high-quality education to students deemed least likely to succeed: students of color and students in poverty.[9] But in a nation of 50 million schoolchildren, we face an enormous, yet-to-be-met challenge: namely, taking such success to scale. There are various theories of change that aim to address this challenge. The theory of change behind authentic, standards-based reform (again, I'm not talking about test-based reform) is that, if you want to improve student learning across the board, then you need to improve the quality of instructional content and practice across the board. In order to do that, you must fundamentally transform schools and school systems so that their focus, energy, and resources are wholly aimed at the primary goal of improving instruction in order to improve learning and improve student performance as measured by a variety of assessments. In short, it is all about quality.

We know that bureaucratic school systems that focus on monitoring mandated inputs for compliance hold little, if any, promise of creating and sustaining good schools for children across the socioeconomic spectrum. An authentic, standards-based system departs radically from this on inputs to a focus on outcomes or performance. It shifts from a focus on quantity to a focus on quality. It shifts from a concern with organizational doings to a singular, systemwide focus on improving the performance of every student. It shifts from what Richard Elmore calls the "loose coupling" approach to educational governance to a system of governance that is structured around public accountability for educational results.[10]

Loose coupling is an arrangement in which governing authorities in public schools–from school boards down to principals–essentially run political interference so that classroom teachers are shielded from public scrutiny and can pursue their idiosyncratic pedagogical approaches. Under this governing structure, which is pervasive in public schools at this time, you can easily find that second-grade teachers in neighboring classrooms are doing completely different things with their students–in terms of content, instructional practice, and even basic objectives.

A standards-based approach departs from this model in two ways. First, it breaks down teacher isolation and calls for collaboration around a common set of standards so that students, parents, and teachers have a widely shared understanding of common educational goals at various levels of schooling. Second, it responds to the demands for public accountability by assuming a results orientation and making those results public.

These shifts mean that structures, roles, responsibilities, and budgets must be rethought and redesigned to dramatically increase the system's investment in high-quality learning for teachers, for school leaders, and for those in the central office whose job it is to support teachers and school leaders. A school system that is not accountable for providing continuous, high-quality, standards-based professional development for teachers and leaders has no business holding students and their teachers accountable for performance against student learning standards.

The urgency of the need for systemic improvement of public education would be difficult to overstate. Any observer of public education whose eyes are even partially open has discerned various currents that represent a potential threat to our public schools. The number of parents who are home schooling their children is growing significantly, as are the number of states that are fostering charter schools, some of which are operated by for-profit firms. Meanwhile, efforts to secure vouchers–including both private and public schools–are not going away.

Over the next decade or two, it is not difficult to imagine a scenario unfolding in which homeschoolers begin forming cooperatives and the number of students participating in them greatly expands.[11] In this scenario, publicly funded vouchers also take off, and the charter school movement increasingly caters to groups of families with specialized interests. We might then find textbook publishers customizing their wares for the narrow interests of parents whose children are being educated in cooperatives or in independent schools organized around parochial values. Meanwhile, the remaining public school systems would find themselves increasingly segregated and educationally crippled. The common school–as a meeting ground for students from diverse economic, cultural, and racial backgrounds–would be lost, as society itself became ever more fragmented. Such a scenario would represent a serious threat to the health of our democracy.

The real potential of authentic, standards-based reform can be seen most clearly against this disturbing backdrop. We live in a time when both politicians and the general public are demanding educational accountability. Public opinion research shows that, while the public favors public schools over publicly funded vouchers, patience is wearing thin.[12] Public schools must demonstrate their ability to help students across the socioeconomic spectrum achieve high-quality educational results. Majorities of the public and of teachers support the movement toward high standards. But, according to poll results recently released by the American Association of School Administrators, a majority of voters reject the idea that a single test can accurately measure students' educational growth.[13]

Authentic, standards-based reform holds the potential for improving the quality of student performance to meet systemwide standards. It is an approach that is designed to make schools accountable to the communities they are meant to serve and to do so by focusing on high-quality teaching and learning, not on test scores. It is an approach that could stand up to the threat of privatization. It is an approach that aspires to reach a goal this nation has never achieved through its systems of public education: a high-quality education for all students, regardless of socioeconomic background. But authentic, standards-based reform–and arguably public education itself–is seriously threatened when high standards get confused with high-stakes, standardized tests.

A 180-DEGREE INVERSION

Identical twins can be difficult to distinguish solely by surface characteristics. But if one is evil and the other virtuous, their character traits or essential natures will stand in stark contrast. So it is with test-based reform and standards-based reform. On the face of it, they are both about moving from an approach to education that values inputs to an approach that values outputs or results. But a deeper look into the essential natures of these twins reveals that test-based reform is nothing less than a 180-degree inversion of its authentic counterpart. This, I believe, becomes readily apparent when their essential characteristics are considered side by side.

Authentic, standards-based reform involves teachers, parents, and others as active participants in developing and refining common learning standards. Test-based reform uses high-stakes tests, written in secret by expert psychometricians, as single indicators for deciding whether students are promoted or graduate, thereby making the tests the real standards.

Authentic standards describe what all students should be learning at each level (not necessarily at each grade level). Test-based reform makes the scores on standardized tests for students at specific grade levels, in effect, the only meaningful standards.

Under a system of authentic standards, the school system invests heavily in high-quality professional development for teachers and administrators in an effort to support their work in teaching to the standards. Under a system of test-based reform, teachers and principals are pressured in a variety of ways to raise test scores, and students are drilled accordingly.

Under a system of authentic reform, student assessments are aligned with the standards, and students have numerous opportunities to demonstrate that they have met the standards. No single test is used to determine whether a standard has been met. Under test-based reform, a single state or national test is used to determine whether students are promoted to the next grade or are allowed to receive a diploma.

High-quality, individualized support for students is a hallmark of authentic, standards-based reform. Such support is rare in test-based reform efforts. When it is present, it tends to focus on test-taking techniques rather than on teaching and learning.

Authentic, standards-based reform has implications for every person, policy, and practice in a school system because it involves a complete abandonment of the bureaucratic, "seat time" approach to education and replaces it with a system of learning communities dedicated to helping all students reach their intellectual, social, and personal potential. By contrast, test-based reform, through its focus on high-stakes tests, narrows the curriculum to what is included on the tests and reduces instructional practice to test preparation.

A still more profound point of contrast between the two movements emerges when we consider what educational purpose is implicit in each kind of reform. In the case of test-based reform, the purpose of education is raising test scores. In the case of authentic, standards-based reform, the purpose is enabling all students to achieve as much of their creative, intellectual, and social potential as possible. Thus the goal of authentic, standards-based reform is to prepare students to live successfully and contribute actively in their communities.

THE WRONG QUESTION

As opposition to high-stakes testing mounts and as negative consequences pile up, observers and policy makers are beginning to ask, "Are we moving too quickly?"[14] But this is the wrong question, and it represents an extreme misreading of the problem at hand. The problem is not one of pacing, quantity, or timing. It is a problem of replacing a reform aimed at systemically enriching and deepening teaching and learning with a reform aimed at raising test scores, regardless of the impact on the quality of instruction or on the number of students being pushed out of schools and onto the streets. At whatever point a high-stakes, standardized test is imposed as the sole basis for determining student success, that test will replace whatever content and performance standards were previously in place. It's something like a computer virus that erases and replaces everything that was stored on one's hard drive.

We could realize significant progress in public education if the proponents of standards-based reform joined hands with the critics of high-stakes testing and effectively outlawed the use of high-stakes tests as sole indicators of student success. Moreover, such a move need not lead to toothless standards. It is possible to require all students to meet a set of rigorous standards in order to graduate from high school without using a single test as the means of determining whether those standards have been met. We should be interested in students who can produce high-quality work rather than students who have mastered the ability to take standardized tests. It is the former who will be rewarded in their personal and professional lives after graduation, when test-taking skills will no longer be relevant.

A PERSONAL NOTE

I hope my use of the "evil twin" metaphor helps bring some clarity to this time of rampant educational confusion. But I want to be clear about what I don't mean, as well as what I do mean, in using this metaphor. I do not intend to call any individuals "evil." I believe that the tendency to demonize people who hold opposing points of view has a coarsening influence on civil discourse and so is bad for democracy itself. What I refer to as the "evil twin" is a set of actions and the consequences I believe these actions can have and are having on children and on schools. Determining whether such consequences are intended or unintended requires discerning what is at work in the hearts and minds of many people who are crafting and enacting such policies. The human hearts and minds of others, I believe, are simply too complex and too inaccessible to be read as a book.

But I see the metaphor as useful in bringing out how sharp the contrast actually is between the two movements. At the same time, it's important to acknowledge the complexity of the relationship between the authentic, standards-based reform and test-based reform. As I noted above, these twins are often essentially joined at the hip. What I mean by that is that most of the districts that I would point to as exemplars of authentic, standards-based reform are operating within state systems that more or less exemplify test-based reform.

THE THEORY IN ACTION

The task of sorting through the complexities of conflicting policy contexts is daunting, but when it is done, what emerges is evidence of what the authentic twin is already beginning to accomplish in a number of school districts. I would point, for example, to District 2 in New York City, which has posted some exemplary early results in its efforts to institute best practices. This story has been Deanna Burney, and others, and I recommend that readers explore their work.[15] Anthony Alvarado, who was the chief architect of the reform effort in District 2, has since become the chancellor of instruction in San Diego. That district is now moving forward rapidly along the same lines and has developed a unique "blueprint" for intervention and for support of students who are failing to meet standards.

As uneven as some of the early results may be at this stage, I would point to a number of other districts whose experience suggests the potential of standards-based reform: Aurora, Colorado; Clovis, California; Edmonds, Washington; Minneapolis; and the three districts constituting the El Paso Collaborative for Academic Excellence, as well as the Houston Independent School District.[16] And there are certainly others.[17]

For an example of a state accountability system that balances the public's need for individual student and school-level results against the school's need for support and for a genuine measure of autonomy in achieving those results, I would point readers to Rhode Island's SALT (School

Accountability for Learning and Teaching), an accountability program that gathers extensive qualitative as well as quantitative data on school quality for the purpose of supporting continuous, standards-based school improvement.[18] Each school in the state engages in self-study and develops a school improvement plan. Periodically, a team of teachers, parents, and administrators from outside the district spends a full week in the school, reviewing the self-study and other data, shadowing students, visiting classes, and interviewing teachers, parents, and administrators. The results of this external review are written up as a report containing conclusions, recommendations, and commendations. The full report is read to the entire faculty by the chair of the visit on the Monday following the visit.

School districts that are working to fulfill the original promise of standards-based reform can play a vital role in the future of public education. They will be more likely to succeed in this critical task if increasing numbers of states adopt approaches to standards and accountability that look more like Rhode Island's SALT and less like a brawny and aggressive twin–wielding a high-stakes weapon.

ENDNOTES

1. Richard Elmore has observed, "We will get standards-based reform. But what kind is in doubt. Will it be the version that proponents envision or a corrupted and poorly-thought-out evil twin?" See Richard F. Elmore, "Building a New Structure for School Leadership," *American Educator*, Winter 1999–2000, p. 8.
2. See, for example, Maureen Kelleher, "Dropout Rate Climbs as Schools Dump Truants," *Catalyst*, June 1999; and Walter M. Haney, *Supplementary Report on Texas Assessment of Academic Skills Exit Test (TAAS-X)* (Los Angeles: Mexican American Legal Defense and Education Fund, 30 July 1999).
3. Sandra Feldman, "Where We Stand," *Education Week*, 12 July 2000, p. 17.
4. Jay P. Heubert and Robert M. Hauser, eds., *High Stakes: Testing for Tracking, Promotion, and Graduation* (Washington, DC: National Academy Press, 1999), p. 15.
5. Quoted in Elaine Sciolino, "Key Missile Parts Are Left Untested as Booster Fails," *New York Times*, 9 July 2000.
6. Scott Thompson, "Shared Accountability–Shifting from Heavy-Handed to Helping Hands," *Strategies*, May 2000, p. 1.
7. Donald B. Gratz, "High Standards for Whom?" *Phi Delta Kappan*, May 2000, p. 684.
8. See, for example, Lynn Olson, "Worries of a Standards 'Backlash' Grow," *Education Week*, 5 April 2000, p. 1; and Drew Lindsay, "Contest," *Education Week*, 5 April 2000, p. 30. For more information on the growing opposition to test-based reform, see Alfie Kohn, "Fighting the Tests: A Practical Guide to Rescuing Our Schools," pp. 348–57, this *Kappan*.
9. The evidence along these lines is enormous. One good example is a study conducted by the Center for Performance Assessment on what it calls the "90/90/90 Schools." These are schools in which more than 90% of students qualify for a subsidized lunch, more than 90% of students are ethnic minorities, and more than 90% of students still achieved "high academic standards, according to independently conducted tests of academic achievement." The results of this study appear in Douglas B. Reeves, *Accountability in Action* (Denver, Colo.: Advanced Learning Press, 1999), chap. 19. See also "Doing What Works: Improving Big City School Districts," AFT Educational Issues Policy Brief No. 12, Washington, DC, October 2000, pp. 1–12; and Scott Justus et al., *Student Achievement and Reform Trends in 13 Urban Districts* (Washington, DC: The McKenzie Group, May 2000).
10. Richard F. Elmore, "Building a New Structure for School Leadership," *American Educator*, Winter 1999–2000, p. 8.
11. I credit the observations in this paragraph to Phillip Schlechty, who outlined a similar scenario in a keynote speech he delivered to the Panasonic Foundation's Leadership Associates Program in October 1999. He has since written up this scenario in the epilogue to his new book, *Shaking Up the Schoolhouse* (San Francisco: Jossey-Bass, 2001).
12. Jean Johnson, *Assignment Incomplete: The Unfinished Business of Education Reform* (New York: Public Agenda, 1995).
13. Lynn Olson, "Poll Shows Public Concern over Emphasis on Standardized Tests," *Education Week*, 12 July 2000, p. 9.
14. "High-Stakes Testing: Too Much? Too Soon?," *State Education Leader*, Winter 2000, p. 1. See also Chris Pipho, "The Sting of High-Stakes Testing and Accountability," *Phi Delta Kappan*, May 2000, pp. 645–46.
15. Richard F. Elmore with Deanna Burney, *Investing in Teacher Learning: Staff Development and Instructional*

Improvement in Community School District #2, New York City (New York: National Commission on Teaching and America's Future and the Consortium for Policy Research in Education, 1997); Richard F. Elmore and Deanna Burney, "School Variation and Systemic Instructional Improvement in Community School District #2, New York City," unpublished paper prepared for High Performance Learning Communities Project, Learning Research and Development Center, University of Pittsburgh, October 1997; idem, "Continuous Improvement in Community District #2, New York City," unpublished paper prepared for High Performance Learning Communities Project, Learning Research and Development Center, University of Pittsburgh, December 1998; "District 2, NYC: Teacher Learning Comes First," *Strategies*, August 1998, pp. 11-13; and Liz Gewirtzman and Elaine Fink, *Realignment of Policies & Resources* (Chicago: Cross City Campaign for Urban School Reform, 2000).

16. "Aurora, CO: A Long, Bumpy Road," *Strategies*, August 1998, pp. 4–10; "Clovis, CA: Thirty Years and Counting–Sustaining Continuous Improvement," *Strategies*, July 1999, pp. 4–7; "Minneapolis: Aligning Assessments," *Strategies*, August 1998, pp. 13–14; Stephen Fink and Scott Thompson, "Standards and Whole System Change," unpublished paper on standards-based reform in Edmonds, Washington, prepared for Panasonic Foundation, December 1998; M. Susana Navarro and Diana S. Natalicio, "Closing the Achievement Gap in El Paso: A Collaboration for K-16 Renewal," *Phi Delta Kappan*, April 1999, pp. 597–601; "Houston, TX: Aiming High," *Strategies*, May 2000, pp. 3–6; and Rod Paige, "No Simple Answer," *Education Week*, 8 November 2000, p. 48. (*Strategies* can be accessed at http:www.aasa.org/publications/strategies/index.htm.)
17. See, for example, "Doing What Works."
18. "Rhode Island: Accountability = School Improvement," *Strategies*, May 2000, pp. 3–6; and "Coming to Judgment," *Strategies*, May 2000, pp. 7–8.

Article 16

REDEFINING RESULTS*

Mike Schmoker

It is time for a more balanced and pragmatic understanding of "results." This redefinition should demystify what happens in schools–for teachers, parents, and students–who need more meaningful indicators of progress and clear descriptions and examples of the kinds of work we want students to be able to do. Test scores and letter grades by themselves do not give us this kind of information. The current revolution in assessment makes a new definition possible–one that includes but is not limited to standardized tests and other traditional assessments.

BEYOND STANDARDIZED SCORES AND DROPOUT RATES

"Results" should take us beyond the exclusive use of such annual indicators as test scores and dropout rates. If we want these to improve (and who do not?), we need to focus on the short-term results and feedback that tell us how we are doing in reaching short-term subgoals and long-term goals. Such efforts give us more timely information and a more informative "report card" for the communities we serve. School report cards are still hopelessly narrow, containing little information about student achievement (Jaeger, Gorney, & Johnson, 1994) and concealing more than they reveal.

"Results" too often refers to the most limited and remote kind of large-scale, annually assembled data. The problem is that such data do not inform or derive from a teacher's ongoing weekly and monthly efforts. Peters (1987) is *almost* right when he says that "what gets measured gets done" (p. 480). Things get done only if the data we gather can inform and inspire those in a position to make a difference. Information must promote purpose, and the right information must be available to practitioners when they need it.

We must be careful to measure what matters, especially what matters to those who can implement change. We need to analyze not only standardized tests, but also local, teacher-generated assessments; not only annual or summative scores, but also ongoing improvement data; not only progress toward long-term objectives, but also progress toward specific short-term or ad hoc subgoals; not only progress toward academic results, but occasionally toward student behavior goals that are linked to those results. All these should constitute the new model for assessment and results.

As we have seen, Csikszentmihalyi (1990) discovered that people will not work eagerly and imaginatively toward goals they do not regard as their own. When we judge schools solely on the basis of a few annual, one-size-fits-all measures, we risk alienating practitioners. They know that test scores

*From *Results: The Key to Continuous School Improvement (2nd Ed.)* by Mike Schmoker. Alexandria, VA: Association for Supervision and Curriculum Development.

and dropout rates, though important, do not tell the whole story.

ACCOUNTABILITY–WITH A HUMAN FACE

We must make sure that accountability focuses primarily on improvement. The information we collect and analyze should help us to understand and improve instructional processes that help get better results. Our constituents should be informed of our work and progress so that we can all work together more effectively.

We have a ways to go. McDonald (1993) provides a telling illustration. Two parents ask how their 14-year-old is doing in middle school. This is, they discover, not a simple request. They need to consult with each of six teachers, who provide anecdotal evidence and grades–both of which can be inflated or which may reflect varying levels of accuracy. Parents want something reliable and objective. The closest thing to reliability and simplicity is standardized test scores–understanding them is easier than trying to negotiate the mysteries of the current reporting system.

By failing to supplement standardized tests with richer, more meaningful alternatives, we unwittingly invite our communities to use only test scores to judge us. We set ourselves up to be judged by an assessment that few of us believe is adequate. The upshot is this weird dance that includes everything from a constructive attempt to improve test scores to outright denial and manipulation of these scores–like we see in connection with the "Lake Wobegon effect"; all the children in every state were found to be above average. Such machinations are hardly the stuff of purposeful, passionate goal-oriented effort. Without abandoning conventional and standardized measures, we have an opportunity to break this game wide open.

DEMYSTIFYING RESULTS: THE RUBRICS REVOLUTION

One of the most promising developments in assessment is the increased use of rubrics–or scoring guides–with their capacity to provide useful, quantitative data on clear, carefully selected, qualitative criteria. "Rubric" simply means a rule or guide. In education, it's the written criteria–or guide–by which student performance or a product is judged. Wiggins includes simple criteria lists under this term. Educators in the Pomperaug Regional School District (1996) in Middlebury/Southbury, Connecticut, rely heavily on such lists in every area and for a host of assignments. Rubrics can also refer to descriptions of quality, which are assigned a weighted numeric value in ascending or descending order. Figure 16.1 shows a rubric for assessing student writing. Notice how it clearly describes expectations and how the elements for "3" and "4" papers are similar to descriptions of good writing in general. The difference is that the rubric nails the criteria down, making them available to schools, teachers, parents, and students while providing clear direction and focus.

Scoring guides have many benefits. First, they promote good performance by clearly defining that performance and showing that such work is achievable. Second, they provide better feedback than the current system by requiring more precision and clarity about criteria for evaluating student work (O'Neil, 1994). Third, they bring a welcome end to the disheartening experience we have all had: handing in an assignment without really knowing how the teacher will evaluate it and with no idea of whether the teacher will think it is excellent or shoddy.

No one wants to "fly blind." "Optimal experience" is a direct function of a "goal-directed, rule-bound action system that provides clear clues as to how well one is performing" (Csikszentmihalyi 1990, p. 71). Goals, rules, and clues are what rubrics provide by giving the kind of clarity that is essential to both enjoyment and productivity. George Hillocks (1987) found that merely using scales (another word for rubrics) was among the most significant factors that favored improved writing skills, second only to the quality and design of the writing assignment itself. If we want to maximize their impact, we should be disseminating–even displaying–rubrics everywhere: in schools, classrooms, homes–on refrigerators.

Rubrics can easily and quickly be created or adapted for any task or subject area. An excellent source for explaining how is *Assessing Student*

Rubric/Scoring Guide for Assessing Student Writing

A "4" paper fully addresses the prompt and is written in a style appropriate to the genre assessed. It clearly shows an appropriate awareness of audience. The paper "comes alive" by incorporating mood, style, and creative expression. It is well organized, containing sufficient details, examples, descriptions, and insights to engage the reader. The paper displays a strong beginning, a fully developed middle, and an appropriate closure.

A "3" paper addresses the prompt and is written in an appropriate style. It is probably well organized and clearly written but may contain vague or inarticulate language. It shows a sense of audience but may be missing some details and examples. It has incomplete descriptions and fewer insights into characters and topics. The paper may show a weak or inappropriate beginning, middle, or ending.

A "2" paper does not fully address the prompt, which causes the paper to be rambling and disjointed. It shows little awareness of audience. The paper demonstrates an incomplete or inadequate understanding of the appropriate style. Details, facts, examples, or descriptions may be incomplete. The beginning, middle, or ending may be missing.

A "1" paper barely addresses the prompt. Awareness of audience may be missing. The paper demonstrates a lack of understanding for the appropriate style. The general idea may be conveyed, but details, facts, examples, or descriptions are lacking. The beginning, middle, or ending is missing.

Figure 16.1. *Source:* Arizona State Assessment Program, Arizona Department of Education, Phoenix.

Outcomes, by Marzano, Pickering, and McTighe (1993) and Grant Wiggins's materials in *Standards, NOT Standardization* (1993).

PROMOTING LEARNING

As Hillocks (1987) and Csikszentmihalyi (1990) have shown, people work more productively if they have clear targets. Using rubrics to establish such clarity has profound implications for educators. We all work more effectively and purposefully toward what we can see and comprehend, and the rules and clues in rubrics enable both teachers and students to understand and hence more effectively work toward higher levels of quality. The levels of achievement the rubrics represent satisfy the psychological need for progress and improvement at every level–for individuals, schools, and districts. The primary value of rubrics is their capacity to provide clear, useful feedback that can be analyzed to identify areas of strength and weakness at any time, at any level, for any number of audiences–from students to whole communities.

PROMOTING PURPOSE

Rubrics and criteria provide schools with the opportunity to begin marking improvement and identifying areas for analysis, discussion, and corrective action. We have seen how rubrics and criteria for targets such as the following can be easily developed by teams of teachers in a small amount of time:

- The number or percentage of students who can achieve proficiency levels in writing an effective position paper for social studies, English, and science.
- The number or percentage of students who can achieve the most essential proficiencies in math, with submeasures in such areas as written demonstration, computation, and application.
- The number or percentage of students who can achieve proficiency in musical and artistic performance.
- The number or percentage of students who can achieve proficiency in oral presentations (a skill increasingly acknowledged as essential to future success).

In the Glendale Union High School District in Glendale, Arizona, students do quite well on standardized tests. But they also take rubric-scored summative assessments in almost every course. They are evaluated for their ability to write, to demonstrate scientific reasoning, and to exhibit oral presentation skills. The state has never required such tests. Glendale had the good sense to develop a system that captures and quantifies the learning that goes beyond the standardized test. With their home-grown assessment system, they can chart and analyze annual progress data for continuous improvement purposes. And they have compelling, quantitative evidence of learning that arguably subsumes and certainly goes well beyond the information provided in the standardized test.

Such an approach enables educators and communities to set the agenda together, based on a broader and richer array of indicators. Again, the good news is that rubrics are underused as part of systematic, goal-oriented improvement efforts; therefore, to the extent that we systematically implement their use, we can redefine results and move toward a better education for more students almost immediately.

SUBGOALS

The criteria made explicit in rubrics can themselves define the subgoals necessary to attain annual and long-term objectives. The English department at Amphitheater High School developed a common rubric for writing improvement. To promote short-term improvement, teachers focused on introductions and thesis statements as their subgoal. They devised a three-point rubric for introductions to ensure consistency for teachers and students. The team began sharing effective strategies and materials at their regular meetings. Almost immediately, members began to see and chart improvement. Between October and December 1994, the percentage of students who were writing introductions at or above standard rose from 35 to 53 percent. By May 1995, the number increased to 82 percent. That is breakthrough improvement.

ASSESSING SUBJECT-AREA CONTENT

Rubrics can be especially useful for assessing content mastery, and many are available for this type of assessment (see Marzano, Pickering, & McTighe, 1993, pp. 94–95). They encourage what is perhaps the best way of demonstrating such mastery: the essay exam, which can be rubric scored. Essays not only allow students to show knowledge of large amounts of content but also emphasize the *meaning of subject knowledge*, which favors retention. The essay exam should be a part of every teacher's arsenal for teaching and assessing content. Richard Stiggins (1994), an advocate of assessing content knowledge as well as processes and skills, speaks of the "vast untapped potential" of essay assessment (p. 134). As many early twentieth century exams reveal, essays assess mastery the old-fashioned way: They promote the critical, higher-order processing of content as they assess mastery of information. Rubrics can help teachers assess such work.

Of course, objective test data serve a vital (and time-efficient) function, too; grades and scores can provide data that we use to derive better, more engaging and effective ways of helping students master material. Objective test results can reveal important information:

- Concepts or content areas that students are having difficulty mastering.
- Knowledge that students don't find arresting or relevant and hence don't retain.
- The need to connect content to life or to a meaningful context.
- The need for review, discussion, or clarification.

Once we establish common goals, we should be able to conduct item analyses that reveal

- The number of students achieving at or above standard (e.g., above a certain percentage) on tests and quizzes.
- The areas of highest and lowest retention of content.

The stage is then set for substantive teacher collaboration, sharing, and brainstorming for more active and engaging ways to teach content and to creatively use or supplement a textbook. Ironically, discussing and analyzing objective test scores can lead us out of some ponderous and unengaging practices.

SUCCESS FROM RUBRICS

States that use rubrics to assess writing have realized profound improvements. In Maryland, writing rubrics are the heart of a more general improvement effort. The rubrics are sent home to parents and posted in schools and classrooms. Teachers use and adapt them for all disciplines. The result? Over the last decade, Maryland has seen the percentage of students who reach proficiency levels rise from below 47 to above 90 percent, with breakthrough improvements occurring after only one year.

Teachers in the Oak Harbor School District in Washington had an incomplete picture of how well their students were writing. Then they developed a district-wide scoring rubric, which immediately identified deficiencies in every category. The data enabled them to begin systematically addressing the deficiencies. After one year, an outside assessor reported that "remarkable improvements" had occurred and that the new program was a "phenomenal success." The following year those gains were "sustained and improved" (Daniel, 1993, p. 44).

In Colorado's Weld County School District 6, the percentage of students who learned to write at or above standard on the district writing rubric rose dramatically after the rubric was introduced during the 1988-89 school year. Rubrics defined these standards and thus motivated students from all backgrounds to achieve them (Waters, Burger, & Burger, 1995). Under such conditions, what gets measured (and clearly defined) does get done.

Rubrics are becoming increasingly available in all disciplines. But despite some encouraging momentum and growing awareness, teachers do not routinely use them in classrooms. Most districts don't routinely collect and analyze writing or other rubric-based performance data. This absence points up yet another huge opportunity. Rubrics may be the catalyst for generating the kind of frequent, focused, measurable improvement and performance data that effectively address professional priorities, as well as the need for accountability.

DEMYSTIFYING RESULTS WITH EXAMPLES OF EXCELLENCE

Not all parents and children know what quality work looks like or understand the criteria for it, because few schools provide representative, intelligible examples of what they expect students to strive for (Wiggins, 1994b). Parents not only want better information about what their children are learning, they want *more of it* (Jaeger, Gorney, & Johnson, 1994). We have underestimated this interest. As our economy becomes increasingly knowledge based, look for this attention to increase.

The emerging interest in exemplary student work or "anchor papers" is especially fortunate. Such examples of excellence clearly exhibit what we want from students. Models and exemplary samples of student work are themselves goals: the clear, concrete expression of the results we wish children to achieve. When accompanied by descriptive rubrics, exemplary student work defines–and promotes–improvement.

We should begin displaying, publishing, and referring to models of achievement within and between every area of study. Wiggins (1994a) thinks that posting models or exemplars in schools creates an atmosphere that promotes improvement almost by itself, without administrative coercion. Seeing what children have actually done extends our sense of students' true capabilities.

A HISTORIC CONVERGENCE

We are witnessing a historic convergence of developments: We are creating, using, and disseminating rubrics and alternative assessments more; parents want more and better information; and we are beginning to recognize that anchor papers and models make desired results less abstract and thus accelerate the ability to learn.

Norm-referenced, standardized scores have their role, but if we take advantage of the moment, the revolution now occurring will add a new dimension to assessment and reporting. Technology is an emerging partner; we may soon be able to collect, manage, and aggregate data on hand-held computers, which can quickly organize the data to reveal strengths and weaknesses on the skills and proficiencies we choose.

Rubrics are key pieces of this change in assessment, allowing us to redefine what counts in schools. Without compromising the qualitative nature of student performance, rubrics enrich and validate quantitative results, even in areas we once thought unmeasurable. No measurement is ever perfect, but rubrics allow us to evaluate more precisely and accurately areas where quality standards have traditionally been ill-defined. Rubrics represent a shift in thinking about how well or reliably we can gauge and assess such intangibles as quality writing, thought, and application. And because they promote the clarity and collective focus that research tells us is essential to improvement, they inevitably favor better results (Rosenholtz, 1989; Little, 1990).

ARE STANDARDIZED TESTS THE ENEMY?

The objective emphasis of standardized tests does not have to drive schools toward "drill and kill." Research shows that students who attend schools where subject matter is made relevant and interesting are retaining more and will therefore earn higher scores on standardized tests. This finding indicates that these tests are indeed useful, especially when we consider the evidence that an abundance of reading, writing, and authentic math experiences is quite possibly the best way to promote success on these tests (Krashen, 1993; Resnick et al., 1991). Standardized tests can reveal both progress and areas needing improvement. Without derailing alternative efforts to gauge student performances and higher-order skills, standardized tests can help us make comparative assessments on how well our students are learning basic knowledge and skills. Such tests have been found to be an impressive predictor of future student success. Their statistical reliability is well documented (Walberg, Haertel, & Gerlach-Downie, 1994).

Because standardized tests are easy to administer and routinely used, they provide a good "first level of analysis" for people wishing to improve their schools (Bamburg & Medina, 1993, p. 36). In a balanced treatment of such tests' worth, Bamburg and Medina found that when used properly, tests can provide the initial leverage for improvement:

> At the school level, the disaggregation [of standardized test data] refocused the staff's purpose, reaffirmed their beliefs, increased the congruence between what was espoused and practiced, focused the instructional conversation, established data-driven priorities, and helped staff affirm that they do make a difference for all children. (p. 38)

Using these tests, people such as Effective Schools consultant Larry Lezotte have helped numerous schools see and then address inequities in the quality of education they provide (Bullard & Taylor, 1993).

RUBRICS AND TRADITIONAL ASSESSMENTS: THE BEST OF BOTH

Schools known for their relevant and enlightened learning activities have also realized exceptional improvement on standardized tests. It is hard to find a school where children are receiving a quality education but where standardized test scores are low.

- Teachers at Westwood School in Dalton, Georgia, undertook to depart from the restraints of a test-driven curriculum. They started with mathematics, refashioning the curriculum and orchestrating an improvement effort that would ensure greater depth, engagement, and application. After one school year, the spring achievement scores were the highest to date (Livingston, Castle, & Nations, 1989.) Their experience is not unique.
- In an inner-city setting, Resnick and her associates set out to improve student math performance, using "as little school drill material as possible" to teach math with manipulatives and other rich, "reasoning-based" methods. In one year, 1st grade math scores rose from a mean of about the 25th to the 80th percentile. The following year, mean achievement with the experimental group was at the 70th percentile (Resnick

et al., 1991, p. 47).

- The Junior Great Books (JGB) program has a long and celebrated reputation for helping students to read and critically assess quality literature through close reading and discussion–what they call "shared inquiry." Until recently, JGB was just "another staff development program without supporting evidence." Now it has acquired "a strong and diverse body of evidence" that includes significant measurable improvement on several state, norm-referenced and cognitive/critical thinking tests (Criscuola, 1998, p. 14).
- The Coalition of Essential Schools' Central Park East Secondary School in East Harlem, New York, saw gains in test scores when former Director Deborah Meier and her new faculty came in with a philosophy that emphasized interactive teaching methods and learning activities: writing workshops, thematic units, discussion, and inquiry (Schmoker & Wilson, 1993).
- According to Stan Pogrow, "The biggest secret in American education is that at-risk students love to learn and be challenged with very sophisticated tasks" (1990, p. 62). Pogrow's Higher-Order Thinking Skills (HOTS) program, emphasizing complex tasks and Socratic questioning and thinking skills, has helped numerous schools get better results on standardized tests in both reading and math (1988, 1990). At 2,000 school sites in 48 states, the HOTS program has realized, on average, twice the gains of alternative approaches used at those same schools; the program has had three times the gains in reading comprehension. Using this carefully researched, metacognitive approach, fifth graders throughout the Detroit Public Schools gained 16 months in reading and 13 months in math during the 1994–95 school year. Recent implementation at Elvira Elementary School in Tucson, Arizona, was successful by several measures. In one year, standardized scores in reading and math went up 13.5 normal curve equivalents (NCEs), as did writing scores and GPAs, irrespective of socioeconomic status.

Standardized tests, if disaggregated and thoughtfully analyzed, can provide feedback and goal-orientation. By themselves, the tests haven't universally inspired teachers to reach viable goals. They don't sufficiently or frequently enough capture the kind of education we should provide. Unless supplemented by other richer and more precise indicators, they have a limited and possibly an unfortunate influence on instruction and its improvement (Smith, 1991; Haladyna, Nolen, & Haas, 1991).

The real problem, as Wiggins points out, "is not [standardized] tests per se but the failure of classroom teachers . . . to be results focused and data driven"–to use these results wisely and as part of a wider array of assessments (Wiggins, 1994a, pp. 17–18).

Another problem is our failure to report on the results achieved with other assessments–like increased rates of success on literary and social studies essays, science performances, and multistep, open-ended math problems. Why not report these? Why not begin making them a part of the public conversation? Schools must take the initiative here.

We must now move toward a new accountability, a new results-orientation, analogous to the baseball card that Wiggins (1994b) uses to illustrate how we should begin marking progress for ourselves, parents, and communities. Win-loss records (like standard grades) are one thing; a baseball card contains a *variety* of significant, specific results, such as stolen bases, batting averages, runs batted in, walks, and strikeouts. Educationally analogous information should be the new norm for education. Like Wiggins's baseball card, the information we gather should enable us to chart and disseminate a richer variety of results. We can thus proclaim the legitimacy of school or district assessments that measure student performance in many areas:

- Musical and artistic performances.
- Quarterly or semester content essay exams.
- Discussion and listening skills.
- Debate and oral presentation skills.
- Student behavior and responsibility.
- Ability to solve multistep math problems and apply math principles.
- Ability to write effective analytical or persuasive papers in social studies and literature.
- Ability to conduct and write up a scientific experiment.

REDESIGNING REPORT CARDS

If we truly wish to change the way we assess, the report card may be one of the main leverage points. The Key School in Indianapolis provides progress reports for each of Howard Gardner's seven areas of intelligence. The Kyrene School District in Tempe, Arizona, reports student levels of development in three activities not typically assessed on report cards:

- Reads fluently.
- Makes sensible predictions.
- Uses word recognition strategies (i.e., phonics structure and context).

As a parent, I'd *love* to get such information on my daughters' progress. The Tucson Unified School District piloted a similar report card in 25 schools, which provides rubrics for everything from the traditional content areas to student progress in learning to become a "collaborative worker" and a "self-directed learner." Parents, predictably enough, gave the report card good reviews (Glarridge & Whitaker, 1994).

For Bob Marzano and John Kendall, a radically different report card–and grade book–are in order: one that reveals strengths and weaknesses relative to specific, carefully designated standards (1996, pp. 125–172). This new report card is being piloted in several school districts.

Bena Kallick (personal communication 1999) points out that we must not expect to jump from traditional assessments to the exclusive use of alternative assessments overnight. Of course, she's right. The key is to exploit the many opportunities we currently have for improvement within the current framework, while earning the additional opportunities that will come with improvement and success.

REFERENCES

Bamburg, J., & E. Medina. (1993). "Analyzing Student Achievement: Using Standardized Tests as the First Step." In *Assessment: How Do We Know What They Know?* edited by J. Bamburg. Dubuque: Kendall-Hunt.

Bullard, P., & B.O. Taylor. (1993). *Making School Reform Happen.* New York: Allyn and Bacon.

Criscuola, M. (Fall 1998). " Achieving the Summit." *Journal of Staff Development 19*, 4: 14.

Csikszentmihalyi, M. (1990). *Flow: The Psychology of Optimal Experience.* New York: Harper Perennial.

Daniel, L. (1993). "Aligning Curriculum, Instruction and Assessment for a K-12 Writing Program." In J. Bamburg (Ed.) *Assessment: How Do We Know What They Know?* Bamburg. Dubuque: Kendall/Hunt.

Haladyna, T.M., S.B. Nolen, & N. Haas. (June-July 1991). "Raising Standardized Achievement Test Scores and the Origins of Test Score Pollution." *Educational Researcher 20*, 5: 2–7.

Hillocks, G., Jr. (May 1987). "Synthesis of Research on Teaching Writing." *Educational Leadership 44*, 8: 71–82.

Jaeger, R.M., B.E. Gorney, & R.L. Johnson. (October 1994). "The Other Kind of Report Card: When Schools Are Graded." *Educational Leadership 52*, 2: 42–45.

Krashen, S. (1993). *The Power of Reading.* Englewood, Colo.: Libraries Unlimited.

Little, J.W. (Summer 1990). "The Persistence of Privacy: Autonomy and Initiative in Teachers' Professional Relations." *Teachers College Record 91*, 4: 509–536.

Livingston, C., S. Castle, & J. Nations. (April 1989). "Testing and Curriculum Reform: One School's Experience." *Educational Leadership 46*, 7: 23–25.

Marzano, R.J., & J. Kendall. (1996). *A Comprehensive Guide to Designing Standards-Based Districts, Schools, and Classrooms.* Alexandria, VA.: Association for Supervision and Curriculum Development.

Marzano, R.J., D. Pickering, & J. McTighe. (1993). *Assessing Student Outcomes.* Alexandria, Va.: Association for Supervision and Curriculum Development.

McDonald, J.P. (1993) "Planning Backwards from Exhibitions." In J. McDonald, E. Barton, S. Smith, D. Turner, & M. Finney *Graduation by Exhibition: Assessing Genuine Achievement.* Alexandria, VA: Association for Supervision and Curriculum Development.

O'Neil, J. (August 1994). "Making Assessment Meaningful." *ASCD Update 36*, 6:1, 4–5.

Peters, T. (1987). *Thriving on Chaos.* New York: Alfred A. Knopf.

Pogrow, S. (February 1990). "A Socratic Approach to Using Computers with At-Risk Students." *Educational Leadership 47*, 5: 61–66.

Resnick, L.B., V.L. Bill, S.B. Lesgold, & M.N. Leer. (1991). "Thinking in Arithmetic Class." In B. Means, C. Chelemer, & M. Knapp (Eds.) *Teaching Advanced Skills to At-Risk Students.* San Francisco: Jossey-Bass.

Rosenholtz, S. (March 1989). "Workplace Conditions That Affect Teacher Quality and Commitment: Implications for Teacher Induction Programs." *The Elementary School Journal 89, 4*: 421–439.

Schmoker, M.J., & R. Wilson. (1993). *Total Quality Education: Profiles of Schools that Demonstrate the Power of Deming's Management Principles.* Bloomington: Phi

Delta Kappa.

Smith, M. (June-July 1991). "Put to the Test: The Effects of External Testing on Teachers." *Educational Researcher 20*, 5: 8–11.

Stiggins, R.J. (1994). *Student-Centered Classroom Assessment.* New York: Merrill.

Walberg, H. J., G.D. Haertel, & S. Gerlach-Downie. (1994). *Assessment Reform: Challenges and Opportunities.* Bloomington: Phi Delta Kappa.

Waters, T., D. Burger, & S. Burger. (March 1995). "Moving up Before Moving on." *Educational Leadership 52*, 6: 35–40.

Wiggins, G. (1993). *Standards, NOT Standardization.* Center on Learning, Assessment, and School Structure. Geneseo, N.Y.: Greater Insights Productions.

Wiggins, G. (July 1994a). "None of the Above." *The Executive Educator 16*, 7: 14–18.

Wiggins, G. (October 1994b). "Toward Better Report Cards." *Educational Leadership 52*, 2: 28–37.

Article 17

THE INVOLVEMENT OF AFRICAN AMERICAN FAMILIES AND COMMUNITIES IN EDUCATION: WHOSE RESPONSIBILITY IS IT?

ROBERT WITHERSPOON

> The diverse and difficult needs of today's children far outstrip the ability of any one institution to meet them. Yet one of the richest resources for understanding a child's early learning experiences–parents–is quite often the most frequently overlooked.
>
> A Path to Follow: Learning to Listen to Parents
>
> –*Dr. Patricia Edwards*

WITH WIDESPREAD AGREEMENT on the importance of the role of families in the education of students, it is surprising that so little emphasis is focused on increasing the involvement of the African American families. Parent involvement has been found not only to improve student achievement but also to produce significant long-term benefits: better school attendance, reduced dropout rates, decreased delinquency, and lower pregnancy rates. A study of low-income high-achieving African American students found that their parents stressed the value of education for their futures, monitored their academic progress closely, and fostered an internal sense of control and responsibility over academic outcomes (Hrabowski, Maton, & Greif, 1998).

Dr. Theresa Perry, President of the University of Maryland, Baltimore County, through her work with the Center on Families, Communities, Schools and Children's Learning, provides a context for the African American community's struggles to ensure their children's school experiences are rich and meaningful and provide opportunities for them to reach their maximum potential. "For the African American child to succeed in school," Perry tells us, "he or she has to negotiate . . . membership in the Black community as a racially discriminated group, membership in a Black cultural group, and membership in the mainstream society" (Perry, 1993). For this to happen Dr. Perry concluded:

> . . . parents must be willing to make explicit, discuss, and share their knowledge about helping African American children develop social and emotional competencies at different developmental periods. It is important for families, community agencies, institutions, and schools to structure learning such that African American children experience biculturality." (p. 3)

The cultural, social, and personal experiences that African American children bring with them to school must be valued and incorporated into the overall school learning experience. Thus, parents and guardians are a tremendous resource that should not be ignored. Schools and families cannot continue to operate in isolation, blame each other for student failure to learn, allow inequities in resources to exist and academic achievement gaps to persist.

SCHOOL RESPONSIBILITIES

Developing a comprehensive, realistic plan to target African American families is a first step to getting parents involved in their children's education. To begin this process, school leaders must hold forums, small-group discussions, focus groups, and informal conversations within the African American community. Other necessary steps school leaders should take include the following:

- **View parent involvement as a shared responsibility**. Help all school staff to rethink and discuss the involvement of families through staff meetings, staff development, and sharing sessions. Involving families is everyone's responsibility and must be an overall part of the culture and climate of the school.
- **Find "nontraditional" ways to involve parents**. Begin to view the involvement of families from nontraditional perspectives. Given the time restraints on families and schools, it is necessary to rethink about how families are already involved in different ways. Parent involvement in education doesn't mean only "coming in" for meetings, parent-teacher conferences, and discipline meetings. School practices that impede involvement, including the use of written communications from the school, must be examined. For example, schools serving families who are English-language learners and/or with low adult literacy levels may require nonwritten forms of communication and may have to ensure that information is translated into languages that meet the needs of all families. Open two-way communication is the foundation of any outreach effort. Involving families in education in meaningful ways requires that we change our traditional behaviors and think out of our traditional boxes.
- **Work collaboratively with other nonschool organizations**. The impact of other parallel reforms throughout our states and communities requires that school leaders actively collaborate and communicate with other agencies, libraries, businesses, and job training efforts. Efforts to engage families must be comprehensive, serving a variety of family needs, so that we do not resort to placing the blame on the family for children's lack of academic progress.
- **Outreach to Head Start and other early childhood programs**. Parents are more likely to be involved in their children's preschool education because of strong family involvement programs. Head Start does a good job of involving families in the classroom, in decision-making committees, and as volunteers. Parents who participate in Head Start often describe their involvement as empowering, important for building many skills and their self-esteem. As they transition into the elementary schools, the feeling is that the schools don't want their involvement and limit opportunities for meaningful participation in their children's education. Other early care and education programs that nurture and support strong connections to families are Parents as Teachers (PAT) Home Instructional Program for Pre-School Youngsters (HIPPY) and Even Start, a family literacy program.

The involvement of families of color must become a central area of focus for public education. Proper planning, resources to support families in their involvement, and training for families and school staff are all necessary ingredients. Opportunities for family members to strengthen their parenting skills, augment their academic knowledge and skills, and develop leadership and advocacy skills should be a part of any long-range plan. To that end, leadership academies/institutes could be implemented through existing organizations and provide a comprehensive curriculum, jointly developed with parents, that is designed to help families develop and improve skills that would be transferable to home, employment, and life situations. An effort of this magnitude is labor intensive, requires resources, and a sustained long-term commitment. It also requires the support of strong visionary school and community leaders and a variety of partners.

Ten Truths of Parent Involvement

- All parents have hopes and goals for their children. They differ in the ways they support their children's efforts to achieve those goals.
- The home is one of several spheres that simultaneously influence a child.
- The school must work with the other spheres for the children's benefit and must not push them apart.
- The parent is the chief contributor to a child's education. Schools can either co-opt the parent's role or recognize the parent's potential.
- Parent involvement must be a legitimate element of education.
- Parent involvement is a process, not a program of activities. It requires ongoing energy and effort.
- Parent involvement requires a vision, a policy, a framework, and a consensus. (Parent Involvement Center, RMC Research Corporation, 1989)

Developing a comprehensive family involvement initiative targeting families of color requires broad-based outreach to the community. In developing a plan of action, convening representatives from all stakeholder groups is essential. A similar approach was used in the development of the Blueprint for Action by the National Council for the Education of Black Children. The Blueprint, although never implemented on a large scale, serves as a model for bringing everyone together and outlining a strategic plan of action with shared responsibilities for all stakeholders.

THE PRINCIPAL'S ROLE

Successful parent involvement programs have one thing in common–supportive principals who understand and foster the need for strong and active participation in their schools by each of the key stakeholders: educators, nonteaching staff, parents, students, and the community. Principals should:

- Set a tone for the school that is positive, friendly, and open–dedicated to helping all children attain their greatest academic and social/emotional potential
- Take time to get to know the community served by the school–the history of community interactions with the school, values and customs, local heroes and leaders, favorite pastimes, child-rearing practices, concerns, aspirations
- Assess school and community perceptions of needs and resources
- Provide formal and informal opportunities for staff, parents, and other community members to get to know each other
- Lead a team of staff, parents, and community members in the design and development of the school's family involvement program. Include students in the secondary grades
- Require, encourage, and support staff members in their efforts to make use of parent involvement as a resource
- Provide high-quality and ongoing staff development opportunities to promote and support meaningful parent involvement
- Provide parent leadership development and training opportunities and parent education on topics of interest to parents and family members
- Appoint staff and parents committed to the broader vision of family involvement to coordinate the school's family involvement efforts
- Establish, encourage, and constantly refine effective, open, two-way communication between the school and the community
- Give parents a voice and authentic shared power in making school management decisions.
- Communicate regularly with all key stakeholders, soliciting their input formally and informally
- Monitor and evaluate progress, revising program activities as necessary
- Acknowledge and reward outstanding efforts by teachers, coordinators, outreach workers, parents, community members, and children

PARENT COORDINATORS

Most school efforts to reach parents are often directed through the use of parent coordinators or liaisons. These growing bodies of staff are often paraprofessionals and work part time. Many often have other responsibilities, such as working in the attendance office or school lunchrooms. Their positions are often funded through federal programs and/or business partnerships. Parent coordinators usually have many schools to support, receive little formal training, have little, if any, support staff, and are often under the supervision of the building principal. Without a strong building leader who understands the value of promoting strong family-school relationships in support of high student achievement, parent coordinators often spend their time getting parents out to meetings and planning a yearly large-scale effort.

THE NEED FOR PARENT AND STAFF DEVELOPMENT

Despite an increasing number of parent education and training programs, there are relatively few efforts primarily targeted to African American families. The most widely known are:

- Effective Black Parenting, designed by the Center For the Improvement of Child Caring based in Studio City, California. The training targets African American parents and family workers and provides a curriculum to enable parents to raise proud and capable children.
- MegaSkills training developed by Dr. Dorothy Rich of The Home and School Institute in Washington, DC. MegaSkills emphasizes eleven key life skills parents must instill in their children to prepare them for school and life.
- The National Black Child Development Institute has also developed a training curriculum targeted to Black parents, *The Spirit of Excellence Power Empowerment Project* (PEP). This curriculum includes three units: Successful Parenting, African American Culture, and My Vision for the Future. Its goal is to help parents assume a leadership role in preparing their children and themselves for a productive future.

Shartrand, Weiss, Kreider, and Lopez (1997), in a major report published by the Harvard Family

Educator's Assumptions

. . . That Hinder Collaboration	. . . That Facilitate Collaboration
Parents who don't attend school events don't care about their children's success in school.	Not all parents can come to school or feel comfortable about it; that doesn't mean they don't care.
Parents who are illiterate, non-English-speaking, or unemployed can't help their children.	All families have strengths and skills they can contribute to their children's school success.
Parents from different ethnic and racial groups don't understand how to help their children.	Parents from different ethnic and racial groups may have alternative and important ways of supporting their children.
It is up to parents to find out what is going on at school.	Schools have a responsibility to reach out to all parents.
Parent involvement is not worth the educator's effort.	Parent involvement pays off in improved student achievement, improved school effectiveness, and increased parent and community support for education.

Adapted from *The "Hard-to-Reach" Parent, Old Challenges, New Insights* (Clark & Dukes, 1996).

Ideas for Overcoming Obstacles to Parent Attendance and Participation in School Activities	
Obstacles	**Possible Solutions**
Inconvenient meeting time	Send home a brief questionnaire asking parents to specify convenient meeting times; provide multiple options for when parents can participate.
Lack of transportation	Arrange car pools and walk pools; provide bus or information about public transportation; arrange for other transportation; take the meeting out into the community; identify other venues in the community for sharing school information.
Lack of childcare	Provide childcare or arrange to car pool children to where a childcare provider is available.
Feelings of personal inadequacy	Arrange informal social events at which parents and staff can become better acquainted Do not discount anything parents say. Acknowledge parental shyness ("We are all initially hesitant to say anything out loud because we think that what we say might not be of interest to the group") but encourage parents to share ideas by keeping the environment respectful. Allow parents to construct solutions to problems and issues.
Inexperienced chairpersons	Conduct training, coach chairpersons; take chairs to observe well-run meetings.
No opportunity to participate at meetings	Ask questions, encourage parents to express their viewpoints; remind staff that they are there in a consulting capacity. Learn cultural customs for participation in public groups to ensure that climate of meeting is inclusive.
Meetings seem to accomplish nothing	Have clear goals and purpose for meeting. Research topic and distribute pertinent information before meeting; close on a positive note. If issue cannot be resolved, research the topic further and present findings at next meeting or by memo; involve other members in getting more information. Make sure meeting topic is of interest and concern to parents. Write "job description" for the group, clearly stating purpose, authority, responsibilities, and communications.
Feeling unwelcome	Brief the staff on ways to put parents at ease (share positive comments about student or compliment parents in some appropriate way). Learn cultural customs that create welcoming environments. Be sincere. Serve refreshments.
Having overwhelming personal problems	Be a good listener. Be sensitive to issues of culture and language. If appropriate, try to help parents resolve their problems. Share information about resources; go a step further and link parents to resources when possible. Arrange time for personal calls or home visits to permit parents to speak openly about their problems.

From *The "Hard-to-Reach" Parent, Old Challenges, New Insights* (Clark & Dukes, 1996).

Research Project called New Skills for *New Schools: Preparing Teachers in Family Involvement*, revealed that teacher certification requirements in most states did not mention family involvement. Not surprisingly, most preservice teacher education programs do not offer adequate training in family involvement for new teachers.

Although studies confirm that educators express positive attitudes toward parent involvement, most school programs and practices do not support those expressed beliefs. Oftentimes, teacher and administrator assumptions about poor students and parents of color stand in the way of educators developing positive, supportive relationships with parents toward the goal of improving the quality and level of their involvement in their children's education (Clark & Decker, 1996).

THE RHETORIC AND THE REALITY

The involvement of parents is riding a crest of popularity, and there seems to be a window of opportunity for increasing the involvement of African American parents in school reform and in support of public education. The rhetoric says we want parents involved; the research supports the rhetoric that the involvement of parents is essential to improving student achievement. It is our beliefs, actions, and practices that don't match our rhetoric. School leaders cannot wait for higher education to change schools of education so that educators are prepared to understand the necessity of and how to work effectively with families from diverse ethnic, cultural, and language backgrounds. Only our genuine actions to truly embrace and support families will make a difference. The National Education Association recently published a series of articles available online and entitled "Priority Schools Resource Guide" (2001). They suggest the following steps be taken to improve family involvement and build effective partnerships with communities and businesses:

IMPROVE FAMILY INVOLVEMENT

- Support public school choice. Inform parents of choices in magnet schools, open enrollment areas, special attendance permits and other options to allow parents' choice in their children's education. Make all schools, schools of choice.
- Make a commitment to families to keep them engaged in their child's progress and take an active role by signing the quarterly learning compacts that set the standards of learning. This compact is a commitment by parents to their child's academic success.
- Create a family-friendly atmosphere in every school.
- Create Parent Centers at each school for parents to have a "place of their own" to meet and confer with each other and the school staff.
- Display signs and symbols of "Welcome to Your School" throughout the school.
- Support and communicate with school site PTO's on issues facing their children.
- Recognize parents for their efforts.
- Inform parents of the curriculum standards for their child's grade and how to use them, along with report cards, to monitor their child's progress.
- Encourage parents to spend 15 minutes a day with their child; reading aloud, listening to them read or discussing homework.
- Encourage parents to keep the television turned off and phone off-limits for two hours a night.
- Encourage parents to assist teachers in class: tutoring, reading to students, sharing experiences, and serving as room parents.
- Encourage parents to become involved in school governance, through the School Site Council and other site-based efforts.
- Encourage parents to provide classroom support at home–by making phone calls for the teacher and preparing materials for class.
- Inform parents of the State's Accountability System and how it impacts their school and their child. Explain how the Accountability System is linked to their critical involvement in the academic progress of their child.
- Encourage parents to serve as translators for other parents and to translate school materials like the school newspaper and other forms of communication from the school.
- Provide parental training on issues:
  - Parenting skills

- English as a Second Language
- Things to Know: Your Local School
- Tips for Student Success
- Family, School, Community Partnerships

- Develop policies to hold parents responsible for student attendance and punctuality.
- Identify and eliminate barriers to family involvement.
- Encourage parents to obtain library cards for their children by the third grade.
- Introduce programs like "family math" to familiarize parents with learning activities and strategies to reinforce school learning at home.
- Establish a "Parent Hotline" or a telephone tree so that families stay in touch with the school. Make sure it is available to all parents, regardless of what language they speak.
- Make all communication (written and oral) with parents and families bilingual; this includes school and district forms, newsletters, and letters from school staff.
- Designate a "family advocate or parent coordinator" at the school site to assist with family involvement activities.

ONGOING SYSTEM OF COMMUNICATION AND OUTREACH

- Identify a cadre of community leaders to build solid ties with parent, community, and religious organizations and to share in the responsibility for outreach to the constituency they represent.
- Mobilize the community to advance quality education and to combat the threats to public education.
- Develop an ongoing system of communication and outreach with parents and the community by building on existing efforts and techniques like:
  - Citizens Organized for Public Service (C.O.P.S.)
  - House meetings
  - Walk for success
  - Door-to-door canvassing
  - House visits
- Develop community training workshops to educate and inform the community about critical local and state school issues (e.g., vouchers, state standards, etc.). The workshop can allow parents to ask questions or request clarification about concepts/issues/programs before consent is given or decisions are to be made.
- Provide translation for non-English-speaking parents and community members at meetings, conferences, and school events.
- Translate big problems into specific, winnable issues.
- Link school issues to broader community issues.
- Implement the NEA Family-School-Community Partnership Program and training:
  - Provide new concepts of partnerships with families and communities in public education.
  - Provide participants with skills and strategies to develop positive relationships between the family, community, and the school.
  - Provide techniques to increase the flow of information to parents and communities.
  - Encourage community members to volunteer in the school at before-and after-school programs, especially those programs implemented to improve student achievement.
  - Encourage community members to serve as mentors to students, providing support and coaching as students begin to think about work, college, and life after high school.
  - Encourage community-based organization, religious congregations, and local business to get to know your neighborhood school, its principal, and school staff.

IDENTIFICATION OF ALLIES AND COALITION BUILDING

- Develop a community-mapping strategy to identify allies and potential allies to broaden the support base for public education.
- Work with existing coalitions to advance public education:
  - Coalition of Public Education
  - Parents for Public Schools
  - Other Coalitions/Task Forces

COMMUNITY POLITICS/ POLITICAL ACTION

- Identify the formal and informal power structures in the community, including the players, their connections and their positions on education issues, especially vouchers.
- Reach out to local politicans/state legislators/ Congress with mailings, briefings, and visits to seek support for public education and the defeat of any voucher legislation. Push for more supportive legislative policy framework around your issues.
- Reach out to African-American and Latino policymakers to build ties and persuade them to become advocates for public education.
- Develop strong ties with other advocacy and community organizations and work on "their" issues, too.
- Support pro-education candidates.
- Participate in statewide legislative activities (e.g., lobby day, hearings, etc.)
- Develop a Parent and Community Guide for pertinent academic issues to inform and educate the community before consent or decisions are made. (NEA, 2001, pp. 5–8)

PARENT RESPONSIBILITIES

Active parent advisory councils bring significant educational, bureaucratic, and political benefits to both educational programs and students. Administrators report that active parents become important political resources at both the state and local levels. As such, African American parents and families can no longer be idle players. They must aggressively organize to ensure that our schools provide the type of education their children and all children deserve.

So often parents believe that the schools are expected to educate and teach their children. We cannot "drop children off" and "pick them up" without asking questions, engaging in dialogue, and finding out what goes on inside the school walls. Parents of color must become more forceful and aggressive in their children's education to ensure that their children are prepared for an increasingly competitive workforce.

The following are issues parents and parent groups must address and overcome if they are going to be recognized as a serious force in the education of children:

- **Turf issues**. Too often parent groups find themselves fighting and competing against each other for recognition in the school. Until parents unite as a body, their efforts will be minimized, groups will be pitted against each other, and a divided parent body will keep other parents from being involved.
- **Connecting with younger parents**. Too often parent organizations are controlled by "veteran" parents. A complaint often heard from younger parents is "they won't let us participate in meaningful ways." We often treat younger parents and parents who may be different the same way we accuse the schools of treating parents.
- **Do the homework necessary to be involved**. Being involved as a parent in today's schools means keeping up with what is going on. Asking questions, forming discussion groups, understanding school reform terms, and continuous reading are all skills parents must use. Consensus building and representing other parents are also essential skills in today's school reform arena. This is a new day and new skills and strategies are necessary.
- **Take advantage of outside training opportunities**. Being an active participant in today's schools requires education and training. Although the school should be responsible for most training and staff development, parents and parent organizations will need to access additional training and information, often not available through the schools. Community-based organizations; federal- and state-supported efforts (e.g., equity assistance centers, educational centers, labs); colleges, universities, technology programs, and libraries are all sources of training and information.

African American parents must mobilize and become active, organized, and informed partners in the education of children. There are numerous examples at the local level. Parents in New York City, Chicago, Illinois, Los Angeles, California, and other communities all have numbers of organized parents involved in education. Community-based organizations and local education foundations often support this involvement.

The Task Force on Minority Achievement (1999) convened by the College Board in an effort to reduce the Black-White achievement gap, recommended the following:

- *"Leaders of national and local minority organizations and minority parents should become much more vocal advocates for increasing the number of African American, Latino, and Native American students who enjoy very high levels of educational success"* (p. 34). In addition to their advocacy for more access to high-quality elementary and secondary school curriculum and teaching and for higher enrollment in colleges and universities, parents should press for growth in the number of underrepresented minority students who are superior performers in school at all levels of the educational system.
- *"Leaders of respected national minority organizations should build or strengthen their capacity to provide information on successful educational strategies for raising the achievement of Black, Hispanic, and Native American students"* (p. 34). As the number of proven higher education, elementary and secondary education, and supplementary education strategies grows, national and local minority organizations and minority parents will need access to these findings from trusted sources as they pursue advocacy work with policymakers and educators. Minority community organizations and parents also will need this information to provide more effective supplementary education for their children.

Advocacy in the Next Millennium: The "Black Think Tank" Symposium, convened by journalist, Tavis Smiley, preceding the Democratic National Convention in August of 2000, recommended the following in relation to the education of African American children:

- Stop buying tennis shoes for our children and buy a computer.
- Start Saturday schools to supplement "formal" education.
- Demand that schools develop academic assembly programs.

FAMILY PARTNERSHIP INITIATIVES

Several national family partnership initiatives are currently underway in communities that serve large numbers of children of color. Although these efforts are not specifically targeted to African American families, they do have the potential to increase their involvement in children's education in a substantial way.

The following represents a snapshot of these efforts:

- *Parent Information Resource Centers (PIRCs)* funded by Congress under Goals 2000 of the Educate America Act. The purpose of the program is to assist nonprofit organizations in partnership with local educational agencies in establishing parental information and resource centers. There is one PIRC in each state and U.S. Territory. They are challenged by the U.S. Department of Education to connect parents and schools and to work with Title I families and in low-performing schools.
- *National Education Association (NEA).* The NEA, through its Urban Initiatives component, has supported and engaged its members through the Family-School-Community Partnership, training a national cadre of F-S-C trainers and state-based contacts to assist local affiliates in reaching out to families and schools.
- *The National Parent Teacher Association (PTA),* often viewed as a White middle-class organization, is engaged in an urban initiative in school districts where there are no PTA units. The initial target districts included Boston, Massachusetts; New York City, and Philadelphia, Pennsylvania. Two of these districts have recently undergone leadership changes, which may necessitate the PTA to begin new conversations. These school districts have large numbers of African American students.
- *The National Urban League (NUL)* has embarked on what may be the most comprehensive effort to increase African American

family involvement in education through its Campaign for African American Achievement. The campaign, supported by a $25 million grant from the Lilly Endowment Inc., targets the involvement of families as a key ingredient to boost academic achievement among minority and urban students. Twenty-five NUL affiliates have been selected on a competitive basis as a part of the initiative; other affiliates have also agreed to participate. The Campaign is in the second year of a five-year effort.

For additional efforts to increase the involvement and effectiveness of families of color in public education see the list of organizations and contact names at the end of this article.

The National Coalition of Title I Chapter 1 Parents, a grass roots parent organization, has for more than 25 years, attracted large numbers of African American parents. Title I, the largest federal assistance to state and local school districts, serves more than 50 percent children of color. Parent involvement is a requirement in Title I. The Coalition, founded in 1973 by 50 parents, has a strong network in many urban school districts serving large numbers of African American children. The Coalition's training efforts, supported by the U.S. Department of Education, are often the only national and regional conferences attended by grass roots African American parents in large numbers.

The words of two of our most prominent leaders provide the guidance to chart the course for our work.

"Education is our Passport to the Future; for Tomorrow Belongs to Those Who Prepare for it Today!"

Malcom X

"These are all our children. We will all profit by, or pay for, whatever they become."

James Baldwin

It is time for the African American community to move the education of Black children to its highest priority. No one else can do it for us.

CONCLUSION

The task of meeting the affective and cognitive needs of a diverse group of students is made considerably easier if parents are successfully encouraged to participate in the education of their children, as well as in the educational environment of the school. Principals can play an important role in setting the tone and establishing the policies and procedures that encourage the involvement of all parent groups. In addition, teachers need to reach out and make the parent a partner. Parents also have a responsibility to try to form partnerships with the school and their child's teacher. Building such relationships and remembering that the common goal is the success of the child's education may require perseverance. Although this is not simple, all stakeholders are responsible for building this relationship. Educators and parents together can make the difference between the success or failure of a child's education.

REFERENCES

Clark, R. W., & Decker, L.E. (1996). *The "Hard-to-Reach" parent: Old challenges, new insights.* Boca Raton, FL: L.E. Decker

Hrabowski, F.A., III, Maton, K.I., & Greif, G.L. (1998). *Beating the odds: Raising academically succcessful African American males.* Oxford: Oxford University Press.

National Education Association. (2001). *Priority schools resource guide.* Retrieved on 6/5/2001 from The World Wide Web: www.nea.org/issues/lowperf/priority schools/appendic/

Parent Involvement Center. (1989). Ten truths of parent involvement: A workshop for use in Chapter 1 technical assistance. Portsmouth, NH: RMC Research Corporation.

Perry, T. (1993). *How racial and ethnic family and community characteristics affect children's achievement–The African American experience.* Research and Development Report No. 3. (pp. 1–3). Baltimore, MD: Center on Families, Communities, Schools and Children's Learning.

Shartrand, A.M., Weiss, H.B., Kreider, H.M., & Lopez, E.M. (1997). *New skills for new schools: Preparing teachers in family involvement.* (report for U.S. Department of Education). Boston, MA: Harvard University Family Research Project.

Smiley, T. (Speaker). (2000). *Advocacy in the next millennium.* (Cassette Recording). Washington, D.C.: The Black Think Tank Symposium.

The College Board (1999). *Reaching The Top–A Report of the Task Force on Minority High Achievement* (Report No. 201635) NY, New York: Author.

RESOURCE ORGANIZATIONS

Center for the Improvement of Child Caring
11331 Ventura Boulevard, Suite 103
Studio City, California 91604-3147
818-80-0903
www.ciccparenting.org

Cross City Campaign for Urban School Reform
407 South Dearborn Street, Suite 1500
Chicago, Illinois 60605
312-322-4880

Even Start
U.S. Department of Education
www.cde.ca.gov/iasa/es.html

Goals 2000 State Parent Information Resource Centers
PACC
1-888-385-7222
www.pacc_pirc.net

Head Start
Administration for Children and Families
U.S. Department of Health and Human Services
330 C Street, SW
Washington, DC 20447
202-205-8572
http://www2.acf.dhhs.gov/programs/hsb/

Home Instructional Program for Preschool Youngsters (HIPPY)
www.cahippy.com
National African American Parent Involvement Day (second Monday in February)
1-800-351-4097

National Alliance of Black School Educators (NABSE)
2816 Georgia Avenue, NW
Washington, DC 20001
800-221-2654
www.nabse.org

National Black Child Development Institute
Building Cross-Cultural Partnerships in African American and Latino Communities
1023 15th Street, N.W., Suite 600
Washington, DC 20005
202-387-1281

National Coalition of Title 1/Chapter 1 Parents
National Parent Center
3609 Georgia Ave., NW, lst Floor
Washington, DC 20010
202-291-8100
Fax 202-291-8200

National Council for the Education of Black Children
P.O. Box 2293
Rancho Palos Verdes, CA 90275

National Education Association
Urban Initiatives
Affiliate Capacity Building
1201 16th Street, N.W.
Washington, DC 20036
202-822-7155

National PTA, Urban Initiatives
330 North Wabash Avenue, Suite 2100
Chicago, Illinois 60611
312-670-6782
www.pta.org

National Urban League
The Campaign for African American Achievement
120 Wall Street, New York, NY 10005
212-558-5360
www.wul.org

Parents as Teachers (PAT)
10176 Corporate Square Dr.
St. Louis, MO 63132
314-432-4330
www.patnc.org

The Home & School Institute
1500 Massachusetts Ave., N.W.
Washington, DC 20005
202-466-3633
www.megaskillshsi.org

Article 18

HIGH-ACHIEVING ELEMENTARY SCHOOLS WITH LARGE PERCENTAGES OF LOW-INCOME AFRICAN AMERICAN STUDENTS: A REVIEW AND CRITIQUE OF THE CURRENT RESEARCH

RAY YAU

INTRODUCTION

WHAT PRACTICES IMPROVE the educational achievement of low-income African American students at the elementary school level? This article examines the literature on high-achieving schools for answers. Our survey of the recent research found a number of studies of successful high-poverty public schools, many with large enrollments of African American students. However, none of these studies focused specifically on African American students or examined race and culture as factors separate from poverty. Given the limited research available, we reviewed studies of high-achieving, high-poverty schools in general and focused on the findings related to schools with large proportions of African American students.

The research that we reviewed falls into two general categories: (1) large-scale statistical survey studies and (2) case studies of exemplary schools. Each has its virtues. The survey studies provide a broad sketch of the characteristics that high-achieving, high-poverty schools tend to share. The case studies provide concrete examples of problems that principals face and detail the actions that they take to solve them.

I. STATISTICAL SURVEY STUDIES

Education Trust Study

The most comprehensive survey study of high-achieving, high-poverty schools in recent years is *Dispelling the Myth: High Poverty Schools Exceeding Expectations* (1999), published by the Education Trust. On the basis of their findings, the researchers in this study recommended the following general policies and practices for principals and school administrators to adopt in improving the achievement of their students:

- Use state standards extensively to design curriculum and instruction and to assess student work.
- Increase instructional time in reading and math in order to help students meet standards.
- Devote a larger proportion of funds to support professional development focused on changing instructional practice.
- Implement comprehensive systems to monitor individual student progress and provide extra support to students as soon as it is needed.
- Focus their efforts to involve parents on helping students meet standards.

- Have state or district accountability systems in place that have real consequences for adults in the schools.[1]

All of the schools in the survey met one of two key criteria. They were either (1) among the ten highest performing high-poverty schools on state assessments in reading and/or mathematics (viz: "high performing") or (2) among the ten biggest gaining schools on state assessments in reading and/or mathematics (viz: "most improved"). Most of the schools used standards to guide practices: 80 percent of the principals surveyed reported using standards to guide curriculum and instruction; an even larger percentage, 94 percent, reported that they used standards to assess student progress; and 77 percent reported that their schools had mechanisms in place for teachers to analyze student work against state standards. The statistics also showed a general increase in learning time and student monitoring: 86 percent of the schools reported an increase in the amount of time students spent on reading; 83 percent reported an increase in the amount of time students spent discussing their work with others; and 81 percent reported that they had systems in place for monitoring and assisting students at risk of falling behind in their achievement.[2]

Limitations of Education Trust Study

Although the report by the Education Trust provides a clear overview of the characteristics common to most successful high-poverty schools, we should note that it has significant limitations. The study identifies a number of school characteristics that tend to *correlate* with high student achievement. Unfortunately, its design and focus is too general to locate *substantive causes* beneath the macro level. First, its survey and analysis includes *all* K through 12 schools, so it does not provide insight into factors that may be specific to elementary schools. Second, although it focuses on poverty as a factor, it does not examine race as a specific factor. Therefore, it provides no information about unique characteristics that may be shared by high-achieving schools with large enrollments of African American students. (Indeed, the average enrollment of the schools examined in the study is 60 percent White.)

Council of Great City Schools Study

Another high-profile statistical study is *Closing the Achievement Gaps in Urban Schools: A Survey of Academic Progress and Promising Practices in the Great City Schools–Preliminary Report*, published by the Council of the Great City Schools in October 1999. This study differed from the one by the Education Trust in two important respects. First, as its title indicates, it examined schools that have been effective in *closing the achievement gap* between White students and students of color, as opposed to focusing on the more general issue of improving achievement.[3] Second, it did not examine high-poverty schools or schools with high enrollments of African American students by specific design. Rather, it concentrated on urban schools. However, because urban schools generally have high proportions of low-income African American students, its research focus overlaps with our interests.

Not surprisingly, the recommendations in *Closing the Achievement Gaps in Urban Schools* include those in the Education Trust report. The study concludes that the most common strategies for closing achievement gaps are:

- Extended professional development for staff
- Reduced class size
- Early identification of at-risk students
- Clear expectations for students and staff
- Establishing and reviewing annual achievement goals
- Increased parent involvement
- Extended learning time: longer school day, longer school year, summer school, after-school tutorials, and Saturday enrichment opportunities
- Increased emphasis on reading in early grades
- Additional use of instructional and curriculum specialists
- Increased community partnerships and minority mentoring programs
- Disaggregating and monitoring student achievement data
- Using multiple assessments
- Increased extracurricular activities
- Developing and implementing content and performance standards
- Implementing school-based improvement plan-

ning and accountability[4]

Limitations of the Council of Great City Schools Study

The report by the Council of the Great City Schools on closing the achievement gap in urban schools is also limited in a number of important respects. Most conspicuously, it does not present information on the number and percentage of schools that reported using the strategies listed previously to successfully close achievement gaps between White students and students of color. Thus, it does not provide an empirical basis for those recommendations. Similarly, although the researchers have identified a number of large urban school districts that have been successful in narrowing the achievement gap between White students and students of color, they did not report on any of the underlying policies and practices (viz: causes). Many of the districts that were recognized as "successful" in closing the achievement gap only closed the achievement gap by a point or two over a lengthy period of time; therefore, the achievement gap was essentially *maintained*, despite a technical improvement. Finally, the researchers sometimes seemed too focused on the issue of *closing the achievement gap*, such that the overarching goal of *achievement* was lost in their analysis. For instance, although the report gave credit and recognition to a number of highly deserving school districts that succeeded in raising the achievement of all students at the same time they closed the achievement gap between White students and students of color, it also gave recognition to a few districts that closed the achievement gap merely by effecting a greater *decrease* in the performance of their White students compared with their African American and Latino counterparts (for example, see the statistics for Miami-Dade County).

Nevertheless, the Council for Great City Schools report is valuable for highlighting the importance of focusing research not only on improving student achievement but also on closing the achievement gap. Furthermore, it points to specific schools and school districts that deserve additional study.

Because some of the schools profiled in the Council for Great City Schools report are Texas schools, we should also mention that some recent articles and reports have strongly criticized the Texas Assessment of Academic Skills (TAAS) system of testing. Most notably, a study by RAND, a nonpartisan policy research group, found some large discrepancies between TAAS and NAEP results among the same pools of students, which convey that the widely reported gains in TAAS scores may not be valid indicators of improved learning and achievement. Rather, they suggest a narrow emphasis on teaching students the test.[5]

What Defines a School as "High Achieving"–Problems with Testing

A basic research issue that requires more attention is how, or by what criteria, schools are judged as "high-achieving." Both of the preceding studies recognized schools as "high-achieving" or "most improved" based on average student scores on standardized tests. For lack of other objective criteria, test scores may be the only measures available for gauging the effectiveness of schools in improving student achievement. However, they can be highly misleading. For instance, a test would not be a valid measure of school performance if any of the following held true:

1. Not all students were given the test. (For example, state- and district-wide reading tests which all students are supposed to take are sometimes administered only to native-born, English-speaking students, leaving immigrant and Limited-English-Proficient students out of the mix.)
2. The school has a high dropout rate, such that at-risk students who would have done poorly on the test were eliminated from the testing pool.
3. The test may be too "easy" in that it does not assess the appropriate level of skill or proficiency.
4. . .Students were trained how to perform well on the test, without necessarily being taught the skills and the knowledge that the test is supposed to measure. (For example, a child can be coached to perform well on a multiple-choice test in reading, but that does not necessarily mean that he or she can complete long reading assignments, make meaning of the literature, or convey the meaning of the literature verbally or in writing.)[6]

Given these possible discrepancies and muddying factors, researchers cannot simply accept that any given set of standardized test scores accurately reflects student content knowledge and achievement. They must examine the form and content of the tests, along with the processes by which the tests are administered, and sort out the factors that may distort aggregate test results. Only then can they appropriately make judgments about the performance of schools based on student test scores. Unfortunately, neither of the mentioned studies analyzed or discussed test methods and test administration processes sufficiently.

II. CASE STUDIES

The virtues of large-scale survey studies aside, recommendations based on statistical trends may be helpful in guiding educational policymakers at the national, state, and district levels toward the right actions, but they are by nature not specific enough to provide clear direction to principals and administrators at the school level–who still have the task of choosing specific courses of action among many that may fit the bill. For this purpose, case studies provide helpful guidance.

The case studies selected for review and analysis in this article are of high achieving, high-poverty elementary schools with large enrollments of African American students. The fourteen schools range from 40 percent enrollment of African American students on the low end to 100 percent enrollment of African American students on the high end. The case descriptions of these schools are gathered from five different sources, each assuming different criteria for "high achieving." Six of the schools on the list qualified as "high achieving," because their student achievement in mathematics and reading was higher than the average of all schools in their state (or higher than the 50th percentile if a nationally normed assessment was used); five other schools were deemed "high achieving," because their students had median test scores above the 65th percentile on national academic achievement tests; and each of the remaining three schools had its own separate criteria for "high achieving."

Two of the selected case studies are of Texas schools. Despite the ongoing debate over the validity of the TAAS testing and accountability system, which casts some doubt on the achievement gains claimed by Texas schools overall, we included these particular schools on our list for the following reasons. First, they were located in urban areas and did not have selective admissions policies. Second, the researchers found no evidence that either of the elementary schools exempted students from participation in the assessment program because of language proficiency or disabilities. Third, the high dropout rates in Texas that artificially "improve" average test scores apply only to high schools and not to elementary schools. Fourth, the case studies of these schools convey evidence of strong performance other than increased standardized test scores (i.e., exemplary student attendance rates, strong parent involvement, and other indicators). Fifth, they were selected as subjects for case studies by experienced educational researchers, who looked into a variety of factors other than TAAS scores in making their choices. Although the TAAS accountability system may be deficient in all the ways that its critics claim, that fact alone does not mean that these two *particular* schools are not excellent and high achieving. The preceding reasons combined suggest that the schools are worthy of our attention.[7]

Our selection of these fourteen schools is based on what was available in the literature. For the purposes of this article, we chose to examine the published case studies that provided the most detailed descriptions of successful practices. No doubt, many other schools are also worthy of recognition for their successes. For instance, the Center for Performance Assessment (CPA) in Denver, Colorado has identified thirteen "90-90-90" schools in the Milwaukee Public Schools System, so-called because they met all three of the following criteria: (1) 90 percent or more of the students were eligible for free and reduced lunch, (2) 90 percent or more of the enrollment consisted of students of color, and (3) 90 percent or more of third grade students scored at/above the basic level on the Wisconsin Reading Comprehension Test. CPA also identified thirteen other schools that were very close to meeting the 90-90-90 criteria. Hopefully, case studies of these schools, as well as other successful schools not referenced earlier,[8] will be conducted in the future, so that we can learn the reasons for their success and apply that knowledge toward improving student achievement at other schools.

Because the case studies reviewed for this article are already published and available in their original sources, the task of summarizing them individually is not necessary. For the purposes of this article, we will outline the *key areas* in which high-poverty schools need to excel for students to be successful, as *abstracted* from the case studies, and describe in detail *specific courses of action* taken by principals that yielded positive results in those areas.

Changing School Culture

Common to the performance of all the schools are the following variables: (1) teacher support, dedication, and morale; (2) student attendance, discipline, and morale; (3) effective curriculum, instructional, and assessment practices; (4) sufficient instructional time; (5) efficient management of resources and funds; and (6) parent involvement. Most of the exemplary schools excelled in all of these areas and achieved their success through what has been called "changing school culture" in the literature on school reform. In general, the principals at these schools directed their efforts at building collaborative relationships among their teachers and uniting them toward the common goal of improving student achievement.

However, some of the schools produced high-achieving students despite less than exemplary performance in one or more of these areas, indicating, perhaps, that there is more than one path to the same goal. (For instance, most of the schools achieved their success with strong cooperation between parents and the faculty, but some schools succeeded despite serious disagreements and tensions between parents and the administration. Arguably, the former is preferable.)

Teacher Support, Dedication, and Morale

The principals at each of the schools faced the daunting task of assembling and maintaining a school staff that was dedicated to their students and had sufficient talent and knowledge to teach them well. All the principals conveyed that having a loyal, dedicated, and qualified staff was crucial to the success of their students. This task is invariably hard to achieve. A principal must have a clear understanding of what needs to be done to improve achievement and have tremendous leadership, communication, and other skills in order to convince most–if not all–of the teachers to share his or her vision and to act in concert with it. In some scenarios, it involves providing incentives (or anti-incentives, as the case may be). In more difficult circumstances, it involves replacing staff with those more dedicated and/or more qualified.

To develop and maintain a dedicated and effective teaching staff, principals directed their attention and resources toward the following tasks and subgoals: (1) increasing collaboration with and among the faculty, (2) getting teachers to focus more directly on the needs of students, (3) assigning teachers to their strengths, (4) providing professional development, (5) encouraging teachers to try new approaches, (6) creating a shared sense of responsibility for improvement, (7) making sound hiring decisions, and (8) employing effective motivational techniques.

Increasing Communication and Collaboration with and among the Faculty

Within the case studies, the following strategies were cited as effective practices for principals to improve their relationships with teachers and to increase communication and collaboration among their staff members.

DEVELOPING THE TRUST AND CONFIDENCE OF TEACHERS. To build the trust of teachers, Principal LaWanna Goodwin of Peck Elementary School in Houston, Texas, adopted the following successful strategies:

- Spent a lot of time with staff; visited classrooms regularly
- Affirmed the strengths of teachers and the school in conversation; did not just point out weaknesses
- Asked teachers to convey and share their concerns
- Was honest—did not promise anything she could not deliver[9]

A number of principals reported that they garnered the support and confidence of their faculty by performing efficiently the job of acquiring the materials that the teachers needed to do their job. A teacher at Hawley Elementary in Milwaukee, Wisconsin, offered the following praise and vote of confidence for her principal:

> One thing I can say about my principal, he does not mind spending money for the kids to support good achievement. When they mentioned computers in the classroom, he was all for it. Now we have them in third, fourth, and fifth grade. You don't see that in a lot of schools. Teachers were willing to do what was necessary to become computer literate, too.[10]

At Goodale Elementary in Detroit, Michigan, one teacher expressed how much the faculty felt supported when they received the materials and equipment they needed in a timely fashion:

> It is wonderful to ask for something and get it. If I need something, they [the school leadership] tell me where I can go get it or if they need to order it, how long it will take. Then, it doesn't take until April to get it. Sometimes you don't even have to ask. All of a sudden something will appear. Someone will come to the room and say, "Hey, do you need this?"[11]

INCREASING COMMUNICATION AND COLLABORATION AMONG TEACHERS. In an effort to increase communication and collaboration among her teachers, Principal Goodwin at Peck Elementary reorganized the master schedule to allow teachers to have more time together to plan joint activities. She also provided opportunities for teachers to become resident experts in assigned areas and for teachers to assist in the staff development of their peers. One teacher explained: "Everyone is allowed to select an area of responsibility, which gives each person an opportunity to learn information, to build his or her own skills, and to report to the staff. Everyone feels like a leader."[12]

Similarly, at E. J. Scott Elementary in Houston, Texas, teachers were allowed to decide among themselves what sort of professional development would be most beneficial to their work. Often, the group would assign individual teachers to research effective practices and to train the whole staff. One teacher said: "If there's something good going on out there, some teacher is going to scout it out and bring it back."[13]

At P.S. 161–The Crown School in Brooklyn, New York, Principal Irwin Kurz instituted a peer evaluation system in which teachers working with the same grade level students observe and critique each other to help improve each other's teaching skills.[14]

Focusing on the Needs of Students

To encourage teachers to focus on the needs of students, Principal Goodwin of Peck Elementary continually conveyed in her speeches and conversations that all activities at the school should be focused on what was in the best interests of the students. She backed this declaration with supportive actions that cemented her credibility and, in turn, gained the respect and cooperation of teachers. For example:

> In response to concerns about the safety of students in Head Start classes, she moved the location of these classes to rooms in the main wing of the school building. She made adjustments to the school schedule to better accommodate students.[15]

Similarly, Principal Carter of Burgess Elementary in Atlanta, Georgia, and Principal Batchelor of Goodale Elementary demanded that their teachers focus on the needs of their students first and foremost and continually reinforced that perspective in their words and their actions. Carter inspired a spirit of giving among her teachers toward their students by exhibiting that generosity herself. She gave rewards and incentives–such as pizza parties, skating parties, and greetings in the morning on the intercom–to her teachers and her students throughout the school year. As a result, the entire school staff was generous in providing extra resources to students that they or their families could not afford. (In one instance, a teacher bought reading glasses for a child who was unable to afford them.)[16]

Principal Batchelor consistently assigned lower priority to school issues that did not relate directly to improving instruction and student learning. One of his teachers recounted: "Recently in our site-based management meeting, Mr. Batchelor asked about concerns. One teacher brought up the idea of redoing the parking lot so that we could get in and out without disturbing neighborhood traffic so much . . . Mr. Batchelor acknowledged that as important, but he rerouted our discussion back to issues that directly affect the academic growth of our students. We have to work on what's most important."[17]

Assigning Teachers to Their Strengths

At Peck Elementary, Principal Goodwin spent a lot of time observing her teachers in the classroom and talking to them about their particular interests. As a follow-up, she gave teachers assignments that matched their strengths and interests–which provided a greater opportunity for teachers to succeed in their jobs and increased teacher morale because each teacher was doing the things that he or she was most interested in doing.[18]

Professional Development Opportunities

IN-SERVICE TRAINING. At Peck Elementary, when it was observed that teachers had problems controlling the behavior of students in the classroom, they were given in-service training on how to improve their instructional practices. Taking the idea of in-service training a step further, Principal Liebes of Spellman Elementary in Cheverly, Maryland, hired instructional specialists on staff who served as in-house master teachers. In addition to teaching students, these teachers provided professional development to other teachers in their specific areas of expertise. These included successful teaching strategies in traditional subjects such as math, science, and reading as well as more recently developed areas of instruction, such as performance-based teaching (viz: teaching that focused on helping students perform authentic tasks).[19]

Similarly, Principal Batchelor of Goodale Elementary hired lab teachers who served as in-house professional development trainers in addition to performing their regular teaching duties. Below is a description of their support role to other teachers:

> The lab teachers also did "push-in" lessons, where they went into classrooms and conducted lessons. Most commonly these lessons were to introduce new materials or methodologies to teachers and students; to model a certain instructional technique for a teacher who requested help in that area; or to provide intensive help to students in areas where state assessment scores were low.[20]

As a means of providing in-house staff development, Principal Alyson Barillari of the Fourteenth Avenue School in Newark, New Jersey, regularly assessed her teachers and assigned the more successful teachers the task of training others in their areas of excellence. In reviewing student test scores, she typically asks: "Is there a pattern to the assessment? Did they do poorly in all areas or only in some?" She recommends, "You then identify the teacher with the best results and get *that* teacher to teach the others."[21]

SCHEDULING TO PROVIDE MORE PROFESSIONAL DEVELOPMENT TIME. Although it is important to provide teachers with professional development opportunities, it is equally important for teachers to have the time to take advantage of them–particularly in cases in which the training opportunities are outside the school and require travel. To allow more professional development time for teachers, some schools adopted innovative scheduling practices. A prime example is Hawley Elementary School, which participated in an optional system offered by the Milwaukee School District called "banking." Under this system, students come to school 10 minutes earlier each day and the extra time is "banked" to allow teachers to have five professional development days per year.[22]

RESOURCE LIBRARIES. To encourage teachers to become more knowledgeable about research-based practices and models, a number of schools created teacher resource centers that housed instructional resource materials and provided space for teachers to meet and share teaching strategies.

TEACHER MOTIVATION. In addition to having professional development resources, opportunities, and the time to pursue them, teachers must want to participate and actually take the steps toward improving their skills. In discussing the exemplary case of Goodale Elementary, Juanita Clay-Chambers, Assistant Superintendent of Curriculum Services for the Detroit Public Schools, expressed:

"Goodale teachers do not necessarily have more professional development opportunities than teachers at other schools in Detroit. They have just become more adept at taking advantage of the opportunities offered."[23] The general question of how to get teachers motivated and interested in giving their best efforts and how to maintain that level of energy is perhaps the most crucial issue that principals and school administrators face. The practices described previously provide some guidance on how to accomplish that goal. Following are more successful strategies.

Getting Teachers to Try New Approaches

Getting teachers to try new approaches requires finesse and, sometimes, a certain amount of guile. Below is an enlightening example. An interesting aspect of this case is that the principal clearly wanted the new approach implemented. She did not really want it to be a matter of choice for the teachers, but she presented the approach as if it were their choice. As a result, the teachers *adopted* it by choice ultimately.

To get her teachers to adopt and accept a block scheduling model, which was new for the school, Sherry Liebes, the principal of Spellman Elementary, took the following strategy:[24]

- She asked teachers to *voluntarily* attend a presentation by Robert Lynn Canady, the creator of the model.
- She made sure that there were some "kingpins" on the staff (viz: teachers who had leadership influence over other teachers) who went with her to the first in-service.
- She worked out a plan to implement the model only *after* interest had been generated among the larger staff.
- She labeled the process a "pilot" implementation, so that the teachers would be more apt to try it and give it consideration.

The virtues of this strategy were:

- It was voluntary and gradual, which made the transition relatively seamless.
- The teachers were involved in the decision making and "owned the process"; therefore, they were more likely to work harder toward making it successful.
- It gave time for reluctant teachers to "wait and see."

(Unfortunately, no comparable "bottom-up" examples existed in the literature. This may be because the case studies were written mainly from the perspective of the principal. This issue is discussed further in the conclusion of this article.)

Creating a Shared Sense of Responsibility for Improvement

Similar to Principal Liebes' strategy, Principal Helminiak of Hawley Elementary School solicited the input of his teachers in planning school activities. Furthermore, he encouraged his staff to take their own initiatives in finding ways to implement their ideas.[25]

Principal Butler of Centerville Elementary School also engaged the input of all staff in deciding new policies and practices at the school. She reported the following results: "The staff became more positive and optimistic when they realized that the decisions they made were valued and taken seriously. They were pleased to discover that they played a significant role in changing the direction of the school, and that their participation was crucial in the process. The staff assumed ownership for the school's success and were willing to work hard to achieve positive results."[26]

At Rozelle Elementary in Memphis, Tennessee, Principal Vivian Dillihunt not only solicited the input of her teachers in planning activities, she gave them responsibility for designing and implementing the curriculum, along with control over how the school funds are spent. Furthermore, she invited her staff to participate in the process of interviewing new teaching candidates and weighed their opinions in her hiring decisions.[27]

Building a Talented and Competent Staff

A number of the principals stressed that it was of utmost importance to have a talented and dedicated staff. A few reported that they sometimes *challenged* candidates to ensure that they were hiring the right people. For example, Principal Helminiak expressed the following to a part-time reading resource teacher on his staff who was vying for a full-time position: "If you want to become full-time, it's not up to me, it's up to all of us [viz: the staff at the school]. It's a committee decision. You have to sell yourself. What are you going to do to show them that this school will not be successful if you're not here full-time?"[28]

In tune with Helminiak's perspective, Principal Batchelor of Goodale Elementary expressed that he would rather leave a position vacant than hire someone who could not help him accomplish the school's goals. In his words, his hiring decisions are based ultimately on the following criterion: "I ask myself, 'Would I want my child in that class?' If I cannot answer, 'Yes,' then I will not hire that applicant."[29]

The forcing out of staff, which was often necessary at these schools, is by no means a trivial matter, because it involves the understanding of union issues and legal constraints that vary greatly by jurisdiction–an area of knowledge that a new principal would likely not have if he or she had not worked within the same district.

The task invariably required some "finesse." In describing how Principal Liebes handled situations in which teachers were not cooperating with her improvement plans at Spellman Elementary, one of her teachers explained:

> She was nice, but stern. All she ever really said was "These are the expectations at Gladys Noon Spellman. This is what we do and this is how we teach. If this isn't something you're interested in doing, then let me know and I'll write you a wonderful evaluation and you can help yourself."[30]

Management Styles

The methods and styles by which the principals at the successful school managed their staffs varied greatly. Some of the principals succeeded with a "soft" management style that presupposed and encouraged a spirit of volunteerism among the staff, whereas some adopted a more "autocratic" style of leadership to achieve their success. In some cases, principals shifted from one management style to another in response to the personalities of the people on staff. Such was the case at Burgess Elementary School, where Principal Gwendolyn Carter found that she had to shift from her preferred "persuasive and persistent" management style to a more direct "autocratic" one to achieve her goals. She explained:

> Some of the problem was that teachers didn't want to lead some of the clubs or participate in some of the parent involvement activities. In the school where I came from, people would volunteer, but that wasn't working here. So finally one of the teachers said, "We would prefer if you just give us assignments." They wanted more structure.[31]

In other cases, principals had to adjust from a stern and autocratic management style to a "softer" one to win the support and cooperation of their staff. Ultimately, it was a mode of success for principals to be open-minded and flexible enough to adjust their management styles and practices to the personalities of their staffs–to motivate them to do their best in attending to the needs of students.

Student Attendance, Discipline, and Morale

In addition to providing support and encouragement to teachers, the principals at the high-achieving schools also implemented practices that produced better attendance, greater discipline, and increased self-esteem among the students.

INCREASING ATTENDANCE RATES. In line with various studies showing that increased attendance correlates with improved student achievement,[32] all of the successful schools had excellent student attendance figures (94 percent or better). Following are some of the strategies that principals and teachers used to achieve that goal:

- In response to the fact that many students were arriving at school late on a consistent basis, Principal Goodwin of Peck Elementary adjusted the school schedule so that classes began and ended fifteen minutes after the official time. Parents were appreciative of the school's willingness to accommodate their needs and became more committed to getting their children to school on time. (It also allowed students more time to eat breakfast provided by the school, which the chronically late students often missed.)[33]
- At Woodson Elementary school in Baltimore, Maryland, students were given rewards for good attendance–every four to six weeks, children with perfect attendance over a specified period

of time were treated to a special event, such as a trip to the movies or to the bowling alley.[34]

- At several schools, classes with perfect attendance the preceding day were noted in the daily announcements and children with perfect attendance were identified in school newsletters and bulletin boards.
- At many schools, the attendance monitor or office secretary would call the parents of students who were absent each day. In some cases, home visits were made to parents who could not be reached by phone.

DISCIPLINARY PRACTICES. To encourage and maintain good student behavior at their schools, principals were compelled to institute policies that were firm but also respectful of students, so that they would not rebel against the rules. The case studies provided the following examples of effective practices:

- To reduce physical conflicts between students at Peck Elementary, Principal Goodwin instituted the rule that students walk with their arms folded when they traveled between classes. Also, she made students wear uniforms (red shirts and blue pants). To counterbalance the strictness of these rules, instead of punishing students who were chronically late in arriving at school in the morning, she made adjustments to the school schedule to accommodate them (as discussed above).[35]
- Another practice at Peck Elementary was a merit system that allowed students to earn various positions of responsibility in the classroom based on their behavior.[36]
- At Hawley Elementary School, Principal Helminiak instituted a strict discipline plan at the beginning of his tenure to address the behavioral problems that existed at the time, but has gradually shifted to a lighter approach, as student self-responsibility and relationships between students and staff have improved over time. In his words, "That strict discipline only works so long, then the kids say, 'I've had enough.'" He has subsequently adopted a program titled "Prevention Is Kid Stuff," offered by the Milwaukee Drug and Alcohol council. In this program, students at the school meet with a social worker to devise ten basic school discipline rules that are upheld at the school, and they reconvene each year to update the rules. In this manner, the students have ownership of their own discipline process.[37]
- At Spellman Elementary, a particular banner was hoisted whenever the school achieved a fight-free day–to celebrate and take pride in the accomplishment.[38]
- At Burgess Elementary, teachers give students the opportunity and time to talk privately with them about their emotional stresses and anxiety, as a way of reassuring them of their support so that they are less likely to seek conflict as a means of expressing their frustrations. Principal Carter explained: "Some schools don't want to deal with that [emotional needs] because it is very time-consuming. But you have to deal with that. If a child comes needing to talk, you have to deal with that before you can teach."[39]
- At Goodale Elementary, students are rarely suspended as a disciplinary measure. Instead, they take part in peer mediation programs and solve conflicts among themselves. The teachers at the school are given training on how to train students to resolve conflicts among their peers.[40]
- At James Madison Elementary School in Pittsburgh, Pennsylvania, Principal Vivian Williams collaborates with the teachers on serious discipline problems, so that teachers are not left to deal with unruly students on their own.[41]

STUDENT MORALE, SELF-ESTEEM, AND HIGH EXPECTATIONS. The following practices were used to improve student morale and self-esteem:

- At Burgess Elementary, student work was put on display and the displays were changed frequently–so that all students have a chance for their work to be publicized and are encouraged to do their best.[42]
- At P.S. 161–The Crown School, kindergarten students who could read and older students who wrote five book reports per year were awarded certificates, which were displayed on walls, and given special buttons noting their achievements.[43]
- As an example of a particularly clever strategy, fourth and fifth grade students at Goodale Elementary who needed *remedial* reading were assigned to *tutor* students in the lower grades. This practice was rather unorthodox and counterintuitive, but it had real positive effects, as Principal Batchelor explains:

With some of our fourth and fifth graders who are having trouble reading, they are not going to read in a second grade book. They just won't do that. But if we have them work as cross-age tutors, they'll read in a first grade book to help a first grader. They will feel empowered to help someone else, and learn along the way. We have to be sensitive to that and allow them opportunities to shine.[44]

- At E. J. Scott Elementary, Principal Hedgemon upheld the standard that all students are expected to succeed and teachers are not to make excuses for them because they are from economically poor backgrounds. She expressed, "I made it clear from the start that it's unacceptable to refer to the status of the students as if disadvantage [viz: being poor] were a handicapping condition . . . There was never any resistance vocalized [by the teachers], but I felt it sometimes."[45]

Curriculum, Instruction, and Assessment Practices

In addition to supporting teachers in their work and preparing students to learn, the principals at the successful schools also implemented curriculum, instruction, and assessment practices that contributed toward improving student achievement. Their decisions regarding curriculum, instruction, and assessment practices were generally guided by two factors: (1) student test data and (2) achievement standards defined at the district and/or state level. The principals and their staff reviewed student test data to gauge the subject areas in which the students needed improvement and referred to state, or district-level achievement standards as benchmarks. Some schools developed structures to provide extra monitoring and support to at-risk students and several schools adopted research-tested model programs to help boost learning in specific areas, such as mathematics and reading.

ATTENTION TO TEST DATA. At all of the successful schools, instructional activities and programs were data-driven. Lesson plans were designed in accordance with student performance data, and the overall instructional plan of the school was aligned to the state or district assessment standards. Furthermore, instructional resources (i.e., teachers, materials) were channeled toward improving those areas that needed strengthening.

For instance, in response to data showing that the students at Peck were achieving poorly in the writing section of the Texas Assessment of Academic Skills (TAAS), Principal Goodwin took the following steps:

- She budgeted funds for hiring a master teacher to train teachers and students on writing strategies.
- She started the "Writing Camp," which all fourth grade students attended on Friday afternoons.

(The results were dramatic: The percentage of students at Peck who passed the writing section of TAAS increased from 15 percent in 1994–1995 to 82 percent in 1995–1996, only a year after these practices were instituted!)[46]

Similarly, at Goodale Elementary, Principal Batchelor reviewed the student test results on the Michigan Educational Assessment Program (MEAP) and noticed that the children were doing well on the narrative writing section, but poorly on the expository writing section. In response, he instructed his teaching staff to focus on expository writing skills. Batchelor also based his teacher and student placement decisions on test data. He allowed teachers who were succeeding with a particular group of students to move with them from one grade to the next (a.k.a. "looping").[47]

ALIGNING CURRICULUM AND INSTRUCTION PRACTICES WITH ASSESSMENT GOALS. The principals at the successful schools adopted various measures to align their curriculum and instruction with their state assessment tests.

- At Spellman Elementary, regular practice tests in preparation for the Maryland School Performance Assessment Program (MSPAP) were instituted as part of the regular curriculum.[48]
- At Hawley Elementary, to get teachers to recognize the skills they need to teach their students in order for them to perform well on the Wisconsin science assessment, a performance-based test which involves applying science to real-world problems, Principal Helminiak assigned his teachers the task of actually *taking* the fifth grade science assessment themselves. As a result, the teachers were more thoughtful in planning their instructional activities to tailor them to the test.[49]
- At Burgess Elementary, Principal Carter spent a good portion of her time in classrooms monitoring teachers to ensure that they were focusing on

the test objectives. Moreover, she hired an outside consultant to supplement her work in this area.[50]

- At Peck Elementary, the computer software used to administer practice tests ("Heartbeeps") was programmed so that its content was aligned with the test objectives of the Texas Assessment of Academic Skills (TAAS).[51]

PROBLEMS AND CONCERNS ABOUT TEACHING TO THE TEST. We should note, however, that many educators are strongly against aligning instructional practices too tightly to test objectives, such that their work in the classroom is focused narrowly on "teaching to the test." They argue that focusing on test objectives too strongly inhibits intellectual growth, because children are only taught the knowledge and skills necessary to do well on standardized tests, which are by nature limited in what they measure. The test scores at James Madison Elementary School in Pittsburgh, Pennsylvania provide a case example. In school year 1996–1997, the students at James Madison performed very well on the Iowa Tests of Basic Skills (ITBS). Specifically, 83 percent of the students scored above the national norm on reading comprehension, and 86 percent of them scored above the national norm on mathematics. However, the same pool of students performed poorly that same year on the Pennsylvania System of Student Assessment (PSSA) tests. On the PSSA fifth grade reading assessment, only 26 percent of the students at Madison scored within the top two levels of proficiency, compared with 31 percent of all fifth grade students in Pittsburgh. On the fifth grade mathematics assessment, only 20 percent of Madison students scored with the top two levels, in contrast to an average of 29 percent citywide. This discrepancy surely indicates that the PSSA tests measure something substantially different from the ITBS tests–even though the named subject areas are identical.[52] More importantly, this discrepancy indicates that educators may have been too narrowly focused on preparing students for one particular assessment–the Iowa Test of Basic Skills–at the expense of teaching the students in a way that nurtures a broader and more substantive understanding of the subjects.

Another example is the discrepancy between student test scores on the NAEP and the Texas Assessment of Academic Skills (TAAS), reported in the study by RAND referenced earlier. The researchers of the study inferred:

> If the discrepancies we observed between NAEP and TAAS were due to some type of focused test preparation for the TAAS, then this instruction must have had a fairly narrow scope. With the possible exception of fourth grade math, it certainly did not appear to influence NAEP scores. In short, if TAAS scores were affected by test preparation for the TAAS, then the effects of this preparation did not appear to generalize to the NAEP exams. This explanation also raises questions about the appropriateness of what is being taught to prepare students to take the TAAS.[53]

The preceding circumstance should indicate to educators that they need to be careful about not having standardized test objectives (determined at the district, state, and national levels) *define* their curriculum choices and teaching practices. If they do, they run the risk of not teaching certain knowledge and skills that might be more valuable to the long-term intellectual growth of their students than what the tests measure. Unfortunately, principals and teachers who have this careful perspective are often pressured by higher-level administrators to apply practices contrary to their beliefs and sensibilities, such as "teaching to the test," for fear of receiving sanctions if their students do not perform well on the standardized tests instituted by the district and/or state.[54]

Despite the problems and concerns about the narrow practice of "teaching to the test," however, the goal of aligning instructional activities to test objectives is not *in principle* counterproductive. According to the case studies, the practice of aligning curriculum and teaching practices to test objectives produces positive effects, ostensibly because the test objectives embody clear standards for measuring student performance and provide a framework for designing instructional plans that are focused on results. However, as noted, no single or limited battery of tests should define all that students should learn in the classroom. Most importantly, educators must acknowledge that standardized testing is one method of *assessment*, not a method for teaching or learning.

SUPPORT MECHANISMS FOR STUDENTS AT RISK OF FAILURE. Finally, there is the issue of providing extra attention and support to students who are at risk of failure. In this area, Hawley Elementary was a model of excellence. At Hawley, individualized attention was given to all at-risk students. A Comprehensive Support Team (CST) was assigned to each of these students, consisting of Principal Helminiak, the reading resource teacher, the social worker, the speech therapist, and two classroom teachers. This group would meet with the child's parents and referring teacher to decide on a specific course of action to aid the student's learning.[55]

At Spellman Elementary, Principal Liebes emphasized the need for teachers and specialists to share responsibility for each student and to share their knowledge of each student. This approach led to better student placement and instruction, because there was a conscious attempt to match teaching activities to individual students' achievement levels and learning styles. A number of teachers at Spellman commented positively on this method. The special education teacher expressed: "This is the first school where I have had 'performance task people' and that makes a lot of difference. In other schools, once teachers know a child requires special education services, they just leave it to the special education teachers. Over here, everybody works with that child."[56]

MODEL PROGRAMS. A number of the schools adopted research-based model programs (i.e., Success for All). One noted educational researcher, Samuel Stringfield, believes that schools are most likely to succeed using an approach such as the Comer Child Development Program, the Success for All progam, the Accelerated School Programs, and other tested models. He expressed: "I think it makes a good deal of sense to choose something that is known to work rather than to try home brewing. . . . I don't think we can base a national school improvement strategy on individual heroism."

Notwithstanding Stringfield's confidence in "research-tested" model programs, no existing research data confirm that a particular research-based model is successful for all or even most elementary schools with high enrollments of low-income African American students. Indeed, Joseph Johnson, Jr., another prominent researcher in the field, has a more qualified view. He explained that several successful schools used research-based models such as those mentioned earlier, but emphasized that these schools were successful because they *adapted* the programs to their specific needs, as opposed to following a rigid formula.[57] Furthermore, we should note that some of the high-achieving schools mentioned in this article developed their own successful programs and practices separate from any preexisting research-based models or practices.

Although model programs were credited with improving student achievement in several instances, none of the reviewed case studies described the implementation processes, methods, and effects of the model programs in sufficient detail to provide any concrete insights into how the programs achieved positive results, under what circumstances they achieved those results, and whether they were more or less effective for certain groups of students compared with others. Also, the case studies did not convey whether the model programs raised student achievement *and* closed the achievement gap, or whether they raised achievement while maintaining the gap.

Because several different model programs were used at several successful schools–coupled with the fact that the model programs vary greatly in their philosophies, approach, and content–a detailed description of each would be a prohibitive task for this article. (And, we still would not have accounts of how these programs produced successes at the *particular* set of schools we are examining.) For a listing of the model programs used at the successful schools, along with brief descriptions of their methods and references to the research studies on which they are based, see Table 18-1.

Increasing Instructional and Learning Time

Principals at the successful schools adopted various measures to make the best use of teachers' instructional time and to expand the amount of structured learning time for students. Below is a listing of some effective practices:

- At Spellman Elementary, a block scheduling model was instituted to minimize classroom interruptions and to allow for more continuous instructional time in reading, the main curriculum focus at the school.[58]
- Similarly, at Earhart Elementary in Chicago,

Illinois, Principal Hellen DeBerry blocked off an hour and a half each morning exclusively for reading. During this period, all physical education, music, art, and library hours were suspended so that the entire staff was freed up to help the children with their reading activities.[59]

- At Peck Elementary, instructional time was supplemented with after school programs such as the Voyager program, which provided tutorials, math enrichment classes, and other activities that supported the regular school day curriculum.[60]
- Hawley Elementary developed an after school Math Club for fourth and fifth grade students to provide extended learning time for students underachieving in math. To accommodate the program, the principal adjusted the school busing schedule. To further increase learning time, the district helped out by providing summer school.[61]
- At Centerville Elementary School in East St. Louis, Missouri, teachers were so dedicated that they worked hours beyond the school day to help students who were falling behind. They often tutored students during their own lunch breaks.[62]
- At Cascade Elementary in Atlanta, Georgia, Principal Alfonso Jessie, Jr. organized a group of retired teachers, business owners, and other professionals from the area around the school to provide one-on-one tutoring to students who needed extra assistance and attention.[63]

Efficient Management of Resources and Funds

Because school funding is particularly limited at schools located in poor communities (becuase of a weak tax base, among other factors), the efficient management of funds is crucial to the success of the enterprise. Several principals supplemented their resources by acquiring funds from outside sources. Others adopted innovative practices to maximize the productivity of their staffs.

VIRTUES OF DECENTRALIZATION. Some principals at the successful schools were aided by changes in district-level policies that allowed them greater control over their school budgets and the freedom to shift surpluses from certain areas to help underfunded areas. Principal Helminiak of Hawley Elementary cited the "decentralization" of his school district as one of the key factors in his school's success, because it enabled him to develop his own budget and use the funds most effectively for his situation:

> [Decentralization is] allowing us to have a little bit more say about what goes on in our building. We don't have enough yet, but decentralization is allowing us to be able to use people in our building to develop our own budget. If it weren't for that, we would have never gotten the reading resource teacher in here full time. He was only half time our first three years. That was a very major issue. . . . Currently, the reading teacher is also the part-time librarian and part-time Title I coordinator. Decentralization allowed for that flexibility in the use of resources.[64]

Although Helminiak credits the district for the change in policy, Alan Brown, the district superintendent, was quick to point out that Helminiak was one of the few principals who saw the opportunities there and took advantage of them. He explained:

> Some schools elected to hire more security, not realizing that the better performing your children are, the more well-behaved they will be. Some schools just completely missed the boat on that. . . . Hawley was one of them who saw the big picture and the long term and hired a reading resource person.[65]

ACQUISITION OF OUTSIDE FUNDS. In addition to managing existing resources efficiently, many of the successful schools also had grant writers on staff working on proposals to acquire funds from discretionary government programs and private foundations to support special services, such as parent training centers and after school math programs.

OPTIMIZING HUMAN RESOURCES. Besides managing and spending financial resources prudently and effectively, some principals also exploited the talents and skills of non-instructional staff who are generally undervalued (and sometimes marginalized) in the school setting. For instance, Principal Batchelor of Goodale Elementary noted the talents of the school's lunchroom coordinator and assigned to her a very important duty:

> I know the main job of our lunchroom coordinator is to prepare and serve food. But we also get our extra money based on her lunch counts [counts of children who qualify for free or reduced-price lunch and generate Title I dollars], so her monitoring is critical. Therefore her *instructional* role is critical, so we involve her. She got a phone back there [in the cafeteria] so she can call homes and keep counts accurate.[66]

In effect, without the efforts of the lunch coordinator, many parents whose children qualify for free or reduced-price lunch would not have filled out the necessary paperwork for it and the school would have received less Title I funding.

Parent Involvement

Finally, a feature common to most of the successful schools is exemplary parent involvement and collaboration with teachers. Following are some of the effective strategies for getting parents involved in their children's education and active in school projects:

Making the School More Welcoming for Parents

In an engaging manner that exemplified the spirit of her goal, Principal Goodwin of Peck Elementary encouraged her staff to be more warm and receptive in greeting visitors at the school. She often provided her staff, including the secretaries and clerks, with donuts and coffee in the morning to lighten their spirits and advised them accordingly:

> We must change the way in which we greet visitors. I try to smile at everyone, including you. I smile everyday and if I can do it, you can do it. If you're having a bad day and you don't want to smile at someone then let that person be me. But to everyone else, you will smile. Let's practice how we will greet visitors to our office.[67]

In a similar vein, teachers at Burgess Elementary School hung pictures of the students' parents–framed with stars formed from construction paper–outside the doors of each classroom.[68]

Providing Training and Enrichment Programs for Parents

To support parent involvement in addition to encouraging it, some of the schools provided structured programs to educate parents and provide them with the knowledge and skills to help their children learn. Some also provided social services for families in need. For instance, Peck Elementary housed the following programs:

- The Project Reconnect Parent Center, which provided computer literacy training and English-as-a-Second Language (ESL) instruction to parents of students at the school
- The Communities in School Program, which provided a social worker to help families in need[69]

Burgess Elementary also offered computer training classes and other programs to build parents' capacity to help their children learn. (These enrichment classes also had the effect of improving the parents' employment prospects and opportunities. In fact, Principal Carter of Burgess Elementary pursued this as an end in itself and used the school's financial resources to create a number of part-time and full-time positions for parents.)[70] At Goodale Elementary, parents and their children were allowed to borrow computers for weeks at a time so that they could work with them at home.[71]

Increasing Outreach

In addition to providing support programs, some of the successful schools also actively solicited the involvement of parents and the larger community via the following means:

- Principal Goodwin of Peck Elementary scheduled periodic meetings with parents, and community and business leaders to discuss ideas on improving the school, as a way of involving them in the process and soliciting their active support in programs at the school. She also distributed a newsletter to update the community on school events and other developments.[72]
- The staff at Hawley Elementary worked with the Parent Council to initiate "Hawley Family

Nights," at which dinner was provided to parents and their children, paid for by Title I funds, to encourage parents to participate.[73]

Resolving Tensions Between Parents and the Administration and Among Different Parent Groups

As noted earlier, despite the fact that exemplary parent involvement was the trend at the successful schools, strong disagreements and tensions between (and among) parents and the administration existed in a few cases. These conflicts, along with the tensions that often exist among and between teachers and school leaders, are perhaps all-too-clear indications of how big a role politics plays in the school setting and how much of an obstacle it can be for principals trying to effect positive change.

AN INSTANCE OF CONFLICT BETWEEN PARENTS AND THE SCHOOL ADMINISTRATION. The circumstances at Peck Elementary are particularly telling. At that school, two racially divided parent-teacher organizations came into conflict because of their separate and opposing agendas. (One group consisted of Latino parents and the other consisted of African American parents.) As a response to the problems at Peck, Principal Goodwin disbanded both parent organizations and helped to assemble a new group, whose president was not involved with either of the previous parent-teacher organizations. Unfortunately, this move was met with hostility by a certain group of parents, who submitted a petition signed by 200 parents to the school district's board of trustees demanding the removal of Principal Goodwin. This was despite the fact that student scores on the Texas Assessment of Academic Skills (TAAS) had risen by double-digits in the prior year because of programs and practices that she had instituted.[74]

DISTRICT-LEVEL SUPPORT. Ultimately, the strong support of the district administrators kept Goodwin in her job, but the incident is a rather disheartening example of how politics can threaten successful improvement and reform efforts. The preceding is, of course, not a case in which the principal's actions solved the problem at hand, and therefore, not an instance of an effective practice at the school level that is promising for other scenarios. However, it is instructive in the sense that it shows that certain matters are too large for the principal to control, no matter how competent and resourceful he or she is, and that prudent decisions must be made at the district level too, in support of the work of principals and teachers at the school level.

The need for district-level support certainly extends beyond resolving issues between school-level personnel and parents. As discussed earlier, the decentralizing of control over school funds is another district-level reform that helped principals make more efficient use of the resources available. Unfortunately, no other case examples concerning district-level support were present in the literature reviewed for this article. As with the dearth of examples involving "bottom-up" reforms initiated by teachers and parents, this is likely because the reviewed case studies were written primarily, if not exclusively, from the perspective of *principals* as leaders of change.

SUMMARY AND CONCLUSION

This article has focused mainly on case studies, because they discuss concrete real-world problems that principals and teachers face on the job and are most enlightening and instructive from a *practical* perspective. In each of the successful schools, the principals played strong and creative leadership roles in bringing about change and improvement. However, as mentioned earlier, their management styles were not identical across the board. Some succeeded with a "soft" management style, whereas others had to adopt an "autocratic" style of leadership to achieve their success. Moreover, some principals were compelled to shift from one style to another to motivate and mobilize their staffs. Ultimately, principals were successful in their efforts not simply because they adopted one management style over another, but because they were able to gauge what motivational strategies would work given the personalities of the individuals on their staffs. They also had the flexibility to adjust their methods and practices accordingly.

LIMITATIONS OF CASE STUDY METHODOLOGY. The fact that contrary management styles and differing practices succeeded in different cases may lead one to suspect that the circumstances at each school are too unique to provide blueprints for other case scenarios. Indeed, the issue of management styles aside, it is not obvious in some cases why and how a particular course of action succeeded. For instance, in reviewing the strategy that Principal Liebes used to get her teachers to adopt the Canady Block Scheduling model at Spellman Elementary School, her actions ostensibly would not have succeeded if the initial group of teachers had not accepted the block scheduling idea. The proposal simply would not have proceeded to the next stage where it was introduced to the whole faculty. Thus, it is easy to imagine a scenario in which a principal adopts the strategy taken by Liebes and fails in the attempt. Knowing this possibility, we might readily infer that we cannot know what will succeed in other cases even if we know what worked in a particular case–because the circumstances vary too much from school to school. A related problem is the difficulty of determining which particular practices are effective in improving student achievement and which are not, if a number of different practices are used concurrently. Thus, principals and teachers need to be organized and scientific in their approach toward assessing their own programs and practices to better understand which practices work best for particular individuals or particular groups. The reviewed case studies provided little or no insight into the methods by which principals and teachers assessed their own practices and weighed the relative merits of their different practices.[75]

The previous concerns aside, the inference that case studies provide no guidance for other scenarios is generally unwarranted. Referring to the same previsou example, although Principal Liebes may have been *lucky* to inherit a staff that was receptive to experimentation and change, she may have had the "people skills" to *read* what she was able to accomplish with her staff and would not have pushed for the same reform or attempted the same strategy with a different group. The case study description provides no information on what was at play in the situation, but that is not to say that there were no real factors influencing the outcome that a more thorough case study description could have captured.

Furthermore, a review of the case studies finds an undeniable "family resemblance" among the school situations examined and clear similarities among the strategies that were successful in effecting improved student achievement. The following features were common to *all* the successful schools that had high proportions of African Americans and high enrollments of low-income students:

- The principal was an effective leader who could motivate his or her staff.
- All children were held to high standards.
- All teachers were held to high standards.
- The principal provided ample staff development opportunities to teachers.
- The teachers took advantage of staff development opportunities.
- Test scores and other assessment data were used to guide instructional practices.
- The school staff defined clear goals for themselves and committed to them.
- The school staff collaborated with each other toward achieving the goals.
- The school had an excellent student attendance record.

Furthermore, the following characteristics were present at *most* of the successful schools.

- The school provided training programs to parent, to increase their capacity to help their children learn.
- The principal and teachers collaborated with parents on school projects.
- The school provided after-school programs to increase learning time for students.
- The school staff acquired grants from outside sources to fund supplemental education programs.
- The school had a discipline plan for maintaining good student conduct.
- The school had in-house instructional experts to provide staff training on a regular basis.

LIMITATIONS OF CASE STUDIES REVIEWED: INSUFFICIENT FOCUS ON AFRICAN AMERICAN STUDENTS. Aside from the issue of research methods, the particular case studies reviewed have some important limitations. First, the successful elementary schools described and listed in this article were culled from studies that examined high-achieving, high-poverty schools in general, not specifically high-achieving, high-poverty schools with large proportions of African American students. In reviewing these case studies, we focused on the schools with large percentages of African American students, but the studies themselves did not examine race as a specific factor in rendering certain practices effective or not effective for certain student populations. Thus, for instance, there were no analyses or reports of practices that were generally effective for improving the achievement of African American students but not so effective for improving, say, the achievement of Latino students. (Although the practices reviewed may in fact be effective for schools of all demographics, it is more than reasonable to assume that some practices, at least, are more or less effective for students of different races and cultures–given that race and culture is a strong qualifying factor in virtually all other areas of sociological study.) Second, most of the case studies did not provide a lot of the data that would be useful in assessing how and why the school was successful. For instance, only one of the case studies gave information on average class size and teacher demographics–two factors that relate strongly to student achievement. Third, as mentioned earlier, all the case studies were written from the perspective of the principal as the primary agent of change; thus, they provided no concrete examples of "bottom-up" reforms achieved by teachers and parents independently of the principal's initiative or direct guidance. Conceivably, successful "bottom-up" initiatives existed in many cases but were not reported.

Finally, the case studies reviewed in this article varied significantly in detail and depth. Some convey that the school succeeded with high proportions of low-income African American students and presented achievement statistics and other baseline data but provide minimal description and insight into the policies and practices that effected positive change. The better case studies provide concrete examples of successful practices for other principals and school leaders to review in planning activities to improve student achievement at their own schools. Although the findings of case studies are difficult to quantify in standard statistical language, the case descriptions themselves are immeasurably more instructive and useful to *practitioners* than general statistical reports–no matter how formally complete the statistical reports may be. Statistics only really tell us the extent of the problem of underachievement among African American students–case studies offer insight on how to solve the day-to-day concrete problems that create the larger one.

Table 18-1. Special programs/practices at high-achieving public elementary schools with high percentages of African American students and students eligible for free or reduced-price lunch programs.

School	Special Programs/Practices and Extracurricular Activities	Reference Information
Centerville Elementary	Accelerated Schools Program	Developed by Hank Levin in an effort to improve the learning of at-risk students. The program involves extensive training in inquiry, planning, teamwork, and working with parents. Hopfenberg, Wendy S. Henry M. Levin, and Associates. *The Accelerated Schools Resource Guide.* San Francisco: Jossey-Bass Inc., 1993. Finnan, Christine, et al., (Eds.) *Accelerated Schools in Action: Lessons from the Field.* Thousand Oaks, CA: Corwin Press, 1996.
Goodale Elementary School	Efficacy Program	Lamberti, Mary Jo. *A Summary of Research Findings on Efficacy Programs for Middle and Elementary School Students.* ERIC, ED368805 1992.
	Sylvan Reading Program	Sylvan Learning Systems http://www.sylvan.net/

Hawley Environmental Elementary School	Banking System	System for creating more professional development time for teachers–students come to school 10 minutes earlier each day and the extra time is "banked" to allow teachers five professional development days per year
	School-to-Work	The School-to-Work Opportunities Act, signed into law in 1994, is administered by the U.S. Departments of Education and Labor. The Act provides funds to States and local communities to develop School-to-Work systems. School-to-Work (STW) is a means of attaining high academic standards through contextual, applied, and focused learning. To help students direct their education, STW encourages, among other things, exposure to a broad variety of career options–starting with speakers and field trips in elementary school and progressing to academically connected internships in a high school student's field of interest. The underlying goal is to provide students with knowledge and skills that will allow them to opt for college, additional training, or a well-paying job directly out of high school. Because STW is locally driven, it also looks quite different from to state to state, and from locality to locality. School-to-Work website: http://www.stw.ed.gov
	Prevention Is Kid Stuff	Discipline program offered by Milwaukee Council on Alcoholism & Drug Dependence Contact: Milwaukee Council on Alcoholism & Drug Dependence, 1126 South 70th Street Milwaukee, WI 53214 Phone: 414/475-2363
James Madison Elementary School	MacMillan/McGraw-Hill series for reading, writing, and spelling	http://www.mhschool.com/student/reading/index.html
	Open Court Reading	A phonics-based reading curriculum Publisher: SRA/McGraw-Hill, 220 East Danieldale Road, DeSoto, Texas 75115-2490, (888) 772-4543 http://www.sra4kids.com/teacher/reading/index.html Reviews: http://www.culvercitylife.com/DECEMBER/december9.htm

James Madison Elementary School (continued from previous page)	University of Chicago School Mathematics Project (UCSMP)	The curriculum emphasizes reading, problem--solving, everyday applications, and the use of calculators, computers, and other technologies. Unnecessary repetition and review are eliminated. UCSMP, The University of Chicago, 5835 S. Kimbark Avenue, Chicago, IL 60637 E-mail: ucsmp@uchicago.edu http://socialsciences.uchicago.edu/ucsmp/
Lora B. Peck Elementary School	Communities in Schools Program	A dropout prevention program launched in 1979 by a non-profit organization based in New York City.
	Graduation Really Achieves Dreams (GRAD)	Initiated in the Houston Independent School District in 1993-94, Project GRAD uses a number of curriculum models that have been widely tested. This model includes: – MOVE-IT-MATH (Math Opportunities, Valuable Experiences, and Innovative Teaching) – Communities In Schools – Success For All (SFA) – Consistency Management and Cooperative Discipline (CMCD) – Harvard Principal Leadership Training Model – University of Chicago School Math Project (UCSMP) Secondary Component GRAD is unique in that it concurrently replicates all models at a single site involving both bilingual and regular classrooms Weblinks: http://www.projectgrad.org/aboutus.html http://www.cgcs.org/services/whatworks/achievement/p1.htm
	Heartbeeps	A computer program used for afterschool tutoring that is aligned with the objectives of the Texas Assessment of Academic Skills (TAAS) Software publisher: Lindy Software (800) 937-8227 http://www.lindyinc.com/lindyweb/heartbeeps/hb.html
	Houston Independent School District Balanced Approach to Reading	Program to train teachers on research-based strategies for developing literacy

Lora B. Peck Elementary School (continued from previous page)	Move-It Math Program	Introduces algebra in the early grades and uses children's literature and science to give meaning and purpose to mathematics; emphasizes understanding of math principles versus memorization; encourages the discovery of "rules" of math through the examination of patterns; and allows flexibility in exposition and acceptance of alternative strategies for problem solving
	Peck Time	School starts and ends fifteen minutes later, to facilitate and improve student attendance
	Project Reach	Program in which teachers go to a local church and provide outreach services to the community
	Project Reconnect Parent Center	Place for parents to meet and attend training/enrichment classes such as ESL
	Success For All	Comprehensive school reform model with a focus on reading Success for All Foundation, 200 West Towsontown Boulevard, Baltimore, MD 21204-5200, (800) 548-4998 http://www.successforall.net/
	Voyager	http://www.iamvoyager.com/
P.S. 161–The Crown School	Open Court Reading	A phonics-based reading curriculum SRA/McGraw-Hill 220 East Danieldale Road DeSoto, Texas 75115-2490 1- 888-772-4543 http://www.sra4kids.com/teacher/reading/index.html Review articles: http://www.culvercitylife.com/DECEMBER/december9.htm

Rozelle Elementary School	Modern Red Schoolhouse Reform Model	Heady, R., and Kilgore, S. 1996. The Modern Red Schoolhouse. In *Bold plans for restructuring: The New American Schools Development Corporation designs*, eds. S. Stringfield, S. Ross, and L. Smith. Mahwah, NJ: Lawrence Erlbaum Associates. Kilgore, S. 1996. *Designing schools for the 21st Century: Essential elements of a Modern Red Schoolhouse.* Arlington, VA: New American Schools. Modern Red Schoolhouse 208 23rd Avenue North Nashville, TN 37203 Phone: 615-320-8804 Website: www.mrsh.org
Gladys Noon Spellman Elementary School	Canady Block-Scheduling Model	Canady, Robert Lynn, and Michael D. Rettig, 1995. *Block Scheduling: A Catalyst for Change in High Schools.* Princeton, NJ: Eye on Education, March 1996 Irmsher, Karen. *Block Scheduling.* ERIC Digest, Number 104, ED393156
E. J. Scott Elementary School	Communities in Schools	A dropout prevention program launched in 1979 by a non-profit organization based in New York City.
Carter G. Woodson Elementary School	Calvert School Program	Children receive instruction at their achievement level, not their grade level. McHugh, Barbara, and Sam Stringfield, 1998 *Implementing a Highly-Specified Curricular, Instructional, and Organizational School Design in a High-Poverty, Urban Elementary School.* Baltimore: Johns Hopkins University

ENDNOTES

1. Patte Barth, et al. (eds). *Dispelling the Myth: High Poverty Schools Exceeding Expectations.* (Washington, DC: The Education Trust, 1999), pp. 2–3.
2. Ibid, pp. 4–9.
3. Recent data show that the achievement of middle-class and upper-income African American students lags behind that of White students of comparable socioeconomic status. More disturbingly, on some tests, African American students from middle-class or upper-income backgrounds have performed no better than White students who live below the poverty line. See Pam Belluck, "Reason Is Sought for Lag by Blacks in School Effort," *The New York Times,* Sunday, July 4, 1999, pp. 1, 12.

   Also, although many states and districts have been successful in improving the achievement of students living in poverty so that they are approaching the same level of performance as students from wealthier backgrounds, the achievement gap between African American and White students tends to remain in those instances. Referring to gains made in the state of Kentucky, Amy Wilkins, a senior associate at the Education Trust, commented: "Kentucky is closing the gap between low-income kids and wealthy kids, and I applaud them for it. But they're not closing the gap between black and white kids." See Kerry A. White, "High Poverty Schools Score Big on Ky. Assessment," *Education Week,* May 5, 1999.

   To address this achievement gap issue, a network of 14 school districts from different places across the country has banded together to research the problem and find solutions. See Caroline Hendrie, "Network of 14 Districts to Focus on Achievement Gap," *Education Week,* July 14, 1999.

   Aside from the moral issue, the benefits of closing the achievement gap outweigh the costs, from a macro-level economic perspective. See Georges Vernez, Richard A. Krop, and C. Peter Rydell. *Closing the Education Gap: Benefits and Costs.* Santa Monica, CA: RAND, 1999.
4. Sharon Lewis, Jack Jepson, and Michael Casserly. *Closing the Achievement Gap in Urban Schools: A Survey of Academic Progress and Promising Practices in the Great City Schools. Preliminary Report.* (Washington, DC: Council for the Great City Schools, October 1999), p. 37.
5. Stephen P. Klein, Laura S. Hamilton, Daniel F. McCaffrey and Brian M. Stecher. *Issue Paper: What Do the Test Scores in Texas Tell Us?* (Santa Monica, CA: RAND, 2000). See also: Linda McNeil and Angela Valenzuela, *The Harmful Impact of the TAAS System of Testing in Texas: Beneath the Accountability Rhetoric* (Cambridge, MA: The Civil Rights Project–Harvard University, 2000); and John Mintz, "Study Disputes Bush Claims on Texas Education Record" (*The Washington Post,* October 25, 2000), p. A19.
6. It is not unusual for teachers to help students prepare for standardized tests by giving them practice questions similar to those that appear on the examinations. In some cases, teachers have helped students cheat by drilling them on the exact same questions that appear in the examinations. See David J. Hoff, "As Stakes Rise, Definition of Cheating Blurs," (*Education Week,* June 21, 2000).
7. We tried to locate NAEP test data for these two schools to compare against their TAAS scores, but that information is not available.
8. Fifteen schools in Colorado with large populations of low-income students received significant press last year for producing reading scores comparable to schools with predominantly middle-class or upper-income students. See Mike Schmoker, "The Quiet Revolution in Achievement," *Education Week,* November 3, 1999.
9. Joseph F. Johnson, Jr. and Rose Asera (Eds.). *Hope for Urban Education: A Study of Nine High-Performing, High Poverty, Elementary Schools.* (Austin, TX: Charles A. Dana Center–University of Texas at Austin, 1999), p. 116.
10. Ibid, p. 107.
11. Ibid, p. 89.
12. Ibid, p. 123.
13. Julie A. Miller, "A Model Urban Elementary School," *Education Week–Quality Counts '98,* January 8, 1998.
14. Samuel Casey Carter. *No Excuses: Lessons From 21 High-Performing, High-Poverty Schools.* (Washington, DC: The Heritage Foundation, 2000), p. 76.
15. Johnson et al., p. 117.
16. Ibid, pp. 60–61.
17. Ibid, p. 88.
18. Ibid, p. 116.
19. Ibid, p. 131.
20. Ibid, p. 91.
21. Carter, p. 72.
22. Johnson and Asera, p. 105.
23. Ibid, p. 90.
24. Ibid, pp. 129–130
25. Ibid, p. 106.
26. Ibid, p. 74.
27. Carter, p. 92.
28. Johnson and Asera, p. 101.
29. Ibid, p. 86.

30. Ibid, p. 130.
31. Ibid, p. 68.
32. S.J. Caldas. "Reexamination of Input and Process Factor Effects on Public School Achievement," *Journal of Educational Research, 86*(4), 1993, pp. 206–214.
    D.J. Lambdin. "Evidence of Student Attendance as an Independent Variable in Education Production Functions," *Journal of Educational Research, 89*(3), 1996, pp. 155–162.
33. Johnson and Asera, p. 117.
34. Barbara McHugh and Sam Stringfield. *Implementing a Highly-Specified Curricular, Instructional, and Organizational School Design in a High-Poverty, Urban Elementary School.* (Baltimore: Johns Hopkins University, 1998).
35. Johnson and Asera, pp. 115, 117.
36. Ibid, p. 118.
37. Ibid, pp. 101–102.
38. Ibid, p. 137.
39. Ibid, p. 61.
40. Ibid, pp. 86–87.
41. Gordon Cawelti. *Portraits of Six Benchmark Schools: Diverse Approaches to Improving Student Achievement.* (Arlington, VA: Educational Research Service, 1999), p. 40.
42. Johnson and Asera, p. 60.
43. Carter, p. 75.
44. Johnson and Asera, p. 87.
45. Miller.
46. Johnson and Asera, p. 120.
47. Ibid, p. 95.
48. Ibid, p. 132.
49. Ibid, p. 106.
50. Ibid, p. 67
51. Ibid, p. 120.
52. Cawelti, pp. 42–43.
53. Stephen P. Klein, Laura S. Hamilton, Daniel F. McCaffrey and Brian M. Stecher. *Issue Paper: What Do the Test Scores in Texas Tell Us?* (Santa Monica, CA: RAND, 2000).
54. Several teachers working in the mid-Atlantic region (District of Columbia, Maryland, Pennsylvania, Virginia and West Virginia) have reported to Mid-Atlantic Equity Center staff that they were pressured by their superiors to teach the standardized tests mandated by their districts and states in the narrow way discussed.
55. Johnson and Asera, p. 103.
56. Ibid, p. 134.
57. Miller.
58. Johnson and Asera, pp. 129ff.
59. Carter, p. 55.
60. Johnson and Asera, pp. 120–121.
61. Ibid, p. 104.
62. Ibid, p. 75.
63. Carter, p. 50.
64. Johnson and Asera, pp. 106–107.
65. Ibid, p. 107.
66. Ibid, p. 94.
67. Ibid, p. 122.
68. Ibid, p. 58.
69. Ibid, p. 122.
70. Ibid, p. 65.
71. Ibid, p. 93.
72. Ibid, p. 122.
73. Ibid, p. 108.
74. Ibid, pp. 114–115.
75. The following is a limitation in *our* method of inquiry. Ironically, although we are purportedly concerned with elementary schools in particular, reviewing case studies of elementary schools exclusively does not provide us with a basis for measuring the characteristics that are *unique* to elementary schools as opposed to middle schools and high schools. To achieve that, we will need to compare our case studies against profiles of middle schools and high schools.

REFERENCES

Barth, P., Haycock, K., Jackson, H., Mora, K., Ruiz, P., Robinson, S., & Wilkins, A. (Eds). (1999). *Dispelling the myth: High poverty schools exceeding expectations.* Washington, DC: The Education Trust.

Belluck, P. (1999, July 4). Reason is sought for lag by Blacks in school effort. *The New York Times*, pp. 1, 12.

Caldas, S. J. (1993). Reexamination of input and process factor effects on public school achievement. *Journal of Educational Research, 86*(4), pp. 206–214.

Carter, S. C. (2000). *No excuses: Lessons from 21 high-performing, high-poverty schools.* Washington, DC: The Heritage Foundation.

Cawelti, G. (1999). *Portraits of six benchmark schools: Diverse approaches to improving student achievement.* Arlington, VA: Educational Research Service.

Hendrie, C. (1999, July 14). Network of 14 districts to focus on achievement gap. *Education Week*, 6.

Hoff, D. J. (2000, June 22). As stakes rise, definition of cheating blurs. *Education Week*, 1, 14–16.

Johnson, J. F., & Asera, R. (Eds). (1999). *Hope for urban education: A study of nine high-performing, high poverty elementary schools.* Austin, TX: Charles A. Dana Center, University of Texas at Austin.

Klein, S. P., Hamilton, L.S., McCaffrey, D.F., & Stecher, B.M. (2000). *Issue paper: What do the test scores in Texas tell us?* Santa Monica, CA: RAND.

Lambdin, D.J. (1996). Evidence of student attendance as an independent variable in education production functions. *Journal of Educational Research, 89*(3), 155–162.

Lewis, S., Jepson, J., & Casserly, M. (1999, October). *Closing the achievement gap in urban schools: A survey of academic progress and promising practices in the Great City Schools. Preliminary Report.* Washington, DC: Council for the Great City Schools.

McHugh, B., & Stringfield, S. (1998). *Implementing a highly-specified curricular, instructional, and organizational school design in a high-poverty, urban elementary school.* Baltimore: Johns Hopkins University.

McNeil, L., & Valenzuela, A. (2000). *The harmful impact of the TAAS system of testing in Texas: beneath the accountability rhetoric.* Cambridge, MA: The Civil Rights Project–Harvard University.

Miller, J. A. (1999, January 8). *A model urban elementary school. Education Week–Quality Counts '98.* Retrieved on November 16, 2000 from the World Wide Web: www.edweek.org/sreports/9c98/soluions/50-n3.htm

Milwaukee Public Schools. (1999). *1998–1999 accountability report.* Division of Research and Assessment: Author.

Mintz, J. (2000, October 25). Study disputes Bush claims on Texas education record. *The Washington Post,* p. A19.

Reeves, D. B. (2000). *Accountability in action: A blueprint for learning organizations.* Denver, CO: Center for Performance Assessment.

Schmoker, M. (1999, November 3). The quiet revolution in achievment. *Education Week.* pp. 32, 35.

Vernez, G., Krop, R.A., & Rydell, C.P. (1999). *Closing the education gap: Benefits and costs.* Santa Monica, CA: RAND.

White, K. A. (1999, May 5). High poverty schools score big on Kentucky assessment. *Education Week,* pp. 18, 20.

Article 19

MIDDLE SCHOOLS: AFRICAN AMERICAN CHILDREN AT THE CROSSROADS

Nathalie Thandiwe

INTRODUCTION

The symbol of the crossroads is a significant metaphor in folklore and literature in many cultures. In the African American folk tradition, it often symbolizes a site for two types of events: rituals that result in mastery of a skill and making choices that mark a transformative point in one's development. Much like the crossroads in folklore, the sixth through eighth grades are a critical turning point in students' academic paths. During these years, ages eleven to fourteen, students' academic and social choices significantly affect the remainder of their K through 12 academic lives. Studies indicate that those students who take courses at the middle level that develop higher-level thinking skills, and who also have the support and information to make healthy personal and social choices, are most likely to experience long-term academic success (Carnegie Council on Adolescent Development, 1989; Lynn & Wheelock, 1997; National Center for Education Statistics [NCES], 1999).

The difference between those middle school students who receive the academic and developmental support to master the skills and content necessary to be successful in school and those who do not is largely racial. It is during these middle years that the achievement gap between African American students and their White and Asian peers widens and becomes set, leaving most African American students behind for the remainder of their school years (College Board, 2000; NCES, 2000). Researchers have found that when African American students are given access to higher-level curriculum and appropriate developmental support, this achievement gap narrows, and instances of long-term academic success increase, making the middle years the crossroads of opportunity and failure for many African American students (Center for Research on the Education of Disadvantaged Students [CDS], 1994; Knapp, 1995; Langer, 1999; Smith 1996).

MIDDLE SCHOOL MOVEMENT AND ITS UNIQUE PURPOSE

Middle schools were developed to provide a transitional environment between elementary and high schools. In middle schools, students between the fifth and eighth grades receive a more challenging curriculum than that offered at the elementary level, in addition to guidance to better prepare them for the coming high school years and the increasing independence and responsibility of adolescence (Alexander & Williams, 1965). The middle school model is unique from both elementary and high school in its emphasis on nurturing students both developmentally and intellectually. In theory, this is achieved through the implementation of middle school concepts, such as varied organizational, instructional, and scheduling approaches based on student needs; moderate enrollment (400–800 students); small student groupings within school; interdisciplinary teaching teams; exploratory curricula that introduce students to a diverse range of subjects; and comprehensive advisory and counseling programs (National Middle School Association [NMSA], 1995).

The actual practices in place at middle schools across the country vary widely in the degree to which they implement middle school concepts. According to a study by the National Middle School Association, 30 percent of middle schools enroll more than 800 students, only 22 percent have instituted the double planning periods needed for interdisciplinary team teaching, 50 percent have teacher-based guidance programs, and most use a schedule of daily class periods of uniform length, rather than flexible or varied scheduling approaches (McEwin, Dickinson, & Jenkins, 1996). Although middle school advocates push for more comprehensive implementation of middle school practices, more recently, critics calling for middle school reform have denounced the model as being too nurture oriented at the expense of academics, pointing to lagging standardized test scores as evidence of its shortcomings (Mizell, 1999b).

WHAT HAPPENS IN THE MIDDLE?

Those who argue that the achievement gap between Black and White students that persists in high school becomes set during the middle school years point out that despite some fluctuations in scores between 9-year-olds and 13-year-olds, the overall trend is shaped by increases in the gap among 13 to 17-year-olds. The push for school reform and measurable improvements has educators, policymakers, reformers, and parents looking for answers as to why academic achievement seems to plateau at the middle grades and why African American students, in particular, actually fall further behind during those grades and stay behind for good. The growing body of middle school reform literature points to issues including tracking, curriculum, middle school concepts implementation, teacher training, and developmental characteristics of middle-level students as critical aspects of both the failure and potential for success of the middle school model and the efforts to close the achievement gap.

TRACKING

Although research has provided mounting evidence of the negative effects of tracking, and most middle level reform theory advises against it, grouping students by perceived ability levels remains prevalent in the middle grades. The practice of tracking is based on the premise that it enables schools to accommodate a diverse range of student ability levels by allowing high-achieving students to receive fast-paced, demanding lessons while low-achieving students receive a slower work pace and more attention. However, studies indicate that when students labeled as low achieving are grouped for instruction with high-achieving peers, it tends to raise the achievement level of the "low achievers" and has no negative effects on the achievement levels of the high achievers (Mason, Schroeter, Combs & Washington, 1992). Additional research indicates that African American students are subject to teachers' assumptions that they have inherent intellectual limitations, attributed to race (Bamburg, 1994; Cotton, 1989; Gonder, 1991; Lumsden, 1997). This means that the many African American students relegated to the lower-level tracks are subject to a double disadvantage, whereby low expectations and negative differential treatment characteristic of teachers at this level may be buttressed by racially biased assumptions about their capacity to learn.

The detracking process requires schools to confront change on three levels: the political, cultural, and technical (Oakes, cited by Lynn & Wheelock, 1997). On the political level, school leaders must convince parents, teachers, and students that the potential and progress of high achievers will not be hindered in mixed-ability classes and that divesting the exclusionary school organization created by tracking is to the benefit of all students. On the cultural level, they must convince everyone that all students are capable of learning in courses geared toward higher-level thinking and establish a culture of high expectations for all students based on this tenet. On the technical level, school leaders must provide the staff development, curricula, school organization, and support necessary for teachers to deliver a rich curriculum and for students to meet the high expectations and excel in heterogeneous classrooms, including academic assistance for those students transitioning from low-level to higher-level curricula. Although middle school leaders have faced challenges in cultivating buy-in for detracking, statistics indicate that support for the process is growing. According to a 1996 study by the National Middle School Association, the percent of middle schools that practice random grouping rose from 25 percent in 1988 to nearly 50 percent in 1993 (McEwin et al., 1996).

In racially mixed schools, where tracking is often practiced, and in predominantly African American schools, where curriculum is characterized by a remedial and basic skills focus, improving curriculum and closing the achievement gap can be approached through instructional and organizational strategies demonstrated to facilitate the achievement of all students. The curriculum that most Black students receive in the middle grades, whether in integrated, tracked schools or predominantly Black schools, reflects the pedagogy of the "back-to-basics movement," which gained widespread momentum in the 1970s. This educational movement emphasized low-level functional skills in reading, writing and math and resulted in a generation of students who, for lack of exposure and experience, performed dismally on measures of thinking and problem solving (Marzano et al., 1993; Schoenfeld, 1992; Strickland & Ascher, 1992). By the time they reach high school, African American students are concentrated in the vocational and general education tracks in preparation for low-level occupations, with little representation in academic, college-prep tracks or gifted and talented programs (Slavin & Braddock, 1993).

Research and practice demonstrate that access to more challenging curriculum beginning in the middle grades can make all the difference in the academic achievement levels and long-term success of African American students.

Improving Achievement for African American Middle School Students

- **Providing early access to algebra:** African American students who are given access to algebra by eighth grade demonstrate increased math skills and achievement and higher rates of advanced/college-track math course taking in high school than those who do not take algebra before high school. (Atanda, 1999; Smith, 1996)
- **Increasing higher-order skills through teaching for meaning:** Poor students and students of color who receive instruction focused on teaching for meaning, i.e., reading instruction for comprehension and writing instruction for composing extended text, are more likely to demonstrate proficiency in both basic and higher-order skills than when they receive traditional basic skills-focused instruction. (Knapp, 1995)
- **Increasing instructional time in reading and math:** Increased reading and math instruction time was found to be a common practice in a study of high-performing, high-poverty schools, most of which have high enrollments of African American and Latino children (Education Trust, 1999). Research indicates that middle schools that offer students the opportunity to take a second period of math or reading during the regular school day instead of other electives show significant gains in standardized test scores in both reading and math. However, only 17 percent of schools in a national representative survey use this approach, and schools with large numbers of disadvantaged students were the least likely to use it. Saturday and summer remedial classes, which also provide students with extra instruction, were also found to help at-risk students. (CDS, 1994)
- **Improving reading and writing skills:** A study of middle and high schools with predominantly poor students of African American and Latino descent that demonstrated high levels of student improvement and achievement in writing and

reading used practices including infusion of culturally relevant reading and writing projects; multiple approaches to teaching skills; test preparation integrated into ongoing instruction; making overt connections among knowledge/skills across lessons, disciplines, and both out-of-school real-world applications. (Langer, 1999)

THE LINK BETWEEN STAFF DEVELOPMENT AND STUDENT ACHIEVEMENT

Clearly curricula and teaching overlap in increasing African American student achievement and closing the gap in the middle grades. A widespread criticism of middle grades instruction is poor teacher preparation and teaching practices. In a national survey of schools with middle grades students, administrators reported that fewer than 25 percent of their teachers had specialized in middle school training (Viadero, 1996). Most middle grades teachers are trained for elementary school or high school teaching, which means that new teachers usually lack training, preparation, and field work in instruction for teaching middle grades content, in middle grades organization, or in developmental approaches to early adolescent education. Although some teacher preparation programs have begun to implement middle grades certification programs, it is not a standard feature of teacher training curricula, and many states have no middle-level teacher licensure and certification (Alexander & McEwin, 1989; Lounsboury, 1996; McEwin, et al., 1996).

The greatest weakness of middle grades teacher training is that most teachers at this level do not have adequate knowledge of the content they are teaching. A recent survey indicates that among students in grades 7 through 12, it is seventh and eighth grade students who are most likely to be taught by teachers without a college major or minor in the subjects they are teaching (NCES, 1999). Myriad of studies point to teacher qualifications such as certification and holding a degree in the subject being taught, as well as knowledge of teaching methods, as the most significant indicators of student achievement (Darling-Hammond, 1997; Ferguson & Ladd, 1996; Strauss & Sawyer 1986). A study of student performance in mathematics and science using data from the National Educational Longitudinal Studies of 1988 found that teacher certification and holding a degree in the subject being taught had a statistically significant positive effect on student test scores relative to the scores of students whose teachers did not have these qualifications (Goldhaber & Brewer, 2000). A Texas study of 900 districts found that teacher quality, as measured by teacher education, licensing examination scores, and experience, accounted for 40 percent of the difference in student achievement in reading and mathematics. The study also found that teacher expertise explains most of the gap in achievement between African American and White students, after controlling for socioeconomic status (Ferguson, 1997). Similarly, a study of schools in New York City found that differences in teacher qualifications accounted for 90 percent of the variation in student achievement in reading and mathematics (Armour-Thomas, et al., 1989).

Research indicates that African American students are nearly twice as likely as their peers to be assigned to the most ineffective teachers (Darling-Hammond, 2000). In racially mixed schools this can be attributed to tracking and the disproportionate placement of African American students in the lower tracks, whereas in predominantly African American schools this outcome can be attributed to hiring practices. In tracked middle schools, inexperienced teachers are often assigned to the lower tracks and "earn" their way up to higher tracks through reputation and seniority. Studies suggest that this informal system of advancement has created a de facto hierarchy in which teacher status is related to the ability-level label of one's students. In turn, there is stigma around working with students labeled low ability, so much so that teachers who actually choose to work among these students may be viewed with suspicion by their colleagues (Rudin & Lane, 1998).

In low-income districts with high minority enrollments, the hiring of underqualified teachers is endemic. Limited budgets and poor school facilities, caused by inequities in school financing, compounded with the challenging teaching conditions of many poor schools, make it more difficult to attract qualified staff. One-third of public school teachers in high-poverty schools taught without a minor in their main field, compared with only 8 percent of teachers in low-poverty schools (Darling-Hammond, 1997). For African American middle grade students, receiving poorly trained teachers is a likelihood that only increases their vulnerability to falling behind their peers, contributing to the achievement gap that has been shown to widen throughout high school.

Given that teacher quality is one of the greatest indicators of student success, better training for middle grades teachers is essential for improving education and raising the achievement of African American students, who are disproportionately subject to poor-quality teachers and instruction. Like teacher preparation and qualifications, staff development is associated with student achievement. For example, a study of the correlation between school expenditures and achievement gains found spending on teacher education to be the most productive investment for schools, even greater than the effects of teacher experience and reduced pupil/teacher ratios (Greenwald, Hedges, & Laine, 1996).

Staff development is an important tool for cultivating culturally responsive instructional practices, particularly in schools where most teachers and staff members are from different ethnic, racial, and socioeconomic backgrounds from their students. Middle schools can provide professional development that gives staff knowledge of backgrounds other than their own and teaches them strategies for providing classroom environments that give a diverse range of students equal opportunities to learn. Cultural awareness can also help teachers to bridge cultural differences to make authentic connections with students from backgrounds other than their own. In a public school system with a majority White teaching force (86.5 percent), African American students are more likely than their White peers to experience alienation from teachers rooted in cultural and class differences (NCES, 1998). This type of teacher-student cultural alienation poses a significant achievement barrier for African Americans, students for whom positive relationships with teachers and positive classroom climate are found to be critical variables in learning and success (Welch & Hodges, 1997).

Among the educational practices that culturally responsive staff development encourages in teachers are establishing a pedagogy rooted in a belief in the ability of all students to learn; creating a positive classroom climate in which students feel comfortable and accepted; using a variety of teaching approaches to meet a diverse range of learning preferences and to strengthen students' range of learning aptitudes, as well as providing frequent feedback and recognition of improvement and achievement (Burnette, 1999; Gorski, 2000; McPartland & Braddock, 1993). These practices speak to the fact that students can be motivated by teacher confidence in and support of their efforts to learn.

EFFECTIVE TEACHING METHODS IN DETRACKED MIDDLE SCHOOLS

Even if excellent staff development better prepares teachers to build student skills to meet or exceed school, district, or state standards, if students don't have access to the same curriculum, it is unrealistic to expect them to meet the same standards. This highlights how middle school improvement initiatives such as detracking and staff development intersect in their potential for raising student and school achievement. The challenge of improving middle grades education and closing the achievement gap between African American students and their peers centers around answering the question, "How can schools successfully assist all students in mastering a higher order, college preparatory curriculum given the reality of varying levels of student preparedness and skills?" Detracking can create heterogeneous classes with students of mixed achievement levels and requires teachers to stimulate all students, while supporting those who are struggling to move ahead and continuing to challenge more advanced learners. Achieving this complex balancing act demands innovations in instruction, classroom organization, and curricula.

Although findings on the effects of heterogeneous grouping are positive in that it can raise the achievement of low achievers without undermining the advancement of high-achieving students, consensus on what teaching methods work best for this model are still formative, because mixed grouping is not yet widespread in public schools at the middle grades level (Mason et al., 1992; Valentine, Clark, Irvin, Keefe & Melton, 1993). According to the National Middle School Association (NMSA), the instructional approaches characteristic of effective heterogeneous middle grades classes emphasize group learning and work, complemented by differentiated instruction to accommodate varying skill levels and support for students when they have not mastered the material and opportunities for advanced work when they have (NMSA Research Summary #6, 1996). Group learning, also referred to as cooperative, collaborative or team learning, uses small groups in which students work together to maximize their own and each other's learning (Johnson, Johnson, & Holubec, 1993). Research on the effects of cooperative learning across content areas in a diverse range of K through 12 classrooms indicates that benefits of group learning include improved comprehension of content and skills; higher academic test scores; improved attendance, behavior, and attitudes toward school; and improved relationships among students from different ethnic backgrounds (Johnson, Johnson, & Holubec, 1993; Slavin, 1980, 1987, 1991; Stahl & VanSickle, 1992).

In middle grades classrooms organized for heterogeneous group learning, the teaching strategy of differentiating instruction allows teachers to acknowledge and work with differences in student skills, learning styles, and cultural contexts (Tomlinson, 1995). Rather than assuming that one method of instruction fits all, differentiated instruction asks teachers and schools to meet students where they are and guide them in mastering core concepts and curriculum in ways that are most effective for the learners. Teachers can do this through providing a variety of within-class grouping and learning options for students to explore, process, and apply curriculum content once they have defined the key concepts and learning goals and provided students with essential background knowledge.

Findings on heterogeneous classrooms, group learning, and differentiated instruction suggest that these approaches to learning are student-centered in ways that may be particularly beneficial for African American middle-level students and in turn may be helpful in closing the achievement gap. The student diversity, consideration of learning preferences and cultural/ethnic and gender perspectives, and the emphasis on higher-order critical thinking skills encouraged by these approaches seem to cultivate positive student interaction and attitudes and to increase achievement among students typically labeled as low ability. (Dentzer & Wheelock, 1990; MacIver et al., 1997; Slavin 1980, 1987; Tomlinson, 2000). For African American students who often fall behind in the middle grades because of racial inequities (either within or among schools) in access to higher order curriculum, these alternative practices may be a key to giving them the opportunity to develop the academic skills that are the foundation for long-term academic success. Ultimately these alternative middle-level practices are promising for all students in that they place student needs, learning, and achievement at the center and are more equitable in intent and outcomes than the traditional middle level curricular, organizational and instructional practices.

IMPLEMENTING THE MIDDLE SCHOOL CONCEPT

The discourse on reform for middle-level education increasingly focuses on improving student achievement and closing the achievement gap, and those who espouse the middle school concept insist that successful reform must include full implementation of middle school philosophy and practices, to support both the intellectual and developmental needs of all adolescents. In the current emphasis on academic improvement, reform efforts have incorporated many elements of exemplary middle-level education practices, such as providing a challenging, integrative, and exploratory curriculum; varied teaching/learning approaches; learning-based assessment and evaluation; and flexible organizational structures. However, critics worry that this academic emphasis has come at the expense of valuing practices that foster the social, personal, and ethical development of students, distinctive and defining factors of a middle-level education (NMSA Research Summary # 4, 1996). Many insist that this trend of partial implementation of middle-school concepts leaves schools short of being true middle schools and reaching their full potential for excellence, given that both academic and developmental exemplary middle school practices have been demonstrated to have positive effects for all students (Mizell, 1999b; NMSA Research Summary #4, 1996).

Characteristics of Successful Middle Schools

Exemplary middle-level schools address the distinctiveness of early adolescence with various instructional and organizational features. Five key components are generally recognized by educators, associations, foundations, state boards of education, and researchers. Both empirical data and conventional wisdom support these components.

1. *Interdisciplinary teaming* refers to the organizational structure of a core of teachers assigned to the same group of students. A variety of configurations have been successful ranging from two to five team members in two, three or four subject areas. Teaming provides the structure to support two essential aspects of middle-level education: (a) **a positive psychosocial environment that allows flexibility and variety** (Keefe et al., 1983) and heterogeneous grouping of students (MacIver & Epstein, 1993) and (b) a structure to plan and deliver a curriculum that balances academic and humane factors (NMSA, 1995). Because teachers share the same students and have a common planning period, they are able to respond more quickly to the **needs of individual students though collaboration, meeting jointly with parents, and designing thematic units that foster the transfer of ideas among disciplines and increase relevance**.
2. *Advisory programs* consist of a small group of students (usually 20 or fewer) assigned to a teacher, administrator, or other staff member for a regularly scheduled meeting to discuss topics of concern to students. The purpose of this program is the development of close, trusting relationships between students and adults and to increase engagement with learning and feelings of positive self-esteem and belonging. Social and academic support activities include "discussing problems with individual students, giving career information and guidance, developing student self-confidence and leadership, and discussing academic issues, personal or family problems, social relationships, peer groups, health issues, moral or ethical issues and multicultural issues/intergroup relations" (MacIver, 1990). Teacher advisories also help create more positive school climates, develop students' self-concepts, and prevent dropouts. (George & Shewey, 1994; MacIver, 1990)
3. *Varied instruction* includes (1) integrating learning experiences, addressing students' own questions and focusing on real-life issues relevant to the student; (2) actively engaging students in problem solving and accommodating individual differences; (3) emphasizing collaboration, cooperation, and community; (4) seeking to develop good people, caring for others, democratic values, and moral sensitivity (NMSA, 1995). Some of the more common programs include multi-age grouping over longer periods of time, cross-age tutoring, cooperative learning, hands-on and student-centered activities; use of block time and flexible scheduling; and positive evaluations. Learning tasks are developmentally appropriate and adapted to individual differences.
4. *Exploratory programs* capitalize on the innate curiosity of young adolescents, exposing them to a range of academic, vocational, and recreational subjects for career options, community service, enrichment, and enjoyment. Exploratory topics include foreign languages, intramural sports, health, clubs, student government, home economics, technological arts, independent study projects, music, art, speech, drama, careers, consumer education, creative writing, and several other special areas.
5. *Transition programs* focus on creating a smooth change of schools for the young adolescent. Eighty-eight percent of public school students begin the middle grades in a new school, a transition that may overwhelm the coping skills of some students and "have pathogenic effects on their psychological adjustment, self-esteem, and motivation to learn" (MacIver, 1990). A common approach is for elementary school students to visit the middle-level school they will be attending, while administrators of the elementary and middle-level schools meet to discuss programs, and the middle school counselors meet to discuss ways to help students make a smooth transition from elementary to middle school and from middle school to high school. Visits to the middle school by fifth graders were used in 90 percent of the six to eight schools. (McEwin, Dickinson, & Jenkins, 1996)

(From *Components of Exemplary Middle Level Programs* as cited in NMSA Research Summary

#4. Exemplary Middle Schools Question: What are the components of an exemplary middle school?)

DEVELOPMENTALLY AND CULTURALLY RESPONSIVE MIDDLE SCHOOLS

The developmentally responsive elements of middle-level education are intended to create a positive, supportive school environment and encourage student motivation, interest, and well-being. This is achieved through practices such as small learning communities, interdisciplinary team teaching, opportunities for academic assistance and recognition, advisory programs for personal guidance, and programs that foster health that engage family and community involvement (Carnegie Council on Adolescent Development, 1989). Research indicates that these middle school concepts encompass key components of school learning environments demonstrated to raise achievement among African American students. (MacIver et al., 1997; McPartland & Braddock, 1993). However, for middle-level programs to be highly effective for African American learners, they also must be culturally responsive in addressing aspects of academic motivation and support needs that may be unique to the experiences of African American students. For many African American students, factors such as inequitable access to learning, being from at-risk environments, or from a cultural context different from that of the dominant culture, can put them at a disadvantage for excelling in traditional learning environments.

Although not all African American students necessarily face these challenges, overall they are more likely than their white peers to be subject to one or more of these circumstances. Perhaps the most distinctive element of the personal development process for African American adolescents that middle schools must be responsive to is the formation of a racial identity. Although it's true that all adolescents go through a process of exploring various aspects of self such as political, religious, gender, sexual, ethnic, and racial identity, not all will think of themselves in primarily racial terms (Tatum, 1997). African American adolescents are more likely than their White peers to be focused on exploring their racial identity, largely because interactions with others around them–teachers, peers, strangers–and their observation of discernible racial patterns, indicate that others increasingly see them in racial terms (Phinney & Tarver, 1988).

In research studies, African American students report interactions with teachers, guidance counselors, and other school officials that reflect racially biased beliefs. Among the racial stereotypes commonly expressed in these interactions are the belief that African American students have limited intellectual capabilities and potential for postsecondary education, or an inherent preference or aptitude for certain activities such as dance or athletics (Tatum, 1997). Concurrently, because African American students experience racial bias in school, they may become sensitized to the racial stereotypes about African Americans perpetuated in the media and the world at large that often associate Blackness with crime, poverty, deviance, aggressiveness, and obtuseness.

Racial patterns that tend to become pronounced by the middle grades that may stand out in the eyes of African American children include:

- *Racially identifiable ability groups or tracks*, whereby each level has a concentration of students from a particular racial group that remains persistent, even as students advance in grade level; in racially mixed schools Black children are most likely to be in the lower tracks (Tatum, 1997)
- *Lack of racial diversity* in the school's teaching and administrative staff
- *Increasing (self) segregation* along racial lines in social groups, events such as parties, in co-ed interactions/dating and extracurricular activities. (Tatum, 1997)

The degree to which establishing a racial identity is a positive or negative process for African American adolescents is in part related to the environment of their school. Just as family and community shape how children see themselves and the world, school, where children spend most of their time away from home, can be equally influential. The education process, school culture, and school actors such as teachers, staff, and peers, influence how students think and feel about themselves and others, as well as their values and beliefs. When the messages African American students receive in the school environment about what it means to be Black are negative, racially biased, or indifferent, the process of developing a racial identity may become difficult and painful, and their strategies for adapting to these circumstances can undermine their well-being.

An example of this observed by researchers is the adoption of an "oppositional identity" in which African American students reject behaviors, activities, events, and symbols believed to be characteristic of White culture in favor of those associated with African American culture (Fordham & Ogbu, 1986). Perhaps the most devastating dynamic of the oppositional identity for African American students is that it often casts academic achievement as a form of "acting White" and discourages students from embracing the behaviors and values that lead to academic success out of devaluing such achievement and fear of peer rejection (Fordham & Ogbu, 1986; Tatum 1997).

Of course, not all Black students have the same process of racial identity development and in turn can exhibit a range of strategies for responding to racism. Many do create a sense of identity that enables them to embrace academic success; however, this process can also cause inner conflict for African American students in a school environment that does not provide positive messages about what it means to be Black. Researchers have observed the use of coping strategies among academically successful Black students in racially mixed schools such as avoiding behaviors and activities seen as characteristically Black, to assimilate and find acceptance among White students (Fordham, 1996). Although this type of assimilation may seem more positive than the oppositional stance with its rejection of academic achievement, it too affirms the notion that being academically successful and being Black are mutually exclusive identities.

Given the middle school concept's emphasis on nurturing the developmental process of adolescence, middle grades educators have an obligation to address issues of racial bias and the question of how it is that academic achievement comes to be viewed as White and develop strategies to prevent African American students from becoming alienated from the education process. This type of school transformation requires creating an inclusive, responsive, and multicultural school environment, one that responds to student needs and experiences, provides all students with equitable learning opportunities, and values diversity in the student and staff population, as well as in the larger society (Gorski, 2000).

CULTURALLY RESPONSIVE STUDENT GROUPING AND STAFFING PRACTICES

To eliminate the widespread belief that academic achievement is the domain of Whites, middle school educators must implement new practices and strategies that will instill belief in the intellectual capability of people of all racial, ethnic, gender, and class backgrounds. Among the common institutional education practices that can perpetuate the primary association of achievement with whiteness are tracking/ability grouping and the absence of African Americans and other people of color on teaching and administrative staff. The effects of these practices are linked to the fact that what we see around us shapes and affirms our notions of how we think of ourselves and others and how we believe others perceive us. When African Americans are persistently placed in the lower tracks/ability groups and the people who provide knowledge and hold power in the school are usually not African Americans, it sends a message that African Americans are not intellectually capable and that knowledge and power are the province of Whites and other non-Blacks.

The importance of having a racially diverse staff, particularly when there is a racially diverse student body, also speaks to the positive effects of providing role models with whom students can identify and connect. For African American students, having teachers and school administrators from their own background affirms their capacity for achievement and leadership and has been shown to contribute to improving teacher-student bonds and students' attitudes toward school and learning (Martinez, 1991; McPartland & Braddock, 1993). At the same time, it's important to note that a teacher's being African American does not guarantee that she or he will have a sense of mutual interest and identification with students. The African American community is not homogenous, and African American teachers, like their colleagues of other racial backgrounds, may have a sense of class, social, and even ethnic/racial identities that differs from that of their students. Ultimately schools will have to be proactive in using racially diverse hiring practices in conjunction with staff development that prepares all teachers to interact with students in affirming and supportive ways to bridge ethnic, racial, and class differences. In addition, providing all students with teachers, administrators, and school leaders of different ethnicities can reverse the idea that only Whites are capable of holding these positions, reduce prejudice, and help build a mutually respectful community.

FACILITATING SOCIAL INTEGRATION

Although schools cannot control students' choices in peer groups, extracurricular activities, or out-of-school activities that may result in racially homogenous groupings, they can foster racial mixing through school organizational structures and activities that encourage participation from all students. One way to do this is to implement required exploratory academic, career, arts, and recreational programs/classes attended by heterogeneous groups of students. The diversity of student participation and interests seen in the course of such exploratory programs can serve to widen students' horizons and challenge stereotypes of what activities, subjects, or preferences are culturally "White" or "Black." This may encourage students to elect to participate in activities or classes that they may have not have considered previously because of race-, class-, or gender biased views of what activities are "appropriate" for them. Exploratory programs can also foster relationships among students who may not have connected otherwise because of outward differences that steer their choices in social cliques, activities, and elective classes, ties that may extend beyond class time and into social settings.

At the same time, it's important for schools to acknowledge that same-race social grouping can be a healthy African American response to being in the racial minority. Same-race social groups serve the purpose of providing connections with peers who can identify with each other's experiences and support them as they explore their racial identity (Fordham & Ogbu, 1986; Tatum, 1997). However, without the context of institutional messages of confidence in the academic capability of African American students and positive African American role models, this type of grouping could seed the negative aspects of oppositional identity that operate against African American students and their educational success. One strategy that schools have used to provide this context is to institutionalize opportunities for African American students to come together on a regular basis with supportive African American education or advisory staff to address issues of racial identity, experiences of bias and isolation, and how to improve and sustain their academic achievement. Schools that have instituted this function report improvements in participating African American students' behavior and attitudes and the development of a peer culture that supports academic achievement, rather than hinders it (Tatum, 1997; Viadero, 2000).

CULTURALLY RESPONSIVE CURRICULUM

Creating a culturally responsive middle school also can be enacted though changes in curriculum. An important aspect of motivating students is providing schoolwork that speaks to their identity, interests, and welfare. African American students often report finding school boring or that they don't see its relevance to them or to their chances for success later in life (McPartland & Braddock, 1993). This is attributed to the absence or marginalization of African Americans and other people of color, as well as women, in texts and other teaching materials, which can be alienating to African American students (Abdal-Haqq, 1994). In particular, African American students without many models of academic and professional success in their own communities are even less likely to be motivated by the notion that learning such material can improve their opportunities for success (Abdal-Haqq, 1994; Tatum, 1997). Studies on Black students, racial identity, and achievement indicate that when young people are exposed to the legacy of achievement and intellectual contributions by African American scholars, politicians, inventors, and other notable figures throughout history and in the present, they are more likely to be motivated to learn and less likely to view academic achievement as characteristically White (Tatum, 1997).

To engage all students, schools must create an inclusive curriculum that reflects the diversity in society and the classroom. Approaches that schools have used to do this include multicultural, antiracist, and conflict resolution education. Multicultural education promotes awareness of racial and cultural differences through education and emphasizes respect and acceptance of differences while valuing one's own intrinsic worth and culture (National Association for Multicultural Education, 2000). Antiracist education consists of instruction that encourages critical thinking to explore the inequities that shape race relations, cultural differences, and the causes of racism (Mitchell, 1990). Conflict resolution education gives school staff, teachers, and students the tools to prevent, resolve, and mediate conflicts that arise because of racial, ethnic, class, and gender issues (Mitchell, 1990). Together, antiracist and conflict resolution education give students the language and tools to explore the origins and effects of racism and to confront racial bias within the "safe" context of mediated resolution.

CULTURALLY RESPONSIVE INSTITUTIONAL PRACTICES

Infusing cultural responsiveness in all aspects of the school environment requires a building-wide effort and the support of committed leaders who consistently demonstrate a belief in the value of providing multiple cultural perspectives and promoting racial diversity for students' well-being. Practices school leaders can use to cultivate cultural responsiveness in the areas of staff, instructional, and policy leadership include the following.

Culturally Responsive Staff Leadership Practices

- Maintain racial and cultural diversity among administrative, faculty, and staff members
- Provide staff development that promotes diversity awareness and increases ability to teach diverse students

Culturally Responsive Curriculum Leadership Practices

- Check textbooks and materials for bias and accuracy
- Design curriculum that provides diverse, accurate perspectives and encourages all students to share their perspectives
- Affirm and acknowledge diverse racial and cultural contributions throughout the curriculum and the school year, not only for occasions such as Black History month

Culturally Responsive School Policies

- Develop and issue antidiscrimination policy statements concerning race, ethnicity, religion, and gender that cover school district policy, hiring practices, and the handling of bias-motivated incidents
- Establish human-relations committees that include students, faculty, and staff to promote an environment that embraces racial and cultural diversity
- Develop systems to monitor and report trends in racial attitudes and bias-motivated incidents
- Provide services for victims of bias-motivated discrimination, harassment, or violence (Abdal-Haqq, 1994; Gorski, 2000; Mitchell, 1990; Tatum, 1997)

Ultimately, the educational practices found effective for addressing the unique developmental needs of African American students reflect the values of the developmental focus central to the middle school concept and strengthen the capacity of middle schools to overcome barriers to African American student achievement and close the achievement gap while fostering excellence for all students.

EFFECTIVE LEADERSHIP FOR CHANGE

A theme echoed throughout the literature on reform efforts is the influence of school leadership in implementing and sustaining meaningful middle-level school reform. In a study of educators across the country with reputations as leaders of effective sustained school improvement efforts, the participants identified the following habits of mind as key to their effectiveness:

Valuing partnership and voice: listening to the voices of a variety of stakeholders; looking for evidence of widespread participation in important aspects of change and developing plans that reflect the legitimate influence of others to energize efforts.

Tying vision and values: establishing a collaborative vision centered on students and academic achievement; operating consistently according to the values and beliefs tied to that vision as "keepers of the dream," and to inspire others.

Knowledge and daring: developing relevant information bases and cultivating human resources to minimize barriers while encouraging risk-taking.

Savvy and persistence: understanding how the system works and how to interact with the central office, local community and others outside of school; learning how to motivate these various actors to move from resistance to cooperation; cultivating a network of supporters within and outside of the system to lean on in times of stress.

Self assessment: using self assessments to demonstrate accountability to values and community expectations; approaches include individual assessment methods such as surveys, mentors, portfolio development and journals; group methods such as collective feedback to identify areas for personal reflection; and tailor-made rubrics that focus on specific elements of the reform process.

Personal qualities: strength of character, reliability, passion, empathy, patience and humor are among qualities that reform leaders identified as instrumental in their success. (From Leighton, M.S. & Nadeau, A. *The Role of Leadership in Sustaining School Reform: Voices from the Field*, 1996)

LEARNING FROM FAILURE

Given that the literature is rich with research-based recommendations on what should work to improve middle-level education and close the achievement gap, it is important to consider why the wave of well-funded middle grades improvement projects during the past decade have not yet had a transformational impact on student achievement. Multimillion-dollar reform projects spearheaded by various foundations and departments of education have channeled money for middle grades reform into schools and school districts across the country to support the implementation of new practices and the establishment of collaborative networks for sharing best practices and shaping reform policy (Lewis, 1996; Norton & Lewis, 2000). Although this has raised support for middle grades improvement in the larger education agenda, improvements have been varied and incremental, because reformers have had to focus resources on overcoming the barriers to change that they encounter in school systems. Among the barriers cited in reports on various reform initiatives are:

- The high rates of turnover in school and district office staff
- Low levels of leadership experience and skills among principals for nurturing sustainable change
- Lack of cooperation from teacher's unions for flexibility in hiring practices
- Low district commitment to supporting school leaders in change efforts
- Poor alignment between curricula and state assessments
- Inadequate data tracking and reporting systems (Lewis, 1996a; Norton & Lewis, 2000; Mizell, 1999b).

In addition, each reform effort has its learning curve in which it discovers with time what approaches to change are least or most effective, how to overcome such barriers, and how to better integrate multiple aspects of systemic change. Learning these lessons has enabled middle grades reform programs to develop a more refined and focused approach and will hopefully increase the level of measurable school improvement and student achievement in the future.

CONCLUSION

Skill, vision, and innovation are essential leadership qualities for answering the mandate of improving middle grades education and closing the achievement gap while meeting the demands of the standards and accountability movement that is increasingly shaping the direction of school reform. Not only must school leaders attend to their roles as "keepers of the dream" reformers, but also as keepers of the crossroads for those African American students for whom the middle grades are often a no return point of academic decline. This means designing schools that apply middle school concepts in ways that provide all students with equitable opportunities to master the skills needed for educational achievement and the support needed to make lasting, positive intellectual and developmental transformations. Out of the efforts that have fall en short of expectations and goals, there are lessons learned and an increasing number of success stories to which leaders can look for direction. In addition, a growing body of research suggests ways to recreate middle-level education to foster equity and provide a balance of academic and personal development for adolescents.

RESOURCES FOR MIDDLE SCHOOL REFORM

NATIONAL MIDDLE SCHOOL ASSOCIATION (NMSA). Established in 1973, the NMSA serves as a voice for professionals, parents, and others interested in the educational and developmental needs of young adolescents (10–15 years of age). NMSA is the only national educational association exclusively devoted to improving the educational experiences of young adolescents. NMSA has more than 20,000 members in more than 50 countries, including teachers, principals, parents, college faculty, central office administrators, educational consultants, and community leaders. The NMSA provides a variety of resources on middle grades instruction, curriculum, organization and leadership. http://www.nmsa.org/

NATIONAL FORUM TO ACCELERATE MIDDLE GRADES REFORM

The National Forum to Accelerate Middle Grades Reform brings together middle-level program sponsors, advocates, educators, researchers, state and local representatives, and leaders of national and regional associations to share ideas and create effective approaches to middle grades improvement. The Forum conducts research and disseminates policy statements on critical education issues that affect the daily lives of students, parents, teachers, and administrators to spur discussion and help others address these issues. In its "Schools to Watch" initiative, the National Forum identifies schools that best meet its criteria to describe high-performing middle-level schools and provides in-depth case studies about these schools on its website. In addition, the Forum website provides an extensive listing of important resources on middle-grades reform and offers assistance in identifying additional resources. http://www.mgforum.org/

NATIONAL STAFF DEVELOPMENT COUNCIL (NSDC). A national nonprofit association of approximately 8,000 educators, NSDC is deeply committed to ensuring success for all students by applying high standards for professional development for everyone who affects student learning. The Council views high-quality staff development programs as essential to creating schools in which all students and staff members are learners who continually improve their performance. Publisher of *What Works in the Middle: Results-based Staff Development* by Joellen Killion. http://www.nsdc.org/midbook/

MIDDLE WEB

This website explores the challenges of middle school reform and provides an extensive array of resources and tools to assist educators and parents in their efforts to improve middle-level education policies and practices. The site provides seminal and cutting-edge information on middle-level education issues, including curriculum and instruction, assessment and evaluation, leadership, professional development, and parent and community involvement. http://www.middleweb.com/

NATIONAL CLEARINGHOUSE FOR COMPREHENSIVE SCHOOL REFORM NCCSR). The Clearinghouse was created to improve the national dissemination of information on comprehensive school reform. NCCSR audiences include school-based staff, educational administrators, researchers, policymakers, and the general public. The Clearinghouse collects, analyzes, and disseminates information on comprehensive school reform in educational institutions serving the K through 12 population, including public schools, public school districts, state education agencies, and private schools in the United States. http://www.goodschools.gwu.edu/abonccsr.htm

URBAN MIDDLE-GRADES REFORM NETWORK. This is a forum for district administrators to support and advance each other's middle grades reform efforts. Thirty-five district administrators from twenty urban districts have participated in the network. The network began in 1995, coordinated by the Academy for Educational Development (AED), a nonprofit educational evaluation and technical assistance organization with offices in Washington, DC and New York City and by the Edna McConnell Clark Foundation, a New York City-based foundation that focuses on youth development. http://www.mgnetwork.org/activities/index.html

MIDDLE LEVEL LEADERSHIP CENTER (MLLC). MLLC identifies, designs, and conducts research about critical issues in middle-level leadership. MLLC disseminates knowledge about effective site-level leadership to practicing school-site leaders, university faculty, and leaders of professional organizations and educational agencies and works with middle-level leaders and school faculty to translate existing knowledge into effective school practices. http://www.mllc.org/about.htm

MERIDIAN. This electronic journal is dedicated to research and practice of computer technology in middle school classrooms. Published twice yearly by North Carolina State University, *Meridian* features research findings, practitioner articles, commentary, and book excerpts by educational researchers, technology designers, middle school teachers, and authors who wish to share and expand teaching and learning experiences with computer technologies in middle school classrooms and beyond. http://www.ncsu.edu/meridian/

REFERENCES

Abdal-Haqq, I. (1994). *Culturally responsive curriculum.* Educational Resources Information Center (ERIC) Digest No. 370 936: U.S. Department of Education.

Alexander, W. M., & McEwin, C. K. (1989). *Schools in the middle: Status and progress.* Columbus, OH: National Middle School Association.

Alexander, W.M., & Williams, E.L. (1965). Schools for the middle school years. *Educational Leadership, 23*(3), 217–223.

Anderson, J.D. (1988). *The education of Blacks in the South, 1860–1935.* Chapel Hill: University of North Carolina.

Armour-Thomas, E., Clay, C., Domanico, R., Bruno, K., & Allen, B. (1989). An outlier study of elementary and middle schools in New York City: Final report. NY: New York City Board of Education.

Atanda, R. (1999). Do gatekeeper courses expand education options? *Education Statistics Quarterly: Elementary/Secondary Education.* U.S. Department of Education: National Center for Educational Statistics. http://nces.gov/pubs99/quarterlyapr/4-elementary/4-esq11-c.html

Bamburg, J. (1994). *Raising expectations to improve student learning.* Oak Brook, IL: North Central Regional Educational Laboratory.

Burnette, J. (1999). *Critical behaviors and strategies for teaching culturally diverse students.* Educational Resources Information Center (ERIC) Digest E584: U.S. Department of Education. http://ericec.org/digests/e584.html

Carnegie Council on Adolescent Development. (1989). *Turning points: Preparing American youth for the 21st century.* New York: The Carnegie Corporation of New York.

Center for Research on the Education of Disadvantaged Students. (1994). *Survey analyses of effective middle grades and high schools for disadvantaged students* (Project #7120). Baltimore, MD: Johns Hopkins University. http://www.ed.gov/offices/OERI/At-Risk/cds1rp13.html

College Board. (2000). *Advancing minority high achievement: National trends and promising programs and practices.* New York: College Board.

Cotton, K. (1989). *Expectations and student outcomes.* Portland, OR: Northwest Regional Educational Laboratory.

Darling-Hammond, L. (1997). *Doing what matters most: Investing in quality teaching.* New York: National Commission on Teaching and America's Future.

Darling-Hammond, L. (2000). Teacher quality and student achievement: A review of state policy evidence. *Education Policy Analysis Archives*, *8*(1), 1–38.

Dentzer, E., & Wheelock, A. (1990). *Locked in/Locked out: Tracking and placement practices in public schools.* Boston: Massachusetts Advocacy Center.

Education Trust. (1999). *Dispelling the myth: High poverty schools exceeding expectations.* Washington, DC: Author.

Ferguson, R. F. (1997). *Evidence that schools can narrow the Black-White test score gap.* (Working Paper, #H-97-04, Malcolm Wiener Center for Social Policy). Cambridge, MA: John F. Kennedy School of Government.

Ferguson, R.F., & Ladd, H.F. (1996). How and why money matters: An analysis of Alabama schools. In H. Ladd (Ed.), *Holding schools accountable* (pp. 265–298). Washington, D.C.: Brookings Institution.

Fordham, S. (1996). *Blacked out: Dilemmas of race, identity, and success at Capitol High.* Chicago, IL: University of Chicago Press.

Fordham, S., & Ogbu J. (1986). Black students' school success: Coping with the burden of acting White. *Urban Review, 18,* 176-206.

Goldhaber, M., & Brewer, D. (2000, Summer). Does teacher certification matter? High school certification status and student achievement. *Educational Evaluation and Policy Analysis, 22*(2), pp.129–145.

Gonder, P. (1991). *Caught in the middle: How to unleash the potential of average students.* Arlington, VA: American Association of School Administrators.

Gorski, P. (2000). *The challenge of defining a single multicultural education.* McGraw Hill Multicultural Supersite. http://www.mhhe.com/socscience/education/multi/define.html

Greenwald, R., Hedges, L.V., & Laine, R.D. (1996). The effect of school resources on student achievement. *Review of Educational Research, 66,* 361–396.

Johnson, D. W., Johnson, R.T., & E. J. Holubec, E.J. (1993). *Circles of learning: Cooperation in the classroom* (4th ed.). Edina, MN: Interaction Book.

Killion, J. (1999). *What works in the middle: Results-based staff development.* Oxford, OH: National Staff Development Council.

Knapp, M.S., (Ed.) (1995). *Teaching for meaning in high poverty classrooms.* New York: Teachers College Press.

Langer, J. (1999). *Beating the odds: Teaching middle and high school students to read and write well.* New York: University at Albany, School of Education, National Research Center on English Learning & Achievement.

Lewis, A. C. (1996a). *Believing in ourselves: Progress and struggle in urban middle school reform, 1989–1995.* New York: The Edna McConnell Clark Foundation.

Lewis, A. C. (1996b). Special issue on middle-grades reform. Urban middle-grades reform: Foundations keep trying. *Harvard Education Letter, 12*(5), 5–6

Lounsboury, J. (1996). *Key characteristics of middle level schools.* Educational Resources Information Center (ERIC) Digest, ED 401 050: U.S. Department of Education.

Lumsden, L. (1997). Expectations for students. Educational Resources Information Center (ERIC) Digest, ED409609: U.S. Department of Education.

Lynn, L., & Wheelcock, A. (1997). Making detracking work. *Harvard Education Letter, 13*(1).

MacIver, D., Plank, S.B., & Balfanz, R. (1997). Working together to become proficient readers: Early impact of the talent development of middle school's student team literature program. Center for Research on the Education of Students Placed at Risk. Report # 15.

Martinez, R. L., Jr. (1991). A crisis in the profession: Minority role models in critically short supply. *Vocational Education Journal, 66*(4), 24–25, 46.

Marzano, R.J., Pickering, D., & McTighe, J. (1993). *Assessing student outcomes: Performance assessment using the dimensions of learning model.* Alexandra, VA: Association for Supervision and Curriculum Development.

Mason, D. A., Schroeter, D. D., Combs, R. K., & Washington, K. (1992). Assigning average-achieving eighth graders to advanced mathematics classes in an urban junior high. *Elementary School Journal, 92*(5), 587–599. EJ 447 688.

McEwin, C. K., Dickinson, T.S., Jenkins, D. (1996). *America's middle schools: Practices & progress: A 25-year perspective.* Columbus, OH: National Middle School Association.

McPartland, J., & Braddock, J.H. III. (1993). A conceptual framework on learning environments and student motivation for language minority and other underserved populations. *Proceedings of the Third National Research Symposium on Limited English Proficient Student Issues: Focus on Middle and High School Issues.* Washington, D.C.: U.S. Department of Education Office of Bilingual Education and Minority Languages Affairs. www.ncbe.gwu.edu/ncbepubs/symposia/third/index.htm

Mitchell, V. (1990). *Curriculum and instruction to reduce racial conflict.* New York: ERIC Clearinghouse on Urban Education. ERIC Document Reproduction Service No: ED 322 274.

Mizell, H. (1999a, April) *The middle school movement: Thirty and counting.* Remarks presented at the Middle Grades Education Conference, Southern Regional Education Board, Atlanta, GA. http://www.middleweb.com/HMsouth.html

Mizell, H. (1999b, December). *A middle grades reformer tells it like it is.* Remarks presented on panel, "What Key Reformers Have Learned About Reform," annual conference of the National Staff Development Council, Dallas, TX. http://www.middleweb.com/HMlessons.html

National Association for Multicultural Education. (2000). *Philosophy and code of ethics.* Washington, DC: National

Association for Multicultural Education. http://www.nameorg.org/philosophy.html

National Center for Education Statistics. (1998). *Digest of education statistics, 1998.* U.S. Department of Education: Author.

National Center for Education Statistics. (1999). *Teacher quality: A report on the preparation and qualification of public school teachers.* U.S. Department of Education: Author.

National Center for Education Statistics. (2000). NAEP 1999 Trends in Academic Progress: Three Decades of Students Performance. U.S. Department of Education: Author.

National Forum to Accelerate Middle-Grades Reform. (2000). Schools to watch. Newton, MA: National Forum to Accelerate Middle-Grades Reform. http://www.mgforum.org/schools.asp

National Middle School Association. (1995). *This We Believe.* Columbus, OH: National Middle School Association.

National Middle School Association. (1996). NMSA Research Summary #4: Exemplary Middle Schools. Columbus, OH: National Middle School Association.

National Middle School Association. (1996). NMSA Research Summary #6: Heterogeneous Grouping. Columbus, OH: National Middle School Association.

National Middle School Association. (1996). NMSA Research Summary #7: Middle Level Licensure. Columbus, OH: National Middle School Association.

Norton, J., & Lewis, A. C. (2000). Middle-grades reform 2000. *Kappan, Special Report, 8*(10). http://www.pdkintl.org/kappan/klew0006.htm

Phinney, J.S., & Tarver, S., (1988). Ethnic identity search and commitment in Black and White eighth graders. *Journal of Early Adolescence, 8*(3), 265-77

Rudin, T., & Lane, L. (1998). *A review of the literature on middle-grade schools' parent and teacher attitudes.* (A Report to the National Forum to Accelerate Middle-Grades Reform.) Middle Web website at: http://www.middleweb.com/MSlitreview.html

Schoenfeld, A.H. (1992). Learning to think mathematically: Problem solving, metacognition, and sense-making in mathematics. In D. Grouws (Ed.), *The handbook for research on mathematics teaching and learning* (pp. 334–370). New York: MacMillan.

Slavin, R. (1980). *Cooperative learning: What research says to the teacher.* Baltimore, MD: Center for Social Organization of Schools.

Slavin, R. (1987, March). Cooperative learning: Can students help students learn? *Instructor*, pp. 74–78.

Slavin, R. E. (1991, February). Synthesis of research on cooperative learning. *Educational Leadership*, pp. 71–82.

Slavin, R., & Braddock, J.H. III (1993). Ability grouping: on the wrong track. *College Board Review, 168*, 11–18.

Smith, J. (1996). Does an extra year make a difference? The impact of early access to algebra on long-term gains in mathematics attainment. *Educational Evaluation and Policy Analysis, 18*(2), 141–153.

Stahl, R. J., & VanSickle, R.L. (Eds.). (1992). *Cooperative learning in the social studies classroom: An invitation to social study.* Washington, DC: National Council for the Social Studies.

Strauss, R. P., & Sawyer, E.A. (1986). Some new evidence on teacher and student competencies. *Economics of Education Review, 5*(1), 41–48.

Strickland, D. E., & Asher, C. (1992). Low income African-American children and public schooling. In P. W. Jackson (Ed.), *Handbook of research on curriculum* (pp. 609–625). New York: Macmillan.

Tatum, D.B. (1997). *Why are all the Black kids sitting together in the cafeteria? And other Conversations about race.* New York: Basic Books.

Tomlinson, C. A. (1995). Differentiating instruction for advanced learners in the mixed-ability classroom. Educational Resources Information Center (ERIC) Digest, No. 389141: U.S. Department of Education.

Tomlinson, C. A. (1999, October) Leadership for differentiated classrooms. *School Administrator.* Vol. 56, No. 9. Alexandria, VA: American Association of School Administrators. http://www.aasa.org/publications/sa/1999_10/tomlinson.htm

Tomlinson, C.A. (2000). The differentiated classroom and African American learners. Unpublished manuscript.

Valentine, J., Clark, D. D., Irvin, J. L., Keefe, J. W., & Melton, G. (1993). *Leadership in middle level education. Volume I: A national survey of middle level leaders and schools.* Reston, VA: National Association of Secondary School Principals.

Viadero, D. (1996, May 29). Middle school gains over 25 years chronicled. *Education Week*, http://www.edweek.org/ew/vol-15/36middle.h15.

Viadero, D. (2000, March 15). Even in well-off suburbs, minority achievement lags. *Education Week*, http://www.edweek.org/ew/ewstory.cfm?slug=27shaker.h19.

Welch, O. M., & Hodges, C. R. (1997). *Standing outside on the inside: Black adolescents and the construction of academic identity.* Albany, NY: State University of New York.

Article 20

MAKING HIGH SCHOOLS WORK FOR AFRICAN AMERICAN STUDENTS

PATRICIA E. ORTMAN AND NATHALIE THANDIWE

> We already know more than enough to successfully educate all students. The question is whether we want to teach all students.
>
> *Ron Edmunds*

IF MIDDLE SCHOOL IS THE CRUCIAL crossroads between academic success and failure, high school often becomes the dead end. Many argue that high schools are failing most students, regardless of race (American Youth Policy Forum, 2000; Carnegie Challenge, 2001; Botstein, 1997; Darling-Hammond, 1997; Kohn, 1999; Commission on Restructuring of the American High School, 1996; National Commission on the High School Senior Year, 2001; Shore, 1997; Sizer, 1984). Although the terrain of high school education should have been transformed (by factors such as the increasing racial and ethnic diversity of students, the advent of information technology, and rapidly changing economic conditions and social and cultural mores), high schools have not changed much during the past century. For the most part, their curricula, instruction, and organizational methods seem mired in the past (Boykin, 2000; Darling-Hammond, 1997; Sizer, 1984).

By high school, the disparities in academic achievement between African American and White students that emerged in kindergarten and grew throughout elementary and middle school remain fixed (Johnson & Viadero, 2000, citing Phillips). Even African American students with socioeconomic advantages that would seemingly exclude them from the "at-risk" category who attend otherwise effective high schools frequently do not do as well academically as their White and Asian peers. In fact, the achievement gap between African Americans and their peers is even greater among students whose parents have college degrees than those whose parents did not graduate from high school (*Reaching the Top*, 1999 College Board Report cited in Viadero, 2000). At the same time, there are resilient African American students who face numerous risk factors but succeed despite the odds against them (Benard, 1996; Ford, 1996, citing Hebert; Wang & Kovach, 1996). In search of answers, researchers have begun to examine the remaining common denominator in the achievement gap equation, schools themselves. They hope to reach a more complete understanding of the causes of the achievement gap to generate viable strategies to raise African American achievement.

HOW HIGH SCHOOLS FAIL AFRICAN AMERICAN STUDENTS

The high school years are characterized by declining levels of student enthusiasm, lower levels of identification with school, and a decreasing correlation between grades and self-esteem (Harris Interactive, Inc., 2000; Osborne, 1997). Researchers have described this process of declining scholastic interest as one of academic disengagement or disidentification. Disidentification is defined as "the lack of a relationship between academic self-esteem and global self-esteem, with the implication that there has been a relationship in the past" (Steele, 1992 as cited by Osborne, 1997, p. 728). The phenomenon of academic disidentification seems more pronounced among African American students, particularly African American males, than among their peers, as they progress through school (Osborne, 1997). In exploring causes of African American student disidentification, researchers have explored the following possible factors: impersonal environments, tracking, a lack of academic support for struggling students, cultural incongruence, weak school links to families and communities, and little support for developmental needs.

The Impersonal Environments of Large Schools

Approximately 70 percent of U.S. high school students attend schools enrolling at least 1,000 students. Nearly 50 percent of students attend schools with enrollments of more than 1,500 (U.S. Department of Education, 2000). Twenty-five percent of U.S. high schools have enrollments exceeding 2,000 (National Center for Policy Analysis, 2000), and New York City has many schools with enrollments approaching 5,000 (Cotton, 1996). Among the recurrent themes in the reflections of students, teachers, and parents on the comprehensive high school experience are complaints about the impersonal, institutional nature of these schools (Kohn, 1999; Harris Interactive, Inc., 2000; Shore, 1997, Sizer, 1999). This kind of educational environment makes it difficult to foster positive, meaningful relationships among students, teachers, and families and may leave parents feeling disconnected from their child's educational experience and unaware of how the system works. For teachers, this can mean they do not know the names of all of their students, let alone have a personal connection with them. Students can easily feel invisible, isolated, and so alienated that their interest in school is eroded (Kohn, 1999; Harris Interactive, Inc., 2000; Shore, 1997, Sizer, 1999).

The lack of close student-teacher relationships is a particular problem, because students are more likely to pursue academic achievement to gain approval and praise when they have good relationships with teachers. (Darling-Hammond, 1997; Nelson-Barber & Estrin, 1995). The establishment of close student-teacher relationships is further compromised by increasingly negative teacher-student perceptions of one another as students progress from elementary through high school (Harris Interactive, Inc., 2000). This disproportionately disadvantages African American students, because negative teacher-student perceptions are even more common between teachers and their African American students, particularly their African American male students, than between teachers and their other students (Roderick, 2000; Harris Interactive, Inc., 2000; Noguerra, in press, citing Ladson-Billings, Foster, & Lee). African American students are even further disadvantaged by the fact that positive personal relationships with their teachers may be even more important to their engagement in academic activities and ultimate academic success than to that of their peers (Ferguson, 1998, citing Casteel and Jassim, Eccles & Madon).

Tracking

High schools have traditionally separated students into college bound and general or vocational education (and remedial) tracks. Historically, African Americans (and other ethnic minorities) have found themselves consigned to the lower tracks. The curriculum and instruction in lower academic tracks is less demanding and stimulating than that of their peers in college-bound tracks. The teachers are also less qualified (Darling-Hammond, 2000, citing Gamoran, Gamoran, & Mare; Oakes, 1985, 1990). Predictably, the outcomes of tracking leave students in lower tracks unprepared for and less likely to move on to higher education opportunities than their higher-track peers.

Lower Levels of Academic Support

Another significant aspect of high school culture that distinguishes it from elementary and middle school environments is the academic "sink or swim" ethos characteristic of large, comprehensive high schools. Once students are grouped according to perceived ability levels or aspirations, most educational resources are put toward maintaining the status quo rather than cultivating academic excellence in all students. For students who enter high school with below-grade-level skills, a circumstance that African American students face at disproportionately higher levels than their peers, the likelihood of being placed in low-level courses or tracks reduces their chances of receiving access to school resources. The high-quality curriculum and instruction, which are key to helping them successfully make the transition to high school and to fulfilling their academic potential, are denied to them (Oakes, 1992). Their low performance, rather than being seen as a sign of needing additional support or varied instruction, is viewed as an affirmation of their placement (Roderick, 2000).

Despite the fact that struggling and underprepared students are often the ones who need the most academic attention and resources, they are usually the students who receive inadequate resources. They are referred in disproportionate numbers to special education (Cotton, 2001; Ford, 1996, citing U.S. Department of Education). Special education has become the high school intellectual burial ground. Students, once labeled, tend to remain in dead-end placements throughout their high school careers (McPartland & Slavin, 1990; Spencer, 2000). Even though individual cases of special education reform have demonstrated that, with appropriate support, many students classified as special education can improve skills and learn mainstream curriculum (Fearn, in press), overall, the special education system does not assist such students in doing so (McPartland & Slavin, 1990). For struggling students, their experiences with the limited, often ineffective, and even stigmatizing academic support systems characteristic of high schools can fuel feelings of ambivalence concerning school and their abilities, undermine their academic development, and contribute to a cycle of failure (Noguerra, in press; Roderick, 2000).

Cultural Incongruence

Although school reform measures typically treat schools as culturally neutral, issues of ethnicity, class, and culture shape the school environment just as they affect the larger society beyond the classroom. To the degree that students' experiences and identities are congruent with the dominant culture, they are more likely to identify with and find affirmation in their school experience. Cultural incongruence can create disadvantages and feed student alienation (Greenfield, Raeff, & Quiroz, 1996).

Lack of Family and Community Links

Additional complicating elements for many African American students are schools' weak linkages to their families and communities. Although parents traditionally reduce their involvement in schools and student learning as children grow older, research shows that parent involvement in schools and the educational activities of their children is important to student engagement and support. African American parents, for the same reasons as their children, i.e., the size and impersonal nature of many high schools, may feel discouraged and disengaged. Traditional Eurocentric assumptions that African American culture has little to offer make some schools less likely to tap culturally relevant community resources, such as parents, African American mentors, or churches, to support student engagement and success (Ford, 1996; Witherspoon, in press).

Lack of Support for Positive Identity Development

Although high school is a time of rapid physical and emotional, as well as cognitive growth, research demonstrates that traditional high school practices and cultures do not meet teenage developmental needs (Darling-Hammond, 1997; Shore, 1997). As discussed previously, it can be argued that high schools are frequently out of touch, alienating youth. This is especially true for those students whose cultural norms differ from White middle-class norms.

PROMISING STRATEGIES FOR IMPROVING HIGH SCHOOLS FOR AFRICAN AMERICAN STUDENTS

Citing the University of California Report of Black Student Achievement, Noguerra (in press), indicates that there are twenty-two public schools in California in which Black students make up 50 percent or more of the population that have achieved aggregate scores of 750 or more (of 1,000) on the academic performance indicators of that state. (He implies, and so we assume, that this is a good score). In addition, however, and perhaps more importantly, he says that when the test score data are disaggregated by race and gender, there is no evidence of an achievement gap. Noguerra cites Sizemore (1988) and Murphy and Hallinger (1985) in saying that researchers who study effective schools have found, for years, "that such schools possess the following characteristics: (1) a clear, sense of purpose; (2) core standards within a rigorous curriculum; (3) high expectations; (4) commitment to educate all students; (5) safe and orderly learning environment; (6) strong partnerships with parents; (7) a problem solving attitude." He goes on to say, "there is no disagreement that such schools consistently produce high levels of academic achievement among minority students" (Noguerra, in press, p. 12). The U.S. Department of Education is studying the characteristics of high schools that are proving to be effective, and several schools with large numbers of African American students have been included in each of two research projects: the New American High Schools initiative (Aiming High) and the educational improvement and Title I in secondary schools study (Stepping up to the Challenge). These studies measure success by improved attendance and graduation rates, improved performance on national standardized tests, and higher enrollment in post-secondary education.

Although their individual plans, programs, and approaches to school improvement often differ, many of the practices these schools used in implementing their various improvement plans are similar in form. Among the features shared by many are school-based initiative to change; a shared vision among stakeholders; visionary, inspirational leadership; dedicated educators; an extensive support structure for the ongoing changes; and in-depth parent involvement. A theme that emerged among the leadership of the schools is that, although they viewed limited resources as a problem, they did not view it as an absolute barrier to change. The success of these schools, many of them high-poverty schools with primarily African American students, demonstrates that obstacles to school reform and student achievement, such as limited resources and low income, and poorly prepared students, can be overcome with the right combination of high expectations, commitment, and collaborative support. In offering words of encouragement and advice to peers, many of the school leaders emphasized the importance of remaining both patient and proactive–because these changes take time, often do not come easily, and require support.

Promising Strategies

SCHOOL ORGANIZATION. Almost half of the schools in the Stepping Up study and virtually all in the Aiming High study moved or are moving to **create smaller learning communities** within the bigger institutions. This is in line with a now sizeable body of research findings that overwhelmingly support the relationship between the size of a school (at any level) and positive educational outcomes (Mitchell, 2001, citing Raywid). Especially for poor children, a small school, in and of itself, seems to mitigate the effects of poverty on test scores by 20 to 70 percent (Mitchell, 2001, citing Howley & Bikel). Central Park East and the Urban Academy, two small public high schools in two of New York City's poorest areas, provide dramatic evidence for this. Approximately 90 percent of their graduates go on to college (Mitchell, 2001). The school personnel in the Stepping Up and Aiming High studies have discovered that there are many ways to create smaller learning communities and that they do not have to involve decreasing or capping student enrollment. Because most schools are not in a position to cap student enrollment, they create "schools within schools" centered around a particular discipline or career interest (i.e., "career academies"), or they create mechanisms to keep groups of students together as much as possible for as long as possible.

Some schools make a commitment to "start small and keep small" when they are first established. What is clear is that smaller learning communities do, in fact, provide a way for teachers and students to get to know and care about each other. They provide the setting for better student-teacher relationships and, thus, respond to the problem of impersonal and alienating school organization and set the stage for improved student learning.

In addition, the Stepping Up and Aiming High schools are exploring various **alternative scheduling and organizing methods**. These new models are often called "block schedules" and involve extending class periods so students have fewer but longer classes each day. This gives teachers more time with their students and decreases the amount of time they spend on classroom management. It gives students more time in class and less in the halls. Schools are experimenting with extending both the school day and the school year. Preliminary findings are promising. Generally, assuming the time is spent in meaningful learning activities, more time in school equals more learning.

SUPPORT SYSTEMS. Most of the schools in these two studies offer a comprehensive array of noninstructional support systems for their students. They share the goals of increasing student attendance; addressing basic human needs; providing students with opportunities for meaningful relationships with caring adults and groups of peers; and, fostering connections between schools, families, and the community. These services range from school support teams that intervene with troubled students and their parents to comprehensive on-site health and social service centers, to career and college guidance counselors and activities. In addition, most of these schools engage in academic interventions such as providing extra instruction during the school day and extending the school day and even the school year to extend learning time.

Burtonsville, Maryland

Paint Branch High School qualified to be a North American High School Status School because of its Academy of Science and Media Magnet, where students can have hands-on experience with biotechnology, medical, and health careers as well as engineering and environmental studies. (Carnegie Challenge, 2001)

ACADEMIC RIGOR. The schools in the New American High Schools study practiced four main approaches to **raising academic standards** as part of broad-based school improvement. They eliminated low-level courses and the general track. They increased the level and challenge of required course sequences. They raised graduation requirements by increasing the number of required credits and the required grade point average. They also raised standards for special needs students. In addition to raising expectations, however, as already discussed, they put in place a comprehensive array of student support services designed to help students meet the raised expectations.

Talent Development High School

This school with Career Academies was developed by the Johns Hopkins University Center for Research on the Education of Students Placed At Risk (CRESPAR). Ninth Grade Success Academy features daily 90-minute, year-long instructional blocks for mathematics and English classes and a Freshman Seminar that teaches study and computer skills. Additionally, it helps students understand the continuity from high school to college and careers. Beginning in sophomore year, students enter a Career Academy that is centered on a specific career choice; each Academy ensures academic rigor by requiring students to take college preparatory courses. (Carnegie Challenge, 2001)

Other schools have reorganized curricula in a way that eliminates the general track and builds in literacy and mathematics supports to ensure that students are able to manage academically rigorous courses.

San Anselmo, California

In the last two years of high school, students at Sir Francis Drake High School have the option of attending learning academies that focus on topics such as engineering, communications, or leadership. Teachers keep a close eye on student achievement and meet with individual students frequently to help forestall academic problems. Students also participate in field projects, with one student recently exploring the world of radio broadcasting and that of webcasts. (Carnegie Challenge, 2001)

RELEVANCE. The schools in both these studies found that **linking classroom learning to real-world and workplace learning** had positive effects on attendance, discipline, student involvement, achievement, and dropout rates. Because students see the relevance between what they are doing in school, their lives, and their futures, they are able to apply themselves better and even do well in subjects they find difficult. Strategies for making these connections vary across schools but include such things are creating schools within schools, career majors, partnerships with employers who offer internships, and job shadowing opportunities. However, they all share the goal of integrating and coordinating learning activities across academic and vocational subjects, between in-school and out-of-school environments, and across grades. An example of such a project is the "Romantic Landscapes Project" at Pine Bluff High School in Arkansas, one of the Stepping Up Schools. This was a hands-on project that combined literature, horticulture, and computer-assisted design (CAD) classes. Students read and compared Neoclassical and Romantic literature. They then used a computerized landscaping software program to design a garden influenced by Romantic design concepts. Teachers evaluated the final designs based on their use of those concepts.

In addition, several schools in the Aiming High study created partnerships with institutions of higher education and took steps to ensure that more of their students enter and succeed at postsecondary education. The most typical strategy was to raise standards and expectations, including offering college-level classes or increasing graduation requirements above local or state requirements. Schools in both studies also provided serious sustained academic and career counseling to their students.

Family and Community Partnerships. Virtually all of the schools in both studies recognize that schools need the active involvement of their students' families to succeed. They use various methods to keep parents informed and provide them opportunities to participate in school activities. Some have parent coordinators who work full time to keep parents in touch. Several involve parents in school decisions. They all offer varied activities in which parents participate or observe. Some offer parent training or workshops. Schools are also partnering with community groups and employers, who can provide mentoring and other resources, including space and expertise that may be of use to schools but is not included in the budgets.

There are examples of public schools jointly sponsored by community-based organizations both nationally affiliated such as the Boys & Girls Clubs of America, the National Association of Service and Conservation Corps, the National Urban League, and National Council of La Raza and local organizations. These collaborations help schools to offer access to a wide range of community resources and support services. For example, at the El Puente Academy for Peace and Justice, a small public school in Brooklyn, students integrate the study of biology and chemistry with projects focused on local environmental health problems such as industrial pollution and asthma. At the Best Practice High School in Chicago, all of the school's 150 students can apply to participate in one-day-a-week field internships at a museum, library, or other local institutions (Carnegie Challenge, 2001).

The Annenburg Rural Challenge

Students spend up to 20 percent of their school day involved in projects such as analyzing clam beds in conjunction with a study of the local watershed, researching the local flora and fauna, developing a history of their community, or practicing journalism skills by writing a local newspaper. (Carnegie Challenge, 2001)

Staff Development

Every school in these studies recognized that teachers needed to be provided with development opportunities to implement reform efforts. Professionals in the Aiming High study learned that the best development activities are designed and delivered by the teachers themselves and address needs that they identify. It also became clear that "abundant" training, resources, and time are necessary both to initiate and sustain reform efforts. The Stepping Up study schools came to similar conclusions. Unfortunately for several of these schools, competing priorities and lack of resources prevented them from effectively using professional development on behalf of their reform efforts. Among the training found important in the Aiming High schools was that which helped teachers to meet the psychological and emotional needs of students, as well as how to know when expert help was necessary.

CONCLUSION

Evidence of the effectiveness of the changes these schools are making in how they educate high school students is based on such outcome measures as improved attendance and graduation rates, improved performance on national standardized tests, and higher enrollments in postsecondary education. Because many of these schools have high percentages of African American students, the reform efforts and positive effects demonstrated by these studies seem promising for improving the education of African American students. There is some compelling inferential evidence for the effectiveness of some of the New American High Schools specifically with their African-American students. For instance, at the Urban Academy Laboratory High School in New York, New York, where 39 percent of its students are African American, 97 percent of its graduates pursue postsecondary education. The John Dewey High School in Brooklyn, N.Y., has a 94.7 percent projected enrollment in postsecondary education (72.2 percent in four-year colleges and universities) figure in a school with an African American population of 38 percent. Paint Branch High School in Burtonsville, Maryland, with a 35 percent African-American or Black population, had higher mean scores for minority students than national averages for minorities in 1999. However, inferential statistics, even with the added weight of past research evidence (Cotton, 2001), theory, and common sense, don't go far enough to ensure that what works for some, works for all equally well. Absent disaggregation of data by race, we cannot claim to know for sure that these strategies work equally well across student ethnic populations. Therefore, we urge that all future studies of promising reform and improvement efforts in high schools disaggregate data on the basis of race, gender, and class to make sure that our attempts at improving education for our students include, as much as possible, all of our students.

We also urge that more research be conducted and include studies of the small but growing and promising group of middle college high schools, that group of schools specifically focused on providing a bridge between high school and college for students placed at risk. On the basis of the scant available initial information on their results, they seem to be successful in providing alternate paths for students of all ethnicities. For example, San Pablo Middle College High School, on the campus of Contra Costra College High in San Pablo, California, has daily attendance and graduation rates of more than 90 percent. In addition, last year the students outscored the highest ranking high school in their district on the Stanford Achievement Test, the one California uses to assess students, by 17 percent in reading, 13 percent in math, and 8 percent in science. In keeping with present belief in the efficacy of smallness, the school has only 240 students. In keeping with the middle high school consortium's philosophical belief that the schools should reflect the demographics of their overall student population, San Pablo's student population is 32 percent Asian American, 24 percent African American, 25 percent Hispanic, and 4 percent white (Gehring, 2001).

It seems, then, there may be reason to hope that high schools are beginning to move in directions that may be beneficial to all students, including African Americans, and educational leaders should not wait for more data to be collected before they begin to implement promising changes as needed. We note with some dismay, however, that many of these changes have been instigated and are supported by federal appropriations for the 1994 School-to-Work Opportunities Act, which was set to expire in Fall 2001. It is unclear how many states will be willing and able to provide funding needed to sustain and expand these efforts. It would be sad if, just as it looked like the United States might be getting a handle on turning around drop-out rates, increasing graduation and postsecondary education rates, and decreasing the achievement gaps between Black and White students, valiant efforts by dedicated educators were undermined and set back by a lack of minimal financial assistance. We still have too far to go, and success depends on everyone playing a part. Although money, as we have seen, isn't everything, it certainly helps. Let's hope we have the national will to build on our successes to date.

REFERENCES

American Youth Policy Forum. (2000). *High Schools of the Millennium: Report of the Workgroup.* Washington, DC: Author

Benard, B. (1996) Fostering resiliency in urban schools. In B. Williams (Ed.), *Closing the achievement gap: A vision for changing beliefs and practices.* Alexandria, VA: Association for Supervision and Curriculum Development.

Botstein, L. (1997). *Jefferson's children: Education and the promise of American culture.* New York: Doubleday.

Boykin, A.W. (2000). Talent development, cultural deep structure, and school reform: Implications for African immersion initiatives. In D.S. Pollard & C.S. Ajirotutu (Eds), *African-Centered schooling in theory and practice* (pp. 143–161). New York: Doubleday.

Carnegie Challenge. (2001). *Creating a new vision of the urban high school.* New York: Joyce Baldwin.

CBO Schools: An education resource whose time has come. Issue Brief 1, Fall 2000. Washington, DC: Center for Youth Development and Policy Research at the Academy of Educational Development.

Commission on Restructuring of the American High School. (1996). *Breaking ranks: Changing an American institution.* Reston, VA.: National Association for Secondary School Principals. Westport, CT: Bergin & Garvey.

Cotton, K. (1996). Affective and social benefits of small-scale schooling. *Eric Digest 401088.* Charleston WV: ERIC Clearinghouse on Rural Education and Small Schools.

Cotton, K. (2001). Educating urban minority youth: Research on effective practices. *School improvement series* (SIRS). Northwest Regional Educational Laboratory. Retrieved April 4, 2001, from World Wide Web: http://www.nwrel.org/scpd/sirs/5/topsyn4.html

Darling-Hammond, L. (1997). *The right to learn: A blueprint for creating schools that work.* San Francisco: Jossey-Bass.

Darling-Hammond, L. (2000). School contexts and learning: Organizational influences on the achievement of students of color. In R.T. Carter (Ed.), *Addressing cultural issues in organizations: Beyond the corporate context.* Thousand Oaks, CA: Sage Publications, Inc.

Fearn, K. (In press). Special Education: What Can Be Done? Programs that Use Promising Practices in Educating Students Who Have been Placed at Risk. In S. Denbo & L. Beaulieu (Eds.), *Improving schools for African American students: A reader for educational leaders.* Springfield, IL: Charles C Thomas Publishers, Ltd.

Ferguson, R.F. (1998). Teachers' perceptions and expectations and the Black-White test score gap. In C. Jencks & M. Phillips (Eds.), *The Black-White test score gap.* Washington, DC: Brookings Institution Press.

Ford, D.Y. (1996). *Reversing underachievement among gifted Black students.* New York: Teachers College Press.

Gehring, J. (2001, March 14). High school, with a college twist. *Education Week, 20*(26), 26–41.

George, P.S., & McEwin, C.K. (1999, April). High schools for a new century: Why is the high school changing? *National Association of Secondary School Principals Bulletin.*

Greenfield, P. M., Raeff, C., & Quiroz, B. (1996). Cultural values in learning and education. In B. Williams (Ed.), *Closing the achievement gap: A vision for changing beliefs and practices.* Alexandria, VA: Association for Supervision and Curriculum Development.

Harris Interactive, Inc. (2000). *The Metropolitan Life Survey of the American Teacher, 2000: Are we preparing students for the 21st century?* New York: The Metropolitan Life Insurance Company.

Jencks, C., & Phillips, M. (Eds.) (1998). *The Black-White test score gap.* Washington, DC: Brookings Institution Press.

Johnson, R.C., & Viadero, D. (2000, March 15). Unmet Promise: Raising Minority Achievement. *Education Week,* 19 No. 27, pp. 1, 18–19.

Kohn, A. (1999, September). Humanizing America's high schools. Constant frustration and occasional violence: The legacy of American high schools. *American School Board Journal,* September, 1999. Retrieved December 19, 2000 from World Wide Web: http://www.asbj.com/199909coverstory.html

McPartland, J.H., & Slavin, R.E. (1990, July). Increasing achievement of at-risk students at each grade level. *Policy Perspectives Series.* Washington, DC: U.S. Department of Education.

Mitchell, S. (2001). Jack and the giant school. *The New Rules Journal: Exploring Community, Mobility, Scale and Trade,* Summer 2000. Minneapolis: Institute for Self-Reliance.

National Center for Policy Analysis. (2000). Are smaller high schools the key to stopping violence? *Idea House.* Dallas, TX: Author. Retrieved December 19, 2000 from World Wide Web: http://www.ncpa.org/ pi/edu/pd041900c.html.

National Commission on the High School Senior Year. (2001). *The lost opportunity of senior year: Finding a better way.* Summary of findings. Washington, DC: Author.

Nelson-Barber, S., & Estrin, E.T. (1995). Bringing Native American perspectives to mathematics and science teaching. *Theory into Practice 34*(3): 174–85.

Noguerra, P. (in press). The role and influence of environmental and cultural factors on the academic performance of African American males. Paper presented at the Department of Education's Conference on African American Males, December 4, 2000.

Oakes, J. (1985). *Keeping track: How American schools structure inequality.* New Haven, CT: Yale University Press.

Oakes, J. (1990). *Multiplying inequalities: The effects of race, social class, and tracking on opportunities to learn math and science.* Santa Monica, CA: The Rand Corporation.

Oakes, J. (1992). Can tracking research inform practice? Technical, normative, and political considerations. *Educational Researcher, 21*(4), 12–21.

Osborne, J.W. (1997). Race and academic disidentification. *Journal of Educational Psychology, 89*(4), 728–735.

Roderick, M. (2000). What's happening to the boys? Early high school experiences and school outcomes among African-American male adolescents in Chicago. Paper written for the National Institute on the Education of At-Risk Students, U.S. Department of Education.

Rubenstein, M.C., & Wodatch, J.K. (2000). *Stepping up to the challenge: Case studies of educational improvement and Title I in secondary schools.* Washington, DC: Policy Studies Associates, Inc.

Shore, R. (1997). *The current state of high school reform: Report to Carnegie Corporation of New York.* New York: Carnegie Corporation of New York

Sizer, T.R. (1984). *Horace's compromise: The dilemma of the American high school.* Boston, MA: Houghton Mifflin Company.

Sizer, T. R. (1999, September). Humanizing America's high schools. Michael alone: Anonymity is the curse of the American comprehensive high school. *American School Board Journal.* Retrieved on December 19, 2000 from the World Wide Web: http://www.asbj.com/199909/0999coverstory.html

Spencer, M.B. (2000). African American males' academic achievement experiences: Assumptions about "opportunities" and facts about normative developmental needs and inopportune structural conditions. Paper commissioned by the Department of Education's Special Task Force on African American Males; presented, DOE Conference, Washington, D.C., December 4, 2000.

U.S. Department of Education. (2000). Smaller Learning Communities: Overview. *Online Grant Application Form.* Washington, DC: Author. Retrieved on December 18, 2000 from the World Wide Web: http://www.ed.gov/offices/OESE/SLCP/overview.html

Viadero, D. (2000, March 15). Even in well-off suburbs, Minority achievement lags. *Education Week, 19*(27), 22–23.

Visher, M.G., & Hudis, PM. (1999) *Aiming high: Strategies to promote high standards in high schools (Interim report).* Berkeley, CA: MPR Associates, Inc.

Wang, M.C., & Kovach, J.A. (1996). Bridging the achievement gap in urban schools: Reducing educational segregation and advancing resilience-promoting strategies. In B. Williams (Ed.), *Closing the achievement gap: A vision for changing beliefs and practices.* Alexandria, VA: Association for Supervision and Curriculum Development.

Witherspoon, R. (in press). The Involvement of African American Families and Communities in Education: Whose Responsibility is It? In S. Denbo & L. Beaulieu (Eds.), *Improving schools for African American students: A reader for educational leaders.* Springfield, IL: Charles C Thomas Publishers, Ltd.

Article 21

DISTRICT-WIDE SYSTEMIC REFORM: EQUITY 2000 SHOWS PROMISE IN NARROWING ACHIEVEMENT GAPS*

VINETTA C. JONES

EQUITY 2000, INITIATED ten years ago, has proven itself to be a highly effective district-wide model for improving mathematics enrollment and achievement, as well as for increasing college attendance. In the late 1980s the College Board commissioned a study to see what variables would facilitate closing the achievement gaps and increasing the college-going and success rates of minority and disadvantaged students. Using the "High School and Beyond Data" of the 1980s and published in *Changing the Odds*, 1990, Pelavin and Kane found completing algebra and geometry by the ninth and tenth grades, respectively, and having some idea about going to college, highly correlated with college-going and success rates. In fact, they found that if these variables were held constant, the differences in college-going and success rates essentially disappeared between minority/nonminority and disadvantaged/advantaged students. They also found that (because of tracking) only 19 percent of African American students and 17 percent of Hispanic students *ever* took both algebra and geometry. This research became the basis for launching a district-wide school reform effort, EQUITY 2000, that offered school districts an alternative to tracking students into dead-end courses and widening achievement gaps as standards were being raised. EQUITY 2000 is built on research and documentation from the last twenty-five to thirty years. This includes such effective programs as MESA (Mathematics, Engineering and Science Achievement), EQUALS, SECME (Southeast Consortium for Minorities in Engineering), and MSEN (Mathematics and Science Education Network). To address the issues of equity and diversity in a whole district, EQUITY 2000 scales up the effective strategies gleaned from these programs.

Thus, ten years ago, the College Board launched a research-based school reform initiative, EQUITY 2000, in six demonstration sites involving all schools in each of the districts. The six sites (Milwaukee, WI, Providence, RI, Prince George's County, MD, Nashville, TN, Fort Worth, TX, and Eastside Union, San Jose, CA) included 14 districts, 700 schools and more than 5000,000 students K through 12. The goal was to close the gap in college-going and success rates between minority and non-minority, advantaged and disadvantaged students. The six-year pilot program ran from 1990 to 1996 and used mathematics as a lever, starting initially at the middle school level to drive reform K through 12 and across all disciplines. Independent evalua-

*This article is adapted from "Effective Programs for Achieving Equity and Diversity in Mathematics and Science Education Outcomes: What Have We Learned? What Do We Need To Know?" by Vinetta Jones and Anne Bouie. Research funded by a U.S. Department of Education grant through the National Institute of Science Education, Madison, WI.

tors found that by the end of the six-year pilot there were more students *passing* the gatekeeper courses of algebra and geometry than were even *taking* them before EQUITY 2000. Enrollment in such accelerated courses as Advanced Placement increased substantially, especially among African American and Latino students, in some cases doubling and tripling. The EQUITY 2000 program is composed of six comprehensive, interrelated components.

1. District-wide policy changes (beginning with the elimination of the dead-end math tracks and a commitment for all students to complete algebra and geometry at least by the ninth and tenth grades)
2. Ongoing professional development for teachers, counselors, and principals (focusing on content, methodology, and equity/expectations)
3. Family involvement
4. Safety nets
5. Partnerships
6. Effective use of student enrollment and achievement data to drive decisions and monitor reforms

It is important to acknowledge the implementation process issues as well. Equity 2000:

- Requires a long-term commitment
- Is focused; it uses the power of math to drive reform
- Builds on what is already working
- Includes guidance counselors as part of the leadership team
- Works at all levels in the district (top-down, bottom-up etc).
- Is data driven
- Establishes ongoing professional development as a norm
- Connects the educators to a network of colleagues across the country
- Is comprehensive
- Makes high expectations for all students a primary focus with a plan

Since 1996, the College Board has been engaged in the national dissemination of lessons learned from EQUITY 2000. The original six EQUITY 2000 sites have become demonstration centers and continue the long-term commitment and work required to address the challenges and institutionalize the policies, practices, strategies, and gains made thus far to close achievement gaps. Meanwhile, new districts joined EQUITY 2000, and district teams attended week-long leadership Adoption Institutes to learn how to use the EQUITY 2000 model as a vehicle in their districts to drive reform and narrow achievement gaps as higher and higher standards are being set for all students. Follow-up professional development workshops are offered throughout the year sharing best practices to foster excellence and equity for school counselors, math teachers, principals, and other administrators. In addition, there are workshops sharing best practices on the effective use of data to drive decisions in school reform and providing "safety nets" for students. Faculty for the "best practice" workshops are drawn from the EQUITY 2000 demonstration centers where they have been developing and honing these efforts for more than 10 years now.

Figure 21.1 shows the dramatic increases in enrollment and passing in algebra for African American students at all EQUITY 2000 sites.

All groups at all sites have made large increases. Results of this district-wide school reform model have been documented in a series of evaluation and case studies by independent evaluators (Harris, 1998). A longitudinal study following the students into college is being conducted now. Preliminary results from senior surveys indicate that these students from high-minority and disadvantaged backgrounds will be attending college at higher rates than the overall national averages for the general population (Bohrnstedt, Jakwerth, & Rodriguez, 1999). Much progress has been made, but much remains to be done and many obstacles remain to be overcome. District-wide reform that achieves excellence and equity requires a long-term commitment. There are no silver bullets. You cannot take AP calculus if you have never taken algebra! Continuing challenges include money for ongoing professional development, an adequate supply of well-qualified teachers, teacher and superintendent turnover, and attempts to retrack the curriculum. And yet the progress that has been made is set in bold relief when the data of the six original pilot districts are compared with the baseline data for new EQUITY 2000 districts. The new districts look like the pilot sites before EQUITY 2000. It is this difference that stimulates new districts to join with

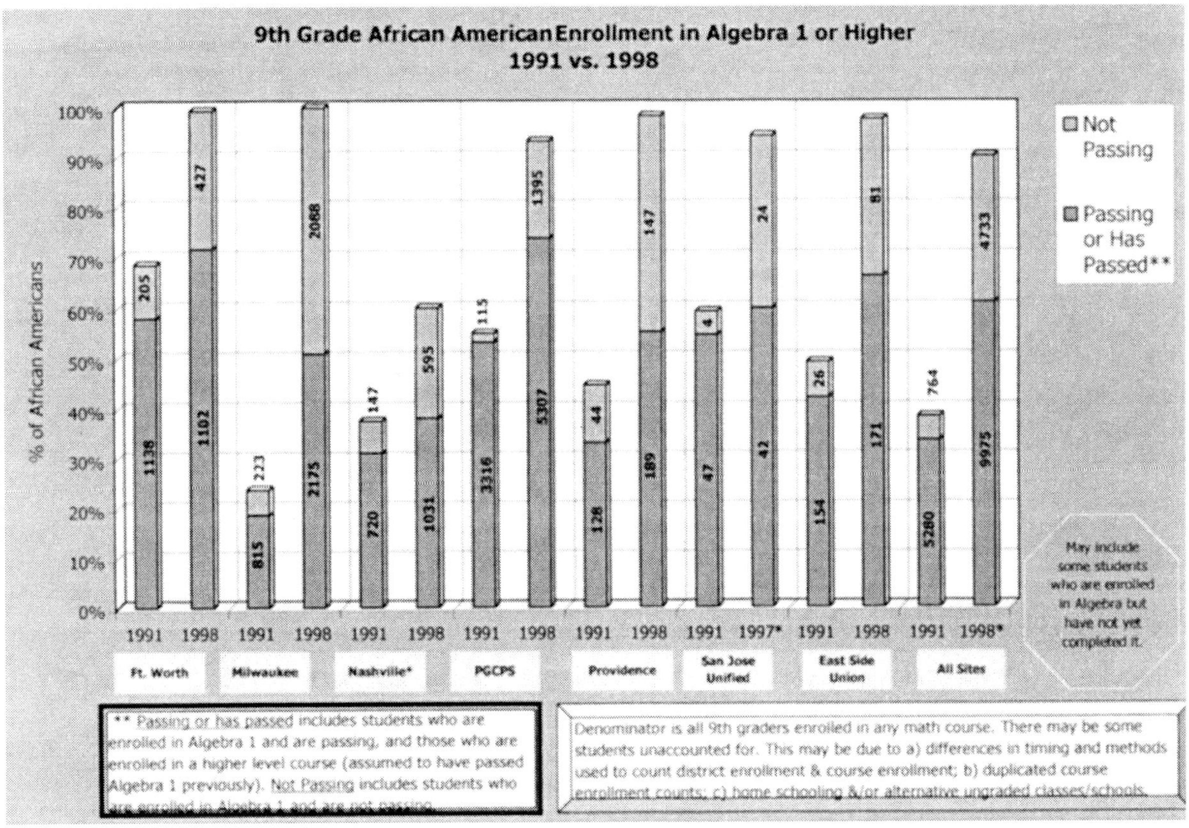

Figure 21.1. Increase in African American enrollment and passing.

their colleagues from across the country to build on lessons learned from EQUITY 2000, rather than wasting time, resources, and lives reinventing wheels.

The longitudinal data from EQUITY 2000 and other effective systemic initiatives suggest that a synthesis of their distinctive characteristics could serve as benchmarks by which districts might assess themselves. Six characteristics of a systemic initiative are as follows:

1. District-wide policy and major practice changes to alter the requirements, assessments, and practices of teaching, guidance, and school administration, beginning with the requirement that all students complete the gatekeeper courses of Algebra 1 by the ninth grade and geometry by the tenth grade, in classrooms in which the teachers embrace the national standards developed by the National Council of Teachers of Mathematics and other discipline-based groups
2. Ongoing professional development for teachers, counselors, and administrators to update their skills and reinforce policy directives and behaviors are explored. The focus for teachers is on content, pedagogy, and equity, where the influence and implications of teacher and school expectations along with their accompanying behaviors are explored
3. The establishment of academic safety nets such as Saturday academies, Summer Scholar programs, and other enrichment experiences that provide supplementary academic support needed to reach high levels of achievement in more rigorous courses
4. The development of parent and familial involvement activities that empower them to be effective advocates for their children's educational achievement
5. The formation of school-community partnerships, which provide broad-based support for the

fundamental goal of academic excellence for all students

6. The effective use of student enrollment and achievement data, which has been analyzed by race, ethnic group, social classes, and genders to drive decisions and monitor the progress of reform

For more information on EQUITY 2000 evaluations, reports, and the professional development workshops being offered to districts based on "Lessons Learned from EQUITY 2000," call Dr. Larry Dolan at the College Board Office in Washington, DC. The telephone number is 202-822-5930.

REFERENCES

Bohrnstedt, G., Jakwerth, P., & Rodriguez, C. (1999). *The EQUITY 2000 Evaluation: The senior survey analysis of cohorts 1, 2, & 3.* Palo Alto, CA: American Institute of Research.

Harris, C.D. (1998) *EQUITY 2000 and district change signs of success.* Alexandria VA: Human Resources Research Organization.

Pelavin, S., & Kane, M. (1990). *Changing the odds: Factors increasing access to college.* New York: The College Board.

NAME INDEX

SUBJECT INDEX

M

N

S